WTO AND INDIAN ECONOMY

WTO AND INDIAN ECONOMY

MANOJ SHANKAR GUPTA

SERIALS PUBLICATIONS
NEW DELHI

First Published - 2007

ISBN : 978-81-8387-106-8

Published by

SERIALS PUBLICATIONS
4830/24, Prahlad Street, Ansari Road
Darya Ganj, New Delhi-110002 (India)
Phone : 23245225. Fax : 91-11-23272135
E-mail: serials@satyam.net.in

CONTENTS

PREFACE

The World Trade Organization (WTO) is the legal and institutional foundation of the multilateral trading system. It provides the principal contractual obligations determining how the governments frame and implement domestic trade legislations and regulations and it is the platform on which trade relation among countries evolve through collective debate, negotiation and adjudication. WTO is expected to administer its trade agreements, provide forum for trade negotiations, handle trade disputes, monitor national trading policies, provide technical assistance and training to developing countries and co-operate with other international organizations.

WTO is reality. There is no escape from its rules and regulations. Even there is no route to approach international court for justice. The decision of its Dispute Settlement Body is final and binding on all the members of WTO. It has introduced competitiveness in the world economy. It is more important for a country like India to realize the challenges imposed by WTO because competition is not only with the already developed nations but also with the newly industrialized countries.

Hence, India cannot come out of WTO. India has to be tough and constructive in the negotiations through uniting developing countries. India should also force high-income countries to open their markets by reducing agricultural subsidies. Initiatives should be taken up to educate the farming community of the country regarding the challenges and opportunities in the WTO regime. Farmers should be encouraged to adopt diversification of crops and larger investment should be encouraged in production where they can have comparative advantage. For achieving international standards, farmers should improve the quality of their agricultural produce. There is a need to change the rural mindset on agro–exports. In this way, India cannot only improve her agricultural base and agricultural export but will also leave a multi-dimensional effect on improving the socio-economic environment of rural India.

The book *WTO and Indian Economy* is a modest attempt to deal with such a debatable subject. It is divided into three sections followed by a glossary of WTO and related terms. Section I deals with impact of WTO on agriculture while Section II and III analyse the impact of WTO on global market and overall Indian economy comprising various sectors. About forty-five eminent economists/researchers from different backgrounds have contributed in this book. The coverage of this book is quite comprehensive; the papers not only study the results of ongoing impact of WTO but also provide futuristic insights too. The scholars have tried to grasp various issues related to WTO in context of agriculture, global market and Indian economy. Various scholars in the book have discussed the pros and cons of WTO. No doubt, the book provides sufficient matters to the readers for understanding WTO.

In this endeavour, I have received help from numerous eminent research scholars across the country who have ably undertaken the tedious task of preparing research papers despite of their heavy engagements well within prescribed time. I would like to place on record my deep appreciation and gratitude to all contributors.

I feel highly privileged to express my profound regard and heartfelt indebtedness to Dr. N.K. Choudhary, Professor & Head, Department of Economics, Patna University, Patna and Dr. Asha Singh, Professor & Head, Department of Economics, Magadh Mahila College, Patna University, Patna for their constant help and encouragement in my academic pursuits. I express my sincere regards to Dr. S.N. Singh, Principal, R.K.D. College, Patna who encouraged me throughout the academic work. I am also thankful to my friends and one-time colleagues, Dr. T.K. Shandilya, Associate Editor (Indian Economic Journal, IEA) and Dr. Rashmi Akhoury, Department of Economics, College of Commerce, Patna for their help and suggestions in finalizing the book.

I am also thankful to all my colleagues, friends and relatives who helped me one way or other. I am very much thankful to my wife, Manju Sahu who helped me to maintain the time schedule in completing the book. Thanks a lot to my children, Mallika Aishwarya and Kumar Manorath whose humour kept me to concentrate in this venture.

Last but not the least, I am grateful to the publishing firm M/s. Serials Publications, Ansari Road, Darya Ganj, New Delhi for bringing out the book in its present form within minimum possible time.

Manoj Shankar Gupta
Patna (Bihar)

[illegible] Indian seed market.

As regards allowing restrictions on textile or food imports by rich countries for ten years, it was felt that the period was not too long. So far as general agreement on trade in services

LIST OF CONTRIBUTORS

Alakh Deo Prasad, Department of Geography, S.G.G.S. College, Patna City.

Anjali Prasad, Department of Economics, T.P.S. College, Patna.

Asha Singh, University Professor and Head, Department of Economics, Magadh Mahila College, Patna University, Patna.

Ashutosh Kumar, A5/32, NABARD Nagar, Thakur Complex, Kandiveli (East), Mumbai.

B.N. Pandey, Principal, Vanijya Mahavidyalaya, Patna University, Patna.

Deepak Bishoyi, Research Scholar, Institute for Social and Economic Change, Nagarabhavi, Banglore-72.

Dinesh Kumar Sharma, Assistant Professor, Department of Management Studies, Galgotia College of Engg & Technology, Greater Noida (U.P.)

Kuldip Kaur, Reader, Punjab School of Economics, GND University, Amritsar.

Kumkum Jha, Department of Economics, B.S. College, Danapur.

Kushwinder Kaur, Ex-student, Punjab School of Economics, GND University, Amritsar.

K.B. Gupta, Indian Institute of Management, Lucknow.

Krishna Kant Jha, P.G. Department of Commerce, C.M. College (L.N.M. University), Darbhanga.

K.K. Sinha, Emeritus Professor, UGC Sr. Fellow, Former Professor & HOD, PG Centre of Economics, College of Commerce, Patna.

Lokbardhan Gupta, Department of Commerce, B.D. Evening College, Patna.

Mahesh Chandra Prasad, Department of Applied Economics and Commerce, Patna University, Patna.

Manoj Shankar Gupta, Department of Commerce, R.K.D. College (Magadh University), Patna.

Md. Imteyaz Hassan, Department of Commerce, College of Commerce, Patna.

Md. Murshid Alam, Department of Commerce, D.A.V.P.G. College (J.P. University), Siwan.

Md. Reyazuddin, Reader in Commerce, Vanijya Mahavidyalaya, Patna University, Patna.

Md. Tarique, University Department of Economics, B.R. Ambedkar Bihar University, Muzaffarpur.

Mridula Kumari, Department of Economics, College of Commerce, Patna.

Neeru Chadha, Senior Lecturer, PG Department of Commerce, BBK DAV College for Women, Amritsar.

N.K. Mishra, Department of Commerce, R.K.D. College (Magadh University), Patna.

Punam, Department of Economics, College of Commerce, Patna.

Pushpa Sinha, Department of Economics, Patna Women's College, Patna University, Patna.

Ramphul, Department of Business Economics, Guru Jambheshwar University of Science & Technology, Hisar (Haryana).

Rashmi Akhoury, Department of Economics, College of Commerce, Patna.

Ratna Mitra, Department of Economics, Patna Women's College, Patna University, Patna.

Reeta Kumari Bhagat, Department of Economics, J.D. Women's College, Patna.

R.C. Choudhary, Department of Economics, College of Commerce, Patna.

R.K. Srivastava, University Department of Commerce, B.R. Ambedkar Bihar University, Muzaffarpur.

R.P. Gupta, Department of Commerce, College of Commerce, Patna.

R.U. Singh, Department of Commerce, College of Commerce, Patna.

Sandhya Rani, Department of Economics, Maharaja College (V.K.S. University), Ara.

Santosh Kumar Sahu, Research Scholar, Department of Economics, Berhampur University, Orissa.

Shaily Verma, Department of A&R Economics, M.J.P. Rohilkhand University, Bareilly (U.P.)

Shamim Akhtar, Department of Economics, Krishna College, Bijnor, U.P.

Syed Eqbal Afzal, Department of Commerce, Oriental College, Patna City.

Shakeel Ahmad Khan, Research Officer, Buddhist Centre for Action Research & Development Studies (BCARDS), Patna.

S.K. Upadhaya, Department of Commerce, T.D.P.G. College, Jaunpur (U.P.)

Vijay Mistry, Department of Geography, College of Commerce, Patna.

Vikas Kumar, Department of Management Studies, G.L.A. Institute of Technology & Management, Mathura (U.P.)

Vikram Chadha, Professor of Economics, Punjab School of Economics, GND University, Amritsar.

Talwar Sabanna, Department of Economics, Karnataka University KRC PG Centre, Belgaum.

Tapan Kumar Shandilya, Department of Economics, College of Commerce, Patna.

Usha Jha, Research Scholar, L.N.M. University, Darbhanga.

INTRODUCTION

Manoj Shankar Gupta

The WTO and its credibility as an international institution promoting multilateral trade system is a much-debated issue as far as the benefits of the developing countries including India are concerned. The World Trade Organization (WTO) is the legal and institutional foundation of the multilateral trading system. It provides the principal contractual obligations determining how the Governments frame and implement domestic trade legislations and regulations and it is the platform on which trade relation among countries evolve through collective debate, negotiation and adjudication. WTO is expected to administer its trade agreements, provide forum for trade negotiations, handle trade disputes, monitor national trading policies, provide technical assistance and training to developing countries and co-operate with other international organizations.

I

WTO came into existence in 1995 but its history goes back to the World War II. The world trade experienced massive disruptions during the Great Depression of the late twenties and the early thirties when economic nationalism reigned supreme. In these years, the government of many nations indulged in competitive devaluations of their currencies, raised their import duties to abnormal heights and imposed various types of trade restrictions to balance their payments, undermining the world's trading system. During the World War II, it was feared that depressed economic conditions of the thirties may return and would create problems for international trade.

Therefore, plans for the reform in international trading system began to take shape during the war. After the war, the allied powers met in Bretton Woods, New Hampshire in 1944 to set some guidelines for the operation of the world economy in the post war years. The International Monetary Fund (IMF) to promote international monetary cooperation and trade and the International Bank for Reconstruction and Development (popularly known as World Bank) to finance economic reconstruction and development–were conceived at the conference. This conference also generated plans for establishment of an International Trade Organization (ITO) to frame rules, eliminate restrictions and settle disputes relating to international trade. But ITO failed to take shape due to the non-approval of its charter by the US Congress. Instead, the US and some other countries agreed to adopt as treaty obligations a set of rules for conducting international trade among them. This treaty was called the General Agreement on Tariffs and Trade (GATT). The GATT was signed in 1947 at Geneva by 23 countries including India and became effective from January 1, 1948.

The GATT framed rules for conduct of international trade among member nations and provided forum for multilateral negotiations on issues relating to it. But despite of various achievements, grievances against the working of the GATT appeared in the early eighties. Its creditability and effectiveness began to be questioned on grounds of its limited success in eliminating non-tariff barriers (NTBs) to international trade and ignoring trade in agricultural goods, textiles and clothing and services. Its weak institutional structure and defective dispute settlement system were considered responsible for impeding further progress in trade liberalization. Its members wanted it to be improved to absorb the complexities of world trade, encompass additional areas of trade address increasingly the concerns of developing countries. The developing countries called GATT as "rich men's club".

These realizations led to a fresh round of trade negotiations –the eighth in the series under the aegis of GATT at Punta del Este, Uruguay in September 1986 with the principle objective "to halt and reverse protectionism and to reverse distortions in trade". This round of trade negotiations popularly known as the Uruguay Round (UR) concluded in 1994 and was unique in several respects. It covered many new areas such as agriculture, textiles, technology, intellectual property rights (IPRs), trade-related investment, services, etc. It included in its scope of liberalization, non-tariff barriers (NTBs) along with tariffs and conceived many new norms and disciplines such as sanitary and phytosanitary measures, anti-dumping measures, dispute settlement procedures, safeguard measures, etc. with a view to ensuring liberalized effective market access and rule-based trade. The conclusion of the Uruguay Round saw the transformation of the GATT into a more formal organization called "WTO" in 1995.

II

The Members of the Agreement have recognized that their relations in the field of trade and economic endeavour should be conducted with a view to raising standards of living along with ensuring full employment. It also endeavours to raise the volume of real income and effective demand while expanding the production and trade in goods and services. It further allows for the optional use of the world's resources in accordance with the objective of sustainable development, seeking both to protect and preserve the environment and enhance the means for doing so in a manner consistent with their respective needs and concerns at different levels of economic development.

Further, they have recognized that there is need for positive efforts designed to ensure that developing countries and the least developed among them, secure a share in the growth in international trade commensurate with the needs of their economic development.

Members being desirous of contributing to those objectives entering into reciprocal and mutually advantageous arrangements directed to the substantial reduction of tariffs and other barriers to trade and to the elimination of discriminatory treatment in international trade relations are resolved to develop an integrated more viable and durable multilateral trading system encompassing the General Agreement on Tariffs and Trade, the results of past trade liberalization efforts and all of the results of the Uruguay Round of multilateral trade negotiations.

The broad issues before the WTO are the following:

1. Agricultural products.
2. Services.
3. Tariffs on industrial products.
4. Implement issues (TRIPS, textile and anti dumping duties and subsides).
5. New issues (Foreign investment, competition policies, transparency in government procurement, e-commerce).
6. Non-trade issues (Linkage between trade and environment, Linkage between trade and labour).

Among these issues, non-trade issues are the most controversial set of issues. The basic underlying philosophy of WTO is that open markets, non-discrimination, most favour nation, national treatment, global competition and rule-based international trade. Rule-based system of international trade outperforms the diplomacy and quota-based trade system. It equally facilitates opportunities and risks to member states for optimum and rational use of their comparative advantages. The process of globalization is irrevocable. States are required to be effective to meet the challenges of the globalization and liberation and aggrandize the benefits arising from it.

III

The WTO structure is dominated by its highest authority, the Ministerial Conference, composed of representatives of all WTO members which is required to be held every two years and can take decisions on all matters under any of the multilateral trade agreements. The First Ministerial Conference held in Singapore on 9-13 December 1996.

The General Council is responsible for day-to-day work and administration of WTO, however the day-to-day work is done in assistance of the number of specialized and competent subsidiary bodies. The General Council is also composed of all WTO members, which is required to report to the Ministerial Conference. The General Council turns itself, as needed, into a body to adjudicate trade disputes (the Dispute Settlement Body) and review trade policies of the member countries (the Trade Policy Review Body).

The General Council observes activities of three other major bodies–namely; the Councils for Trade in Goods, Trade in Services and TRIPS. The Council for Trade in Goods oversees all agreements covering trade in goods, though many such agreements have their own specific overseeing bodies. The other two councils have responsibility for their respective WTO Agreements. There are three other bodies established by Ministerial Conference and report to the General Council, the Committees on Trade and Development; Balance of Payment Restrictions; and Budget, Finance and Administration. The General Council, in January 1995, established the Committee on Trade and Environment, pursuant to a Marakesh Decision. And in 1996, the General Council established a Committee on Regional Trade Agreements.

Each of the four plurilateral agreements–on civil aircraft, government procurement, dairy products and bovine meat–have their own management bodies which report to the General Council.

IV

The Article III of Agreement Establishing the Multilateral Trade Organization/WTO has specified five specific functions of WTO. They are following:

1. **Administrative Functions:** Under this function, the WTO facilitates the implementation, administration, operation and advances the cause of objectives of WTO Agreement, Multilateral Trade Agreements and provides framework for implementation, administration, operation of Plurilateral Trade Agreements. It provides a framework for the implementation of the results of negotiations, as may be decided by the Ministerial Conference.
2. **Platform for Negotiation:** WTO works as a platform where its members joining their helping hands can advance negotiations among themselves concerning their multilateral trade relations in matters dealt under the WTO agreements and enlisted in its annexes. Members can use this platform for negotiation not only for the issues under WTO agreements but for new issues concerning multilateral trade.
3. **Execution:** WTO administers the Understanding on Rules and Procedures Governing the Settlement of Disputes.

4. **Administering TPRM:** WTO administers the Trade Policy Review Mechanism.
5. **Economic Coherence:** WTO works with a view to achieve greater economic coherence in global economic policy-making, cooperating as appropriate with IMF and World Bank.

When the WTO took over from the GATT, it did not have the luxury of a relaxed beginning and a gradual build-up to its new and greatly expanded mandate. The demanding pace of work in its first and second year is a good indication of the central role, which the WTO is playing in the on going integration of the world economy.

V

The World Trade Organization is not a simple extension of GATT. On the contrary, it completely replaces its predecessor and has a very different character. Among the principal differences are the following:

1. The GATT was a set of rules, a multilateral agreement, with no institutional foundation, only a small associated secretariat that had its origins in the attempt to establish an International Trade Organization in the 1940s. The WTO is a permanent institution with its own secretariat.
2. The GATT was applied on a 'provisional basis' even if, after more than forty years, governments chose to treat it as a permanent commitment. The WTO commitments are full and permanent.
3. The GATT rules applied to trade in merchandise goods. In addition to goods, the WTO covers trade in services and trade-related aspects of intellectual property.
4. While GATT was a multilateral instrument by the 1980s, many new agreements had been of plurilateral, and therefore selective in nature. The agreements, which constitute the WTO, are almost all multilateral and thus, involve commitments for the entire membership.
5. The WTO dispute settlement system is faster, more automatic and thus much less susceptible to blockages than the old GATT system. The implementation of WTO dispute findings will also be more easily assured.

VI

The first Ministerial Conference in Singapore in 1996 added three new working groups to this structure. They deal with the relationship between trade and investment, the interaction between trade and competition policy and transparency in government procurement. At the second Ministerial Conference in Geneva in 1998, ministers decided that the WTO would also study the area of electronic commerce, a task to be shared out among existing councils and committees. The third Ministerial Conference held in Seattle during 30th November-3rd December 1999 was being looked up by many, specially in the developing countries, as a launching pad for a comprehensive round of negotiations. In the preparatory process in the General Council of the WTO (September 1998-September 1999), new issues which were proposed for the negotiating agenda by some Members under paragraph 9(d) are as follows: (a) Industrial Tariffs (b) Global International Commerce (c) Trade and Labour Standards (d) Trade and Environment and (e) Coherence in the interaction of WTO and other international organizations. The fourth Ministerial Conference held in Doha, Qatar from 09-13 November 2001. In Doha Deceleration, WTO members agreed to negotiations on the relationship between WTO members and specific trade obligations set out in Multilateral Environmental Agreements (MEAs), procedures for regular information exchanges between MEA secretariats and the relevant WTO committee and the reduction, or as appropriate elimination, of the tariff and non-tariff barriers to environmental goods and services. The fifth WTO Ministerial Conference was held in Cancun, Mexico from 10-13 September 2003.The main task was to take stock of progress in negotiations and other work under the Doha Development Agenda. The fifth Ministerial meeting reflected serious polarization of views and positions with wide divergence of views and lack of convergence amongst the developed and developing countries, especially on Agriculture and the Singapore issues. The Ministerial meeting concluded on September 14, 2003 without reaching a consensus. But the members have adopted a Framework Agreement on 1 August 2004 outlining the elements and principles that will guide the future negotiations. The sixth Ministerial Conference held in Hong Kong, China from 13-18 December 2005 and major outcomes and timelines of this Ministerial Deceleration are as follows:

1. Resolve to complete the Doha Work Programme fully, and to conclude the negotiations in 2006.
2. To establish modalities in agricultural and non-agricultural market access (NAMA) by April 30, 2006 and prepares draft schedules by July 31, 2006.
3. To eliminate export subsidies in agriculture by 2013, with a substantial part in the first half of the implementation period. Developing countries without Aggregate Measurement of Support (AMS), such as India, will be exempt from reductions in de minimis and the overall cut in trade-distorting domestic support, consisting of AMS, the Blue Box and de minimis, that is entitlement to provide Amber Box subsidies up to 10 per cent of value.
4. To submit a second round of revised services' offers by July 31, 2006 and submit final draft schedules by October 31, 2006.
5. Amendments to TRIPS Agreement reaffirmed to address public health concerns of developing countries.
6. Duty-free, quota-free market access for all LDC's products to all developed countries. Developing country declaring itself to be in a position to do so, to also provide such access, though flexibility in coverage and in the phase of their commitments are provided.
7. In cotton, export subsidies to be eliminated by developed countries in 2006 and trade-distorting domestic subsidies to be reduced more ambitiously and over a shorter period of time.

VII

Federation of Indian Chambers of Commerce and Industry (FICCI) has welcomed the Draft Hong Kong Ministerial Declaration as a significantly positive step towards successfully completing the Doha negotiations by 2006. Dr Amit Mitra, FICCI Secretary General, complimented the Commerce Minister, Mr. Kamal Nath for successfully negotiating several provisions and clauses, which are of vital interest to developing countries in general and India in particular. Particularly welcoming India's initiative to build the unprecedented alliance of a large number of developing and least developed countries (LDCs), Dr. Mitra said "To form such a coalition cutting across levels of development and interests through a process of inclusion, engagement and commitment would not only strengthen the multilateral trading system but also safeguard a number of legitimate concerns of the developing world in agriculture, services and industrial goods".

In the area of agriculture, it is important for the developing countries that an end-date (2013) has been specified foe elimination of all forms of export subsidies by developed countries, with substantial reduction in the first half of implementation period, FICCI added. Dr. Mitra observed that the Declaration has adequately addressed concerns of Indian farmers by providing for 'flexibility' to 'self-designate' an appropriate number of products as Special Products (SP) and a Special Safeguard Mechanism (SSM) that would enable India to protect its large population of small and marginal farmers from the unfair competition of subsidized imports from developed countries. The Chamber is also pleased to see the mandate for review of Green Box criteria that will help towards keeping out most of the trade-distorting support measures.

In non-agricultural market access (NAMA), FICCI is happy with the explicit mention of'paragraph 8 flexibilities' that would allow us to place a number of vital items outside the ambit of tariff reduction formula. In addition, the draft provides for reduction/elimination of tariff peaks and tariff escalation in products of developing countries' export interest. This will go a long way, FICCI said, towards expanding our access in the markets of developed countries. The 'non-mandatory' participation in sectoral negotiations as specified in the draft would also be in our interest, as felt by the Chamber. As regards services, the Chamber pointed out, there were concerns about the 'square brackets' on the whole of Annex C in earlier draft; the absence of this Annex would have resulted in very little movement in service liberalization. The Draft Declaration has preserved the integrity of Annex C that would facilitate much freer temporary movement of professionals and more liberalized commitments on cross-border supply of services (Mode-1). FICCI expressed satisfaction that the draft now specifies clear time lines for concluding negotiations based on different approaches. Regarding unprecedented alliance among a large number of developing and least developed countries (LDCs) having diverse interests, FICCI termed this among the most significant developments so far in the Hong Kong Ministerial Conference. On the issue 'coalition building', FICCI was of opinion that this could be vital to achieve a more equitable and pro-development outcome from the Doha Round of negotiations. The alliance would effectively counter some developed countries concerted attempts to divide the developing countries in the WTO context.

VIII

WTO is reality. There is no escape from its rules and regulations. Even there is no route to approach international court for justice. The decision of its Dispute Settlement Body is final and binding on all the members of WTO. It has introduced competitiveness in the world economy. The fact is that only those countries can create a niche and survive at the international level, which upgrade their technology and improve the quality of their products. It is more important for a country like India to realize the challenges imposed by WTO because competition is not only with the already developed nations but also with the newly industrialized countries.

The developed countries enjoy several advantages over the developing countries. Their access to international capital, trained personnel, innovative technology and superior management techniques place them in the advantageous position as compared to the latter countries. WTO agreements agreed upon and signed by all the member countries have compelled developing countries to improve their capabilities, ignored for long time, in order to enhance their productive capacity and improve their well-being.

Hence, India cannot come out of WTO. India has to be tough and constructive in the negotiations through uniting developing countries. India should also force high-income countries to open their markets by reducing agricultural subsidies. Initiatives should be taken up to educate the farming community of the country regarding the challenges and opportunities in the WTO regime. Farmers should be encouraged to adopt diversification of crops and larger investment should be encouraged in production where they can have comparative advantage. For achieving international standards, farmers should improve the quality of their agricultural produce. There is a need to change the rural mindset on agro-exports. In this way, India cannot only improve her agricultural base and agricultural export but will also leave a multi-dimensional effect on improving the socio-economic environment of rural India.

SECTION - I

WTO AND AGRICULTURE

WTO AND INDIA'S AGRICULTURAL TRADE: AN EMPIRICAL ANALYSIS

Ramphul

INTRODUCTION

Historically, India's agriculture sector is a net foreign exchange earner. During the year 2004-05, agriculture is accounted for 10.64 per cent of the total export earnings and 21.58 per cent of the gross domestic product (GDP) (triennium ending 2004-05) is come from agriculture sector and is still provides livelihood to the large proportion of population. This sector provides employment to 56.7 per cent of country's total work force and is the single largest self-employment occupation. A large number of industries like textiles, silk, sugar, rice, flour mills and milk products are getting raw material from agriculture. A nation of more than one billion people cannot be dependent on imports for the staple diets like wheat and rice. The agriculture sector, therefore, acts as a bulwark in maintaining food security and, in the process, national security as well. The allied sectors like horticulture, animal husbandry, dairy and fisheries are most important in improving the overall economic conditions and health and nutrition of the rural masses. Further, India's agriculture is the key sector for poverty reduction. Majority of the Indian poor (74%) are in the rural economy (Tenth Five Year Plan) and draw the bulk of their income directly from agriculture and those do not mostly rely on it indirectly by providing goods and services to farmers. Thus, any change in the agriculture sector, has a spill effect on the entire Indian economy. The world agricultural trading system has been experience a tremendous change in the last decade of the twentieth century. The Agreement on Agriculture (AoA) of the WTO signed in 1994, and implemented since January 1995 with the establishment of WTO, strives to establish a fair and free market-oriented world trade in agricultural commodities. The AoA in its Article XX incorporated the provision to review the experience of the member's countries in its implementations, and start fresh negotiations for continuing the process of opening up of world agricultural markets and reducing distortions. The AoA provides that one year before the end of the implementation period for the AoA commitments of developed countries i.e. 2001, negotiations should start on continuing the reform process to achieve the long run objective of substantial progressive reduction in agricultural support and protection. The committee on agriculture of WTO began renegotiations on agriculture in March 2000 and now is at advanced stage. India, being a signatory to the AoA for negotiating effectively in the future rounds, it is necessary to assess the impact of AoA on India's agricultural trade. It demands for an intensive study to analyze the impact of AoA on India's agricultural trade performance.

REVIEW OF THE LITERATURE

There are few studies, which had tried in recent past to analyze the trend and pattern of India's international agricultural trade. Some important studies are mentioned in this paragraph. Das (2001) discovered that in India the farm products constitute a sizeable component of foreign trade despite of a steady decline in their share over time and the largest contribution to the agricultural export is made by fish and fish preparations, followed by rice and oil cakes. Prasad (2001) analyzed the impact of structural adjustment programmes on India's agricultural trade and found that agricultural exports in total exports varied between 16.6 per cent (1994-95) and 20.4 per cent (1996-97). Kishor (2004) estimated the trend of India's agricultural exports and found that the contribution of India's agricultural export to the world agricultural export is increased in WTO period. Bhattacharya (2004) found that India's trade surplus in agriculture is due to the high growth of export of non-traditional commodities viz. fruits juices, vegetables, processed foods and beverages, etc. on the other hand, have been some what offset by the continuing dismal performance of India's traditional products like cashew nuts, tea, coffee, spices, tobacco, etc. Bhalla (2004) in his study explored that agricultural exports witnessed acceleration in their growth notably during the fist half of the nineties but the agricultural imports has grown faster than agriculture export. Chand (2005) analyzed the India's agro-export performance in the changed international scenario and concluded that decline in value of India's agriculture exports in post WTO period is much more than decline in world trade in agriculture. Chakrabarty (2006) found that the surge in imports in the post-WTO phase indicate that Indian agriculture (or at least parts of it) is prone to high cost; which creating inconvenience to Indian producers in exporting the agricultural goods.

From these studies, it is observed that to analyze trends of India's agricultural export majority of these studies has included fish and forestry products in total agricultural export, despite the non applicability of AoA on these products and to analyze the impact of AoA on India's agricultural trade majority of these studies has undermined the impact of AoA on agricultural imports, which is one of the most important part to draw comprehensive conclusions. It demands for more evidences to know the impact of AoA on India's agricultural trade. The present study is an attempt for empirical analysis of the impact of AoA on India's agricultural trade.

OBJECTIVES

The objectives of our present study are:

(i) To estimate the trends and patterns on India's agricultural trade.

(ii) To assess the impact of AoA on India's balance of agricultural trade.

(iii) To identifies the sources of growth of India's agricultural export.

METHODOLOGY

To estimate the trend in the data, following semi log-linear regression model is used

$$\log Y = \log A + \log B\ T$$

Where,

Y = dependent variable,

B = 1+g,

g = compound growth rate,

T = time.

The values of parameters log A and log B in the model are estimated by using Ordinary Least Square (OLS) method.

The compound annual growth rate (CAGR) is computed by employing following formula:

CAGR = [Antilog (log B)-1] 100

Nominal Export Growth

Let f_1 be the ratio of the world imports in last year to the first year of the period under consideration. Thus, f_1 measures the growth due to expansion of world market for the country's agricultural exports, which will be called 'passive expansion'.

Let f_2 be the ratio of the country's share of world trade in the agricultural export at the end of the period to its share at the beginning of the period. Thus, f_2 measures the growth due to expansion of market share in the world agricultural exports, which will be called 'active expansion'.

Let f_3 be the trade diversification factor defined as reciprocal of the change in the share of the agricultural exports from the beginning to the end of the period. Thus, f_3 captures the growth in export due to diversification into non-agricultural exports.

The nominal export growth rate is now defined as the product of the f_1, f_2 and f_3 i.e.;

$$G = f_{1} \times f_{2} \times f_{3}$$

Where,

G = Nominal growth rate

$f_1 = W_1/W_0$;

Where, W_1 = World imports in last year,

W_0 = World imports in first year,

$f_2 = (T_1/T_0)/(W_1/W_0)$;

Where, T_1 = Country's agricultural exports in last year,

T_0 = Country's agricultural exports in first year,

$f_3 = (T_0/X_0)/(T_1/X_1)$;

Where, X_0 = Country's total exports in first year,

X_1 = Country'stotal exports in last year.

It is being noted that individual values of f_1, f_2 and f_3 identifies the sources of the nominal export growth.

Net Terms of Trade

The net term of agricultural export is calculated by the following measure:

$$N_T = (Px/ Pm)\ 100$$

Where,

N_T = Net terms of trade,

(Px)= Value index of agriculture export,

(Pm)= Value index of agriculture import.

Specialisation in Agricultural Trade

The specialization in agricultural trade is assessed by the following moasure:

$$S_T = \frac{E - I}{E + I}$$

Where,

S_T = Specialisation in agricultural trade;

E = Value of agricultural exports;

I = Value of agricultural imports.

SOURCES OF DATA

The analysis is carried out for a time span of 15 years from 1989-90 to 2003-04. To analyze the impact of AoA on India's agricultural trade before and after approach is used and the whole period under analysis is divided into pre (1990-95) and post (1996-2004) WTO phase. In the present study, the terms "agricultural products", "agricultural exports", "agricultural imports" and "agricultural trade" relate to the definition of agricultural products under the AoA. The data on the values of India's agricultural exports and imports of agricultural products is compiled from various volumes of Food and Agriculture Organization of the UN (FAO) Trade Yearbook, Foreign Trade and Balance of Payments a publication of CMIE and Economic Survey, Ministry of Finance, GOI. The exports values are taken at FOB prices and imports values are based on the CIF prices.

EMPIRICAL RESULTS AND INTERPRETATION

The analysis of the India's agricultural trade performance during pre and post WTO period in the light of information generated by different mathematical, statistical and econometric techniques is given as below. Results in Table 1 reflect that after a relative strong expansion in mid 1990's, India's agricultural exports have declined in value terms during the period 1998-2000. During the year 1994-95, agricultural exports were accounted for US$ 3239.5 billion, which have become US$ 6504.4 billion during the year 2003-04. In the WTO regime, India's share in world agricultural exports has increased but it is less than that of for imports.

The average annual growth rates of India's agricultural exports and imports have decreased but it is higher in former case. As a result, the net agricultural exports have declined in value term and self-reliance in agriculture is worse affected. The share of India's agriculture export in its total merchandised trade is decreased, while it is increased for agricultural imports. In the WTO regime, India's specialization in agricultural trade is deteriorated (Table 2).

INDIA'S NET TERMS OF AGRICULTURAL TRADE

The net term of trade has become unfavorable for India's agricultural trade. The net term of trade was 150.8 during 1991-92, which has become 53.11 in 2003-04 (Table 2). The average annual growth rate of agricultural net exports has worsen in the WTO regime and reduced to -5.89 per cent during 1996-2004 in comparison to -2.03 per cent during 1990-95 (Table 1).

INDIA'S AGRICULTURAL TRADE RELATIVE TO SIZE OF AGRICULTURE

India's agriculture export as a percentage of GDP agriculture is increased but it is less than that of for imports. As a result, India's agricultural net export as percentage of GDP agriculture has decreased. In the WTO regime, share of India's agricultural exports required to finance agricultural imports is shot up and

Table 1
India's Agricultural Trade Performance: Before and After WTO

(Million $ and percentage)

Year	India's agr. export	Annual % change	Share in India's total export	Share in world agr. export	India's agr. import	Annual % change	Share in India's total import	Share in world agr. imports	Net agr. exports
1989-90	2657.10	-	16.00	0.88	1063.90	-	5.01	0.34	1593.20
1990-91	3074.70	15.72	16.88	0.94	1084.70	1.96	4.48	0.31	1990.00
1991-92	2796.20	-9.06	15.49	0.85	742.40	-31.56	3.78	0.21	2053.80
1992-93	2947.50	5.41	14.45	0.82	1366.60	84.08	5.67	0.35	1580.90
1993-94	3357.40	13.91	15.04	0.99	1044.20	-23.59	4.46	0.29	2313.20
1994-95	3239.50	-3.51	12.24	0.83	1910.30	82.94	6.85	0.47	1329.20
1995-96	4529.60	39.82	13.74	1.02	2225.00	16.47	5.85	0.48	2304.60
1996-97	5849.50	29.14	17.78	1.26	2205.50	-0.88	5.76	0.46	3644.00
1997-98	5315.80	-9.12	15.52	1.16	4053.70	83.80	9.88	0.87	1262.10
1998-99	5225.30	-1.70	15.43	1.19	3832.90	-5.45	8.87	0.84	1392.40
1999-2k	4642.00	-11.16	12.53	1.11	3969.60	3.57	7.94	0.90	672.40
2000-01	4949.60	6.63	10.93	1.20	2377.40	-27.51	5.60	0.66	2072.20
2001-02	5233.90	5.74	11.82	1.27	3923.30	36.35	7.55	0.89	1310.60
2002-03	5521.60	5.50	10.31	1.25	4019.40	2.45	6.44	0.87	1502.20
2003-04	6504.40	17.80	11.42	1.25	4903.90	22.01	6.88	0.89	1600.50
Annual average growth rate	1990-04 6.29%, 1990-1995 3.81%, 1996-2004 2.00%				1990-04 13.66%, 1990-1995 10.27%, 1996-2004 7.99%				1990-04 -2.48 1990-1995 -2.03%, 1996-2004 -5.89%

Source: Computed on the basis of data available from FAO Trade Year Book, various issues (1989-2003).

become 75.4 per cent in 2003-04 in relation 31.1 per cent during 1993-94 (Table 3). The above analysis reflects that in the WTO regime, there is a deceleration in agricultural export and import growth but it is higher in former case. Here, all these evidences support the hypothesis that AoA of the WTO did not have a significant impact on the India's net agricultural export.

Table 2
India's Net Terms of Agricultural Trade

(Million $ and per centage)

Year	*Speciali-zation in agricul-ture*	*Export used to finance import*	*Value index of agr. import (Pm)*	*Value index of agr. export (Px)*	*Net term of trade =[(px/pm)* 100]*
1989-90	0.43	40.04	100.00	100.00	100.00
1990-91	0.48	35.28	101.96	115.72	113.50
1991-92	0.58	26.55	69.78	105.24	150.81
1992-93	0.37	46.36	128.45	110.93	86.36
1993-94	0.53	31.10	98.15	126.36	128.74
1994-95	0.26	58.97	179.56	121.92	67.90
1995-96	0.34	49.12	209.14	170.47	81.51
1996-97	0.45	37.70	207.30	220.15	106.20
1997-98	0.13	76.26	381.02	200.06	52.51
1998-99	0.15	73.35	360.27	196.65	54.59
1999-2k	0.08	85.51	373.12	174.70	46.82
2000-01	0.26	58.13	270.46	186.28	68.88
2001-02	0.14	74.96	368.77	196.98	53.42
2002-03	0.16	72.79	377.80	207.81	55.00
2003-04	0.14	75.39	460.94	244.79	53.11

Notes: Net export is the export minus import; specialization is the ratio of net agriculture export to the total trade in agriculture.

Source: Computed on the basis of data available from FAO Trade Year Book, various issues (1989-2003).

SOURCES OF INDIA'S AGRICULTURAL EXPORT GROWTH

The nominal growth rate of India's agricultural export in pre and post WTO period along with its sources is presented in Table 4. The results in this table reflect that India's agricultural export during the pre WTO period (1990-95) grew by 59 per cent and during the post WTO period (1996-2004) by 71 per cent.

Table 3
India's Agricultural Trade Relative to GDP Agriculture

Year	*Agr. export as % of GDP agr.*	*Agr. import as % of GDP agr.*	*Net trade as % of GDP agr.*
1989-90	3.88	1.56	2.33
1990-91	3.84	1.35	2.48
1991-92	3.94	1.05	2.89
1992-93	3.85	1.79	2.07
1993-94	4.59	1.43	3.16
1994-95	3.97	2.34	1.63
1995-96	5.26	2.58	2.68
1996-97	6.25	2.36	3.90
1997-98	5.37	4.10	1.28
1998-99	5.36	3.93	1.43
1999-2k	4.78	4.09	0.69
2000-01	5.31	3.09	2.22
2001-02	5.38	4.03	1.35
2002-03	5.76	4.19	1.57
2003-04	6.79	5.12	1.67

Source: Computed on the basis of data available from FAO Trade Year Book and Economic Survey, various issues (1989-2003)

Table 4
Decomposition of India's Agriculture Nominal Export Growth

Factors	*1990-04*	*1990-1995*	*1996-2004*
f1	1.73	1.27	1.18
f2	1.42	0.96	1.21
f3	1.40	1.31	1.20
G	3.43	1.59	1.71

Source: Computed on the basis of data available from FAO Trade Year Book, various issues (1989-2003).

The decomposition of growth of India's agricultural exports reveals that the bulk of India's overall export growth during the period 1990-2004 was due to expansion of world market for the country's agricultural exports products (f_1) and active expansion of market share of its agricultural exports (f_2). The growth in export due to active expansion of market share of its agricultural exports (f_2) in WTO regime dominated the other sources of nominal growth rate.

COMPOSITION OF INDIA'S AGRICULTURAL TRADE

The share of different commodities in India's agricultural export and import during pre and post WTO period is presented in Tables 5.1 and 5.2.

Table 5.1
List of India's Major Agricultural Export Items

(Million $ and percentage)

Commodity	*1993-95*	*2002-04*
Wheat	5.89 (0.19)	454.61 (7.9)
Rice	389.44 (12.24)	938.21 (16.3)
Onion	56.51 (1.78)	127.18 (2.2)
Tea	351.11 (11.04)	342.41 (6.0)
Pimento	19.04 (0.60)	59.23 (1.0)
Ground nut	30.04 (0.94)	69.82 (1.2)
Tobacco	121.41 (3.82)	208.95 (3.6)
Sesame seed	20.59 (0.65)	118.06 (2.1)
Castor oil	80.01 (2.51)	115.41 (2.0)
Sugar	72.18 (2.27)	335.49 (5.8)
Coffee	148.20 (4.66)	153.57 (2.7)

Note: Figures in parenthesises are the share in total agricultural exports.
Source: Computed on the basis of data available from FAO Trade Year Book and CMIE publications, various issues (1989-2003).

In the WTO regime, the importance of commercial crops like sugar, sesame seed, onion and ground nut and cereals like rice, in the India's agricultural exports basket is increased while the share of traditional items like tea, coffee, castor oil and tobacco is declined (Table 5.1).

Table 5.2
List of India's Major Agricultural Import Items

(Million $ and percentage)

Commodity	*1993-95*	*2002-04*
Fruits and nuts	81.97 (5.7)	155.74 (3.6)
Pluses	169.06 (11.7)	576.82 (13.5)
Spices	14.19 (1.0)	116.98 (2.7)
Edible oil	106.61 (7.4)	1909.44 (44.6)
Cotton raw	84.24 (5.9)	343.68 (8.0)
Cashew nuts	175.76 (12.2)	215.38 (5.03)

Note: Figures in parenthesises are the share in total agricultural imports.
Source: Computed on the basis of data available from FAO Trade Year Book and CMIE publication, various issues (1989-2003).

Among the agricultural imports, the share of fruits and nuts and cashew nuts has declined while edible oil, pluses and raw cotton are emerged as India's major agricultural imports during the WTO phase (Table 5.2). During the period 2002-04, the palm oil was accounted for 27.31 per cent of total agricultural imports. Increased in the imports of edible oil, pulse and raw cotton may be reasoned because of deceleration in their domestic production and increased in their demand on account of higher growth rate of population.

INDIA'S TARIFF RATES FOR AGRICULTURAL COMMODITIES

Under the market access provision of AoA of the WTO, India has bound its agricultural tariffs at sufficiently higher level. But for a large number of agricultural commodities, India's actual tariff rates are significantly lower than that of final bound rates. During the year 2005-06 for 82 per cent of commodities numbering 533, the difference was more than 50 percentage points and above, and the average basic duty rate for all agricultural tariff lines was 39 per cent (Table 6).

Table 6
Difference in MFN Tariff Rates and WTO Final Bound Rates: Number of Lines by Different Range Groups (FY 2005-06)

Range (WR-TR) percentage points	*No. of Lines*	*Percentage Distribution*
WR-TR > = 75	210	32.41
50 = < WR-TR < 75	323	49.85
25 = < WR-TR < 50	46	7.10
10 = <WR – TR < 25	14	2.16
0 = < WR – TR < 10	45	6.94
WR-TR < 0	10	1.54
Total	648	100.00

Notes: (i) TR = Most Favored Nation Tariff Rates i.e. Basic Custom Duty as announced in GOI, Budget 2005-06, read along with other notification in force (ii) WR = WTO final bound rates (iii) Tariff lines at 6-digit HS or sub-groups of 6-digits HS and (iv) Includes only agricultural products.

Source: Computed on the basis of data available from Big Easy Reference Customs Tariff, Arun Goel, 2005-06 and WTO secretariat.

In the light of the computed results, it may be argued that the India has failed to take the advantage of signing on AoA in term of the agricultural trade.

SUMMING UP

The trends and patterns on India's agricultural trade in pre and post WTO phase were analyzed by using the both least square growth model and nominal growth model. It is found that in the WTO regime, the average annual growth rates of India's agricultural exports and imports have decreased, but it has worst for agricultural exports. As a result, net agricultural export has reduced and self-reliance in agriculture has badly affected. The share of agricultural export required to finance agricultural import has shot up implying deterioration in the specialisation of agricultural trade as a whole. The performance of the export and import of agricultural products shows that AoA has failed to encourage an expansion in India's net farm trade. The bulk of India's overall export growth during the period 1990-2004 was result of the expansion of world market for the country's agricultural exports products and active expansion of market share of its agricultural exports. It may be reasoned that the decease in growth rate of India's agricultural exports is due to the deceleration in agricultural growth. There may be other reason also, that is, the huge amount of domestic subsidies provided by developed countries to their farmers. It is evident by the facts that during the year 1998-99, domestic subsides provided by Norway, USA, EU, Japan and Switzerland to their farmers was 102.92, 33.21, 57.67 and 56.98 per cent of the their GDP agriculture respectively (WDI and WTO, 2005). The subsides provided by developed countries cause excess supply of agricultural products in these countries, which make the producer to dump it into developing economies by cutting prices below long run marginal cost. In this situation, it is rightly argued by Patibandla (2002) that "By imposing high tariffs on imports of agricultural products, developed countries subsidies can be transferred into tariff revenue of the Indian Government, without disturbing the domestic consumer surplus". The tariff revenue generated through developed countries subsides can be utilised to increase the public investment in Indian agriculture sector to enhance its productive efficiency that is a necessary conduction for increase in the growth rate of agricultural exports in the WTO regime. The implications from this study suggest that to safeguard the productive efficiency of Indian agriculture based on true comparative advantage; India needs to maintain its agricultural tariff rates at WTO final bound level.

REFERENCES

Bhalla,G.S. (2004), "Globlisation and Indian Agriculture", Academic Foundation Publication, New Delhi.

Bhattacharya B.B. (2004) "Agricultural Exports", Academic Foundation Publication, New Delhi.

Chand Ramesh (2005) "India's Agro Export Performance and Competitiveness in Changed International Scenario" in Hanumantha Rao, C.H., Bhattacharya B.B. and Siddharthian N. S. (Editors), Indian Economy and Society, Academic Foundation, New Delhi.

Chakrabarty Pravel (2006), "Agriculture Sector: Trend in Export and Import", in Beyond the Transition Phase of WTO: An Indian Perspective on Emerging Issues, (editors) Dipankar Sengupta, Debashis Chakraborty and Pritam Banerjee, Academic Foundation, New Delhi, pp. 129-137.

CMIE, "Foreign Trade & Balance of Payments", Mumbai, various issues.

Das Hem Chandra Lal (2001), "Globalisation and India's Farm Export Trade", in Sinh Kumar Jiwitesh (editor), International Trade and Business: Emerging Issues and Challenges in 21st Century, Deep & Deep Publication, New Delhi.

Food and Agricultural Organisation, (FAO), "Trade Year Book", Rome, Italy, Various Issues (1989-03).

Government of India, "Economic Survey", Economic Division, Ministry of Finance, New Delhi, various issues.

—— (2002), "Tenth Five Year Plan 2002-07", Planning Commission, New Delhi.

—— (2004), "Agricultural Statistics at a Glance", Directorate of Economics and Statistics, Department of Agriculture and Cooperation, Ministry of Agriculture, Government of India, New Delhi.

Kishor, Nawal (2004), "World Trade in Agricultural Commodities and India's Strategy in the Post Globalized Economy", Indian Journal of Commerce, Vol. 57, No. 3, July-September 2004, 27-41.

Patibandla, Murali (2002), "Imports of Food Products: Need for High Tariffs", Economic and Political Weekly, May 11, 2002, 1781-1783.

Prasad Jagdish (2001), "Structural Adjustment, Indian Agriculture and International Trade: Challenges and Prospects", in Singh Kumar Jiwitesh (Editor), International Trade and Business: Emerging Issues and Challenges in 21st Century, Deep & Deep Publication, New Delhi.

World Bank, "World Development Indicator" Washington, D.C, Various Issues.

—— "World Development Report" Washington, D.C, various issues.

World Trade Organization (1998), Trade Policy Review of India, Geneva.

—— (2002), Trade Policy Review of India, Geneva.

WTO AND INDIAN AGRICULTURE

Ashutosh Kumar

INTRODUCTION

There was no multilateral or international organization that dealt with trade issues between countries until the end of 1994. The international trading system had functioned without such an organization for almost fifty years under the aegis of the General Agreement on Tariffs and Trade (GATT). But it did not have the standing of international organization like International Monetary Fund (IMF) or the World Bank. However, the scenario changed in 1994, when the Uruguay Round of trade negotiations under the GATT ended with an agreement to establish the World Trade Organization (WTO), along with considerable progress in strengthening the international trading system. The WTO came into existence on 1 January 1995.

PRINCIPLES UNDERLYING THE GATT AND THE WTO

The key principle of GATT was to establish an open and non-discriminatory trade, thus giving rise to the term "open multilateral system". It enjoins each signatory to commit it to treat all other signatories according to the most favoured national standard. *Most Favoured Nation (MFN)* treatment requires that tariffs and other regulations should be applied to imported or exported goods without discrimination among countries. *National Treatment* rule prohibits countries from discriminating between imported products and equivalent domestically produced goods. However, member countries did not commit to free trade with zero tariffs. Under GATT, all member countries agreed to undertake a series of negotiating rounds in which 'tariff concession' would be exchanged. The contracting parties would negotiate with their key trading partners for reduction of tariffs on items they export in return for 'concessions' on items of interest to their trading partners. Once tariff concessions were agreed, they extended to all contracting parties (the MFN or non discrimination, clause). The tariff rates were subsequently 'bound' so that tariffs could not be raised unless the 'escape clause' was invoked. As per provisions, the WTO is also to administer the provisions of Dispute Settlement Understanding (DSU) and also Trade Policy Review Mechanism (TPRM). It would also work in coherence with IMF and World Bank for achieving greater coherence in global economic policy making.

THE AGREEMENT ON AGRICULTURE (AoA) UNDER WTO

Although there were many agreements under WTO regime, the Agreement on Agriculture (AoA) is of importance for agriculture-based economies like India. The AoA is basically intended to liberalize world trade in agriculture and free it from governmental measures that distort trade and lead to inefficiency. For example, take the case of Western Europe; here domestic cultivators are protected from foreign competition through export subsidies to get rid of surplus agricultural commodities in world markets at prices, which are lower than the actual cost of production. Internal prices are supported through the Common Agricultural Policy (CAP) if they are above world prices.

Following are the three pillars of Agreement on Agriculture (AoA) under WTO regime:

(a) Market Access Commitments

(b) Reduction in Domestic Support and

(c) Requirement on Export Subsidies.

(a) Market Access Commitments

First of all, there is a requirement of tariffication. What it amounts to saying is that all non tariff measures like quantitative import restrictions, minimum import prices, discretionary import licensing, variable import levies, non-tariff measures maintained through state trade enterprises, voluntary exports restraints and other such measures must be replaced by tariffs. Once this tariffication requirement is complete, developed countries have the binding to reduce the tariffs by an average of 36 per cent over a period of six years. Similarly developing countries have the commitment to reduce the tariffs by an average of 24 per cent over a period of ten years. For each line, the minimum tariff reduction has to be 15 per cent apart from the average reduction. In case of developing countries, minimum tariff reduction for each line is 10 per cent. The tariff reduction does not apply to least developed countries.

Other market access commitments require that the countries that maintain quantitative restrictions on agricultural imports must provide for minimal imports at low customs duties. This minimal limit is defined as 3 per cent of domestic consumption rising to 5 per cent of domestic consumption at the end of six years. A lot of myth prevails regarding this commitment. It is generally perceived that, India must import 3-5 per cent of domestic consumption requirement but this is not true for two strong reasons. These market access commitments apply only to those countries that maintain quantitative restrictions that are inconsistent with GATT. Under article XVIII B as long as any country has Balance of Payment (BoP) problem, they are exempted from the above commitments. Further, assuming that India no longer has BoP problem, the minimum market access clause will be really relevant. But even then there is no compulsion that 3-5 per cent consumption needs must be imported. What the market access commitment stipulates is that 3-5 per cent of consumption needs must be opened up to imports. In other words, 3-5 per cent of consumption cannot be on the negative list, but will have to be on the Open General License (OGL) list, subject to whatever tariff exists. However, there are certain safeguard provisions if the market access leads to an import surge or if imports take place at an extremely low price. There are also disciplines on export prohibitions and restrictions but these do not apply to developing countries.

(b) Reduction in Domestic Support

As envisaged in agreement, calculation of Aggregate Measure of Support (AMS) has to be made by each Government and to be reduced over a period of six years. The AMS is to be calculated separately for subsidies, which are product specific and subsidies, which are non-product specific. As mentioned above, in the case of developing countries, a limit of 10 per cent has been stipulated separately for product specific and non-product specific AMS below which there is no obligation to make any reduction.

The benchmark for product specific support is 5 per cent of the total value of production of the agricultural products. In simple words, if product specific support is greater than 5 per cent of the total value of the production of the agricultural product then it has to be brought down by 20 per cent over a period of six years, beginning in 1995 and if it is less than 5 per cent, then there is no reduction commitment. Similarly for non-product specific support, the benchmark is also 5 per cent of the value of total agricultural production. If the non-product specific support is less than 5 per cent, there are no reduction commitments. However, for developing countries like India, there is special clause, which stipulates 10 per cent as the benchmark figure for reduction commitments. It means, for developing countries, a limit of 10 per cent has been stipulated separately for product specific and non-product specific AMS below which there is no obligation to make any reduction.

(c) Requirement on Export Subsidies

There are certain export subsidies, which are subject to reduction commitments. The proposals under AoA stipulate that Budgetary Outlay on such export subsidies must be brought down by 36 per cent over a period of six years. The volume of agricultural exports that receive subsidies must be brought down by 21 per cent, also over a period of six years. However, these commitments are for developed countries. There is a differential and special treatment again for developing countries. That is, the timeframe for reduction is ten years and not six years. For developing countries, budgetary outlays on export subsidies must be brought down by 24 per cent and the volume of exports that receive subsidies must be brought down by 14 per cent. In case of least developed countries, there are no reduction commitments on export subsidies. The benchmark year for all these reductions is 1986-90.

A summary of commitments under AoA of WTO by Member Countries are given below:

Table 1
Reduction Commitments under the AoA of WTO by Member Countries

Particulars	*For Developed Countries*	*For Developing Countries*
Period of Commitment	*6 years (1955-2000)*	*10 years (1995-2004)*
Tariffs		
Average cut for all agricultural products	- 36%	- 24%
Minimum cut per product	- 15%	- 10%
Domestic Support		
Total AMS cuts for Agriculture Sector (Base period: 1986-88)	- 20%	- 13.3%
Exports Subsidies		
Value of subsidies	- 36%	- 24%
Subsidised Quantities	- 21%	- 14%

Source: CMIE, (Various Issues)

IMPLICATIONS OF AoA ON INDIAN AGRICULTURE

1. Since the Aggregate Measure of Supply (AMS) calculated by various experts for India turned out to be negative, there is no ground to reduce the domestic support for India. Hence, the product specific and non-product specific subsidies shall largely be untouched for the time being.
2. As opposed to the prevalent myth that the PDS will have to be scrapped, there is no reason to worry on this account. The PDS will very much be there in place. However, greater disciplines on the PDS are on the cards, which do not conflict with the Indian objective of better targeting and revamping of the PDS. It must be more transparent and directed at urban and rural poor on the basis of clearly defined nutritional criteria. The export subsidies listed for reduction does not include export incentives. Therefore, while industrialised countries would have to reduce export

subsidies, there is no requirement for India to reduce these incentives. There is also a view that elimination of subsidies by the industrialised countries will create market opportunities for the Indian products.

3. As per the general safeguards and exceptions, there is no obligation to convert non-tariff measures into custom duty equivalent for those countries, which are having BOP problems. Since India maintained QRs (Quantitative Restrictions) for BoP reasons, the removal of QRs was done in phases. It was done gradually only on a few commodities to begin with. Subsequently, India made a series of commitments to remove QRs. With the removal of QRs, foreign trade is expected to pick up in the coming years.

INDIA'S AGRI-EXPORT IN THE POST-LIBERALIZATION REGIME

The agricultural sector has undergone enormous changes over a period of time. The share of Gross Domestic Product (GDP) in agriculture to total GDP has come down from 58.9 per cent in 1951 to about 23 per cent in 2005. However, the employment in agriculture has come down from 72 per cent of total labour force in 1991 to approximately 65 per cent in recent years.

Agricultural exports are the major components of the international trade in India. The proportion of agri-exports to total exports came down from 11.9 per cent in 2003-04 to 10.2 per cent in 2004-05. It hovered around $ 3.2 billion in 1990-91 to 1992-93. It jumped to $ 4 billion in 1993-94 and witnessed further jump to 6.1 billion in 1995-96. This tempo of growth continued till 1996-97, which took agricultural export close to $ 7 billion. The spectacular increase in agricultural exports during 1992-93 to 1996-97 raised export surplus of this sector from a modest $ 1.4 billion to $ 4.5 billion. Agricultural imports including fertilizer showed a mixed trend during this period. Agricultural exports took a down turn after 1996-97 and plummeted to $ 5.6 billion during 1999-2000. In contrast to this, agricultural imports witnessed 80 per cent increase in dollar terms after 1996-97. Due to this, net foreign exchange earnings of agriculture declined. However, the declining trend of agri exports has reversed since 2000-01 and it has again gone up to $ 8.01 billion in 2004-05.

Table 2
India's Agricultural Trade in the Post Liberalization Regime

	Year	*Exports $ million*	*Imports $ million*	*Net exports $ million*
Pre WTO Period	1991-92	3338	1256	2082
	1992-93	3028	1618	1410
	1993-94	4023	1317	2706
	1994-95	4227	2544	1683
Post WTO Period	1995-96	6120	3001	3119
	1996-97	6868	2303	4565
	1997-98	6634	2893	3741
	1998-99	6033	4012	2021
	1999-00	5615	4402	1213
	2000-01	6256	2738	2275
	2001-02	6146	3350	2796
	2002-03	6734	2804	3930
	2003-04	7532	3708	3824
	2004-05	8001	3811	4190

Source: GOI, Economic Survey, Ministry of Finance, New Delhi (various issues).

The import of agricultural and allied products during 2004-05 was at $ 3.81 billion as compared to $3.70 billion during 2003-04. The proportion of agri-imports to total imports came down from 4.7 per cent to 3.5 per cent in 2004-05 and a declining trend is discernible in 2005-06.

AGRI-EXPORT TRENDS

During early 1990s, marine products topped the list of agricultural export followed closely by export of oil meal. Other import items of export are tea, cashew nut, basmati rice, spices, tobacco etc. Liberalization of non-basmati rice in mid 1990s provided big boost to its exports. As a result of this, rice export figured at the top during 1995-96 and during 1998-99. Out of two grades of rice, basmati rice showed a steady trend in its export but non-basmati rice showed violent year to year fluctuations.

Export of marine products has been consistent around $ 1.1 billion and gone up to $1.3 billion and $1.26 billion in 2003-04 and 2004-05 respectively. Export of traditional items like tea, cashew and spices did not show adverse impact in post WTO regime but coffee exports has been hit badly. Castor oil and guargum meal are emerging as important items of exports. However oil meal is the worst affected export item. After witnessing 90 per cent growth between 1992-93 and 1996-97, oil meal exports dwindled to less than 40 per cent of level attained in 1996-97 by end of 1990s. Exports of cotton have declined from $ 444 million in 1996-97 to meager $ 19 million in 1999-2000. Almost similar has been the case with export of sugar.

AGRI-IMPORT TRENDS

India no more depends upon rice imports and import of cereal preparations has reduced to very low level. As far as import of food grains is concerned, India occasionally imports wheat. This, according to some researchers, is due to export of wheat in previous year, besides production fluctuation. Import of pulses was increasing till 1997-98 and declined thereafter. Like wheat, India some times goes for huge import of sugar and raw cotton. Import of vegetable oil has increased drastically after 1993-94. As a result, vegetable oil import now constitutes about 2/3rd of import of all agricultural items including fertilizer. Vegetable oil import during late 1990s has reached staggering level of more than $ 1.8 billion. It is reported that India is now biggest edible oil importer in the world except China and 40 per cent of total requirement of edible oil is met through import. Among agricultural inputs, India has imported fertilizers to the tune of $ 1.28 billion during 1999-2000. However, this has dropped to almost half during 2000-01 ($ 0.66 billion) and 2001-02 ($ 0.62 billion).

ISSUES FOR AGRICULTURE AND AGRO-BASED INDUSTRIES IN THE WAKE OF WTO AGREEMENTS

To increase India's share in the world trade from its existing level of 0.7 per cent, some of the issues need to be highlighted and addressed suitably. They are as follows:

Raising Quality Standards of Indian Agri-Exports

- With WTO agreement and consequent Sanitary and Phytosanitary (SPS) measures, Indian agro-processing sector may face non-tariff barriers for its products. Several past instances are there to prove this. Interestingly, many countries are setting their health standards at a level higher than the internationally prescribed ones. For example, in case of tobacco exports, the internationally prescribed level of Dichloro-Dimethyle-Trichloro-ethane (DDT) residue is 4 parts per million (ppm), while Japan and the USA had set their permissible level at less than 1 ppm. The idea is to block tobacco exports originated from countries like India. Another instance is shrimps' exports from India. The USA had placed restrictions on the ground that these are not caught with turtle excluding devices. This may well be a ploy for blocking shrimps' exports knowing well India's fisherman lacks adequate resources to catch shrimps with turtle excluding devices.

- There should be a proper mechanism to monitor the entire commodity chain to maintain quality and hygiene standards. There is a serious need to link up farmers with processing and exporting agencies and firms so that quality can be ensured right from the raw material production stage. This can be achieved through appropriately designed arrangements like contract farming or the procurement cooperative alignment with processing and marketing companies.
- There has to be an all round realization at every level that quality production of international standards is the watchword for survival now. The processors, small or big, have to take steps to improve quality right from the selection of the raw material and that of the ingredients. Steps have also to be taken to upgrade the hygienic and sanitary conditions of the workers, plant and machinery so as to ensure quality of the finished products. There has to be much greater emphasis to invest in research and development and also in product innovation.

Raising Production and Export Base of Agro-Processed Commodities

- The production and export base of all agro-processed commodities has to be enlarged. Based on the past trends of exports, natural advantages, quality and productivity parameters, India has a comparative advantage and is the world leader in producing certain good quality agro-products, like fruits and vegetables and certain other cash crops. These products are usually low volume and high value, not essential food and India's production capacity is higher than the competitors. The productivity of certain crops has to be improved for greater value addition, export and to cut the unit cost.

Post Harvest Management Practices

- Post Harvest Management practices is important for prevention of post harvest losses, value addition, maintenance and improvement of quality, enhancing the shelf life of food and ensuring remunerative price for farmers. With production of about 600 MTs of food, India is the second largest producer after China in the world. However, post harvest management of food products in India has not kept pace with the progress achieved in the production. The need for high degree of efficiency in the post harvest management is as essential as in the production of agricultural commodities as the wastage and value losses in India's food production is estimated at about Rs.50,000 crore per year. The cold chain may be provided to help in retaining quality, freshness and to reduce post-harvest losses. These developments would result in the greater availability of quality raw materials to the industry, thus, resulting in better capacity utilisation and producing a wider range of products and of international quality. The multinationals now entering into food industry have an international marketing network and their brand loyalties all over the world. This will enable the Indian products reaching all over the world in the form and packing required.

Livestock Sector

- There is a regional imbalance in creation and utilization of processing facilities for milk in the country. Moreover, only a few processing plants are meeting the ISO standards. In order to maintain the quality of milk, bulk milk coolers have to be installed by the milk unions/dairies. Further, Indian dairy products have to compete with the international players like EU, USA and Oceania countries like Australia and New Zealand. In the absence of import restrictions, domestic dairy products have to compete with cheaper imported products in the domestic market. If this happens, it will totally *topsy turvey* the pattern of dairy development in the country, affecting income distribution.

Poultry Sector

- As for the poultry sector, with quantitative restrictions (QRs) being lifted, domestic producers will be exposed to the threat of uneven competition from developed countries. No subsidies exist for this sector in India, although the governments of developed countries give their industry heavy subsidies on production as well as exports. In USA, the exported poultry meat is subsidized to the extent of \$394.7 per ton (approximately Rs.18 per kg.). The poultry meat is subsidized to the extent of \$295.2 per ton in EU (Rs.13.50 per kg.). It is reported that in Orissa, West Bengal, the farms are small, with about 500 birds per farm. The poultry gives employment to about 1.6 million people. Many ancillary industries support the poultry industry. Agriculture that provides many ingredients essential for poultry feed will be hard hit along with the poultry industry if the foreign players are allowed to bring in cheap chicken.

SUGGESTIONS TO ENSURE GREATER COMPETITIVENESS OF INDIAN AGRICULTURE

(i) While India has some surplus for export of agricultural products, our international competitiveness is adversely affected because of the existence of heavy subsidies in developed countries and the non-tariff barriers faced by Indian exports of agricultural products. India should maintain sufficient level of border protection for our farmers who are largely subsistence and marginal producers. At the same time, we want substantial reduction in the domestic support, lowering tariffs and export subsidies by developed countries with a view to eliminating export subsidies within a reasonable period of time.

(ii) There is a need for finding greater market access for Indian agricultural products especially in the markets of developed countries.

(iii) Food security of our people, protection of interest of domestic farmers and their livelihood as also to boost our exports should be given due importance.

(iv) There is need to raise productivity, providing better irrigation facilities, developing rural infrastructure including cold chains, increasing expenditure on agricultural research and strengthening the market net work and effectively managing the supply chains.

(v) Public investment in agriculture should be accelerated by adopting the cost reducing technologies and by removing restrictions on agricultural trade, marketing and processing in the country. This can be achieved through appropriate policy framework and institutional arrangement. Institutional reforms for augmenting and managing infrastructure and other services through Self Help Groups, Watershed Development Committees, etc. needs to be strengthened.

(vi) Indian agricultural sector needs to be diversified. Farmers should grow and export cereals, fruits, dairy products, vegetables and flowers in a big way. The increased revenue from exports could then be used for new investment in agriculture. Through the multiplied effect, this new investment can double or triple agricultural output for further exports.

(vii) A shift of sizeable proportion of the work force to the non-agricultural sectors such as industrial and services sector is also needed. This is because of the fact that share of agriculture in India's GDP has fallen to about 24 per cent, while 65 per cent of the work force is still employed in this sector.

CONCLUSION

With the advent of WTO regime, we need to prepare our agriculture and allied activities for the global competition with cost effective production and efficient management. It is obvious that benefits to developing countries like India in terms of increasing their exports will occur only after the elimination of export subsidies and substantial adoption in domestic support in the developed countries has been effected. The opening up of agricultural trade should be looked at as a major opportunity for raising the overall economic growth rate by exploiting India's competitive as well as comparative advantage in agriculture for improving the efficiency of resource use in agriculture and technologically upgrading the rural sector. We need to devise a multi pronged strategy to face the emerging challenges under the WTO regime and make Indian agriculture a sustainable and internationally competitive.

REFERENCES

Bhattacharya, B. (1995), World Trade Organisation, Yojana, February 28, Vol. 39, No. 3.

Centre for Monitoring Indian Economy (CMIE) (2002), Foreign Trade and Balance of Payments, October, Mumbai.

Centre for Monitoring Indian Economy (CMIE) (2003), Foreign Trade and Balance of Payments, September, Mumbai.

Centre for Monitoring Indian Economy (CMIE) (2004), Foreign Trade and Balance of Payments, September, Mumbai.

Economic Survey, Ministry of Finance, Government of India (Various Issues).

IMPACT OF WTO ON INDIAN AGRICULTURAL EXPORTS

Manoj Shankar Gupta

INTRODUCTION

The establishment of World Trade Organization (WTO) is a trend towards globalization of world economy. The world economy has been experiencing a progressive international economic integration since the last quarter of the twentieth century. After seven years of protracted negotiations-called Uruguay Round of Trade Negotiations-the most powerful World trade regulating agency, named World Trade Organization (WTO) came into existence on January 1, 1995. It covered many new areas such as agriculture, textiles, technology, Intellectual Property Rights (IPRs) and trade related investment services. Gradually the canvas of WTO negotiations expanded (Koushik and Karol, 2005).

Indian agricultural trade has been facing serious challenges under the globalization. Though Indian agriculture contributes one-fourth in country's GDP, and source of livelihood of more than two third of the population but its share in global agro trade has been diminished to about 9 per cent only over the period of time. Agricultural trade was an exception to liberalization before the WTO agreement. It was the highly protected sector in the developed countries. Remunerative prices, subsidies, quantitative restrictions were the order of the day. As a result, the agricultural exports of the developing countries like India, suffered a lot (Madaan, 2005).

The Agreement on Agriculture of WTO recognizes free and market oriented trading system in agriculture. During 1986-88 (the base years of WTO), the international prices of most agro products were more than India's domestic prices. Then, India was expecting stability in international agricultural prices due to reduction of subsidies by the developed countries under WTO commitments. But international agricultural prices have declined except paddy, and now India's domestic prices are more than international prices. India's competitiveness in agricultural exports has been lost. The share of agro products in India's total exports has not increased during the post WTO period (1995-2004). This paper is an attempt to analyze and discuss the emerging trend of Indian agricultural trade during post WTO period. Besides, an effort has been made to work out India's global terms of trade in agriculture.

WTO AND HONG KONG MEET

The WTO was established on 1st January 1995 after converting General Agreement on Tariffs and Trade (GATT) of 1947-94, as a result of the Uruguay Round Agreement on April 15, 1994 in Marrakesh, Morocco. It is the highest body for setting rules for international trade. It encompasses GATT plus a lot more, and has acquired a much wider and ever increasing scope and coverage. The legal text of the WTO agreement is a list of about 60 agreements, annexures and decisions. At present, 148 countries are its members including India and China. About 29 countries including Russia are waiting eagerly to become the WTO members. A Ministerial Conference that meets at least once every two years directs WTO. Till date, six Ministerial Conferences have been held in Singapore (December, 1996), Geneva (May, 1998), Seattle-USA (November-December, 1999), Doha-Qatar (November, 2001) and Cancun-Maxico (September, 2003) respectively (Madaan, 2005). The sixth Ministerial Conference held in Hong Kong during December 13-18, 2005 and major outcomes and timelines of this Ministerial Deceleration (Government of India, 2005-06) are as follows:

1. Resolve to complete the Doha Work Programme fully and to conclude the negotiations in 2006.
2. To establish modalities in agricultural and non-agricultural market access (NAMA) by April 30, 2006 and prepare draft schedules by July 31, 2006.

3. To eliminate export subsidies in agriculture by 2013, with a substantial part in the first half of the implementation period. Developing countries without Aggregate Measurement of Support (AMS), such as India, will be exempt from reductions in de minimis and the overall cut in trade-distorting domestic support, consisting of AMS, the Blue Box and de minimis, that is entitlement to provide Amber Box subsidies up to 10 per cent of value.
4. To submit a second round of revised services' offers by July 31, 2006 and submit final draft schedules by October 31, 2006.
5. Amendments to TRIPS Agreement reaffirmed to address public health concerns of developing countries.
6. Duty-free, quota-free market access for all LCD's products to all developed countries. Developing country declaring itself to be in a position to do so, to also provide such access, though flexibility in coverage and in the phase in of their commitments are provided.
7. In cotton, export subsidies should be eliminated by developed countries in 2006 and trade-distorting domestic subsidies to be reduced more ambitiously and over a shorter period of time.

WTO AND EXPORT SUBSIDIES

The WTO is based on the principles of non-discrimination, free trade and promotion of fair competition among the member countries. About 95 per cent of the global trade is governed by the rules and regulations of WTO. The Quad countries (USA, EU, Canada and Japan) with their share of 80 per cent of the global trade, dominate the decision-making of WTO. The WTO Agreements have been implemented fully since January 1, 2005.

The long-term objective of the Agreement is "to establish a fair and market oriented agricultural trading system and that a reform process should be initiated through the establishment of strengthened and more operationally effective GATT rules and disciplines". It has been further stated that the long term objective is to provide for substantial progressive reductions in agricultural support and protection sustained over an agreed period of time, resulting in correcting and preventing restrictions and distortions in world agricultural markets.

WTO agreement envisaged two kinds of support to agriculture viz. domestic support and export subsidies. The domestic support further classified into five categories:

1. Green Box Support
2. Blue Box Support
3. Deminimis Support
4. Aggregate Measure Support (AMS), which includes product specific and non-product specific support.
5. Special and Differential Treatment Box (S&D)

AGRICULTURAL EXPORTS–AN APPRAISAL

(a) Agricultural Exports

There is a remarkable increase in the agricultural exports during economic reform period. According to the World Bank study, economic reforms created favourable conditions to agriculture through the trade policy reforms and devaluation of rupee (World Bank, 1996). Table 1 reveals that aggregate agricultural exports rose from $2.6 billion in 1980-81 to $ 6.3 billion in 1995-1996 but thereafter declined to $ 6.1 billion in 2001-2002 and again registered an increase to the tune of $ 7.8 billion in 2003-2004. The country's export basket in the past was heavily dependent upon items like tea and mates and coffee which in recent years has widened to include commodities like rice, marine products, fruits and vegetable etc. It is also evident from the table that rice, other cereal preparation, fruits and vegetables and processed fruits and vegetables have high potential for exports for India.

The study further shows the buoyancy in rice export of India with large fluctuations due to devaluation of Indian rupee in 1991, abolition of quota system, quantitative restrictions on export of rice in 1992, burgeoning stocks and exports subsidy.

Regarding export of coffee, India has been able to improve its position from less than one lakh tonnes (0.87 lakhs tonnes) in 1980-81 to 1.88 lakh tonnes by 2003-2004. The export earnings increased from $ 270.9 million in 1980-1981 to $ 449 million in 1995-1996 but registered a decline after that and reached $ 236 million during 2003-2004. During the period 2000-2001 to 2003-2004, despite an increase in the volume of coffee export; India's export earnings from coffee followed a steep decline due to a crash in global coffee prices, which has put coffee industry in a challenging position to face the crisis.

The tea export of India witnessed fluctuations in the period 1980-81 and 2003-04. For instance, its export first declined substantially from 229 thousand tonnes in 1980-81 to 158.1 thousand tonnes till 1995-96 and again registered growth after that. The unit value realization from export of tea and mate also exhibited a considerable year-to-year variation and were close to $ 3.5 billion in 2003-2004 (Table 1).

Sugar is also one of the export items of India. Export of sugar has shown serious fluctuation during the reform period. Due to sharp rise in its domestic demand, even a marginal decline in its production has led to occasional import of large size. The reason for which seems to be mismanagement of supply and lack of clear policy on trade and pricing of sugar. Spice export has shown a steady increase from 84 thousand tonnes in 1980-1981 to 278 thousand tonnes in 2002-2003 and then declined to 267 thousand tonnes in 2003-2004. In value terms, the export earnings from spices have shown about a 2.5 times increase during the same period.

(b) Agricultural Exports–Growth and Trends

Table 2 reveals the estimated annual compound growth rates for the agricultural exports for the Period I (1986-87 to 1994-95), Period II (1995-96 to 2003-2004) and Period III (1986-1987 to 2003-2004). It shows that export earning from India's agricultural and allied products grew at the rate of 7.78 per cent per annum in Period I (Pre-WTO) and plummeted to 0.81 per cent in Period II (Post-WTO). Growth rate in the overall Period III was however, 7.35 per cent. Appreciable increase in export has come about mainly due to the devaluation of the Indian rupee and opening up of the economy due to significant reduction in the import duties. The decline in agricultural exports in the latter half of the nineties is probably due to sharp reduction in the international prices of agricultural commodities (Chand, 2002).

Among the various agricultural export groups, the growth rates registered by fish and fish preparations were significant both in volume and value in all the three periods followed by

Table 1
Composition of Indian Agricultural Exports

(Qty in '000 tonnes
Value in '000 US $)

Commodity	1980-81		1990-91		1995-96		2000-01		2001-02		2002-03		2003-04	
	Qty	*Value*	*Qty*	*Value*	*Qty*	*Value*	*Qty*	*Value*	*Qty*	*Value*	*Qty*	*Value*	*Qty*	*Value*
Coffee	87.3	270.9	86.5	141	156.1	449	184.9	259	176.3	230	184.9	205	188	236
Tea & Mate	229.2	538	199.1	596	158.7	350	202.4	433	180.1	360	184.4	344	178	356
Oil Cakes	886	158	2447.8	339	4331	702	2417.8	448	278.2	474	177.6	382	325	729
Tobacco	91.3	178.7	87.1	147	87.1	134	108.3	191	97.9	169	100.5	211	121	238
Cashew Kernels	32.3	177.2	55.5	249	70.8	370	83.8	412	92.4	346	129.4	424	99.7	370
Spices	84.2	140.8	103.3	133	204.1	237	244.9	354	239.3	314	278	343	267	336
Sugar & Molasses	97	50.4	191	21	734.4	151	769	112	1677.5	374	1870.2	375	1299.2	269
Raw Cotton	131.6	208.6	374.4	471	33.3	61	30.2	49	8.2	9	11.7	10	179.6	205
Rice	726.7	283.2	505	257	4914	1366	1534.4	644	2208.4	666	4967.8	1205	3412.1	1025
Fish & Fish Preparations	69.4	269.2	158.9	535	310.1	1011	502.6	1394	–	1236	–	1432	–	1329
Meat & Meat Preparations	–	70.81	–	78	–	187	–	322	–	250	–	284	–	373
Pulses, Fruit & Vegetables	–	277.8	–	120	–	240	–	239	–	327	–	350	–	513
Others	–	101	–	119	–	223	–	906	–	259	–	307	–	305
Total		2601		3521		6320		6256		6146		6962		7888

Source: Directorate General of Commercial Intelligence and Statistics, Kolkata.

cashew kernels and meat and meat preparation. The results reported in Table-2 showed that during Period I, the quantity exported of coffee rose at the rate 5.80 per cent per annum while in terms of value; it registered a negative growth rate to the tune of 0.49 per cent. Similar trends were recorded for the Period II also. Tea and mate witnessed a negative growth rate both in volume and value in Period III. During Period I, the export of tea (in quantity terms) declined at an annual rate of 3.4 per cent, while it recorded a positive growth rate of 6.33 per cent in Period II. Tea industry's capacity to increase export substantially in terms of volume has been threatened by steady spurt in domestic consumption. Export of Indian tea has also received a setback due to war in Iraq and due to disintegration of erstwhile Soviet Union.

Table 2
Growth Trends in Export of Agricultural Products (1986-87 to 2003-04)
(Compound Average Rate CAGR in per cent)

Commodities	*Period I*		*Period II*		*Period III*	
	(1986-87 to 1994-95)		*(1995-96 to 2003-04)*		*(1986-87 to 2003-04)*	
	Qty	*Value*	*Qty*	*Value*	*Qty*	*Value*
Coffee	5.8	-0.49	3.07	-10.14	6.65	3.05
Tea & Mate	-3.4	-4.87	6.33	-0.69	-0.70	-1.48
Oil Cakes	14.14	18.86	-13.76	-6.66	7.24	5.44
Tobacco	0.34	0.51	3.26	2.02	4.03	4.6
Cashew Kernels	9.34	5.97	4.68	0.50	6.18	4.28
Spices	8.04	-3.72	1.16	1.51	7.65	5.23
Sugar & Molasses	45.43	3.87	-20.42	16.18	21.7	22.14
Raw Cotton	6.08	1.40	-24.97	-19.74	-5.12	-6.85
Rice	15.49	10.29	-30.95	-3.63	14.37	11.51
Fish & Fish Preparations	15.75	12.41	6.35	3.56	12.38	8.65
Meat & Meat preparation	–	9.41	–	8.65	–	11.62
Fruits & Vegetables	–	4.28	–	-1.68	–	8.22
Agricultural & Allied Products	–	7.78	–	0.81	–	7.35

Source: Directorate General of Commercial Intelligence and Statistics, Kolkata.

The export of oil cakes reported positive growth rates (14.14 per cent in quantity and 18.86 per cent in value) during Period I whereas in the second period under study both turned negative (-13.76 per cent and -6.66 per cent) respectively.

The exports of Tobacco showed a higher growth rates in volume as well as value during Period II as compared to Period I. The exports of sugar, cotton, and rice witnessed higher rates of growth during Period I, whereas these turned out to be negative in Period II.

The exports of fruits and vegetables grew at the rate of 4.28 per cent in Period I and plummeted to -1.68 per cent during Period II but registered an annual growth rate of 8.22 per cent in the overall period.

During Period III export of sugar and molasses registered the highest annual growth in quantity (21.7 per cent) as well as in value (22.14 per cent) followed by rice (14.37 per cent in quantity and 11.51 per cent in value) and fish and fish preparation (12.38 per cent in quantity and 8.65 per cent in value).

Spices constitute a major commodity of export in agricultural sector and it grew by 7.65 and 5.23 per cent per annum respectively in quantity and value. Exports of other items in value term such as meat and meat preparation, fruits and vegetables, tobacco, cashew kernels, oil cakes and coffee grew in the range of 3 to 12 per cent annually. Tea and mate showed a negative growth rate.

Period-wise analysis of Table 2 indicates that the performance of agricultural exports in almost all the commodities was much better during the Pre-WTO period than the Post-WTO period.

(c) India's Share in World Exports of Selected Agricultural Commodities

India's share of agricultural exports in different years is presented in Table 3. However, it reveals that India's share of some of the traditional items in world exports has been declining rapidly in the Post- WTO period. In the case of tea and mate, India's share in world exports declined from 26.2 per cent in 1985 to 12.6 per cent in 2002. Earlier India enjoyed a respectable place in spice exports with its share in world exports around 19.3 per cent in 1985 but it came down to 8.5 per cent in 2002.

A mixed trend was observed in the case of tobacco. India has had a reasonable presence in the world exports market of rice with India's share around 5.1 per cent in 1985. It further increased to 18.1 per cent in 2003-04, which is really commendable.

Table 3
India's Share in World's Exports of Selected Agricultural Products

(In per cent)

Commodity	*1985*	*1990*	*1995*	*2000*	*2001*	*2003*
Coffee	1.9	1.7	2.8	2.3	2.6	2.3
Tea and Mate	26.2	22.1	14.3	14	13.3	12.6
Cereals & Cereal Preparation	0.6	0.6	2.7	1.5	1.8	2.8
Tobacco & Tobacco Manufacture	1.8	0.8	0.5	0.7	0.6	0.7
Unmanufactured Tobacco	3	2.1	2.1	2.7	2.1	2.9
Spices	19.3	7.7	9.5	10.3	9.2	8.5
Sugar and Molasses	0	0.1	0.8	0.9	2.4	2.4
Rice	5.6	6.4	18.6	10.2	9.7	18.1
Fish & Fish Preparations	2.4	1.6	2.1	2.7	2.4	2.6
Meat & Meat Preparations	0.4	0.2	0.4	0.7	0.5	0.6
Fruits & Vegetables	1.4	0.8	1	1.3	1.1	1.1

Source: Directorate General of Commercial Intelligence and Statistics, Kolkata.

On the other hand, India's share in the world fisheries export hovered around 2.5 per cent in value terms. India thus does not have a substantial presence in the world exports of fishery products. But India's output is large and it is the seventh largest producer, and an opening up of her large fisheries sector to world trade may have considerable effect on the nature of the world equilibrium in terms of prices and subsequently outputs. India's share in world coffee export increased from 1.9 per cent in 1985 to 2.8 per cent in 1995 and remained close to it in the subsequent period.

(d) Share of Agricultural Exports in India's Total Exports

In India, agricultural exports contribute significantly to the trade balance. While, the share of agricultural exports in the total exports is eroding, for examples from 30.65 per cent in

1980-81 to 12.36 per cent in 2003-2004 (Table 4), the net export earning (difference between value of exports and imports) has improved (Economic Survey, 2005). The share of all the agricultural products in total exports of India has shown a consistent decline from 1980-81 till 2003-2004. The data in Table 4 reveals that until 1980-81, the traditional products like tea and mate, rice, coffee, raw cotton, tobacco, oil cakes, cashew kernels and spices occupied predominant place, each of which contributed nearly 5 to 10 per cent to the country's total agricultural exports with the exception of tea. Tea contributed 20.68 per cent alone.

Agricultural exports accounted for about 12.36 per cent of total annual exports of the country in 2003-2004. Agricultural products valued at more than US $7.8 billion were exported from the country, 16.85 per cent of which was contributed by the marine products alone. The percentage share of fisheries exports in total agricultural exports varied from 10 per cent to 20 per cent during 1980-1981 to 2003-2004. The share of fisheries sector in total merchandise exports in India remained around 2 to 3 per cent. The commodities whose share in total exports declined since 1980-81 were coffee, tea, tobacco, cashew kernel, raw cotton, rice, pulses, fruits & vegetables while the share of oil cakes, spices, sugar, meat and meat preparation remained more or less stable. Fruits and vegetables, meat and meat preparation, have recently shown strong growth but they are currently not among the dominant foreign exchange earners.

The stagnating agricultural exports from India in recent years can be traced partly to distorted domestic prices for products like rice, oil meals, tea, coffee etc. Weakness in export infrastructure specific to agricultural products such as storage, port handling facilities and lack of large scale processing technology, makes Indian supply sources unreliable and hinder the exploitation of full potential of Indian agricultural exports. India's efforts of raising exports of traditional agricultural products suffered a server setback primarily since the markets were expanding very slowly. In view of the fact that the prices of Indian products tended to be higher than those of competitors, the demand for Indian products did not grow substantially. The sharp fall in jute exports is mainly due to growing competition from Bangladesh, Brazil in tea, Hong Kong in cotton.

Table 4
Percentage Share of Agricultural Products in Agricultural and Total Products

Commodity	*1980-81*		*1990-91*		*1995-96*		*2001-02*		*2002-03*		*2003-04*	
	Agril Exports	*Total Exports*	*Agril Exports*	*Total Exports*	*Agril Exports*	*Total Exports*	*Agril Exports*	*Total Exports*	*Agril Exports*	*Total Exports*	*Agril Exports*	*Total Exports*
Coffee	10.42	3.19	4.00	0.78	7.10	1.41	3.74	0.53	2.94	0.39	2.99	0.37
Tea & Mate	20.68	6.34	16.93	3.29	5.54	1.10	5.86	0.82	4.94	0.65	4.51	0.56
Oil Cakes	6.07	1.86	9.63	1.87	11.11	2.21	7.71	1.08	5.49	0.72	9.24	1.14
Tobacco	6.87	2.11	4.17	0.81	2.12	0.42	2.75	0.39	3.03	0.40	3.02	0.37
Cashew Kernels	6.81	2.09	7.07	1.37	5.85	1.16	5.63	0.79	6.09	0.80	4.69	0.58
Spices	5.41	1.66	3.78	0.73	3.75	0.75	5.11	0.72	4.93	0.65	4.26	0.53
Sugar & Molasses	1.94	0.59	0.60	0.12	2.39	0.47	6.09	0.86	5.39	0.71	3.41	0.42
Raw Cotton	8.02	2.46	13.38	2.60	0.97	0.19	0.15	0.02	0.14	0.02	2.60	0.32
Rice	10.89	3.34	7.30	1.42	21.61	4.30	10.84	1.52	17.31	2.29	12.99	1.61
Fish & Fish Preparations	10.35	3.17	15.19	2.95	16.00	3.18	20.11	2.83	20.57	2.72	16.85	2.08
Meat & Meat Preparations	2.72	0.83	2.22	0.43	2.96	0.59	4.07	0.57	4.08	0.54	4.73	0.58
Pulses, fruit & vegetables	10.68	3.27	3.41	0.66	3.80	0.75	5.32	0.75	5.03	0.66	6.50	0.80
Others	3.88	1.19	3.38	0.66	3.53	0.70	4.21	0.59	4.41	0.58	3.87	0.48
Agricultural & Allied	100.00	30.65	100.00	19.41	100.00	19.88	100.00	14.06	100.00	13.21	100.00	12.36

Source: Directorate General of Commercial Intelligence and Statistics, Kolkata.

(e) Share of Export and Import in GDP

The information regarding the share of total exports and imports as well as agricultural exports and imports in the total GDP and GDP for agriculture and allied respectively is given in Table 5. The share of total exports in the total GDP was 7.48 per cent in the year 1991-92, which increased to 11.55 per cent in 2003-04. Similarly, the share of total imports in the GDP increased from 8.12 per cent to 14.03 per cent in the same period. Thus, the share of international trade was about 26 per cent in the total GDP of India during the year 2003-04.

A perusal of the data given in Table 5 showed that the share of agricultural exports in the GDP from agriculture and allied products was to the extent of 4.22 per cent in the year 1991-92 which increased to 6.58 per cent in 2003-04. Similarly, the share of agricultural imports in the GDP from agriculture and allied products increased from only 0.80 per cent to 3.91 per cent in the corresponding period. On account of liberalization, privatization and globalization of the Indian economy, the growth rate of GDP (at factor cost at 1993-94 prices) has increased in the post-reforms period. The growth rate of GDP was 1.3 per cent in the year 1991-92 which increased to 6.8 per cent in 2003-04 (Tata Services Ltd., 2004). There is overwhelming evidence in favour of the export led growth hypothesis if one looks at cross-section studies alone. The results of studies by (Michaely, 1977), (Heller and Porter, 1978), (Balassa, 1978), (Ram, 1985, 1986) and (Feder, 1983) support the view that export growth promotes overall economic growth. The post-reforms experience of the Indian economy also supported the viewpoint of these studies. The export growth in India was (-) 1.5 per cent during the year 1991-92 which had increased to 11.5 per cent in 2003-04.

(f) Destination of India's Farm Exports

The information about country-wise export of agricultural and allied products for 1996-97 to 2003-04 is given in Table 6. The data given in the table clearly showed that the maximum exports had been to the USA (12.87 per cent) followed by Bangladesh (9.25 per cent), UAE (5.99 per cent), Japan (5.23 per cent) and Saudi Arabia (5.05 per cent) during the year 2003-04. The other important importing countries were Indonesia, Malaysia and

Table 5

Share of India's Total Exports and Imports and Agricultural Export and Import in the Gross Domestic Product at Factor Cost (at current prices) 1991-92 to 2003-04

Year	*Total GDP at factor cost (Rs. in Crores)*	*Total Exports*	*% share of total exports in GDP*	*Total Imports*	*% share of total imports in GDP*	*GDP from agriculture & allied (Rs. crores)*	*Exports of agri-cultural products*	*% share of agri. export in GDP from agricul-ture & allied products*	*Imports of agri-cultural products*	*% share of agri. import in GDP from agricul-ture & allied products*
1991-92	589086	44041.81	7.48	47850.84	8.12	185712	7838.04	4.22	1478.27	0.80
1992-93	673221	53688.26	7.97	63374.52	9.41	208265	9040.30	4.34	2876.25	1.38
1993-94	781345	69748.85	8.93	73101.01	9.36	241967	12586.55	5.20	2327.33	0.96
1994-95	917058	82673.40	9.02	89970.70	9.81	278773	13222.76	4.74	5937.21	2.13
1995-96	1073271	106353.35	9.91	122678.14	11.43	303102	20397.74	6.73	5890.10	1.94
1996-97	1243546	118817.32	9.55	138919.88	11.17	362605	24161.29	6.66	6612.60	1.82
1997-98	1390148	130100.64	9.36	154176.29	11.09	387008	24832.45	6.42	8784.19	2.27
1998-99	1598127	139751.77	8.74	178331.69	11.16	442494	25510.64	5.77	14566.48	3.29
1999-00	1761838	159095.20	9.03	215528.53	12.23	461964	25313.66	5.48	16066.73	3.48
2000-01	1902998	201356.45	10.58	228306.64	12.00	468479	28657.37	6.12	12086.23	2.58
2001-02	2090957	209017.97	10.00	245199.72	11.73	521907	29728.61	5.70	16256.61	3.11
2002-03	2249493	255137.28	11.34	297205.87	13.21	509907	34653.94	6.80	17608.83	3.45
2003-04	2523872	291581.93	11.55	353975.61	14.03	560482	36893.90	6.58	21894.37	3.91

Source: (I) CMIE, (2004), (ii) Goverment of India (2004)

Table-6
Destination of India's Export of Agricultural & Allied Products 1996-97 to 2003-04

(US $million)

Country/Year	1996-97	% share in total export	1997-98	% share in total export	1998-99	% share in total export	1999-2000	% share in total export	2000-01	% share in total export	2001-02	% share in total export	2002-03	% share in total export	2003-04	% share in total export
World	6868.5	100.00	6634.20	100.00	6033.11	100.00	5614.87	100.00	5982.94	100.00	5921.3	100.00	6727.44	100.00	7425.33	100.00
USA	660.09	9.61	651.53	9.82	677.62	11.23	851.27	15.16	790.92	13.22	749.89	12.66	954.09	14.18	955.65	12.87
Bangladesh	100.68	1.47	150.51	2.27	570.34	9.45	173.80	3.10	230.54	3.85	298.65	5.04	407.92	6.06	686.72	9.25
UAE	403.49	5.87	422.34	6.37	354.00	5.87	317.14	5.65	380.60	6.36	328.69	5.55	350.01	5.20	445.00	5.99
Japan	699.49	10.18	736.26	11.10	648.08	10.74	642.28	11.44	651.26	10.89	447.41	7.56	440.08	6.54	388.29	5.23
Saudi-Arabia	336.65	4.90	384.10	5.79	440.31	7.30	372.94	6.64	372.57	6.23	326.46	5.51	312.51	4.65	375.27	5.05
Indonesia	325.51	4.74	205.01	3.09	75.66	1.25	116.49	2.07	137.60	2.30	251.81	4.25	247.10	3.67	314.59	4.24
Malaysia	191.85	2.79	162.83	2.45	129.83	2.15	142.91	2.55	169.01	2.82	220.55	3.72	319.44	4.75	308.31	4.15
UK	285.35	4.15	301.03	4.54	257.10	4.26	294.27	5.24	312.92	5.23	243.78	4.12	273.08	4.06	284.48	3.83
Sri Lanka	148.52	2.16	116.67	1.76	63.67	1.06	93.97	1.67	65.69	1.10	149.28	2.52	171.00	2.54	202.46	2.73
China	271.18	3.95	362.58	5.47	114.68	1.90	148.49	2.64	160.92	2.69	126.18	2.13	151.17	2.25	195.71	2.64
Germany	171.35	2.49	212.93	3.21	175.79	2.91	183.11	3.26	156.57	2.62	129.19	2.18	153.89	2.29	186.76	2.52
Russia	339.76	4.95	448.25	6.76	335.60	5.56	340.98	6.07	228.53	3.82	206.18	3.48	157.22	2.34	168.33	2.27
Netherland	284.32	4.14	227.41	3.43	202.00	3.35	267.90	4.77	221.49	3.70	183.99	3.11	163.26	2.43	162.63	2.19
Belgium	62.80	0.91	74.31	1.12	83.91	1.39	76.69	1.37	78.57	1.31	82.17	1.39	126.09	1.87	145.91	1.97
Italy	157.92	2.30	141.32	2.13	129.69	2.15	116.22	2.07	97.57	1.63	93.14	1.57	101.96	1.52	123.68	1.67
Vietnam	35.64	0.52	31.70	0.48	21.26	0.35	35.17	0.63	55.78	0.93	70.15	1.18	107.98	1.61	121.75	1.64
Singapore	329.04	4.79	184.13	2.78	108.79	1.80	104.67	1.86	152.05	2.54	161.12	2.72	117.33	1.74	121.31	1.63
Korea Republic (South)	133.16	1.94	146.34	2.21	69.88	1.16	65.85	1.17	90.01	1.50	62.21	1.05	105.03	1.56	118.21	1.59

Contd...

Country/Year	*1996-97*	*% share in total export*	*1997-98*	*% share in total export*	*1998-99*	*% share in total export*	*1999-2000*	*% share in total export*	*2000-01*	*% share in total export*	*2001-02*	*% share in total export*	*2002-03*	*% share in total export*	*2003-04*	*% share in total export*
France	106.04	1.54	83.83	1.26	94.95	1.57	99.90	1.78	133.46	2.23	85.81	1.45	99.27	1.48	114.23	1.54
Spain	87.06	1.27	81.57	1.23	80.58	1.34	91.01	1.62	90.79	1.52	102.26	1.73	122.57	1.82	114.07	1.54
Yemen	73.59	1.07	23.87	0.36	19.17	0.32	26.09	0.46	48.10	0.80	63.39	1.07	67.10	1.00	112.13	1.51
Thailand	118.69	1.73	93.70	1.41	65.49	1.09	70.46	1.25	77.78	1.30	120.32	2.03	63.36	0.94	106.83	1.44
Philippines	101.41	1.48	107.98	1.63	59.04	0.98	45.49	0.81	80.57	1.35	125.47	2.12	309.47	4.60	99.39	1.34
South Africa	87.81	1.28	108.40	1.63	149.75	2.48	57.93	1.03	34.57	0.58	71.79	1.21	178.28	2.65	87.55	1.18
Kuwait	72.91	1.06	91.44	1.38	59.24	0.98	65.41	1.16	92.79	1.55	83.19	1.40	79.02	1.17	86.47	1.16
Pakistan	-	-	74.59	1.12	45.91	0.76	34.58	0.62	93.35	1.56	57.45	0.97	28.78	0.43	85.33	1.15
Nepal	-	-	16.97	0.26	11.23	0.19	24.50	0.44	22.43	0.37	26.32	0.44	29.53	0.44	80.44	1.08
Canada	41.59	0.61	52.87	0.80	48.26	0.80	61.41	1.09	63.12	1.05	57.61	0.97	63.00	0.94	74.79	1.01
Taiwan (Taipei)	86.24	1.26	52.88	0.80	40.60	0.67	34.84	0.62	63.99	1.07	59.10	1.00	61.54	0.91	65.83	0.89

Source: CMIE, (2004)

U.K. Recently, the USA has decided to restore generalized system of preferences (GSP) to India that allows a host of items to be imported under duty free tariff (IANS, 2005). This decision of the USA will give a boost to the exports of India to the former. Moreover, it will improve bilateral economic and trade relations between two biggest democratic countries of the world.

As far as export of farm produce to different trade blocks is concerned, Organization of Economic Cooperation and Development (OECD) is the biggest importer of Indian agricultural and allied products. In percentage terms, our farm exports to the OECD was about 49 per cent of the total exports during the year 2003-04. The next important trade block was European Union having a share of about 23 per cent in our farm exports. The share of NAFTA and OPEC was about 20 per cent and 15 per cent respectively during the same year. Our farm export to the SAARC countries was about six per cent of the total export. With the improvement of political and diplomatic relations between India and Pakistan there is big potential for our exports to Pakistan. Similarly, Pakistan can also increase its exports to land blocked countries like Nepal through India. In this way, the trade will be mutually beneficial to both the neighbouring countries, i.e. India and Pakistan.

In the last ten years, the Food Corporation of India (FCI) has exported more than 30 million tones of foodgrain. India has thus, attained the status of the second largest exporter of rice in the world after Thailand and sixth largest exporter of wheat. The rice stocks were exported to 29 countries and wheat to 62 countries (Rangi and Sidhu, 2004). These exports have been mainly from the foodgrain surplus states like Punjab and Haryana. Besides, India has exported about 52 lakh tones of fresh fruits and vegetables from 1993-94 to 2001-02. In this way, our annual export of fresh fruits and vegetables was to the extent of about 5.73 lakh tones per annum during the last nine years. The value of these exports was about Rs 615 crore per year in this period. Moreover, India has also exported processed fruits and vegetables of about Rs 721 crore per annum from 1993-94 to 2001-02.

As already discussed, Punjab is the principal surplus state for wheat and rice. But the varieties of wheat mainly cultivated in the state have low protein and gluten content. Therefore, it fetches fewer prices in the international market. On this account, some countries do not prefer our wheat. The plant breeders should develop such wheat varieties, which have high protein and gluten content as demanded in the world market. Our future thrust should be on quality and not on quantity alone. As already stated, duplicate varieties of basmati rice are sown in certain pockets of northern states. Unscrupulous rice traders/exporters use these varieties to mix with high-grade basmati for quick profiteering. But it has adverse affect on our basmati rice export to the developed countries and such malpractices should be checked.

It appears in the press from time to time about rejection of our wheat and rice lots meant for exports even by developing countries. This rejection has mainly been on account of poor quality. During the year 1996, the Food Ministry of Bangladesh decided to dump into sea our 3700 tonnes of rice purchased from India, which was found unfit for consumption (Anonymous, 1996). Similarly, a cargo of 23500 tonnes of Indian wheat has been barred from the port of Swinoujscie in Poland after the tests showed it was infested with Karnal blunt (ANI, 1996). Again Iraq rejected a consignment of 35000 tonnes of wheat during the year 2001 (Anonymous, 2001). More than the marketing embarrassment, such events put hurdles in our efforts for large-scale exports of wheat and rice in the international market. The exports of wheat to Iraq were under agreement 'Wheat for Petrol" and thus, India had to export 3.50 lakh tones of wheat to that country (ENS, 2001). Anyway, our country's credibility as a reliable exporter of quality wheat has been dented.

FACTORS OF SLOW AGRICULTURAL EXPORT

The slow growth of India's agro-exports is attributable to numerous reasons. The major causes are lower prices of agricultural commodities in foreign markets, economic crisis in South East Asian countries and Japan and the decrease in exports to some of India's trade partners such as Indonesia and Bangladesh. The developed countries continued subsidizing exports of farm products in the interest of food security, maintaining farm incomes and preserving the farming population distorting agriculture trade unfavorable to the developing countries. The market access was thwarted by these countries retorting to Tariff Rate Quota (TRQ) i.e. importing certain amount of the product at low rate of tariff duty and the successive import of the same products at higher rate of tariff making the imports from the developing countries costly in their market.

India has followed low tariff rates compared to the negotiated tariff rates so far as imports of several agricultural products is concerned from abroad (Gulati, 1999). In the year 2000-01, the average basis duty rate was 34.9 per cent as compared to UR Bound Tariff Rate 114.9 per cent. After the lifting of QRs on the remaining 715 items as part of WTO commitment, India's agriculture sector is likely to have far reacting impact.

Under this scenario, some of the far-reaching implications on agriculture are highlighted below:

- The Indian markets has faced with the problem of low cost import of most of the agricultural commodities from several countries, which has caused considerable anxiety among the domestic producers.
- The gradual reduction in subsidies in a developing country like India as against the high level of subsidies provided by developed countries, result in high costs of production for comparable agricultural crops and affects adversely the growth of agriculture and allied export in India.
- Liberal import of agricultural commodities may create difficulties for supply-demand balance for essential commodities, especially food grains in a developing country like India in the event of natural calamities like flood and drought.
- The shift in cropping pattern from subsistence farming labour intensive into commercial or export oriented farming (capital intensive) will adversely affect the employment opportunities in India.
- Finally, increased investment in modernized and export oriented agriculture would require re-allocation of financial resources, which would pose a problem to our policy makers and planners, as they are already facing the fiscal deficit in their budgets.

FUTURE COURSE OF ACTION

Although, odds are many with reference to AoA, India cannot come out of WTO. We have to be tough but constructive in the negotiations and do not retreat to isolation, which would deeply damage out interest in the long run.

- Most important requirement of India in the context of WTO system is that not only preparedness for negotiations but also bringing unity among developing countries. Recent Cancun meeting failed because African Countries did not agree with India on Singapore issues. (Aloka, 2003)
- We should some how force high-income countries to open their markets by reducing the agricultural subsidies. We should convince them that trade barriers put by developed countries. We have adverse effects on job generation all over the world in developing countries in particular. For instance, it is calculated that in the textile sector alone, saving a job in industrial countries through trade protection costs 35 jobs in developing countries with the total number of jobs lost because of tariff and quotas in rich countries estimated at 27 million (Vasudev, 2002).
- In the next round negotiation on WTO, India should seek clubbing of all kinds of support to agriculture in one category and seek some parity among developed and developing countries.
- Huge investment in agriculture is needed to boost up the productivity and production in general and special emphasis needs to be given on the promotion of production and productivity of the selected export oriented crops in particular. The previous and present government at the Centre is rightly thinking in the direction of bringing a Second Green Revolution in agriculture. (Jashwant Singh, 2004).
- Air cargo transportation facilities needs to be stepped up to meet the delivery of schedule of products. Stringent measures should be adopted to see that the material being exported is of desired quality. India has to throw money and brain to study all parts of what goes by the generic name of International Law.

- There is a need to change the rural mindset on agro-exports. The farmer as well as the labourer working in the field should be made to think labour exports and quality of the products.
- In the past, experts were of the opinion that India cannot fight her battle with mighty US, Japan and EU on the basis of her own limited economic strength. She will have to join an economic block and the naturally is South Asia Free Trade Association (SAFTA) for her (Biplab, 2001).

CONCLUSION

The formation of the WTO is the right step at the international level. It has provided both the challenges and opportunities to all countries particularly the developing countries/economies. The world market would gradually be distortion free and those countries pursuing International competitiveness be able to take advantage of the free and fair trade. It is important to point out here that the developing countries would need more time to bridge the gap in their developmental pursuits as compared to the level of development in advanced countries. The two types of economies would not be able to compete with each other on reciprocal basis for longer period because the real reciprocity differs from the conventional reciprocity. In real terms, the developing world is far behind of the developed world and the farmer needs assistance on the part of the latter if the two are to be brought at par.

A country like India with vast and sizable in population and poverty will face acute problems on extreme dependence on external markets for food. Hence, we have to safeguard our interest and make pointed references to this later. It is being argued that WTO and similar other trade liberalization measures threatens the national sovereignty. Thus; technically speaking, there are costs and benefits. If the benefits exceed the cost we have to opt for it. Further, it has to be reckoned that Indian cannot walk out of WTO, as bilateral and trilateral agreements are difficult to strike. In this predicament, the best course that India can follow is to equip our agriculture to trade along the road of liberalization with our own built in checks and balances for which policies and programmes have to be carefully crafted.

India should maintain sufficient level of border protection for farmers who are mainly subsistence and marginal producers. There must be substantial reduction in domestic support, lowering tariffs and export subsidies by developed countries with a view to eliminate export subsidies within a reasonable period of time. India should raise productivity, provide better irrigation facilities, develop rural infrastructure including cold chains, more expenditure on agricultural research, strengthen the market network, manage the supply chains effectively and find a greater market access for her agricultural products especially in the markets of developed countries. For this, public investment in agriculture should be accelerated by adopting the cost reducing technologies and removing the restrictions on agricultural trade, marketing and processing in the country. This can be achieved through appropriate policy framework and institutional arrangement through Self-Help Groups, Watershed Development Committees, etc. which is to be strengthened more. Apart from this, Indian agriculture sectors also need to be diversified. Indian farmers should grow and export cereals, fruits, dairy products, vegetables and flowers in big way. This increased revenue from export can be used for new investment in agriculture resulting in more agricultural output for further export.

REFERENCES

Aloka Mukherjee (2003), The Hindu, October 4, p. 17.

ANI (1996), "Poland Ban Indian Wheat", The Sunday Tribune, Chandigarh, Vol. 116 (215), August 4, p. 18.

Anonymous (1996), Bangle Scam Over Import of Rice from India, Indian Express, Chandigarh, Vol. 43 (620), July 22, p. 10.

Anonymous (2001), "Wheat as a Reject Maal", The Tribune, Chandigarh, Vol. 121 (127), May 2, p. 10.

Balassa, Bela (1978), "Export and Growth: Future Evidence", Journal of Development Economics, 5 (2), pp. 181-189.

Biplab Dasgupta (2001), "WTO and India's Reform Agenda: One Step Forward and Two Step Backward", Indian Economic Association, 84th Conference Volume, Vellore, pp. 36-42.

Chand, Ramesh (2002), "Trade Liberalisation, WTO and Indian Agriculture: Implementation of Agreement on Agriculture Contentive Issue", Mittal Publication, New Delhi, p. 89.

CMIE (2004), Foreign Trade and Balance of Payments, Economic Intelligence Service, Mumbai.

Express News Service (ENS) (2001), "Rejection of Wheat by Iraq to be Proved", The Indian Express, Chandigarh, Vol. 24(268), May 6, p. 4.

Feder, G. (1983), "On Exports and Economic Growth", Journal of Development Economics, 5, pp. 59-73.

Government of India (2004), Agricultural Statistics at a Glance, Department of Economics and Cooperation, Ministry of Agriculture, New Delhi.

Government of India (2005-06), Economic Survey, Ministry of Finance, New Delhi.

Gulati, Ashok (1999), "From Maarakash to Seatle – Indian Agriculture in Globalising World", Economic and Political Weekly, October 9-15.

Heller, P.S. and R.C. Porter (1978), "Export and Growth: An Empirical Reinvestigation", Journal of Development Studies, 5, pp. 191-193.

IANS (2005), "India Welcomes US Decision on Preferential Tariff", The Financial World, Chandigarh, Vol. V(87), July 6, p. 2.

Jaswant Singh (2004-05), Budget Speech, Business Standard, February 4, 2004, p. 11.

Kaushik, K.K. and Sanju Karol (2005), World Trade Organisation and its Impact on India's Agricultural Exports", 88th IEA Annual Conference Volume, Vishakhapatanam, Andhra Pradesh.

Madaan, D.K. (2005), "Impact of WTO on Indian Agricultural Trade", 88th IEA Annual Conference Volume, Vishakhapatanam, Andhra Pradesh.

Michaely, M. (1977), "Export and Growth: An Empirical Investigation", Journal of Development Economics, 4, pp. 49-53.

Ram, Rati (1985), "Exports and Economic Growth: Some Additional Evidence", Economic Development and Cultural Change, Vol. 33 (2), pp. 415-425.

Ram, Rati (1986), "Government Size and Economic Growth, A New Framework and Some Evidence from Cross-Section and Time Series Data", American Economic Review, Vol.76 (1), pp. 191-203.

Rangi, P.S. and M.S. Sidhu (2004), "Development of Market Infrastructure for Globalisation in India", Indian Journal of Agricultural Marketing, Vol. 18(3), pp.1-22.

Srivastava, Roopali and J.N. Purwar (2005), "A Review of Indian Agricultural Export Scenario in the Context of WTO Regulation",

88th IEA Annual Conference Volume, Vishakhapatanam, Andhra Pradesh.

Tata Services Ltd. (2004), "Statistical Outline of India 2003-04", Development of Economics and Statistics, Bombay House, Mumbai.

Vasudeva, P.K. (2002), "WTO Lead by Example", Business Standard, December 15, p. 6.

WTO AND MARKET ACCESS FOR NON-AGRICULTURE SECTOR

Shamim Akhtar

INTRODUCTION

A major concern of developing countries with the process of trade liberalization for non-agricultural products in the Uruguay Round has been the persistence of high and peak tariffs, tariff escalation and non-tariff barriers in developed countries on goods of export interest. It has also been shown that process of trade liberalization has been asymmetric with developing countries taking deeper commitments compared to developed countries. The Doha Ministerial conference sought to address this asymmetry by proposing negotiations on the market access for non-agricultural goods to be agreed by May 2003 to eliminate barriers to market access in particular on products of export interest to developing countries. Subsequently, a Negotiating Group on Market Access (NGMA) has been set up at the WTO and different countries have presented proposals on modalities for liberalization.

Against that background this chapter reviews the Doha Mandate on non-agricultural market access (NAMA). It then discusses the priorities for developing countries in NAMA. The different proposals on modalities are summarized. The implications of the Draft Paper on Modalities of Negotiations prepared by Chairman of NGMA in May 2003 on the basis of various proposals are then commented upon from a developing country perspective. Subsequently, the Chairman of NGMA issued a Revised Draft Paper on Modalities on 19 August 2003 where a number of provisions of the May Draft were changed. The implications of the changes are also commented upon. Some concluding remarks are made at the end.

THE DOHA MANDATE: A COMMENT

The Doha Ministerial Meeting had agreed to reduce industrial tariffs under the agenda item "Market Access for Non-Agriculture Products". We agree to negotiation which shall aim, by modalities to be agreed, to reduction of eliminate tariffs peaks, high tariffs and tariff escalation as well as non-tariff barriers in particular on products of export interest to developing countries. Product coverage shall be comprehensive and without a priori exclusions. The negotiations shall take fully into account the special needs and interests of developing and least-developed country participants including through less than full reciprocity in reduction commitments, in accordance with the relevant provisions of Article XXVIII bis of GATT 1994 and the provisions cited in paragraph 50 below. To this end, the modalities to be agreed will include appropriate studies and capacity building measures the assist least-developed countries to participate effectively in the negotiations (WTO, Ministerial Declaration, WT/MIN (01)/DEC/W/1, Nov, 2001 Doha, 9-14, November 2001). Even though the Ministerial Declaration proposes about reduction in and elimination of high and peak tariffs, there is some ambiguity. The Definition of high and peak tariffs has not been made very clear in modalities before negotiations start. Peak tariff in the literature is defined at a specified level, i.e., 10 per cent, 12 per cent 15 per cent.[1] The level of the peak tariffs cannot be assumed as being the same for developed countries, developing countries LDCs. In fact, this should be related to average tariffs rates.[2]

The Declaration also mentions reduction of elimination of tariff escalation as well as of non-tariff barriers. In the Uruguay Round negotiations, actually tariff escalation increased in developed countries particularly for the products in which developing countries have an export interest.[3]

The Declaration does not make any reference to an increase in transparency and predictability through a significant expansion of the scope of tariff bindings and through simplifying members' tariffs. A large number of developed countries are defining tariffs in the form of specific and compound duties, which have been found to be relatively high. It is very difficult to put them in the negotiations without knowing ad valorem equivalence and the other implications of such duties.

PRIORITIES FOR DEVELOPING COUNTRIES

In the pre-Doha era, many developing countries were opposed to comprehensive WTO negotiations on market access for industrial sector. They had taken this stand probably from the consideration that the level of developed countries average tariff was low, and a further reduction (or even complete elimination) in industrial tariffs of developed countries would not lead to a substantial increase in market access for developing countries. On the contrary, there was a lurking fear that developing countries would have to give in return substantial market access by significantly cutting down their present level of tariff rates and spread of tariff bindings.

A large number of developing countries as a part of trade policy reforms have been unilaterally reducing their custom tariffs on industrial products. Table 1 shows that applied tariffs of a large number of developing countries are significantly lower than the UR commitment level. Nonetheless, the negotiation process is expected to put pressure on developing countries to reduce/eliminate their tariffs. In the light of a number of studies,[4] developing countries should give emphasis on the following aspects:

Elimination of Tariffs: A symmetric framework of elimination of all tariffs completely would not be in developing countries' interest, as it will lead to very high reductions by developing countries as compared to those of developed countries. It will not be consistent with the development dimension and with the principle of 'less than full reciprocity'. Elimination of low/nuisance tariff in developed countries also should not be considered as equivalent to high or deeper reduction by developing countries.

Focus of Tariff Reduction: Developing countries should not concentrate on reduction in the average tariff but their concerns should be on other aspects like peak tariffs, tariff escalation, 'credit for autonomous liberalization' and non-ad valorem duties, etc.

Table 1
Tariff Reduction on Industrial Products by Select Developing Countries

Country	*Trade-weighted Tariff averages (%)*			*Simple Average (%)*
	*Pre-Uruguay**	*Post-Uruguay* (based on UR commitments)*	*Applied, 1999*	*Applied, 2000*
Argentina	38.2	30.9	15.4	13.4
Brazil	40.6	27.0	16.2	14.78
Chile	34.9	24.9	10.0	8.96
Colombia	44.3	35.1	11.6	10.99
India	71.4	32.4	27.09	30.82
Indonesia	20.4	36.9	10.5	9.68
Korea Rep.	18.0	8.3	7.6	7.62
Malaysia	10.2	9.1	9.0	
Philippines	23.9	22.2	8.0	8.87
Thailand	37.3	28.0		14.61
Venezuela	50.0	30.9	11.9	

*Notes:** Pre-and post-Uruguay Round tariff averages are computed as the trade weighted average of tariff rates on bound tines and applied tariff rates on unbound rates. Due to the significance of ceiling bindings in the post-Uruguay Round tariff averages, no reduction are reported. It excludes the Petroleum sector.

Source: Mehta (2003), Indian Industrial Tariffs: Towards WTO Development Round Negotiations, RIs.

Bringing Greater Transparency in Tariff Rates: A large number of developed countries are used to the practice of imposing specific and complex duties rather than ad valorem duties. The total number of commodities for which custom duties are given in the form of specific duties, is very large for developed countries, for instance, EU (1780 tariff lines), US (1455 tariff line). In most cases, non-ad valorem duties[5] consisting of several specific and ad valorem tariffs associated with a condition of relationships between them. There are any variants of specific duties in schedules of different countries. Some of these variants are very complex.[6]

It has been noticed that the developed countries have imposed specific duties on a larger number of commodities as compared to developing countries. Although most of the countries believe that the specific duties should be replaced by ad valorem rates, no decision was made in the UR. In fact, a significant number of UR bound rates had been committed in the form of specific duties. It has been noticed that these specific duties conceal the fact that the countries are indirectly, imposing high tariffs[7] mentioning them in different forums.[8]

The specific duties are not suitable for analytical and comparative purposes, and require more common ad valorem tariffs. Hence, these specific duties are converted to ad valorem equivalences[9] (AVEs). A study by UNITAD (1999-2000) has computed ad valorem equivalence of specific duties for 18,000 commodities (of different counties) for the year 1996. It shows that the ad valorem equivalence of a large number of products with specific duties are much higher than the average ad valorem rates.

The custom tariff database of the US for August 1999[10] also corroborates the above observation. In this database, the US defines specific duties for around 600 industrial commodities (national lines) and provides the corresponding ad valorem equivalent rates of most of specific duties. It shows that the average tariff rate of the commodities with non-ad valorem duties is almost three times higher than the average tariff of the rate of commodities whose custom duties are defined in form of ad valorem rates. In this context, it is worth highlighting that adverbial equivalence of found rates is still not available in the literature.

Dealing with the Tariff Peaks: Even if the tariff are reduced by developed countries, tariff peaks seem to be the major hurdle in the market access for certain sector where the developing countries have good export potential.

In the literature,[11] a cut-off point is generally taken as 12 per cent (and sometimes 10 per cent or 15 per cent). All those commodities, whose tariff rate is more than 12 per cent ad valorem rate, are called commodities with peak tariff. In the existing literature, the selection of cut off point is arbitrary and has no relationship with average tariff. Further, it does not make any distinction among different groups of countries.

Besides number of attempts have been made to identify the commodities with peak tariff. Notably the study by UNCTAD[12] concludes that, "both frequency and levels of tariff peak rates remain a matter of concern. Over 10 per cent of tariff universe of the quad countries, corresponding to an aggregate 4,000-tariff line, will continue to exceed 12 per cent ad valorem. All four countries maintain high variance in tariff rates. One fifth of the peak tariff of the US one quarter of those in EU and Japan and about one tenth of those of Canada exceed 30 per cent. In the four selected developing countries, tariff peaks are more frequent but reach less extreme rates than in the major developed countries." (Emphasis added).[13]

Disciplining the Tariff Escalation: Tariff structures of many countries have traditionally displayed significant escalation favouring domestic processors for large number of commodities. It was expected that tariff commitments in the UR would provide for gradual reduction of escalation by applying relatively higher cuts to finished goods. However, rapidly rising tariff have been noticed from low rates for raw material to higher rates for intermediate goods and sometime peak tariff for finished products. A number of studies[14] have confirmed that tariff escalation has continued after UR for a large number of sector, particularly, fish & fish products, textile & textile products, leather & rubber products, footwear and to some extent wood & wood products. Basically, the result confirms that tariff escalation is still a major constraint for export industries of India and developing countries.

Addressing the Non Tariff Barriers: The developed countries employ an impressive array of new measures of protection and government interventions. These have been imposed through different instruments, including non-tariff barriers (NTBs). The agreement of the UR have changed the intensity of different types of NTBs. As a result, while some measure of NTBs have lot their significance while significance of some NTBs measures has been increased.

The non-tariff barriers continue to affect the growth of world trade and the UR could not tackle these issues successfully. On the one hand, the importing countries generally term them as NTBs, the imposing countries insist that "these instruments are policy objectives." Developing countries should look for a coherent approach for dealing with such issues and participate actively in setting up new and clear provision.

In short, the priorities of developing countries should be focused on peak tariff, tariff escalation and NTBs to get market access and to see that it is consistent with development dimension and "less than full reciprocatory."

PRESENT STATUS OF NEGOTIATION ON MODALITIES

To initiate negotiation on market access for non-agriculture products, the Negotiation Group on Market Access (NGMA) has been formed, such negotiations could be concluded by 1 January 2005. The Fifth Ministerial Conference in Cancun will take stock of these negotiations and recommend appropriately. As part of negotiations, a number of meetings of NGMA have held and many proposals,[15] particularly relating to Modalities, have been submitted by member countries. These proposals include those submitted by China, EU, India Japan, Korea and the US. The different modalities can be categorized into following five board categories.

1. Request and offer, 2. Formulae, 3. Sector by sector, 4. Zero for zero, 5. Mixed.

Proposals submitted by these members to NGMA are summarized blow:

Proposals

(a) China[16]

The Chinese Formula is specified as:

$$t_1 = \frac{\{t_a + (B \times P)\} \times t_o}{(t_a + P^2) + t_o}$$

Where,

t_a is the simple average of the base rates (A in TN/MA/20).

P is a peak factor defined as the ratio of the tariff rate over the average rate (t_a/t_a)

B is an adjusting coefficient for the year of implementation. B=1 for 2015 of B =3 for 2010.

The formula is very similar to the Swiss formula but instead of a fixed coefficient, a variable factor based on the simple average of the base rates t_a, a peak factor and an additional parameter for the year of implementation has been used. The properties of the Chinese formula are similar to what is known about the properties of the Swiss formula discussed in paragraph 16, such as higher cuts for higher rates. Furthermore it can be shown that for B=1 the formula reduces any initial tariff rate below a maximum level which is the current average of the base rates. This is equivalent to the effect of the standard Swiss formula using the tariff average as coefficient.

The percentage cuts for any given tariff rate will depend on the tariff average of the Member concerned. For the same tariff rate, Member with lower tariff averages will experience relatively higher reduction rates. Therefore, the overall result of applying this formula will depend on the statistical properties of different member tariff profiles.

(b) European Communities[17]

European Communities proposal is within the class of linear tariff dependent formulae, however, with an adjustment, which gives it the properties of a step-wise linear function. The formula is applied across a set of tariff intervals and the tariff rate cuts depend upon the upper and lower bound of the applaudable interval.

The formula is specified as:

$$t_1 = B_1^L + (t_o - B_o^L) \times \left(\frac{B_1^U - B_1^L}{B_o^U - B_o^L} \right)$$

Where B^i_j are the upper and lower bounds of the respectively tariff intervals. The super-scribed letter U and L are, respectively, the upper and lower bounds of the interval. The intervals are defined as follows:

	Base			Final
	B_o^L	B_o^U	B_1^L	B_1^U
Interval 1	0	less than 2	0	0
Interval 2	2	15	1.6	7.5
Interval 3	15	50	7.5	15
Interval 4	50	More than 50	15	15

(c) India[18]

India proposes a simple linear cut on the individual bound tariff lines of each member, with a higher percentage cut for developed countries than for developing countries. In addition to the linear cut, any tariff in excess of three times the national average tariff shall be reduced to no more than three times the national average which results after applying the initial linear cut. The formula is specified as:

Step (1) $t_o = c't_o$

Where c= {1 – (A' Y/100)} and

Step (2) $t_1 \leq 3\ t_a$

Where

A is defined as 'less than full reciprocity' parameter with

A = 1 for developed countries and

A = 0.67 for developing countries,

Y is the reduction percentage (to be negotiated)

t_{al} is the simple average tariff after applying the linear cut.

The following supplementary modalities are proposed for developing country Members: (a) The actual reductions of at least 15 per cent of currently bound rates can differ from the rates calculated under step (1) under condition that the overall percentage reduction still meets the reduction percentage resulting from step (1). (b) The flexibility in the application of formula shall also apply for step (2).

(d) Japan[19]

Japan proposes that each member sets a target level of a trade-weighted tariff average according to a formula and that each member reduce its trade-weighted tariff average to that target level. Each member will retain flexibility on ways to realize the target tariff level. The formula is specified as:

$$t^{w}_{1a} = \frac{A \times t^{W}_{0a}}{A \times t^{W}_{0a}} + \alpha$$

Where, t^{W}_{0a} is the weighted tariff average prior to the application of the formula and t^{W}_{0a} is the weighted average after the application of the formula. A is a constant whose value varies as follows:

t^{W}_{0a} £ 10%, A = 10

$10\% < t^{W}_{0a} \leq 20\%$ A = 20

$20\% < t^{W}_{0a} \leq 30\%$ A = 30

$30\% < t^{W}_{0a}$ A = 40

The term á in this specification has been proposed as a constant equal to 0.3.

The formula applies to the reduction of the trade-weighted tariff average as opposed to a reduction of the tariff rates on a line-by-line basis. This means that the formula is used to determine the end result, or the objective of the tariff negotiations. A lower coefficient will yield a higher cut and a higher coefficient a lower cut.

(e) Republic of Korea[20]

The objective of this proposal is to lower the weighted tariff average of members by 40 per cent. This is achieved by applying a reduction formula that results in a higher reduction formula that results in a higher reduction of tariff peaks. The starting point is a 20 per cent minimum reduction by tariff line, which is followed by a further reduction aimed at harmonising the tariff profile. Two criteria are used to distinguish which tariff rates should be addressed and the applicable methodology. These are twice the national average and 25 per cent.

For the case where tariff rates are above twice the national average but less than 22 per cent, the following formula is applicable which includes the initial 20 per cent reduction:

$$t_1 = (t_0 \text{ X } 0.8) - \{0.7 \text{ X } (t_0 - 2 \text{ X } t_a)\}$$

If the tariff rate is less than twice the national average but, still above 25 per cent the following formula is applicable which includes the initial 20 per cent reduction:

$$t_1 = (t_0 \text{ X } 0.8) - \{0.7 \text{ X } (t_0 - 25)\}$$

In cases where the tariff rate is two times the simple national average and at the same time above 25 per cent, the final tariff rate shall be whichever is lower after the reduction.

The formula reduces higher tariff rates in a way that takes into account individual tariff profiles since the cut is dependent of the tariff average. This means tariff profiles that have duties predominantly below 25 per cent but above twice the national average will still be subject to further tariff reductions. Alternatively, profiles with duties predominantly above 25 per cent, but with high overall averages will still be subject to reductions since the 25 per cent rule will apply.

The overall result of applying this formula will, therefore, depend on the statistical properties of each member tariff profile. It should be noted that for all tariff profiles with an average of above 12.5 per cent the tariff rate reduction in per cent are identical for a given tariff rate because the 25 per cent rule applies in all cases where twice the national average is greater than 25 per cent.

f) United States[21]

The United State has proposed a modality, which includes the elimination of tariff rates at or below 5 per cent and the application of a Swiss formula on the tariff proposed coefficient is 8, which converts the general Swiss formula[22] into the following specification:

$$t_1 = \frac{8 \times t_0}{8 + t_0}$$

What is important to note about the US proposal is the value of 8 of the coefficient. This implies a maximum tariff rate of 8 per cent after tariff reductions for any tariff profile.

DRAFT MODALITIES BY CHAIRMAN, NGMA: SOME COMMENTS

Based on different submission as summarized above, Chairman of NGMA has presented a document 'Draft Elements of Modalities for Negotiation on Non-Agricultural Products', WTO, TN/MA/W/35, 16 May 2003. There are four major components of the NGMA Chairman Draft (NGMA-CD).

1. **Formula (Core modality):** All non-agricultural tariffs shall be reduced on line-by-line basis using the formula applied to the base taste:

$$t_1 = \frac{B \times t_a \times t_0}{B \times t_a + t_0}$$

Where,

t_1 is the final rate, to be bound in ad valorem terms

t_0 is the base rate

t_a is the average of the base rates

2. **Sector-by-Sector/Zero-by-Zero Approach:** The NGMA CD has also proposed a sectoral elimination approach, in addition to the application of formula, for seven sectors Electronics & Electrical goods, Motor Vehicle parts & components, Stone, Gems & Precious Metals and Textiles & Clothing.
3. **Supplementary Modalities:** In addition to the above two approaches, the NGMA-CD proposes that member countries should adopt other procedures for additional tariff reduction and elimination.

Table 2
Summary of Alternative Liberalization Proposals

EU	Initial tariff under 2 per cent are eliminated, tariffs between 2 and 15 per cent are reduced by 55 per cent with final tariffs capped at 15 per cent. No reductions in agriculture or services in least development countries.
Korea	For industrials, as specified by formula. No reductions in agriculture or services in least developed countries.
India	50 per cent reduction in bound import tariffs in developed countries and 33.3 per cent reduction in developing countries for industrials. No reductions in agriculture or services in least developed countries.
China	For industrials, as specified with B=1, No reductions in agriculture or services in least developed countries.
US	All tariffs eliminated. No reductions in agriculture or services in least developed countries.
WTO	Tariffs reduced according to a Swiss formula with maximum coefficient equal to country average. Tariffs eliminated for electronics & electrics goods, fish and fish products, textiles, clothing, footwear, leather goods, motor vehicle, parts and components, stones, gems and precious metals. No reductions in agriculture or services in least developed countries.

Note: (Based on proposals, modified to take account of undefined LEMENTS) under the "WTO" simulation, the binding of developing country tariffs at double the applied rate follows the WTO proposal except that the WTO proposes to bind 95 per cent of tariff lines and imports. Obviously, it could be very important which lines are excluded.

Source: RIS based on Laird et.al. (2003): Market Access proposals for Non-Agricultural Products (Draft). Trade Policy Branch, UNCTAD, Geneva, 16 July, 2003.

4. **Non-Tariff Barriers:** The Chairman summaries some elements for deductions of elimination of non-tariff barriers.

The above components so not summarise elements of 'special & differential treatments', 'newly acceded members' and appropriate study and capacity building'.

Table 3
Bound and Applied Non-Agricultural Tariff Before and After Application of Various Proposals

	Developed Countries		*Developed Countries*	
	Bound %	*Applied %*	*Bound %*	*Applied %*
nitial	3.0	2.0	14.6	8.3
Proposal				
Eu	1.6	1.5	5.6	4.6
Korea	2.1	1.8	11.5	7.0
ndia	1.4	1.3	10.8	7.5
China	1.1	1.1	5.7	5.0
VTO NGMA-CD (B=1)	0.7	0.6	5.8	4.1
JSA	0.0	0.0	0.0	0.0

A comparative summary of the different proposals is provided in Table 1, Table 3 present simulations of tariff reductions resulting from different proposals to get a comparative perspectives.

Keeping the priorities of developing countries, the following paragraphs give some pointed observations on NGMA-CD modalities:

The core modality is based on formula. The formula proposed in NGMA-CD is a modified version of Swiss Formula. Swiss formula does not incorporate the structure and average level of tariff rates of individual member Countries, while the NGMA-CD proposed formula fakes care of average tariffs of member countries, however, this formula (like Swiss Formula) also depends upon the (magic) Value of coefficient B. in the Tokyo Round, the value of B was taken as 14 (and 16 in some cases). In this modified formula of NGMA-CD, we cannot take B=14 or 16; because it will not lead to deeper reduction as per guidelines of the Doha Declaration. The draft proposal is silent on the value of coefficient B.

To understand the implication the NGMA-CD proposed formula, we have calculated post-development round binding tariff rates under alternate scenarios depending on value of Band averag tariff (t_1). Figures 1.1-1.5 give select broad scenarios based o NGMA-CD proposed formula using alternate values of B=0.25 0.5, 1.0, 1.5 and 2.0 respectively; and average tariff rates o t_a=5, 10, 15, 20, 25 and 30 per cent. One can notice from thes figures that the post-development round bound rates fo countries with average tariff of 5 per cent and B=1.0 per cen (Figure-1.4), will be 70 per cent lower than the pre-developmen round. In case the uppermost tariffs is 50 per cent, the post development round tariff will be round 4 per cent. This scenari is close to the tariff structure of a large number of develope countries. On the other hand, a scenario with average tariff o 25 per cent and B=1, will lead to reduction of around 50 pe cent. In case peak tariff is 50 per cent in pre-development round it will be reduced to 17 per cent in post-development round This scenario is close to the countries whose average tariff i high. Basically it show that the NGMA-CD formula can take care of (i) reduction of tariffs, (ii) peak and high tariff and (iii structure of pre-development round binding rates. In othe words, if the average tariff of a country is low the declining rat of peak tariff will be substantial.

The NGMA-CD formula is sensitive to co-efficient value o B. If the value of B is high (say-2) the reduction will not b significant (figures 1.1 to 1.5). This can be illustrated through a case study. Let us suppose the average tariff of a country is 5 per cent. If we take B=2, we can expect that it will lead to a decline from 10 per cent level (of a commodity) to 5 per cent level; and a B=0.25 will lead to a decline from the 10 per cent level to 1 per cent level. Keeping these factors in view, it is clear that the co-efficient value for developed and developing countries should not be unique. In fact, the value of B for developing countries should be higher as compared to that of developed countries.

The zero-by-zero approach for tariff elimination of seven sectors, i.e. Electronics & Electrical goods, Fish & Fish products; Footwear, Leather goods, Motor Vehicle parts & components, Stones, Gems & Precious Metals and Textiles & Clothing is similar to information technology agreement (ITA). Although the NGMA-CD talks about S & D treatment for implementation period in these sectors, it adds, however, very specifically that

Figures

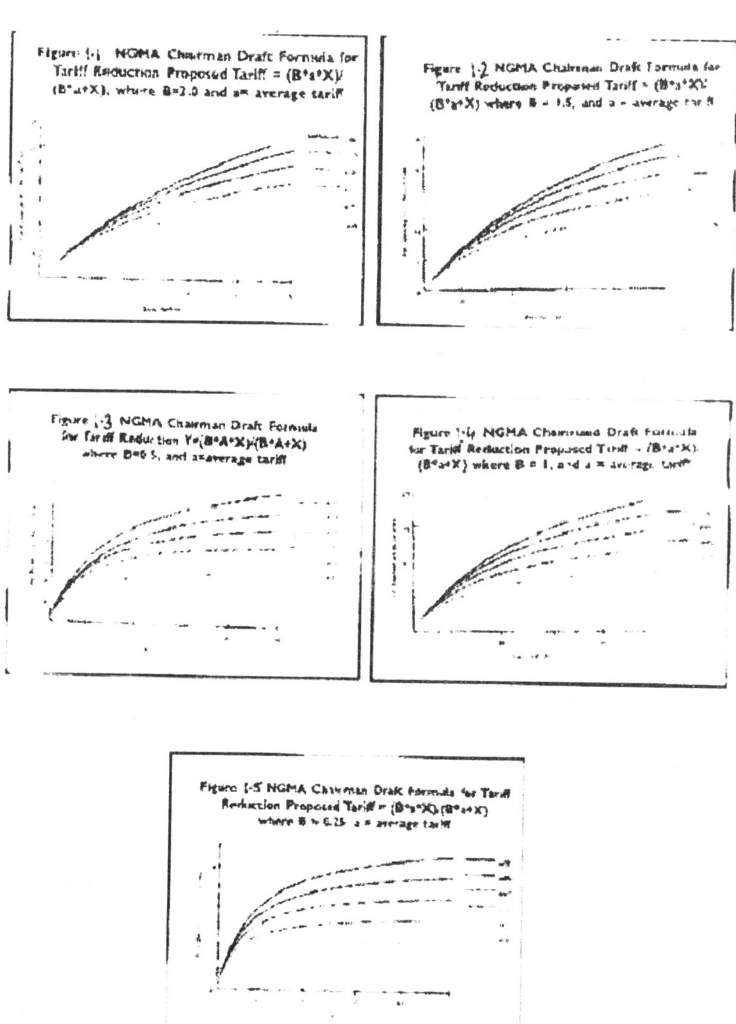

approach will be applicable to all the products of these sectors, even for developing countries.

The NGMA-CD is completely silent on tariff escalation of non-agricultural products. The formula does indirectly capture it. In case the NGMA-CD formula is used, the rate of the tariff escalation may decline as compared to as that of Uruguay Round.[23] The 'supplementary modalities' of NGMA-CD may lead to increase in tariff escalation. This may not meet the priorities of developing countries. In this context the draft proposal for market access or agricultural[24] is very clear. The proposal says that "for developed countries where the tariff on a processed product is higher than the tariff for the product in its primary form, the rate of tariff reduction for the processed product shall be equivalent to that for the product in its primary form multiplied, at a minimum, by a factor of 1.3". In other words, the proposal for market access for agriculture suggests that the binding rate of finished products should be reduced by more than 30 per cent as compared to that of raw materials, if the pre-development round tariff of the final product is higher than that of the raw material.

The NGMA-CD proposal is very clear that all items whose duties are defined in the form of specific and complex forms should be included in negotiations. It says "Non-ad valorem duties shall be converted to ad valorem equivalents (AVEs) according to the procedures" The NGMA-CD proposal also mentions the formula for working out ad valorem.

Equivalence of specific duties using simple methods, however, it is well known how some of these specific duties are defined and it is very difficult to calculate ad valorem equivalence of these duties.[25] The NGMA-CD proposes that in such case of "Non-ad valorem tariffs for which AVEs cannot be calculated by the Secretariat because of the technical nature of the duties concerned shall be assumed to have an AVE equivalent to the tariff average (ta) as used in the formula". India and developing countries should keep a close watch on this, because it has been noticed that the ad valorem equivalence of specific duties, indeed, is relatively very high as compared to those commodities whose duties are defined in the form of ad valorem rates.

NGMA-CD is still not clear about coverage of NTBs to be dealt with. It is probably not very clear about how to deal with non-tariff barriers. It is talking about (i) identification and examination of various types of NTBs, (ii) categorization, (iii) collection of information and (iv) inter linkage with other bodies of WTO. It says that modalities could include request/offer, horizontal or vertical approaches. Developing countries should ask for clear interpretation of such steps towards NTBs.

The NGMA-CD proposal says that "for developing countries up to 5 per cent of tariff lines may remain unbound provide that they do not exceed 5 per cent of the total value of a member's imports". Both these conditions of per cent tariff lines and 5 per cent import value are very strict. The developing countries should demand either a 5 per cent tariff line or 5 per cent imports value.

A revised version the May 2003 Draft Modalities Paper by Chairman, NGMA was issued on 19 August (TN/MA/35/Rev/1). In this revision, a number of provisions were changed. For instance, the flexibility offered to developing and least develop countries to keep up to 5 per cent of tariff lines unbound, provided they do not exceed 5 per cent of the total value of imports. Amending it to 5 per cent of tariff lines provided that no more than 1 per cent could be taken in one HS Chapter has curbed this flexibility. Another change is the exception allowed to countries having binding coverage of less than 35 per cent from the reduction commitment provided they bind 100 per cent of tariff lines at 27.5 per cent or less.

CONCLUDING REMARKS

Market access for non-agriculture products is one of the principal agenda items in the WTO negotiations. The basic mandate in the Doha Declaration under the category 'tariff and trade of industrial products' is both broad and comprehensive. Developing countries should concentrate on reduction in peak tariffs and tariff escalation. They should also demand that all the countries should define their binding rates in the form of ad valorem rates because it has been noticed that ad valorem equivalence of non-ad valorem duties are very high.

After the adoption of the Doha Agenda, member countries to NGMA submitted a number of proposals relating to 'modalities'. The Chairman of NGMA submitted a draft proposal of modalities after a series of formal and informal consultations. The core modality/formula submitted by NGMA-CD does attempt to address: (i) tariff peaks, (ii) tariff escalation, and (iii) non-ad valorem duties. However, it also seeks drastic reductions in tariff rates in developing countries. It is not easy for developing countries to completely accept the tariff elimination in seven sectors, even in an extended framework. They should be either made 'zero-for-A', where A is a positive number or alternatively, the coverage of lines in identified seven sectors should be 75 per cent of lines for developing countries. The thrust could be to grade the product tariff according to the developing countries capabilities.

Keeping in view the prevailing level of developing and their infrastructure in the developing countries, it needs to be appreciated that tariff is an important instrument for making domestic and trade policies. On the domestic front, tariff elimination, it may be recalled, will lead to substantial reduction in customs revenue that is the main form of revenue receipt for the developing countries. The developing countries, therefore, should be given full advantage of "less than full reciprocity".

NOTES

1. WTO, (2001), US Trade Policy Review, Geneva.
2. Mehta, (2001), WTO, Liberalization and Industrial Sector: The Case of Market Access, RIS Occasional Paper No. 63.
3. Mehta, (2003), Indian Industrial Tariffs: Towards, WTO Development Round Negotiations, RIS.
4. UNCTAD, (1999-2000), The Post-UR Tariff Environment for Developing Counties: Tariff Peaks and Tariff Escalation, TD/B/COM/1/14/1, 14 September. Mehta (2001), ibid; Mehta (2003), ibid, UNCTAD (2003), Back to Basics: Market Access Issues in the Doha Agenda, UNCTAD/DITC/TAB/Misc, 9, and Bacchetta, M. and B. Bora (2003), Industrial Tariff Liberalization and the Doha Development Agenda, WTO Discussion Paper.
5. Amount of Value per unit of imported commodity.
6. UNCTAD, CDROM TRAINS Winter (1998) and Mehta, R. and S.K. Mohanty (2001), WTO and Industrial Tariff: An Empirical Analysis for India, Reprint, RIS.
7. ibid, Mehta, Rajesh and Mohanty, S.K. (2001), ibid UNCTAD.
8. ibid, Mehta, Rajesh and Mohanty, S.K. (2001), ibid UNCTAD.
9. ibid, Mehta, Rajesh and Mohanty, S.K. (2001).
10. ibid, Mehta, Rajesh (2001).
11. UNCTAD, (1999-2000), IBID and UN, Market Access since UR, Implications, Opportunities and Challenges, Report prepared by UNCTAD and WTO, May 1998.

12. ibid, UNCTAD, (1999-2000), for instance.
13. Mehta and Mohanty, (2001) also prove this point using detailed data of five developed countries.
14. ibid, UNCTAD, and ibid, Mehta 2001.
15. Different countries have submitted a number of proposals. Among these proposals three submissions have been made by India.
16. TN/MA/W20
17. TN/MA/W/11/Add. 1 and Add 2.
18. TN/MA/W/10/Add. 2; suggestions for the treatment of unbound lines are beyond the scope of this document and have therefore not been included.
19. TN/MA/W/15.
20. TN/MA/W/6/Add. 1.
21. TN/MA/W/18.
22. Hoda, A. (2001), Tariff Negotiations and Renegotiations under the GATT and the WTO, Procedures and practices, Cambridge University Press, UK and Mehta, R 02003), ibid.
23. Uruguay Round led to increases in tariff escalation particularly for products in which developing countries have export potential. Mehta and Mohanty (2001) and UNCTAD (1999/2000), among others.
24. WTO, (2003), Negotiations on Agriculture First Draft of Modalities for the Further Commitments, Committee on Agriculture, TN/AG/W/1/Rev. 1, March 18, 2003.
25. UNCTAD, TRAINS, Winte (1998); and Mehta and Mohanty (2001).

INDIAN AGRICULTURE: BETTER FUTURE OPPORTUNITIES UNDER WTO

R.K. Srivastava and Md. Tarique

India is a founder member of the General Agreement on Tariffs and Trade (GATT) 1947 and its successor, the World Trade Organization (WTO), which came into effect on January 1, 1995 after the conclusion of the Uruguay Round (UR) of Multilateral Trade Negotiations. India's participation in an increasingly rule based system in the governance of international trade is to ensure more stability and predictability, which ultimately would lead to more trade and prosperity for itself and with more than 150 other nations which now comprise the WTO. India also automatically avails of MFN and national treatment for its exports to all WTO Members.

India, which followed the socialistic pattern of development and built a vast but controlled and regulated economic system had to follow the trends in the world trade. Though late, the National Policy of Economic Reforms and Liberalisation was announced in 1991-92. In fact, limited reforms and liberalisation had already been initiated during 80s. After signing the WTO agreement, India is bound to go for full-scale economic reforms and liberalisation of trade and commerce. Initially, economic reforms and liberalisation covered the industrial and service sectors. After the agreement on Agriculture (AoA) under the WTO regime, we started reforms and liberalisation in the agriculture sector. From 1st April 2001, as per the AoA, all Quantitative Restrictions (QRs) have been removed.

With the liberalisation of trade in agriculture and removal of QRs, the Indian agriculture is now exposed to the competitive environment in the global market under the WTO regime. The opportunities opened up in the new environment could be rewarding as well as threatening to farmers. In fact, the questions related to the effectiveness of AoA under the WTO regime to Indian farmers, the efficiency of Indian agriculture to face the challenges of competition in the global market, impact of Trade Related Intellectual Property Rights (TRIPS) and patenting on the accessibility to advanced farm technologies, particularly high quality seeds and plant material and other related matters are hotly debated these days. This paper tries to find out the impact of WTO on Indian agriculture. Though the period for WTO starts from 1995, the paper analyses the impact since the inception of new liberalisation era in the Indian economy i.e. since 1991.

GLOBALISATION OF INDIAN AGRICULTURE

India's total agricultural exports were at $ 3.35 billion during 1990-91, which corresponds to 4.91 per cent of GDP of agriculture sector. Devaluation of exchange rate by 22.5 per cent in two quick stages in 1991 followed by subsequent depreciation in the exchange rate, coupled with lifting of some restrictions on export, helped the country to double its exports in next six years (Table 1). Imports also moved on a rising trend in the same period but increase in export was much higher than the increase in agricultural imports. Consequently, the net exports increased from $ 2.72 billion during 1990-91 to $ 5.45 billion by 1996-97.

The increase in export and import raised the proportion of trade in agricultural GDP from less than 5 per cent in the beginning of reforms to close to 8.76 per cent by 1995-96. After 1996-97, value of export started shrinking as international prices started falling (Chand 2003). Due to falling international prices, imports into the country became more attractive and were facilitated due to liberalisation of imports followed due to WTO commitments. Thus, after 1996-97 imports kept increasing further and were doubled in the next three years. This way the net earning from agriculture trade in the post WTO period dropped to a very low level. The post WTO period showed

Table 1
Trade Orientation of Indian Agriculture

(Million US $)

Years	*Agricultural Exports*	*Agricultural Imports*	*Total of Agricultural Exports and Imports*	*Agricultural Exports / Agricultural GDP (Per cent)*	*Agricultural Imports / Agricultural GDP (Per cent)*	*Agricultural GDP (US million)*	*Agricultural Trade / Total Agricultural GDP (Per cent)*
(1)	(2)	(3)	(4)	(5)	(6)	(7)	(8)
1990-91	3,354.4	631.2	3,985.6	4.13	0.77	81,220.53	4.91
1991-92	3,202.5	382.9	3,585.4	4.59	0.55	69,774.67	5.14
1992-93	3,135.8	636.6	3,772.4	5.02	1.02	62,397.79	6.05
1993-94	4,027.5	480.6	4,508.1	5.69	0.68	70,724.35	6.37
1994-95	4,226.1	1,364.3	5,590.4	5.2	1.68	81,274.24	6.88
1995-96	6,081.9	1,196.6	7,278.8	7.32	1.44	83,063.08	8.76
1996-97	6,862.7	1,407.7	8,270.4	7.29	1.49	94,092.68	8.79
1997-98	6,626.2	1,689.8	8,316.0	6.96	1.78	95,113.68	8.74
1998-99	6,034.5	2,754.5	8,789.0	5.99	2.74	1,00,603.03	8.74
1999-00	5,608.0	2,693.4	8,301.4	5.47	2.63	1,02,444.56	8.10
2000-01	5,973.2	1,642.8	7,616.0	6.24	7.96	95,672.23	7.96
2001-02	5,901.2	2,294.4	8,195.6	5.37	2.09	1,09,765.78	7.46
2002-03	6,710.0	2,803.4	9,513.4	5.91	2.47	1,13,564.32	8.37
2003-04P	7,405.7	3,568.3	10,974.0	—	—	—	—

Source: (a) CMIE India Trade Database.
(b) Economic Survey, 2003-04.

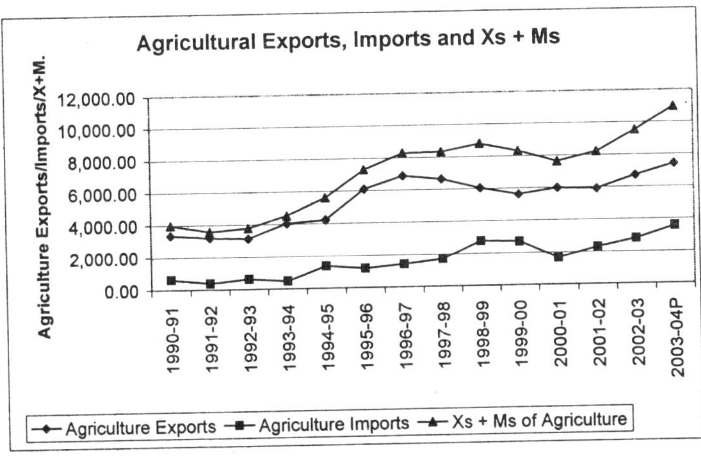

increase in ratio of imports to GDP whereas ratio of exports to GDP for agriculture sector followed small decline. This shows that post WTO period has been adverse to export but favourable for imports. This pattern shows sharp contrast with the first five years of reforms period when share of exports in GDP experienced sizable increase.

What is more important than sudden and short-term import penetration is the long-term trend that can be differentiated with respect to the increasing openness of the Indian economy. The following table provides data on India's agricultural exports, imports and agricultural gross domestic product (GDP) and some ratios. The data brings out several important trends:

- In value terms, both agricultural exports and imports have increased consistently over the last decade-the growth rates are, however, widely divergent: 85 per cent for exports and 166 per cent for imports. The higher growth rate of imports is partly due to a lower base.
- As a consequence, the ratio of agricultural exports to imports has consistently deteriorated over the period.
- What is most significant, however, is the rising share of agricultural exports and imports to agricultural GDP. This is what reveals the extent of openness due to trade policy reforms. The ratio has shot up from about 5 per cent to 8 per cent during the period. It is almost similar to the overall trade/GDP ratio of the Indian economy.

The latest Mid-Term Appraisal of the Tenth Five Year Plan[1] gives the following facts regarding the exports and imports performance:

> India's agricultural exports had performed extremely well in the first half of the 1990s. But since 1995-96, this has shown extreme fluctuations. Exports growth accelerated 45 per cent in 1995-96 over the low base of the previous year, to US $ 6,081.9 million, further increased to US $6862.7 in 1996-97 and then registered negative growth for three years in succession. This recovered somewhat in 2000-01 but suffered another setback in 2001-02. However, there has again been a turnaround during 2002-03 and 2003-04 and indications are that this favourable trend will continue in 2004-05 (Table 1).

As in the case of agri-exports, India's agri-imports have also displayed extreme fluctuations, having varied in the range of 58 per cent to (-) 29 per cent in the post 1995-96 period. The percentage share of agri-imports in total imports also has shown very high volatility, having moved in the range of 28 per cent to less than 2 per cent during the same period. There was, in fact, a negative growth of 29 per cent in 2000-01 but since then, agri-imports have grown at a relatively high rate of about 23, 22 and 27 per cent in 2001-02, 2002-03 and 2003-04 respectively. In recent years, imports of only two items, namely, pulses and edible oils have recorded consistently high volumes. Import of pulses, which used to vary in the range of 3-6 lakhs in recent years except in 1997-98 when over 1 millions were imported surged to over 2 millions in 2001-02 and has been close to that level since then, essentially reflecting shortage of domestic production. Similarly, import of edible oils surged from 1 millions in 1995-96 to over 4 millions in 1999-2000 and has since been moving in the range of 4.2 to 5.3 millions per year, accounting for about half of domestic consumption. As in the case of agri-export items, concerted efforts are required to raise the productivity and production of both pulses and oilseeds in the country.

COMPARISON OF PERFORMANCE OF INDIAN AGRICULTURE VIS-A-VIS OTHER LEADING ECONOMIES IN THE PRE AND POST REFORM ERA

On the basis of above-mentioned facts we find that all is not well with regard to the performance of the Indian agriculture in the post liberalization and WTO era. The reasons are various bottlenecks faced by the Indian agriculture. However, if we compare the growth rates of various indices as mentioned in Table 2, we find a silver lining in the tunnel as the growth rates of these indices in India are higher than the growth rates in other leading economies.

A comparative study of some of the other countries in the world with that of India clearly explain how much India lags behind with respect to the variables like crop production index, food production index, livestock production index, cereal yield and agricultural productivity in both pre and post liberalisation era (Table 2). India is even behind civil war devastated country Sri Lanka in terms of crop production index, cereal yield and agricultural productivity in both pre and post liberalisation era. The agricultural productivity in Sri Lanka in 1979-81 was 2.38 times and even in 2000-02, it is 1.8 times higher than India. In terms of food and livestock production index though Sri Lanka was in a better position in 1979-81 but India has improved with a higher value in the post liberalisation era in 2000-02. China was below India in terms of crop production index, food production index and livestock production index in the pre reform era but after making a spectacular performance in the post liberalisation era, it is not only far ahead of India but also even in a better position than many developed countries in terms of these indices. The crop production index during the mentioned period has increased at a compound rate per annum in China by 4.08 per cent, in Australia by 3.11 per cent, in India by 2.7 per cent, more than the increase in world average by 2.45 per cent. An impressive compound growth rate is seen for food production index (livestock production index) with the figures of 3.19% (4.2%) in India against 5.46% (7.96%) in China, 2.01% (1.4%) in Australia, 1.24% (1.39%) in U.S., almost zero (-0.25%) in U.K. and 2.5% (1.71%) as world average. The cereal yield (kg./hectare) was just 25per cent of Japan in the pre liberalisation era but increased to 40.65 per cent in the post liberalisation era. The value is 35% of U.K. value, highest in the table in the post liberalisation era. However, the compound growth rate in productivity shows a dismal figure. It is just 1.92 per cent per annum in India as against 4.8 per cent in Canada and 4.67 per cent in United States.

Table 2
Agricultural Output and Productivity

Country ↓	*Crop Production Index*[2]		*Food Production Index*[3]		*Livestock Production Index*[4]		*Cereal Yield*[5]		*Agricultural Productivity*[6]	
	1989-91=100						*Kilogram per hectare*		*Agriculture value added per worker 1995 $*	
	1979-81	*2000-02*	*1979-81*	*2000-02*	*1979-81*	*2000-02*	*1979-81*	*2000-02*	*1979-81*	*2000-02*
Australia	79.9	152.2	91.3	138.8	85.6	116.1	1,321	1,758	20,872	36,327
Canada	77.6	106.7	79.7	123.5	88.3	142.2	2,173	2,521	16,002	43,064
China	67.1	155.6	60.8	185.9	45.4	226.7	3,027	4,845	161	338
India	70.9	124.2	68.2	131.8	62.6	149.8	1,324	2,390	269	401
Japan	108.3	87.1	94.1	91.6	85.1	93.2	5,252	5,879	17,378	33,077
Sri Lanka	99.3	114.8	98.1	117.2	92.0	147.7	2,462	3,520	642	725
U.K.	80.1	97.2	92.2	92.4	98.1	93.1	4,792	6,841	20,326	32,918
U.S.	98.6	118.3	94.5	122.5	89.0	123.6	4,151	5,830	20,672	53,907
World	79.1	131.5	78.8	133.1	79.6	136.4	1,605	2,233	—	—

Source: World Development Indicators, 2004.

On the basis of above analysis we find that India has done well in terms of the growth rates of various indices (except productivity index), the country lags far behind if given a look at the absolute figures. Some of the reasons for these lower absolute values and a dismal compound rate of increase in the overall productivity level are:

- The arable land in India in 1999-01 is just 0.16 hectare/capita as against the values of 2.58 in Australia and 1.48 in Canada.
- The irrigated land, as percentage of cropland is just 32.2 per cent in India as compared to 54.7 per cent in Japan and 40.7 per cent in Australia during 1999-01.
- The fertilizer consumption (hundreds of grams per hectare of arable land) is merely 1074 in India in comparison to the values of 3162 for Japan and 2170 for European Union.

If we compare the use of agricultural machinery in terms of the availability of tractors per 100 square kilometer of arable land it is merely 94 in India against the figures of 4601 in Japan and 984 in European Union.[7]

INDIAN AGRICULTURE AND ENVIRONMENTAL ISSUES UNDER WTO

A policy of trade liberalisation is often suggested as a means of stimulating economic growth in developing countries. Trade liberalisation consists of policies aimed at opening up the economy to foreign investment and lowering trade barriers in the form of tariff reduction. However, while trade may stimulate growth it may simultaneously lead to more pollution either as a result of relocation of polluting industries from countries with strict environmental policy or owing to increased production in dirty industries. Given the potential benefits of trade liberalisation policies, it is important to examine whether such policies are actually in conflict with the environment as they expand production and accelerate economic growth.

Thus, what happens to the environment when international trade is liberalised is a matter of debate. Economists and environmentalists commonly assume it alike that greater economic openness will lead to increased pollution in developing countries, as free trade will increase environmental degradation in developing countries. Among environmentalists, one common concern is that liberalised trade regimes and market-driven exchange rates by increasing the incentive for export, will lead to a greater exploitation of natural resources. Secondly, free trade will increase industrial pollution in developing countries through the displacement of dirty industries from developed countries with stricter environmental regulations and through competitive pressure on developing countries to reduce further their environmental standards.

An attempt has been made by Mani and Wheeler (1999)[8] to link pollution intensity with capital and labour intensity of goods on the basis of the work of Hettige and others (1995).[9] Emission intensity (emission per unit of output) has been calculated and the sectors that rank high on actual emission intensity. To determine high-ranking sectors by this criterion the authors have used detailed emissions intensities by medium for manufacturing in the United States by three digit standard industrial classification (SIC level) computed by the World Bank in collaboration with the United States Environmental Protection Agency and the United States Census Bureau (Hettige and others, 1995). They have computed average sectoral rankings for air pollutants. They have found that the following sectors which rank high are pollution-intensive industries: iron and steel, non-ferrous metal, non-metallic mineral products, miscellaneous petroleum, coal products, pulp and paper, petroleum refineries, industrial chemicals and other chemicals, wood products and glass products. In addition, they have estimated the capital intensity of these dirty industries and found that dirty industries are relatively intensive in capital because capital intensity is substantially higher in the dirty sectors with an average ratio of around 2:1 for capital output and investment output. Following the criteria, they have identified that iron and steel, metal products and chemical products are highly capital intensive as well as pollution intensive. They have also found that the clean sectors are about 40 per cent more labour intensive on average.

In the light of the above results, we can argue that India has a comparative advantage in exporting labor-intensive environment friendly goods. The argument can also be supported by famous factor endowment theory of international trade given by Hekscher-Ohlin. Hence, we suggest that the production of labour-intensive goods should be emphasised. This will generate employment opportunities in a labour surplus economy such as India, which in turn will help to reduce poverty, as the eradication of poverty in the developing countries including India is being given top priority in recent years. So; to increase exports, the tariffs on the tradable sector especially primary sectors-agriculture, allied and agriculture-based industrial sector, consumable non-durable goods sector that includes textiles, and leather industries with high social profitability, should be lowered appreciably. A policy of selective, chief credit extension for these goods will be of great help for enhancing production capabilities.

In conclusion, we can say that although India missed the opportunity to open up two decades ago, its attempts to do so now must be regarded as better late than never. Others such as Desai (1999)[10] observe that, "the logic of the global economy as well as India's interests dictate that India become proactive in its liberalisation policies. India must liberalise not because it has no choice but because it is the best choice". His lament that India has adopted a 'victim mentality' when it really needs to adopt a 'winner mentality' has become less of a concern as over time, India has shown commitment to stay on the bandwagon of globalisation. Having realised that globalisation is a necessary but not a sufficient condition for high growth production; India has undertaken economic reforms, both internal and external. However, it must be ensured that these reforms are synchronised so that the pace of both reforms is set right in order to work hand in hand to promote agricultural productivity growth and definitely India will be a net gainer in the long run.

NOTES AND REFERENCES

1. Mid Term Appraisal of 10th Five Year Plan (2002–07), Government of India, Planning Commission, New Delhi, June 2005.
2. Shows agricultural production for each period relative to the base period 1989-91. It includes all crops except fodder crops. The regional and income group aggregates for the FAO's production indexes are calculated from the underlying values in International Dollars, normalized to the base period 1989-91. The data in this table are three years average.

3. Covers food crops that are considered edible and that contain nutrients. Coffee and tea are excluded because, although edible, they have no nutritive value.
4. Includes meat and milk from all sources, dairy products such as cheese, eggs, honey, raw silk, wool and hides and skins.
5. Measured in kilogram per hectare of harvested land, includes wheat, rice, maize, barley, oats, rye, millet, sorghum, buckwheat, and mixed grains. Production data on cereals refer to crops harvested for dry grain only. Cereal crops harvested for hay or harvested green for food, feed, or silage, and those used for grazing, are excluded.
6. Refers to the ratio of agricultural value added, measured in constant 1995 U.S. dollars, to the number of workers in agriculture.
7. The analysis is based on the data obtained from World Development Indicators, 2004.
8. Mani, M. and D. Wheeler, 1999. In Search of Pollution Havens? Dirty Industry in the World Economy, 1960-1995, document presented to the OECD Conference on Foreign Direct Investment and the Environment, The Hague, 28-29 January.
9. Lucas, R.E.B., D. Wheeler and H. Hettige, 1992. Economic Development, Environmental Regulation and the International Migration of Toxic Industrial Pollution: 1960-88 in Low, P. (ed.) International Trade and the Environment. World Bank Discussion Paper No. 159.
10. Desai, M., 1999. "What should be India's Economic Priorities in a Globalized World?", Indian Council for Research on International Economic Relations, New Delhi.

WTO POLICY FRAMEWORK'S IMPACT ON AGRICULTURE: INDIAN EXPERIENCE

Shaily Verma

INTRODUCTION

The great depression of 1920's and the Second World War during 1939-45 experienced shrinking of world trade in the first half of the twentieth century. This reduction of trade was adversely affecting the living standards of the people, as deteriorating trade slowed the pace of economic development. The stabilization and the promotion of international trade was the immediate need of the time. International trade, which was originally in private hands, came under State control/State trading agencies in the first half of twentieth century. After Second World War, steps were taken to regulate it by setting up an International Trade Organization (ITO) on the lines of the International Monetary Fund (IMF) and World Bank (*Rao, 2001*). The ITO failed to take off due to non-ratification of the Charter by the US Senate. Instead of ITO, a new Multilateral Trade Agreement was made in 1947, which was known as General Agreement on Trade and Tariff (GATT). It only dealt with trade in goods and excluded services. It provided momentum to international trade and new sectors emerged like service, for which there were no provisions in the GATT. The Uruguay Round, the last under the aegis of the GATT, a proposal was mooted and member countries finally resolved to establish a new organization on April 1994, which was named as World Trade Organization (WTO). It started functioning from 1st January 1995. The evolution of the WTO as a new officiating agency for smooth functioning of multilateral economic relations is not the result of single discussion. The seeds of the formation of this new organization can also be traced to the Ministerial discussions of GATT since 1986.

The major objective of this round was to halt and reverse protectionism and to remove distortions in trade (*Sachdev, 2000*). In fact the need for such a global agreement arose because there were signs of the world moving towards protectionism as far as trade was concerned (*Sengupta and Wadhwa, 1994*).

WTO is more ambitious than any other Multilateral Trade Negotiations (MTNs) that include not only the traditional concerns like trade in Agriculture and Textiles in its negotiations but also new areas like Trade in Services, Trade Related to Intellectual Property Rights (TRIPS) and Trade Related to Investment Measures (TRIMs) (*Debroy, 1996*).

THE BEGINNING: URUGUAY ROUND & INDIAN SCENARIO

When the Uruguay Round commenced agriculture featured in a major way. "In the Uruguay Round, countries recognized the long term solution for agriculture and did not lie in administered price, trade restrictions, supply controls and export subsidies but rather in open, non-distorted markets (*Schumacher, 1999*). It was decided to take the bold steps for revolutionizing agriculture trade especially in the 21st century by accelerating agricultural trade reforms. The Uruguay Round agreement sought to bring order and fair competition to this highly distorted sector of world trade by establishing a fair and market oriented agricultural trading sector.

The inclusion of agricultural commodities in MTN's in the Uruguay Round is watershed in the history of the international trade. The world trade in agriculture, which has been conducted without a rule based system and was heavily distorted due to high degree of protection in most countries, has now become subject to the WTO discipline. The agreement is supposed to be the last bastion of restricted trade era. In Agreement on Agriculture (AoA), three distinct areas have been identified as the immediate concerns. They are Domestic Support, Market Access and Export Subsidy Commitments.

An international Agreement on Agriculture is bound to affect a large segment of population of India, being an agricultural economy. The inclusion of agriculture for the first time in the MTN's of Uruguay Round proved most fortuitous and a God given opportunity for India (*Dattatreyulu, 1994*). Exporting agricultural commodities from India is an idea that was unbelievable few years ago. Importing foodgrain under PL-480 was a hard reality for the country, which has now been getting ready for agricultural exports in a modest way (Banerjee, 1994). In recent decades, India has rapid strides in the area of agricultural production and exports. The production of foodgrains has considerably increased from 82 million tones in 1960-61 to 212.0 million tones in 2003-04. The exports of agricultural and allied products have increased significantly from Rs. 284 crore in 1960-61 to Rs. 36247 crore in 2003-04 (Economic Survey, 2004-05). Although India's share of agricultural exports in total exports of India has been declining i.e. from around 45 per cent in 1960-61 to 12.35 per cent in 2003-04, yet agricultural exports constitute an important segment of India's exports.

The WTO Agreement on Agriculture is a multifaceted agreement therefore, its impact on Indian economy will also be multifaceted. It is a known fact that India enjoys the advantages of low wages in agriculture in comparison to most of the developed countries. However, at the same time India also faces the problem of low productivity per man/hectare, in comparison to developed countries. It is worth mentioning that in most of the agricultural commodities, domestic prices are already lower than world prices. Therefore, due to trade liberalization, a large-scale import of agricultural commodity is not feasible. Contrary to that in certain cases especially in oil seeds, sugar, Indian prices are higher than world prices. Coming to the exports, due to WTO led liberalization India may gain market of developed countries provided, government agencies make all out efforts to ensure that the marketable surpluses is exported without affecting the economically backward section of the society. There would be various kinds of pressures generated through different groups, for example, farmers would try to pressurize for higher prices to narrow the gap between the domestic and external prices in search of higher profits while the exporters and industrialists would like to keep the domestic prices at a lower level to maintain the dominance in exports market. In this paradoxical situation, India has long experiences of higher prices affecting the PDS system and creating a pressure on food subsidy bill of the Finance Ministry. Therefore, the state would have to strike a balance between the competing interest of farmers, exporters and economically backward section of the society.

It must be remembered that world trade in agriculture is expected to increase at a rapid rate because of the Uruguay Round agreement. This could mean around 300 billion US dollars worth of additional exports beyond the year 2005. Of this, 90 per cent is expected because of the agricultural agreement alone due to the removal of domestic subsidies and easing of border measures, particularly in developed countries. It means, around 270 billion US dollars worth of additional agricultural exports per year. Because of the liberalization, it is also expected that world agriculture prices will go up by an average of 10 per cent, subject of course to the caveat that all these estimates tend to be somewhat arbitrary. This makes India's agricultural exports even more price competitive-not only in US and Western Europe but also in Eastern Europe, a region that was earlier catered to by agricultural exports from the West (*Sachdev, 2000*)[1].

The likely impact of the Agreement on Agriculture on India can be illustrated as under:

> It is implied from the AoA that reduction in farm subsidies and export subsidies by developed countries would lead to higher agricultural prices in developed countries. This would enable Indian products to be more competitive on the one hand and would improve the terms of trade of the country on the other hand. Thus, exporters of farm subsidies will get higher remunerative prices. Agricultural subsidy and non-product subsidies would allow India greater maneuverability to provide subsidies for increasing agricultural production. India can increase subsidy because Indian subsidy level is below the allowed subsidy level up to 10 per cent in the agreement. In case of market access to farm products India will have to lift QRs* (Quantitative Restrictions) on imports within 6 years as agreed with Australia (*Vasudeva, 2000*). India will have to open its market for the imports of agricultural commodities up to 3-5 per cent of the domestic consumption needs. Removal of

QRs on agricultural imports would promote competition that will benefit the consumers as well as improve the social welfare specifically of economically backward section of the society.

Beside the above-mentioned facts, it is also a reality that the last round of negotiations did not bring about trade liberalization in agriculture to the desired extent. The farmers in developed countries, with massive support of governments through domestic and export subsidies and high tariffs and some other advantages in terms of higher financial resources, access to technology and benefit of modern infrastructure clearly have unfair advantage over the developing countries (*ASSOCHAM, Sep-Oct, 2000*).

In the Uruguay Round, it was expected that AoA would improve the distortion in agricultural trade and hence, there would be a scope for manifold increase in agricultural exports of developing countries. Besides, it was anticipated that free market forces would improve the prices; contrary to this it was found that definite decline in prices of most agricultural products viz. cereals, pulses and sugar took place. Assuming that cereal production would shift to developing nations from developed ones, if the reduction in subsidies to agriculture by developed nations is realized. However, the expectations were not fulfilled, hence change in pattern of world cereal production and exports have been hardly visible.

THE CONTROVERSY

Food and livelihood security of people, protection of the interest of domestic farmers and maximizing export opportunities for Indian agriculture products have been the guiding principles of India's proposals at the WTO negotiations on agriculture.

The Ministerial Conference of WTO at Doha in 2001 affirmed the long-term objective already agreed in the present WTO agreement: to establish a fair and market oriented trading system through a programme of fundamental reform. The programme encompasses strengthened rules and specific commitments on government support and protection for agriculture. The purpose is to correct and prevent restriction and distortions in world agriculture markets (GOI: Economic Survey, 2001-02).

The Ministerial Conference of Cancun in 2003 flagging agriculture as the key concern, India sought elimination of distortions in world agriculture created through high level of subsidies in the developed countries. At the meeting, urgent needs to bring down the high tariff and non-tariff barriers on products of export interest of developing countries was also underlined, to secure for these countries sufficient gains from liberalization (GOI: Economic Survey, 2003-04).

Moreover, the subsequent formation and consolidation of the G-20 on agriculture has emphasized that any new market access commitments on developing countries must not cast a disproportionately higher burden on them as compared to developed countries (GOI: Economic Survey, 2003-04).

However; during recent ministerial conference from Doha to Cancun under WTO negotiations, liberalization did not materialize, as was required. Developed countries are not ready to reduce the domestic support, export subsidies whereas developing nations do not agree to open the market to the desired extent. Developed countries have continued to provide high domestic support to their agriculture sector. At the best, policies in many developed countries have only been cosmetically altered by shifting the support from Amber to Green and Blue boxes (Ministry of Commerce and Industry, 2001). The continuation of the high domestic support to agriculture in many developed countries is a cause of concern as they encourage over production in these countries leading to low levels of international prices.

The agreement has ensured that developing countries take time bound initiative to open up their domestic markets for cheep and highly subsidized imports of agriculture commodities to encourage competitiveness. But developed countries have not fulfilled their commitments of opening up agriculture sector for developing countries (Markande and Jaiswal, 2005). Eventually, developing nations achievements in regard to access in marketing is still limited. Market access in developed countries is hampered by their maintaining high tariffs on products of interest to developing countries beside a plethora of non-tariff barriers. Stringent Sanitary and Phytosanitary Measures* (SPS) continue to be a major barrier in diversifying exports in horticulture and meat items. These non-tariff barriers are acting in favour of developed countries. The United States is the country aggressively pursuing for a lowering of agriculture tariffs, has the largest number of SPS measures, accounting for more than a fourth of the total, put in place by all WTO members (Dhar and Kallumal, 2004).

In case of subsidy reduction commitment, it is the most surprising that developing countries including India has been phasing out gradually these subsidies but USA, EU and Japan have done little in this regard. This is clearly an act of denying to developing countries market access to their market (Agarwal, 2003). According to an estimate, the subsidy provided by the developed country is over US$ 500 billon a year, the daily subsidy comes out to be of more than US $ 1.4 billion. This has led to dampening in world prices of agricultural commodities putting at stake the livelihood of billions of marginal farmers in developing countries (Markande and Jaiswal, 2005). The OECD countries subsidies their agriculture to their true of a billon dollar a day, yet they insist on developing countries removing the agriculture protection and opening up their markets (Pingali, 2002). Therefore, expected gains for developing world are still a nightmare and these conferences resulted in a stalemate between developed and developing countries.

CONCLUSION AND SUGGESTIONS

The Ministry of Agriculture as well as the Ministry of Commerce has officially admitted that the hopes from an international regime that aimed at establishing a fair and market oriented agricultural trading system have been belied (Francis, 2001).

To review its existing stand on Agriculture on Agreement, the Government of India presented a paper on 15th January 2001 to the Committee on Agriculture. In fact, it is realizing that in WTO, the concerns of developing countries regarding agriculture were not placed properly. The Government of India's paper wishes to bring certain very important aspects before the Committee on Agriculture to provide additional flexibility to the States like India in implementing Agreement on Agriculture. The first important concern is related to food security and protection of environment as 26 per cent of India's population still lives in absolute poverty conditions. So, the issue of food security is of vital importance, which involves excess of food, adequate supply of food and stability in supply, which is necessary for the protection of environment also. Further, food subsidy for food security and rural employment is of vital importance and any such products reserved for the above mentioned reasons should not be included while measuring Product Specific or Non-Product Specific Aggregate Measurement Support.

Similarly reduction of bound tariff should be negotiated under a special and differential treatment clause and the discussion on such issues should be granted highest priority in coming round. The modalities in regard to Tariff Rate Quota (TRQ) should be ascertained in the coming ministerial conference.

Another important contentious issue regarding Sanitary and Phytosanitary, standards must be discussed on priority. With progressive reduction of high tariff on Sanitary and Phytosanitary are being increasingly used to restrict imports by developed countries. Against the spirit of liberalized WTO, no developed country should be allowed to use the impractical standards to restrict market access. These SPS are acting like non-tariff barriers in favour of developed countries. The developed countries must provide longer transitional period (at least 10 years) to affect any change in SPS.

A review of measures listed under green box is also necessary. In fact, the present green box measures are not linked to production decision and also do not influence the type and the volume of agricultural products. The Government of India thinks that the Agreement on Agriculture should not stand in the way to provide food security to the poor environmental security and support to small farmers while it should stand in way of unfair non-tariff barriers in the name of SPS.

If the concerns of the developing countries as projected by India in its review paper submitted to Committee on Agriculture is accepted, almost all developing countries including India are likely to gain a lot from WTO Agreement on Agriculture. But these measures would not be enough to sustain in a globalized world. The Indian agricultural sector must get the status of an industry. In India, diversification of agriculture sector is the need of hour. Therefore, efforts should be made to bring agriculture sector to its zenith with the help of new investment in higher level of consumption of chemical fertilizers, pesticides and insecticides, development of new varieties of seeds, better irrigation facilities, bringing more and more land under cultivation, research and development, easy agricultural credit facilities, etc.

The inferences drawn may be listed as the new agreements on agriculture have more gains than losses to India. The proper implementation of the agreement can provide enormous support to Indian farmers. It will improve the production capacity and export opportunity to the producers and exporters. The improved market access condition through reduction in tariff and non-tariff barriers and competitiveness in the industrialized and developed market will provide new opportunities to Indians. Only making some major changes both at the government as well as stakeholders level can materialize this advantage of growing opportunities.

Thus, agriculture sector should be declared and treated as an industry. Trade in agriculture should be totally liberalized. Import of commodities that cannot be competitively produced in the domestic market should be liberalized. Exporters should intensify their efforts to enhance the exports rather than to look short-term gains in the domestic market. Specific commodities should be identified that can be produced competitively in India and offer substantial export potential. The new agriculture policy should make more vigilant to strengthen the positive signals and treat the side effects.

The percolation of benefits from Agreement on Agriculture to developing countries can be realized with the absolute elimination of export subsidies and substantial reduction in domestic support in developed countries. Thus only then the outcome of the Uruguay Round would help in bringing new dynamism to step up the growth of agriculture sector.

REFERENCES

Aggarwal, M.R. (2003), *"Economic Reforms in India: A Critical Appraisal & Agenda for the Next Decade"*, Indian Journal of Economics, Allahabad.

ASSOCHAM (2000), *"Implementation of the WTO Agreement"*, WTO Update, p. 3, September-October.

Banerjee, Pranab K. (1994), *"Uruguay Round Agreement on Agriculture-An Overview"*, Trade in Agriculture: Uruguay Round and After, ed. by Bhattacharya, B. and Sengupta, A.K., IIFT, New Delhi, p. 26.

Dattatreyulu, M. (1994), *"Uruguay Round–New Opportunity for Boosting Agro-Exports"*, Trade in Agriculture: Uruguay Round and After, ed. by Bhattacharya, B. and Sengupta, A.K. IIFT, New Delhi, p. 33.

Dhar, Biswajit & kallumal Murali (2004), *"Trade Liberalisation and Agriculture: Challenges before India"*, online at networkideas.org.

Debroy, Bibek (1996), *"Beyond the Uruguay Round: The Indian Perspective on GATT"*, Sage Publication, New Delhi, p. 30.

"Focus" (2001), Ministry of Commerce & Industry.

Francis, Sheelu (2001), *"Trade Libralisation in Agriculture and Food Security: Impact on Peasant Women"*, in Asian Women Workshop on Globalisation in Manila online at www.isgnweb.org., November 22-24.

GOI: Economic Survey (Various Issues), Ministry of Finance, Economic Division, Government of India.

Markande, R.K., and Jaiswal Vidhan (2005), *"The Concerns of Developing world on Agricultural Trade in Pre and post WTO Regime: W.S.R. to in India."* in a National workshop on WTO and Indian Economy, Allahabad. Page 4, April 23-24.

Pingali, Prabhu (2002), *"Food Security Challenge: Plauged by Complex Issues"*, The Hindu Survey of Indian Agriculture, p. 43, 45.

Rao, M.B. (2001), *"WTO and International Trade"*, Vikas Publishing House Pvt. Ltd., p. 31.

Sachdev, Santosh (2000), *"Agricultural Exports of India: Lessons from East Asia"*, Century Publication, New Delhi, p. 199.

Schumacher, August, (1999), *"The Future of Agricultural Trade"*, Economic Perspective Electronic Journal, (Focus, Public Affairs Office, US Embassy), p. 6, October.

Sengupta, A.K. and Wadhwa, R.K. (1994), *"Impact of Uruguay Round on Agro Exports"*, Trade in Agriculture: Uruguay Round and After, ed. by Bhattacharya, B. and Sengupta, A.K., IIFT, New Delhi, p. 54.

Vasudeva, P.K. (2000), *"India and World Trade Organization: Planning and Development"*, A.P.H. Publishing Corporation, New Delhi, p. 210.

WTO AND AGRICULTURE: INDIAN CASE

K.K. Sinha

WORLD FREE TRADE ORGANISATIONS: INDUSTRY VERSUS AGRICULTURE

The rich industrial countries of the west had first the problem of expanding their industrial goods trade to outside world. Britain, the first industrially rich country in late 18th century found it easy to exchange industrial goods with the primary goods of its colonies. The balance of trade was achieved by Ricardo's concept that let all countries, rich or poor, exchange goods in which they had comparative advantage. India having comparative advantage in agricultural products like cotton, jute or indigo could exchange it with finished goods and capital goods from Britain. Both the countries were said to be in advantage by trade.[1]

As between the industrial countries of Europe, inter se, which developed as equals, the trade was for finished goods both ways. Here, deficits or surpluses were marginal and would be corrected through the mechanism of gold flows. This game, known as Gold Standard would deflate the trade-losing country with loss of gold and this in turn, resulted in price fall and the resultant increase in trade demand. At the same time, the trade gaining country would have more gold leading to inflation and price rise. This would reduce its demand in foreign market. Thus, these countries could maintain trade balance by deflating or inflating their economies for a short term and a net gain eventually.

Gold standard was tortuous if the imbalances in trade were not corrected by reciprocal policies. Further, the emergence of

America as a powerful trader made such adjustments by the European Countries difficult. Gold Standard after the World War I period (1914-18) and the Great Depression of 1930 collapsed and the World War II (1939-44) created the need for IMF and World Bank, the nearest substitutes for Gold Standard. Here, the trade surpluses of US dollars would flow to debtor countries through these new international organisations as short term measures of assistance and loan to the debtors. This was a balancing system in the beginning and even when the supremacy of dollar was fading in the world market, IMF made a basket of important currencies (special drawing rights or SDRs) for lending to the debtors. But this had created a North South divide of rich and poor traders and a third world of dependencies and indebtedness. The trade deficits were no more marginal and the poorer countries had now to trade with comparative disadvantage with increasing foreign debts.[2]

The second world of communist Russia, however, remained a closed economy with no outside trade and some of the poorer countries too wanted to close their economy to trade, as Russia did, by tariffs and protect their agriculture and diversify their economy with industrial growth. Now, the World Bank assured longer term loans to correct fundamental disequilibrium. But the IMF was hardening its role as lender by putting conditionality to the poor trading members so that exports and imports balanced on rules of comparative advantage. The conditions became tortuous to the debtors who needed protection against the highly competitive richer world. There was a wide demand for a new world order, which could be more cooperative to the third world. But this would not happen as the rich countries were themselves facing competition as well as resistance with the coming in of east and south-east nations in world market. The developing countries in general on their turn had started to plan their economy and protect it.

ROLE OF GATT AND WTO

USA had initiated in 1947 a membership organization for more compromises and concessions in trade and tariffs with 23 member countries, mainly European, in the first round. By its seventh round in 1973 in Tokyo, with tariff cuts for the most favoured nations (MFNs) and principle of non reciprocity and a generalized system of preferences to the LDCs, the membership widened to developing countries covering 107 countries and 75% of world trade.

There was, however, a U-turn with Dunkel's Declaration in the 8th Uruguay Round of the GATT in 1986 when 117 countries had joined it with 85% of world trade. Dunkel's proposals went pro rich nations with its widened control and compulsory nature of new agreements.[3] The trade terms earlier used to be optional. It took about 7 years for poor countries to accept it as a package in 1993 under its new name, WTO and another 7 years, i.e. 2001, when Agreements on Agriculture (AoA) were also pushed in. The unique feature of the new Dunkel package was that trade would include agriculture and services along with industry. The poorer countries had their agriculture trapped under the terms due to the ongoing trade war between rich countries in agriculture, where it had contracted to 7-10% of their GDP, while services were outgrowing over 60-70%. Another trade necessity of the industrial world was to cash its technology and secure market access of finished products like textiles and clothing based, as they were now on new substitutes of cotton or jute which agricultural countries provided earlier. Their new need was to get market access also of various services like investments, finance, banking, insurance, travels, etc.

All this required rich country's right of trade related intellectual properties (TRIPS) and TRIMs, i.e. trade related investment measures. This also required reduction in existing tariffs by at least 1/3rd in phased way for a free trade. It also required a phased reduction in farm subsidies as input support or price support, so that no artificial pressure was put on terms of trade in agriculture. Further, provision of cross retaliation was brought in. All this happened because developed countries were reacting more aggressively to poor countries restricting imports. The growth of new competitors like Russia, abandoning communism, and various other countries in the east, was pushing back USA as a "diminishing giant syndrome."[4]

WHY WAS DUNKEL ACCEPTED?

India had to accept the terms due to a give and take policy involved in the tortuous negotiations. Agreement on reducing subsidies in agriculture was reached on the hope that rich countries would also do it and that existing subsidies were much less in India than the 10% limit imposed on it, when it was over 50-70 in rich countries. An aggregate of support measures (ASM) was divided on product specific (seeds, fertilizers, irrigation, credit and support price) and non product specific (research, pest, extension, infrastructure) areas. Here, investment subsidies and input subsidies for low-income farmers were to be exempted. The task before the rich countries was in fact much difficult, as they had to reduce subsidies to 5% of value of production.

Maintaining buffer stocks for food security and subsidy to below poverty line (BPL) cardholders were exempted with the condition that procurement prices should be not more than market prices and PDS should be only for BPL population. This was to ensure food security to rural poor against the current flow of food in urban markets. Similarly, the export subsidy would not include export incentives. All this would give some relief to poor countries.

TRIPS (PATENT RIGHTS)

It may be noted here that the Indian Patent Act, 1970 differed from Dunkel not in copyrights, trademarks, industrial designs or trade secrets but only in patents. Thus, product patent would affect 10% of the drug industry in the main, extending to 20 years, which in practice may not be more than 10 years. Bio technology was exempt. Further, patent on tropical diseases could be possible only in India, as rich countries were not to explore this area. Similarly, tropical crops (pulses, oil seeds, cotton and cereals) or spices, fruits, vegetables had also not such fears. But outside seeds, if patented, would sell at high prices covering up to 10% of product value. It is doubtful that small farmers could increase production with such seeds higher than 10%. Further, farmers were not allowed to save seeds for next cropping, as it would harm the interest of big seed firms. But governments could rescue the farmers by their own stocks here and it was felt that big seed firms would not have any dent in Indian seed market.

As regards allowing restrictions on textile or food imports by rich countries for ten years, it was felt that the period was not too long. So far as general agreement on trade in services

(GATS) was concerned, both the trading parties had equal chances to reciprocate so that opening of investments and personnel services was concerned. This, however, was not true and the big countries got a comparative advantage in these areas. Any way, the 1993 cut off for agreeing to these terms were complied and could be effective by 1995. Unfortunately, these agreements were made at ministerial levels (trade negotiations committees or TNCs) with little exposure to general public. The agricultural terms were accepted only in 2001 for implementation.[5]

What helped the acceptance of the agreement was that during the 1990s, the Indian food problem was almost solved and higher value farm goods could be exported against cheaper imports from rich countries. This would ensure better return to farmers and capital formation in the agricultural sector through such trade. This would also help in employment generation and diversification of agriculture.

What again was helpful that India adopted economic reforms in the same period as rich countries had rigorously done and the objective was utilitarian for getting through its huge debt problem. Thus, globalisation matched with economic reforms, opening markets within and without. Many public sector undertakings had to go to allow private enterprises to compute with ass open world trade.

WTO REGIME: ASSESSMENT

It is only 5 years when in April 2001, India started liberalisation in agriculture under the AoA of the WTO by removing all non tariff restrictions. It is too early to study the impact of the AoA of WTO on Indian agriculture. But this made some impact on India against its psychological sticking to protection and was expected to push down imports from 10% of GDP to 2% as foreseen by the World Bank and the OECD (Organisation for Economic Cooperation and Development) which calculated an increase of global income at 217-230 billion dollar with India's share at 4.6 billion dollar (about 2% of it). Obviously, the major share of growth goes to the rich countries only.

Further, Dunkel's scheme could only be seen as a package and agriculture cannot be studied in isolation with other areas, even if agriculture gets integrated to global technology. The optimists hope that the second generation of green revolution may get the benefits of increased productivity in agriculture but will it click at all? Whole brunt of development falls on government policy for small farmers and adequate food security for the poor and not on big farms and borrowed technology. The recent rise in food stocks and poor delivery system at the same time exposes the high rise in procurement prices and the rising issue prices, thus, explaining the poor off take from FCI.

SUBSIDIES

As regards agricultural exports and imports, where as imports have increased in the WTO regime, exports could not be pushed up due to a highly protected agriculture in the rich OECD countries (a group of 30). Rich countries were giving huge export subsidies to their farmers and their exports, Under the AoA, export subsidies are restricted through reduction in subsidy outlay in the budget by 36% for developed and 24% for developing countries, while the volume of subsidized exports is to be reduced by 21% for developed and 16% for the developing countries within a time limit of 5 years. But big players in the game, however, enjoyed very high export subsidy at the initial base itself.

As distinguished from it, the domestic support subsidies have a different story to tell. These are grouped under green and amber boxes, in which the latter constituted trade distorting subsidies with limits laid down at 5% for developed and 10% of developing countries. The green box subsidies in rich countries is however huge, covering income insurance and safety nets, food security and research and plant protection. Known as producers support equivalent, this subsidy was 30-40% of agricultural output in OECD countries by 1998-2000, which poor countries could not cope with. It was here that a "subsistence box" subsidy was suggested for the poor farmers in agricultural countries as an equivalent to the green box so huge to protect the interest of the farmers in rich countries.

The amber box subsidies are product specific in term of price support to the poor and non product specific in terms of input support like fertilizers, irrigation, electricity and credit. Here, the two subsidies taken together are so low that there could not be any trade-distorting effect, while reaching the 10% limit was too remote. It is, therefore, felt that rich countries are not using markets as any measure of efficiency and are highly protectionists. It is here that even the non trade issues in the name of welfare in rich countries need to be capped, in the same way as the rich countries are demanding minimum standards of sustainable development, health and hygiene, pollution and labour standards in poor countries (Rio Declaration in the Earth Summit, June 1992). Is it not necessary to evolve a level playing field and a multilateral discipline? The Rio terms for India is sure to put barriers to increasing agricultural exports.[6]

PATENT

Patent rights in agriculture have been an unusual feature where agriculture is mainly for subsistence and not tuned to commerce. But the OECD countries where a small percentage of population managed it had a commercial interest and cold have an exporting system. They could have a geographical interest in protecting the plant varieties. India had to amend its patent laws under die WTO terms for implementing a product patent regime, covering improved plants and seeds. Earlier; it protected only processes, not products. In fact; agriculture, food and health are supposed to be related to life itself and so were kept free from anybody claiming it to be his property to be sold.

For agricultural countries, such rights for selling and earning a profit would only make the traditional agriculture face cut throat competition if it does not join the race itself. Here, again India may have to trade in agriculture with comparative disadvantage. The great fear is the emergence of MNCs in food processing and seeds that would work against the interest of small and marginal farmers in an open market and may own the genetic resources of the country for them. The need is to protect the unique process (su generis) adopted by these farmers to create their brand.[7]

REFLECTIONS ON TRIMS

Increasing Debts of Poor Countries and Neo Colonial Stances

The best way to assess the results of the world trade system is to assess why poor countries and India could not be able to check their growing foreign debts in spite of global adjustments against that. It may here be noted that the area of world trade is not only trade flows but also investment (capital) flows and more conspicuously the financial flows. As regards trade flows, it increased more than world output, meaning thereby that more and more of output were being traded. Thus, exports of about 60 billion dollar in 1950 increased by 5 times in 1970 and 58 times in 1990. This was due to 20-40% tariff rate on industrial goods imports in industrialized (OECD) countries and still stronger non tariff barriers. This clearly meant that rich countries were strong exporters in manufactured goods through tariffs and quantitative regulations (QRs) in spite of GATT and had net advantage in comparison to poor countries.[8]

Similarly, direct foreign investment inflows in industrial countries were dropping but in developing countries, it rose sharply during 1980-92. Thus, in the former, it remained low at 2.3% of world fixed capital formation in 1980 to 2.9% in 1992; it increased in the latter from 2.5 to 8%. The cross liability of paying interest was high in the latter.[9]

It may be noted that the growth in international finance was the sharpest and rather explosive, so much so that the growth in trade or investments looked dwarfish. In foreign exchange market, the sale and purchase of foreign exchange to world trade rose in the ratio of 9:1 in 1973 to 12:1 in 1983 and 90:1 in 1992. This meant that the demand for foreign currency for export trade was only 10 billion dollars per day when for speculation or short term capital gains; it was 900 billion dollars per day. Thus, what was growing was not trade or investments but speculative money transactions just for earning short-term gains.

Thus, international financial market has three dimensions–bank lending, sale and purchase of bonds and equities by institutional investors (pension funds and mutual funds) and sale and purchase of government bonds. Between 1964-1991, international bank loans increased from 7.5% of world trade to 43% in 1980 and 105% in 1991. Thus, cross border inter bank liabilities increased from 455 billion to 5560 billion dollars. This naturally reflects increase of international debt liabilities.

Regarding growth of international sale and purchase of financial assets like bonds and equities between foreign and domestic residents, the total cross border ownership of tradable securities was 2500 billion dollars in 1992. Similarly, government bonds also became tradable and the proportion of government bonds held by foreigners rose from 1% to more than 20% in some industrial countries (Germany, USA). All show large scale borrowing in capital markets of rich countries.[10]

WHAT IS BAD IN TRIMs

It may be pointed here that free trade before and after GATT have a sea of difference. It was not debt creating to the poorer nations earlier, based as it was on absolute advantage, but it became a vast accumulation of debts after 1950s and more so after 1970s because it was based on factor endowments and technological superiority of industrial nations. Further, trade today is not between nations but between firms of the same transnational corporations, placed across national boundaries and such trade covered 1/3rd of' world trade. These are big competing oligopolies producing similar products and reaping the trade profits between themselves through intra firm trade and aggressive advertisements and dumping. This aggressively restricts other domestic firms to compete in trade and trade gains. Further, primary goods in trade have been losing their place due to intermediate goods substituting primary raw materials of poor countries.

Similarly; the investment flows, direct or portfolio after the GATT, have concentrated in industrialized countries so that the ratio between rich and poor groups has changed from the earlier ratio of 55:45 to 78:22. Here also, distribution of investment is tilted heavily to service sector and then to manufacturing but not more than 10% in primary sector.[11]

As already told, the financial flows are no more capital flows to under developed countries but to industrialized countries which give high interest for government deficits and welfare expenditures rather than for productive investments. How so little flowing to developing countries, the aim is to get short term capital gains due to changing exchange rates or interest rates. Thus, capital enters into stock markets for speculative gains, through institutional investors in pension or mutual funds and not through regular banking for bond of long maturity. Thus, the game of short maturing securities may enjoy a bullish market or lose or suffer a bearish market in spite of specialized financial intermediaries in the game.

FALL OF THE NATION STATE AND AGRICULTURE

As told earlier, MNCs have become the real players of free trade and nations are no more in a position to regulate trade in their own interest. At the same time, nations with most of the MNCs situated in them are invariably the richer nations and have nothing to lose even if they are ruled by the economic interest of their MNCs. The poorer nations with hardly any giant oligopolies of the type could never be able to counter the rule of the game.[12]

POLICY IMPLICATIONS

This explains how there is a strategic role of nation state of developing countries to see that their primary sector, agriculture is saved from the onslaughts of rapidly growing world market for capital and consumption goods with agriculture reduced to insignificance. The WTO represents such onslaughts and to tune Indian agriculture to the needs of the competitive trade dominated by rich countries would only leave a small morsel for the vast village poor for subsistence.

No doubt, appropriate technology and the trickles of development could be widened to rural sectors with diversification to non farm sectors but the aim of it could not be a share in the world trade but only in increased domestic income. As already noted, the income from agriculture in India has started the process of losing agricultural share in GDP, down to 25% now but population dependent on it is still 60%. Is it not time to see that agriculture is regulated more by the micro policy of the Indian government than the macro package of the WTO? Such policies would not deny either a second Green Revolution or diversification of farm incomes or strategic support to agriculture but will need more land reforms and reconstruction of the rural sector. The imminent need is to have a comprehensive agricultural policy parallel to the WTO, which may not mismatch but would keep agriculture more a domestic concern than a package with industrially rich countries.[13]

In India, social inequality is more pervasive and "detrimental to competition" than anywhere in western world.

Industrial revolution and competition were indigenous to the West but not do in the UDs. So any such reforms like globalization often remain on paper "till inherent pattern of life would persist." Further, westerners are accustomed to the kind of permanent industrial revolution in which they live today. Such a globalised system in the UDs will only have the "same colonial impact small islands of industrial production in the ocean of backwardness and poverty."[14]

NOTES AND REFERENCES

1. V.R. Panchmukhi, "Recent Development in Trade Theories and Practice", Indian Economic Association, Presidential Address, 1994.
2. K.K. Sinha, "Growth Through Globalization: Policy Riddles", in H.K.Sinha (ed.) Development at Crossroads, pp. 114-5.
3. A.N. Prabhu, "Dunkel Proposals and India", Yojna, Independence Day Issue, 1993.
4. Nitya Chakravarty, "Differences over Dunkel's Proposals", HT, May 12, 1993; Also Panchmukhi, op.cit.
5. Chakravarti, ibid.
6. R.K.P. Singh, "GATT: Whose Losses Were It Any Way", HT, March 19, 1994.
7. L.P. Singh, "Living With Global Giants", HT, January 6, 1996.
8. Deepak Nayyar, "Globalisation: The Past in Our Present", Indian Economic Association, Presidential Address, 1995.
9. Ibid.
10. Ibid.
11. Ibid.
12. A.M. Khusro, The New Economic Disorder, Indian Economic Association, 1993.
13. The package must revert back to more reciprocity between rich and poor nations so that a dominating Centre promotes the Peripheries. Such development culture and behaviour would assure social stability and help in doing away with the evenness of development mal behaviour of mass production at the Centre, in which the common masses are made the market. The mass man should not be treated as an element of the market but as value creator. (Quoted Amalendu Guha, Warning Against Americanisation: The WTO Debacle in Seattle, *HT, December* 9, 1999.
14. G. Myrdal, Asian Drama, 1968, pp. 583-595.

WTO AND INDIAN AGRICULTURE

Syed Eqbal Afzal & Sandhya Rani

The new economic policy of 1991 aims at making the Indian Economy competitive and much better integrated with the world economy. It introduced the reform packages namely liberalization, privatization and globalization to revitalize the economy. The economic reform measures have the short-term and long-term measures. The short-term measures aim at stabilization of the economy while the long-term measures are designed for structural adjustment (Kallur and Rasure: 2005). The birth of WTO is indeed a major turning point in the history of world trading and investment system and the developing countries including India are almost surely benefited from it. What is needed is a cautious optimism, rather than euphoria, in evaluating its potential benefits and knowing its drawbacks (Srinivasan 1999).

The global agri-business, governed by the WTO-regime, would have far-reaching implications for Indian agriculture. Its full effect would be realized with effect from January 1, 2005 when GATT Agreements 1994 would stand fully implemented. In fact, this Agreement has brought, for the first time, agricultural sector and international trade of agricultural commodities within the purview of GATT and WTO, thus, integrating agriculture fully with the global market. The Agreement on Agriculture (AoA) under WTO, pertaining to subsidies, market access, and sanitary and phytosanitary measures would have a direct bearing on Indian agriculture. The bringing of intellectual property right (TRIPS) in the purview of WTO would also have euros effects on Indian agriculture through patenting of seeds and the upcoming signers system. Changing the period of patent from 7 (as per India's Patent Act, 1970) to 20 (under WTO) years would make the situation from bad to worse. There is, thus, an urgent need to evolve appropriate picky measures and undertake a serious research so that ways and means could be found to prepare Indian agriculture for the fast changing domestic and global scenarios. We would have to devise a multi-pronged strategy to face the emerging challenges and make Indian agriculture sustainable and internationally competitive.

However, having completed a decade of existence, during which it has evoked the entire spectrum of opinion from being the saviour of the global economy to the destroyer of less developed countries (including India). During this period of ten years, much has been already written and said about the World Trade Organisation (WTO) and Indian agriculture. Many concerns have been voiced about the fact that Agreement on Agriculture (AoA) of WTO is disadvantageous for developing countries like India. Now, what needs to be ascertained and determined is that, whether these concerns are genuine, based on a cogent analysis of the provisions and arguments or these mere rhetoric uttered for the sake of negating the role of WTO (Kallur and Rasure: *ibid*). Hence, in this paper, an attempt is made to look at the relative merits and demerits of AoA in a logical manner.

PATTERN OF INDIAN AGRICULTURAL DEVELOPMENT

India continues to be predominantly an agrarian economy in terms of population dependency and labour force proportion even after more than five decades of independence. Though the primary factor's contribution to GDP has witnessed a substantial fall, yet, the desired structural change with respect to the proportion of labour force has taken place. During the first tow decades of the planned economic development, the proportion of labour force in agriculture remained constant, close to 70 per cent. It came down to 66.5 per cent in 1981 and to 64.8 per cent in 1991. Thus, there has been a mere 5 per cent labour shift from agriculture to non-agricultural activities over the period of four decades and only 1.7 per cent during eighties. In net terms, about 65 per cent of the workforce engaged in agriculture contributes (consumes) 32 per cent of GDP (1951). The share of primary sector in GDP declined from 56 per cent in 1951-52 to about 28 per cent in 1995-96. The share of agriculture in GDP declined from 48.6 per cent in 1950-51 to about 26 per cent in 1995-96. (Clearly, the share of agriculture in the primary sector decreased only marginally. Contrary to it, the share of agriculture in gross capital formation (GCF) witnessed a serious decline. This brings out the fact that Indian agriculture, with 65 per cent labour force, contributes only 28 per cent to GDP, and about 10 per cent to GCF. This had made rural-urban gaps sharper over time, and the persistence of widespread poverty, especially in rural India (Planning Commission, 1999). In fact, agriculture has certain upper limit beyond which it cannot help the development of the economy. But the problem with Indian agriculture is that it has diversified in terms of Sectoral share in GDP but not in terms of the proportion of work- force. Moreover, low productivity of labour has also been on of Indian agriculture's weaknesses till more, about 90 per cent of operational holdings in 1990-91 were less than four hectares 13.1 per cent). The future of these cultivators along with the landless agricultural laborers (74.6million) is a cause of worry to Indian policy makers, especially after the WTO regime has come up in recent years.

The rural-urban or farm-non-farm hiatus would be rather large if we look at the break-up of labour force into cultivators and agricultural labourers. The proportion of agricultural labourers went up to 26.3 per cent in 1971 from 19.7 per cent in 1951 and remained close to 26 per cent in 1991. Thus, while the global economy has achieved a remarkable level of diversification and structural change during the past few days, rural India has been seeing through the proliferation of the landless agricultural labour households.

Nonetheless, in terms of total arable land, population and production of major crops, India is very well stationed in world agriculture. India owns 11.8 per cent of total global arable land area and occupies the second position in the world. It also has the second rank in the world with its 16.4 per cent share of population. It produces 10.6 per cent of the total world cereals for which it stands third. Its ranking in the global community is second in the production of wheat (11.3 per cent), rice (21.5

per cent), groundnut (26.7 per cent), sugarcane (21.4 per cent) and vegetables (9.2 per cent). In terms of tea (28.9 per cent and pulses, it ranks first in the world. It stands third in the world in cotton and fruits production with 14.5 per cent and 8.6 per cent of global production, respectively (GOI, 2000).

All this has improved the per capita availability of cereals and food rains in India over the period of time, from 334 (in 1951) to 428 (in 1993) grams per day. However, compared to China's 730 grams per capita per day in 1993, India is far behind. According to an estimate (Govt. of India, 1996), India's population would rise to 1329.1 million by 2020. The food and feed requirements for cereals, projected for 2020, under three different scenarios, is 257, 296 and 375 million tons, respectively, at 2, 3.7 and 6 per cent per capita income growth rats (Bhalla, 1999). The available supply of cereals in 2020 is projected to be between 219 and 321nukkuib tons under eight different scenarios (Bhalla, 1999). Comparing the requirements and availability, it seems that India would hardly have any export surplus in cereals in future. Keeping in view the present state of technology and rural infrastructure, it is not an easy takes that the cereals production would be raised to the required projected level. In case we fail to achieve it, there can be a serious threat to India's food security.

Agreement on Agriculture

Agreement on Agriculture forms a part of the Final Act of the Uruguay Round of Multilateral Trade Negotiations, which was signed by the member countries in April 1994 at Marrakesh, in Morocco and came into force on 1st January, 1995. It is a set of rules that govern international agricultural development and policy. The purpose of it is to liberalise agricultural trade on a global level by curbing policies that have created distortions in agricultural production and trade. This will go a long-way in fighting against world poverty (Annual Report, IMF: 2003). The commitments under the AoA may broadly be categorized into (1) market access commitments (2) domestic support commitments and (3) export subsidy commitments. These are highly described as three pillars (Saimwalla: 2000). In all AoA means to march ahead to free trade through agricultural trade liberalization.

Market Access

Market Access Commitments deal with policies that relate to the removal of trade restrictions that confront exports. It states that, market access for agricultural products is to be governed by a 'tariff only' regime. In other words, it means that there can be no restrictions on farm trade except through tariffs. This means that, non-tariff barriers such as quantitative restrictions on imports, i.e., quotas, import restrictions through permits, import licensing etc., which were in existence before the agreement came into being are to be replaced by 'tariffs' only (Misra: 2001). Further tariffs are to be reduced by a simple average of 6 per cent over six years totaling to 36% in the case of developed countries and 24 per cent over ten years in the case of developing countries (Table 1). It was stipulated that, such countries would also provide minimum market access opportunities to the extent of 3 per cent of their domestic consumption going upto 5 per cent at the end of the implementation period.

Reducing Domestic Support

These measures under AoA aims at: (a) Curbing such domestic policies through the quantification of all trade destroying domestic policies, (b) Translating them into the aggregate measures of support (AMS), and (c) progressively reducing these quantitative measures. AoA has clearly defined that, AMS is consisting of all such subsides which have a distortion effect on trade or on production and has classified them into three separate boxes, namely (a) Amber box, (b) Green Box and (c) Blue box. The base cleared for calculating total AMS could be either taken as the year 1986 only or the same as in other cases i.e., years 1986-88.

(a) **Amber Box:** In includes those policies that provide domestic support, which have a substantial impact on the flow of trade and production of agriculture commodities. Input subsides, market cost reduction measures, some part of deficiency and direct payments and many other equivalent measures of support.

(b) **Green Box:** It consists of those measures, which provide domestic support that are not having major effect on production and trade. General services like research programme, pest & disease control measures, training facilities, advisory services, marketing and promotional services, infrastructural services etc,. Besides these general services, other measures like public stock holding for food security purposes, domestic food aid, direct aid relief from natural disaster, resource retirement programme, environmental protection programmes and regional assistance programme providing to disadvantaged region are included in this box.

(c) **Blue Box:** It has all those measures permitting due payment under production limiting programmes which have relevance for a few developed countries. Domestic support refers to all the three boxes and it is called Total Aggregate Measurement of Support (AMS) (Mathur: 2003).

WTO AND INDIAN AGRCULTURE

As a founder member of WTO, India is committed to implement various agreements and provisions pertaining to Agreement on Agriculture (AoA). On an objective reckoning, Indian agriculture is going to be influenced by the WTO regime, both positively and negatively. Based on the available estimates of support to agriculture, many experts are of the view that AMS would not affect Indian agriculture as the total Indian AMS is much below the stipulated limits (Bhalla, 1996; Gulati, 2000). It many be so in the present context, but given the falling trend in the global primary commodity prices (as shown in Table 1), and measuring the AMS at border prices, the total AMS may exceed the upper limit over at border prices, the total AMS may exceed the upper limit over the period of time. That may tantamount to reduction of subsidies and, thus, affect the global competitiveness of Indian agriculture. Just to mention a few, wheat price in the global market declined from US $ 240 per ton in 1980 to 121 per ton in 1998. The corresponding prices of rice were US $ 570.5 against 292.5; of sugar US $ 877 against 189; and of cotton US $ 2843 against 1389, respectively. Again, certain studies (Parikh, 1998) find that as a result of India's intervention in global rice market, global export prices would further fall and import prices would rise. This change, both in export and import prices, in likely to affect India adversely. Certain studies (Bhattacharya, 2000;

FAO, 1999) are apprehensive of food insecurity in many developing countries, like India, owing to liberalization of agricultural trade under the WTO regime. However, there are some studies (Gulati, 1994; Bhalla, 1996), which support the view that India would gain from its participation in liberalized trade in agriculture. Their conclusions are largely based on the expected rise in the prices of world agricultural commodities. Another study (Gill and Brar, 1996) concludes that the global competitiveness of Indian agriculture, in general, and that of Punjab agriculture, in particular, has been adversely affected under the liberalized trade regime.

Table1
Trend of Primary Commodity Prices in the Global Market

Year	*Wheat*	*Rise*	*Sugar*	*Cotton*	*Tea*
1970	250	574	323	–	–
1980	240	571	877	2843	2305
1990	136	271	277	1819	2058
1995	149	269	246	1785	1249
1998	121	293	189	1389	1968

Source: World Bank, World Development Indicators, 1993 & 1999.

With regard to market access clause, if 3 per cent of the total consumption of, say, 200 million tones, is imported in India then agricultural prices in India may nearly collapse. As regards, exports subsidy' effect on Indian agriculture, it is largely non-applicable to the Indian situation, and is likely to remain so in the near future. It may, however, be mentioned that intellectual property rights pertaining to seeds and seed-technology may also adversely affect the Indian agriculture. Given the size of India's population, almost stagnating yield, diminishing returns, declining global prices of primary commodities, rigid cropping pattern and shrinking expenditure on research and development, Indian agriculture may have smaller export surplus and limited export competitiveness.

AGRICULTURAL EXPORTS OF INDIA UNDER AoA

The impact of free trade on Indian Agriculture will determine whether it will enhance prosperity or poverty in the country. Agriculture is the lifeline of rural livelihood security. It is also the foundation for National Sovereignty. Most Indian Formers are resource poor, struggling to produce, and market more with poor production and post–harvest infrastructure. Even today, the road and roof are the primary spaces available to most of them for drying the harvested grain or the other farm produce. Exposing our hard working but resource–poor small farm families to the challenge of comparative advantage in world trade without assisting them through integrated package of technologies, services & public polices to bridge the wide gap between actual and potential yields currently prevailing in most farming systems, will result in importing unemployment perpetuating the growing rich–poor divide (Vethirajan: 2004). However, it was expected that, under AoA India's export would be increasing without any difficulties owing to market excess, reduction in AMS and export subsidies. But actual performance has been moderate one.

Share of Agricultural Commodities in Total Exports

In reality, the share of agricultural commodities in total exports for the period from 1995-1996 to 2000-2001 is given in the Table 2. The percentage share of agricultural commodities in the total exports increased from marine products (16.54 to 23.22), basmati rice (4.16 to 7.81), tea (5.73 to 7.20), cashew (6.05 to 6.85), spices (3.88 to 5.92), meat (3.07 to 5.36), tobacco (1.85 to 2.86), seasame nigerseeds (1.26 to 2.18), guargum (1.11 to 2.15), processed fruit (1.00 to 2.18), pulses (0.64 to 1.96) and others (8.92 to 10.98). The maximum increase was for marine products. On the other hand, there was a negative percentage change in the share of oil seeds (11.49 to 7.46), coffee (7.35 to 4.34), castor oil (3.63 to 3.47), now basmati rice (18.19 to 2.86), sugar and molasses (2.48 to 1.83), and miscellaneous (2.64 to 1.82) during the same period. It is a pleasant surprise that exports of basmati rice and non-basmati rice increased again in the financial year 2005.

- India's in financial year 2005 touched an all time high of 11.2 lakh tonne up 45% informed Agriculture Minister.
- Export of rice has emerged as a significant foreign exchange earner for the country, fetching \$1.48 billion in financial year 2005 against \$ 918 million in previous financial year.

Table 2
Share of Agricultural Commodities in Total Exports.

(percentage)

Years	Marine Products	Basmati Rice	Oil Seeds	Tea	Cashew	Spices	Meat	Coffee	Castor Oil	Non Basmati Rice	Tobacco	Sea same and Niger seeds	Guar-gum	Processed Fruit	Pulses	Sugar & molasses	Misc	Others	Total Exports
1995-96	16.54	4.16	11.49	5.73	6.05	3.88	3.07	7.35	3.63	18.19	1.85	1.26	1.11	1.00	0.64	2.48	2.64	8.93	100.00
1996-97	16.54	5.12	14.35	4.26	5.28	4.93	2.91	5.86	2.57	7.90	2.71	1.13	1.46	0.86	0.54	4.42	3.14	16.11	100.00
1997-98	18.22	6.84	13.95	7.62	5.68	5.72	3.28	6.89	2.34	6.84	3.73	1.23	2.21	1.11	1.47	1.04	1.04	10.79	100.00
1998-99	17.21	7.39	7.65	8.92	6.41	6.43	3.10	6.81	2.65	17.35	2.25	1.29	2.87	1.15	0.88	0.10	1.00	6.54	100.00
1999-00	21.09	7.33	6.74	7.34	10.11	7.27	3.37	5.96	4.39	5.54	3.34	1.54	3.35	1.54	1.73	0.17	1.22	8.04	100.00
2000-01	23.22	7.81	7.46	7.20	6.85	5.92	5.36	4.34	3.47	2.86	2.41	2.18	2.15	2.18	1.96	1.83	1.82	10.98	100.00

Source: Foreign Trade and Balance of Payments, July 2000 & 2001.

- The exports to Rs. 2,741.94 crores compared with the previous years figures of Rs. 1,990.92 crores.
- Earning of foreign exchange from basmati has increased to $612 million from $442 million. (Business Standard–2005). India has benefited from disputes settlement process, most famously in the basmati rice case (Business Standard–2005).

Some experts argue that, we have been exporting fresh fruits and vegetables, mango, grapes etc., in a substantial quantity. For instance, export of mangoes has increased from 30 crores in 1999-2000 to Rs. 70 crores in 2001-2002. So is the case of Grapes, Pineapples and Apples where India has the competitive advantage. In the field of vegetables also, India enjoys one of the greatest competitive advantages despite a substantial transport cost, she exports fresh vegetables to number of countries in EU and with ever-growing interest in India's cusine, the demand for her vegetables will increase (Anil 2002). Further, we need to focus on non-traditional farm export in future as they present a welcome diversification in our export basket and reduce dependence on smaller number of products and market. The focus on value–addition and agro-processing highlights the need to improve infrastructure such as roads, storage warehouses and refrigerated transport. We need to setup a credible Certification Mechanism to guarantee quality and to maintain the health standards of our agriculture exports (Nath: 2003).

Share of Agriculture and Allied Products in World Exports

In the shares of selected agricultural commodities in the world exports, the growth rates were positive for the shares of all the items except rice, cereals and cereal preparations, sugar and sugar preparation. The data regarding India's share in world exports of agricultural and allied products are given in Table 3.

For instance, the percentage increase in the shares of agricultural commodities in the world exports for vegetables and fruits (1.0 to 1.3), spices (9.6 to 11.9), coffee and coffee substitutes (2.8 to 2.9), tea and mate (14.5 to 17.2), and feeding stuff for animals (3.5 to 4.8), between 1995-96 and 1999-2000. The negative percentage change in the shares of cereals and cereal preparation (2.7 to 2.3), rice (18.7 to 12.1) and sugar and sugar preparation (0.8 to 0.5) during the same period. It shows that the increase in the share was more for spices, and tea and mate. But the decrease in the share was more for rice in the world exports. Spices had the maximum positive growth and rice had the maximum negative growth in the world exports.

Table 3
India's Share in World Exports of Agricultural & Allied Products

Years	*Cereals & Cereals Preparation*	*Rice*	*Vegetables and Fruits*	*Spices*	*Sugar and Sugar Preparations*	*Coffee and Coffee Substitutes*	*Tea and Mate*	*Feeding Stuff for Animals*
1995-96	2.7	18.7	1.0.	9.6	0.8	2.8	14.5	3.5
1996-97	1.6	12.0	1.0	11.2	2.0	2.7	11.1	3.7
1997-98	1.5	12.5	1.1	12.1	0.4	2.6	18.5	3.8
1998-99	1.6	10.4	1.0	11.2	0.4	2.7	16.4	4.3
1999-2000	2.3	12.1	1.3	11.9	0.5	2.9	17.2	4.8
2000-2001								

Source: Foreign Trade & Balance of Payments, July 1999 & Economic Survey, Ministry of Finance, New Delhi, 2001-02.

DIFFICULTIES EXPERIENCED BY INDIA IN EXPORTING AGRI PRODUCTS

(i) Low Productivity, Illiterate Farmers and Lack of Adequate Market Infrastructure

A comparison of productivity in Indian Agriculture with the levels in other countries shows how low the productivity in Indian Agriculture is: Average world yield is higher, compared to India in many crops and it is 27% higher for paddy, 249% for maize, 41% for pulses, 61% for rapeseed etc. The country lacks adequate marketing infrastructure, rural storage facilities, cold chains and the like even in the 21st century, there is also non-availability of timely credit at reasonable rates of interest to the farmers. Farmers have not taken to 'precision farming', bio-control of pests and post harvest management techniques on a large scale even after eight years of joining of WTO, Investment is the key to the growth of agricultural sector, However, it has been falling since more than a decade. All these have made the country poor in having export surplus both in quantity and quality.

(ii) Absence of Quality Consciousness

In terms of quality, most of the Indian farm products do not conform to international standards, because of sanitary and phytosanitory restrictions, processing and packaging specifications and so on. This is evident from the recent rejection of our mangoes by Japan on the ground that they had organic, inorganic residues on the skin and we had to import special machines for further processing.

(iii) Slow in Registering Patents

Our government is rather slow in enabling farmers and others to register patents for products. But, to maintain the status in the domain of knowledge, we have to rush to register patents for which awareness and training among the cultivators is essential.

(iv)Lack of Awareness of International Laws

India and other developing countries will always be outmaneuvered by the developed world, if they do not throw money and brains in the struggle for global trading. The developing countries have to acquire greater expertise in fields beyond trade and commerce and in particular, in "International Law". The Shrimp/Turtle case of June 2001, which went against India, Malaysia, Pakistan and Thailand, is the best example where USA defeated these countries by its superior knowledge pertaining to the International Law (Fali: 2004).

(v) Slow on Clearing Customs, Port Congestions

India has to be quick in clearing customs, which takes three times longer, time than in high-income countries. In China the longest delay experienced by firms in 2003 was just twelve days while in India, the average longest delay was twenty-one days. The port congestions and delays are increasing transport cost in India. For instance, the cost of shipping container of goods from India to the US is 35% higher than shipping from China and 20% higher than shipping from Thailand. (Vasudev: 2002).

(vi)Inadequate Preparedness

Inadequacy of preparedness of India has been quite evident in the various Ministerial Review Meetings held in Singapore and afterwards. For instance, even in recent meeting at Doha, India had no clear plan and the then Union Commerce Minister, only talked rhetorically. The lack of proper strategy robbed India of making any substantial gains in that meeting (Ravikant: 2001)

CONCLUSION

In the liberalized trade scenario, backed by WTO-regime, Indian agriculture would be fully integrated with the global trading system. Aggregate measurement of support and sanitary and phytosanitary measures, patenting of seeds and technology and food security, etc. are the areas of real concert. In fact, WTO-regime has many safeguards, relaxations and exemptions for the developing countries, which India must exploit to its favour. The new regime would have far-reaching implications for Indian agriculture, both positive and negative. India should try to maximize its gains and minimize its losses in the changing scenario.

Thus, Indian agriculture faces serious challenges both from within and from outside. From within, it would have to shift a sizeable proportion of work force to non-agricultural sectors. Along with it, Indian agriculture must be diversified. Another important challenge to Indian agriculture is to raise per hectare yield to the global level. Protecting its dairy and poultry sectors, from the onslaught of foreign competition, arising due to the removal of quantitative restrictions, is still another great challenge. In order to meet this challenge, the Indian Government would have to take serious and bold steps at the policy level. This is imperative to prepare Indian agriculture to face the internal and global challenge. There is a need to change the rural mind set on agro-exports. The farmer as well as the labourer working in the field should be made to think labour exports and quality of the products.

REFERENCES

Anil Swarup (2002), Indian Export Performance and Their Prospects: Souvenir of 62nd Annual Conference of Indian Society of Agricultural Economics, IARI, New Delhi, pp.16-22.

Annual Report (2003), International Monetary Fund, Washington DC, USA, p. 44.

Bhalla, G.S. and Gurmail Singh (1996), Impact of GATT on Punjab Agriculture, Ajanta Book International, New Delhi.

Bhalla, G.S., Peter Hazell and Hohn Kerr (1999), "Prospects of India's Cereal Supply and Demand to 2020", (Washington, International Food Policy Research Institute, Discussion Paper 29).

Bhattacharya, B. (2000), "food Security in India in the Context of Agreement on Agriculture", paper presented at the seminar on Consultation on Agreement on Agriculture, Ahmedabad, 31st January.

Bureau of Business Standard, Volume VI No. 117. 9th August 2005.

Bureau of Business Standard, Volume VI, No.118. 10th August 2005 p. 16.

Fali S. Nariman (2004), The WTO Tug of War. Business Standard, 7th Feb., p. 6.

FAO Report (1999), The State of Food Insecurity in the World.

Gill, S.S. and J.S. Brar (1996), "Global Market and Competitiveness of Indian Agriculture: Some Issues", Economic and Political Weekly, Vol. 31, No. 32.

Government of India (1996), Population Projections for India and States, 1996-2016, New Delhi.

GOI (2000), Agricultural Statistics at a Glance, New Delhi.

Gulati, Ashok and Anil Sharma (1994), "Agriculture Under GATT: What is hold for India", Economic and Political Weekly, Vol. 29, No. 29.

Kallur, M.S. and K.A. Rasure (2005), "Impact of WTO on Indian Economy", 88th Indian Economic Association (IEA) Annual Conference, Vishakhapatanam, Andhra Pradesh.

Kallur, M.S. and K.A. Rasure (2005): ibid.

Mathur V.C. (2003): "Indian Agriculture in the New Regime of Global Trade : Issues and Concerns" in WTO and New International Trade Regime ed. by Vasisht A.K. and Alka Singh, Advance Publishing Concept, New Delhi, 2003, pp. 21-48.

Misra, R.S. (2001), "WTO Agreement on Agriculture and Agricultural Crisis in India", Indian Economic Associations 84th Annual Conference Volume, Vellore, p.29.

Nath, Siddahartha (2003), Business Standard, 27 December, p. 7.

Parikh, Kirti S. (1998), "Food Security: Individual and National", in Isher Judge Ahluwalia and I.M.D. Little (Eds.), India's Economic Reforms and Development: Essays for Manmohan Singh.

Ravikant (2001), The Deccan Herald, 8th October, p. 12.

Saimwalla, Ammar (2000), "World Agriculture Trade after the Uruguay Round" in Global Trading System and Developing Asia ed. by Aravind Panagariaya et al. University Press, Hongkong, pp. 437-76.

Srinivasan,T.N. (1999), WTO and Developing Countries. Journal of Social and Economic Development, 2 (1): Jan-June, pp.1-32.

Vasudeva, P.K. (2002), WTO Lead by Example, Business Standard, 15th December, p. 6.

Vethirajan, C. (2004), "WTO: The Impact on India", Fact for You, Volume 24, No. 7, April pp. 3640.

WTO: AGREEMENT ON AGRICULTURE AND INDIA

Pushpa Sinha and Ratna Mitra

Indian agriculture accounts for about one-fourth of the Gross Domestic Product (GDP) and is source of livelihood of more than two-third of the population. This made it important to study the impact of WTO on Indian agriculture as the clauses of WTO is related to it. The main aim of WTO is to promote multilateral trade which includes various measures as tariffication, market access, domestic support, export competition which effects the export of the country in the international as well as in the domestic market.

The WTO, which succeeded and subsumed the General Agreement on Tariffs and Trade (GATT, 1974), came into existence on January 1, 1995. This is a rule-based organisation governing multilateral trade relations. The high decision making body within the WTO is the ministerial conference. It meets at least once every two years. Four ministerial conferences have already been held: Singapore (December 1996); Geneva (May 1999); Seattle (November-December 1999); Doha (November 2001). The ministerial conference at Cancun between September 10-14, 2003 was the fifth in the series.

The World Trade Organization is a buzzword today. For the first time ever a world body dealing with trade and involving overwhelming number of countries has come into being. There has always been a legitimate doubt that the US is trying to dominate the WTO in accord with its habit of policing the world, and there are enough examples and experiences of such a policing. The US seems ever ready with offer of advice to other countries about how to manage their internal affairs.

The information of WTO synchronizes the beginning of economic reforms in India. WTO has a definite agenda of global trade and economic development of the member countries both rich and poor. The principles on which the WTO is based are mainly the classical economic premises of free trade. The classical free trade was directed for exchange and accumulation from international trade relations. Modern trade relations among the nations are largely directed by GATT guidelines. The Dunkel modification of that agreement and latter development of the World Trade Organization is the final outcome of trade relation of the contemporary capitalist world. But successive meetings of WTO have indicated that there was a sharp conflict of interest among member nations. It is also to be noted that alongside the global netting of trade under the WTO, there are strong regional trading groups and their interests are irreconcilable with the WTO, agenda as it stands today. India also belongs to that dissenting group as to regional blocks. India is in a paradoxical position; whether to swim with the WTO rules along with the advanced countries which may entail loss to her interest, or to stand against the dominating clauses of advanced countries and to hold her own along with the developing countries, or to pursue any mixed strategy and hold her own development objectives.

After GATT, WTO is the new organization for disciplining the multilateral trade among the member states. Ministers of the member countries meet from time to time in order to thrash out the rules and regulations of multilateral trade. WTO insists on integration of capital market, free movement of capital and investment of multinational companies on land and other natural resources. It is urged that such free and liberal trade among nations will improve the economic conditions of the nation. The argument is clear that free trade will hasten the process of growth. In different ministerial meetings, the rich and developing nations sit across to negotiate the reduction of tariff and free flow of capital. The developing countries are coarsed to agree on such free trade transaction; the developing countries also fear that failure of WTO will be disastrous on their part. By now, the WTO has made some agreements among member nations in different meetings, which have lent a distinct, a pro-capitalist character to this global trade organization. The Agreements on Agriculture (AoA), General Agreement on Trade Services (GATS), Trade Related Intellectual Property Rights (TRIPS) and Anti-Dumping and Subsidies Agreement are some of the issues that have been partly formulated and debated in different ministerial meetings; the latest one is the Hong Kong meeting.

The AoA is a major debating issue not yet settled even in the fifth ministerial meeting at Cancun (Mexico). According to this agreement it is proposed to reduce the tariff and subsidies. The USA and other pro-liberal countries want all the countries to stop their farm subsidies and export tariffs so that free trade of agreement products of advanced countries to all developing countries becomes possible. Opinions on this are divided. India and other developing countries now formed a group called as G-17, which is fighting against this proposal. As most of the farmers are at subsistence level in these countries, the free entry of agro-products of advanced countries to the poor countries will jeopardize the interest of their farmers. This was the central issue of debate in the recently held Cancun conference. However, the issue could not be resolved against the vehement opposition of the developing countries. The General Agreement on Trade in Services and related issues cover a wide range of services such as medical and health services, tourism, architecture, computer and maritime services. GATS also cover other computer related services like accountancy, auditing, book keeping, urban planning, land scope services, construction and audiovisual services. India and other developing countries demand higher commitments of developed countries under this mode of trade so that they increase their access to the developed country market.

Under TRIPS, geographical specificity of only wine and spirits has been considered. But there is large variety of geographical specification of different countries. Under trips multilateral system for notification and registration of geographical indications are provided and the developing countries demand the inclusion of provisions regarding biotechnological inventions, traditional knowledge and pharmaceuticals. The implications are that developing countries that have attained progress in biotech inventions in agriculture, medicine and other traditional products will face competition and extinction. Developing countries who have attained advantage in R&D in several fields should be given legal protection.

Serious issues are involved with agricultural and the services sector provision which developing countries can hardly ignore. The free trade agenda pursued by many developing countries of Africa and Latin America has brought about serious damage to their productive system and employment. In agriculture, the call for reduction of Aggregate Measure of Support (AMS) by 20 per cent by developed countries and 13.3 per cent by developing countries over a period of ten years is very negative approach on the part of the developing countries, where as this base (AMS) for the advanced countries will be high. This itself is an unequal principle institutionalized. The developing countries market excess will be hindered. The negotiations on these issues depend on the attitude of the OECD countries on trade negotiation. On the structure of subsidies also, there are significant differences. India has reduced her farm subsidies in respect of fertilizer, credit and electricity. USA has maintained the farm subsidies on various devices. The organization of subsidies in various boxes under AoA favours the developed countries. (Agricultural subsidies are categorized into green, blue and amber bases). While subsidies payment to the farmers by the USA on efficiency principle is considered as non-distortionary, the same in the developing countries are considered as trade distortionary. Again, there are sharp differences regarding the modalities to be adopted for negotiations. India and many other countries (about 75 countries) prefer the Uruguay Round (UR) formula of request offer approach under this formula the countries can adopt the wait-and-watch approach and can negotiate with the respective countries. The USA and Cairns group (Australia, New Zealand etc.), on the other hand, back the Swiss formula, which calls for steep reduction in the commitments wherever the existing tariff levels are higher than the norm (RBI: Annual Report, 2002-03, p. 22).

On WTO, there is agreed principle of foreign direct investment (FDI), which is considered important for development of developing economies. Although, investment is the most important item the negotiation on this issue has not developed at all in the Cancun Ministerial conference. The matter has been deferred in the Fourth Ministerial conference of WTO at DOHA, Qatar. While the developed countries like to bring the FDI issue under the multilateral framework, the developing countries would like to have necessary protection to their local enterprises instead of opening the entire space to the foreign multinational enterprises. In a sense, the Multilateral Frame on Investment (MFI) is a general principle to spread the investment net of MNE in the developing countries. In that case, the developing countries will have to consider their own interest in terms of employment and balance of payment positions. The issue is particularly important for employment generation. While capital and labour are mobile factors of production, the MFI proposes to liberalize the capital movement but not the labour movement. This is an asymmetry. The EU members, allow movements of capital and labour among their member countries, Under the WTO, MFI issue is only unilateral, i.e. the capital will flow from the developed countries to the LDC, but movement of labour from the later to the former is not allowed.

We can make some reflections on the course of the operations of the WTO so far proposed and practiced. There is no logical development of WTO as is such. The eight round of GATT Agreement started on First January 1988 is known as Uruguay Round (1986-1994). Uruguay Round prepared the ground for multilateral trade agreement and the WTO was instituted on January 1st in 1995 in Geneva.

The Uruguay Round Agreement on Agriculture (URAA) calls for the initiation of negotiations for continuing the process of agricultural trade reform in 1999. Article 20 of the agreement states that member countries of the World Trade Organization (WTO) recognize that the long-term objective of substantial progressive reductions in trade distorting support and protection of agriculture resulting in fundamental reforms is an ongoing process.

The Uruguay Round Agreement on Agriculture, which entered into force in 1995 along with other Uruguay Round accords including the agreement to establish the World Trade Organization, was an important step toward applying multilateral rules and disciplines to global agricultural trade. Most assessments of the agreement hail it as a historic shift in the way agriculture establishes new multilateral trade agreement. The agreement establishes new multilateral rules governing market access; export subsidies and domestic support for agriculture. In terms of future trade liberalization, its most important provisions may be those requiring the elimination of quantitative trade restrictions and their conversion to bound tariffs. These bound tariffs, even if some of them are extremely high, can provide a starting point for future negotiations of tariff reductions.

MARKET ACCESS

The agreement requires all WTO members to convert non-tariff trade barriers to tariffs and to reduce them by a simple average of 36 per cent over six years (with a minimum tariff reduction per tariff line of 15 per cent). The agreement prohibits the introduction of new non-tariff barriers to trade. Where non-tariff barriers restrict imports, the agreement requires that importing countries offer minimum access of usually 3 per cent of consumption rising to 5 per cent over the six-year implementation period for the agreement.

Most assessments of the agreement conclude that it provides little in the way of expanded access for agricultural products. Its importance lies in extending the principle (already applied to trade in industrial products) of protection by bound tariffs to agricultural trade and establishing at least a base for further tariff reductions in future negotiations.

EXPORT SUBSIDES

The agreement requires that export subsidies be reduced by 21 per cent in terms of quantities and by 36 per cent in terms of budgetary outlays by the end of the six-year implementation period. WTO members may continue to use their existing export subsidies within the limits established but may not introduce any new export subsidies.

DOMESTIC SUPPORT

The agreement also includes rules and commitments for domestic support. Domestic subsidies are to be cut by 20 per cent from average levels of support aggregated across all commodities for the base period 1986-88. Support reduction commitments are also to be made over the six-year implementation period on the basis of this Aggregate Measure of Support (AMS).

Trade policy experts contend that the rules established for domestic support policies are more important than the reduction commitments required. The agreement defines which domestic policies are permitted ("green box" policies), such as income support provided to farmers independently of participation in production limiting programs, advisory services, or domestic food assistance. Policies that are not eligible for the green box are automatically prohibited ("amber box" policies).

SANITARY AND PHYTOSANITARY MEASURES

An Agreement on the Application of Sanitary and Phytosanitary (SPS) Measures reaffirms the right of WTO members to adopt and enforce that they deem appropriate to protect human, animal or plant life or health as long as such measures are not applied in an "arbitrary and unjustified" manner. The agreement states that such measures may not be used as disguised barriers to trade. SPS measures may be based on international standards where they exist. WTO members could impose higher standards than those derived from these sources if based on scientific justification and risk assessment. All WTO members agree to recognize the equivalence of different standards that result in a comparable level of SPS protection. Dispute settlement panels should seek advice from relevant international organizations when scientific or technical matters are at issue.

The SPS Agreement, though binding on WTO members, is started in broad language. Specific will come from interpretation of the agreement and adjudication of sanitary and phytosanitary issues in WTO dispute settlement.

DISPUTE SETTLEMENT

New and strengthened dispute settlement procedures agreed to as part of the Uruguay Round also apply to disputes that may arise under either the Agreement on Agriculture or the SPS Agreement. An important change in WTO dispute settlement procedures is the elimination of a member's right to veto a dispute panel's decision and effectively block implementation of the panel's recommendations for resolving the dispute. Potentially, this strengthens the ability of the WTO to enforce panel judgments. The right of WTO members to negotiate compensation rather than change its challenged policies remains in place, however.

As the Agreement on Agriculture relates to domestic subsidies, export subsidies (including volume of subsidies exports), minimum market access commitments, domestic support, sanitary and phytosanitary and food aid operations as discussed above.

The Agreement seeks to open national markets to international competition by replacing non-tariff measures with normal customs duties that would be progressively reduced. Second, it seeks to check over production by progressively reducing government aids that encourage overproduction and hence surpluses, which are either disposed of through, export subsidies or destroyed. Third, it seeks new disciplines on export competition and reduction in subsidies along with the volume of exports subsidies.

The WTO determines the following provisions to promote trade in agricultural products:

1. All non-tariff barriers like quantitative restrictions (QRs) would be converted to tariffs.
2. The reduction of tariff in agricultural products will be implemented over six years for developed and more than ten years for the developing countries, effective from January 1, 1995.
3. Countries with closed farm markets will have to import 3 per cent of products of domestic consumption. This share will rise to 5 per cent over six years effective from January 1, 1995.
4. Trade distorting support for farmers will be reduced by 20 per cent over six year for the developed countries and 13.3 per cent for the developing countries.
5. The value of direct export subsidies will be reduced by 36 per cent and volume wise by 21 per cent over six years.
6. The poorest nations are exempted from all these provisions of farm products.

After giving a glance on the provisions of the WTO, a concrete perception that can be drawn is that being a predominantly agricultural economy, India will be a mixture of experience gainer as well as looser due to the nature of the WTO provisions. As a founder member of WTO, India is committed to implement various agreements and provisions pertaining to Agreement on Agriculture. These include commitments on market access, domestic support and export subsidies, the agreement on sanitary and phytosanitary measures etc. that are already discussed above. As a result of the Agreement, all the quantitative retractions are to be abolished and non-tariff measures are to be replaced by the tariff measures during the implementation period that is from January 1, 1995 to 31 December 2004. The minimum market access quota is to be expanded to 3 per cent of total domestic consumption by 31 December 2004. However, there are certain protection provisions in the form of "safety trigger", custom duties, anti-dumping clauses and countervailing duty rights, etc. available to India, as to other members of the WTO family.

As a result of the commitment to subsidy reduction, the upper limit of total aggregate measurement to support (total AMS) for the developing countries like India would be 10 per cent of the total value of agricultural production. Nevertheless, the domestic support measures the have a minimum impact on trade is excluded from reduction commitments. Such policies include general government services in the area of research, disease control, infrastructure and food security. Besides, direct payments to producers under various programmes and certain government assistance to encourage agriculture and rural development in developing countries are also excluded from total AMS. As regard the export subsidies, the developing countries are required to reduce the value of direct subsidies to a level of 24 per cent below the 1986-90 base period and the quantity of the subsidized exports is to be reduced by 14 per cent over a 10 year period.

On an objective reckoning Indian agriculture is going to be influenced by the WTO regime, both positively and negatively. Based on the available estimates of support to agriculture, many experts are of the view that AMS would not affect Indian agriculture as the total Indian AMS is much below the stipulated limits (Bhalla, 1996; Gulati, 2000). Experts say that since India's per capita income is less than US $ 1000 and, thus, product specific and non-product specific subsidies given by Indian Government on agricultural inputs would not be withdrawn. The reduction obligation to non-specific subsidies, which are given on chemical fertilizers, irrigation, electricity, seeds, pesticides, bank's interest and cost of credit given to all crops, and product specific subsidies, which are given through support price to all agricultural products applies only if subsidies exceed 10 per cent of the value of total agricultural production which is incidentally not the case with Indian agriculture.

The WTO also ensures that Indian farmers do not have a problem of keeping portion of crops as seed for succeeding crops and in exchanging seeds with other farmers of the country. However, the WTO restricts the desire of those Indian farmers who attempt to adopt seed production as their productive occupation. The Indian economy which eventually not be deprived of selling seeds either in domestic or international market, if the norms of the WTO are not violated by Indian planners.

It may be so in the present context, but given the falling trend in the global primary commodity prices, and measuring the AMS at border prices, the total AMS, may exceed the upper limit over the period of time. That may tantamount to reduction of subsidies and, thus, affect the global competitiveness of Indian agriculture.

With regard to market access clause, if 3 per cent of the total consumption of, say, 200 million tones, is imported in India then agricultural prices in India may nearly collapse. As regards, exports subsidy's effect on Indian agriculture, it is largely non-applicable to the Indian situation and is likely to remain so in the near future. It may, however, be mentioned that intellectual property rights pertaining to seeds and seed technology may also adversely affect the Indian agriculture. Given the size of India's population, almost stagnating yield, diminishing returns, declining global prices of primary commodities, rigid cropping pattern and shrinking expenditure on research and development, Indian agriculture may have smaller export surplus and limited export competitiveness. Another factor, which adversely affects the global competitiveness of Indian agriculture, is the comparatively low average yield compared to other countries.

In concluding lines, apart from the productive arrangement in the short run, there is a fear among the developing counties like India regarding patenting of seeds. Trade Related Intellectual Property Rights (TRIPS) as applicable to agriculture concerns with patenting of seeds. Patent is of two types – product patent and process patent. While product patent is followed in US, Europe and other countries, process patent is followed in India. Patenting refers to granting of monopoly to the innovator of any new product. In the field of agriculture, patenting of seeds is the major area of controversy. As implied, seed patenting is supposed to restrain Indian farmers from using seeds, which they retain out of output to be used as seed. They also have the practice of selling surplus seed to fellow farmers in that or neighboring villages. The farmers cannot commercially sell seeds. However, with the establishment of a Plant Breeder's Rights (PBR) system in the near future (end of 2005), provision will be made for "farmer's privilege" whereby "a farmer is completely free to use the farm-saved seed of a protected variety for growing subsequent crops either on his own land or on leased-in land or for traditional exchange in the village community. As long as the farmer continues to be a grain producer and does not convert himself into a 'commercial seed seller' of the protected variety, he would be unaffected by the PBR". Researcher's privilege produces the freedom for Indian researchers to use own protected varieties to breed another new variety, without any specific consent of the original plant breeder.

Another question that might crop-up is whether prices of these seeds, particularly from MNCs, could be so high as to exploit the farmers? As could be observed, hybrid varieties of seeds are more productive, which could influence the farmers' decision to go for these seeds. Another view held is that the WTO regime provides an opportunity to Indian farmers to get latest seeds from any part of the world. This could be true only in the long run, if more attention is paid by international scientists on the invention of new seeds that confirm to the cropping pattern in India.

The second important concern relating to agriculture is liberalization of agriculture trade. This has two dimensions. Firstly, reduced protection to agriculture in the developed countries where subsidies range from 20 per cent to 30 per cent, provides increased scope for agricultural exports from developing countries. Ultimate elimination of tariff and non-tariff barriers on agricultural imports into developed countries provides price advantage to developing countries. India can take advantage in enhancing agricultural exports. However, India has to compete with other developing countries. The age-old contention of cherry that developing countries will have to compete for the limited market in these goods may still appear to be relevant even today. Further, trade liberalization in agricultural goods is also than trade liberalization in manufactured goods. There also exists scope under WTO to restrict agricultural imports into developed countries under anti-dumping legislation. The import duty on agricultural products in India is given in Table 1 and Table 2.

Table 1
Import Duties on Agricultural Products in India
(As on 2001) (Per cent)

Sl. No.	*Commodity*	*WTO's Bound Rate*	*Applied Rate*
1.	Wheat	100	50
2.	Spelt Wheat	80	50
3.	Rice	70 & 80	70 & 80
4.	Pulses	100	5
5.	Maize	60 & 70	50
6.	Sugar	150	60
7.	Oilseeds (Rapeseed/Sunflower)	75	75
8.	Raw Cotton	100	10
9.	Crude Palm Oil	300	65*
10.	Refined Palm Oil	300	92.4*

* Fixed tariff US$ 432/tonne w.e.f. 26/11/2002.
** Fixed tariff US$ 460/tonne w.e.f. 26/11/2002.
Source: Govt. of India. Economic Survey 2001-2002

Secondly, every country irrespective of its output and consumption pattern, will have to import at least 3 per cent of its food consumption requirements. In situation of excess food stocks, this may really hurt the interests of farmers, as import supply would depress the prices, which are already low and unremunerative to farmers. In its present situation, Indian agriculture may be negatively affected because of this clause WTO.

Table 2
Import Duties on Agricultural Products in India

Country	*T.E. 1986-88 (WTO's Base Period)*			*1999*		
	Per Farmer	*Per Hectare (UIS $ in mn)*	*Total Subsidies*	*Per Farmer*	*Per Total Hectare*	*Subsidies (US$ in mn)*
Canada	12000	75	5645	9000	52	3093
EC	11000	707	95214	17000	831	114450
Japan	15000	10048	53637	26000	11792	58885
USA	17000	98	41890	21000	129	54009
OECD	11000	187	246226	11000	218	282780
India	11	8	1058	66	53	7247

T.E.= Triennium Ending Average per annum
Source: Govt. of India, *Agricultural Statistics at a Glance 2002,* Ministry of Agriculture.

At present, India is exporting wheat and rice living in the deficit on less than cost price with the support of subsidy. Now, there is a question with the poor countries like India that what is the justification of providing cheap grains to the foreigners by granting subsidy at the cost of neglecting her own people being in the condition of hunger, malnutrition, impoverishment and deprived of minimum needs? On the whole, international trade system of agriculture is far unequal. It is very harmful and disadvantageous for the role of the poor countries. This is the real world economic order emerged after establishment of the WTO. Like in India, western subsidies are iniquitous (unfair and unjust). The largest 2 per cent of Europe's farms receive 24 per cent of all direct payments from their respective governments while the smallest 60 per cent get only 10 per cent. Even in the US, the richest 7 per cent of farms soak up half of government support. Both the EU and the US dole out cheques as 'deficiency payments' (the gap between the low global prices and high cost of production) to farmers. The EU combines this with 'price support' and 'export subsidies'. All these countries also use import tariffs as a barrier. Japan's import tariffs on rice go up to 1,000 per cent, while America's $4 billion cotton subsideies to 25,000 well-off farmers is more than the value that they produce, besides helping to pauperize 10 million African farmers in four countries Burkina Faso, Mali, Chad and Benin. It is these African nations, which scuppered a deal at Cancun.

The poor nations should not go in the trap of rich nations. They should not assure to any extent in lieu of reducing subsidy by the rich countries (if they do it also really). India along with other developed nations should retake its right to raise import duties as well to impose quantitative restrictions on their imports. It is in the interest of billions of rural dwellers of the world depending on the agriculture related lives. It is only way to save their agricultural lives and right to get food. Developed nations are neglecting development issues in WTO. They try to thrust developing nations towards non-trade issues cleverly. What is observed in 'Doha Talk' or 'Cancun Talk' seems to be double tracks procedure in which the issues related to the interest of rich countries are taken on 'fast track' but the issues and anxieties of poor countries are kept on 'slow track'. The developing countries always try to outline those disparities, but they reluctantly neglect it. In the 'Cancun meet', India along with its G-21 allies as well as G-15 allies stressed boldly on these issues. The developing nations kept "Alternative Reform Proposal" in the leadership of India, China, Brazil and Argentina (G-21 Group) etc. The other members of G-21 Group, who supported the developing nations' issues such as abolishing subsidy by the rich countries, are Bolivia, Chile, Columbia, Costa Rica, Cuba, Ecuador, Al-Salvador, Guatemala, Mexico, Pakistan, Paraguay, Peru, Philippines, South Africa, Thailand, Venezuela and Egypt. The courage of very poor countries was also stronger. The small African counties like Benin, Burkina, Faso, Mali and Chad also strongly demanded for abolition of subsidy from cotton to which they are affected adversely. After the strong opposition of developing countries also, USA alongwith other developed countries interpret the abolition of subsidy on their own way. They always tried to be fool the poor countries. They stressed on reducing subsidy of some commodities only. The USA and other developed countries could not stick on the 'Doha Talk'. To the contrary, they opposed the voice of Arun Jaitly, the Indian Commerce Minister and other developed countries by saying, "You stick to the word like clever pleader but neglecting and overlooking its background and context ". By saying so, it is evident that 'might is right' policy will provoke in near future also. In the past too, USA, by pursuing developing nations to reduce subsidy and import duties, has continued its huge agriculture subsidy. On the contrary, it has raised its quantity. Very cleverly, the agriculture subsidy divided into three categories:

A. Orange Box Subsidy

B. Green Box Subsidy

C. Blue Box Subsidy

Out of these only 'Orange box subsidy' is considered as obstacle in trade. 'Green box subsidy' and 'Blue box subsidy' have been kept out of the curtailment jurisdiction of WTO. As a result, the subsidy of rich countries remained constant. In some items, 'green box' and 'blue box' subsidies has been raised in lieu of reduced 'orange box' subsidy. This is the charismatic and deceitful behaviour of USA and other rich countries on the line of force theory of sovereignty. As a result of 'Uruguay talks' of GATT, the agriculture subsidy has been increased in lieu of being diminished. In 1986-88, the agriculture subsidy of World was $23,800 crore, it became 24,800 crore by being raised in 1999-2002. After 'Cancun Meet' it was observed that in lieu of expressing dedication towards heavy subsidy in the agriculture sector and slowly abolishing at completely by the developed countries, it provided to continue 'the blue box of subsidy' (a category of subsidy), although it has made it comprehensive. The 'Declaration of WTO' at Cancun remained totally full of despair and agony. Until the favorable atmosphere is not made for removing the anxieties of developing countries, this document cannot be the basis of future talk. There is no possibility of any meaningful talk further in the 'Cancun Document' (13 September 2003). In that document the worries of developing nations of talks like EU full of heavy subsidies, dumping of agricultural products of USA in developing nations and Singapore issues were set aside. India, Malaysia and seventy other countries had opposed vehemently of this issue. In that draft document developing nations were directed to open their markets absolutely. The benefits gained by 'Doha Round of Talks' for the development of developing countries were taken in the grab by the developed countries.

The subsidies given by the developed countries in their agricultural sectors affect adversely to the agricultural of the developing nations. Indian Commerce Minister, Arun Jaitly appealed US to reduce $3 million per year subsidy to its agriculture sector in the ministers level meet of WTO at Cancun. The developed countries should abolish their high rate of subsidies given to their agricultural sectors. It will be very damaging and harmful for the economies of poor countires. All this activities of developed nations represent as unequal deal that will force the poor to do more and the rich less. The Cancun, the G-23 asked the rich nations to reduce the unreasonably high subsidies given to their farmers and allow greater market access to agro-products sold by poor nations. However, the developed world – notably European Union, Japan and the USA instead of an agreement on the contentious Singapore issues on investment and competition that required poor nations to further liberalize rules governing foreign investment, corruption and bureaucratic cutback. Since, neither side was willing to yield an inch, the Cancun talks failed. Thus, the size of the disparity between rich and poor widened at WTO.

Actually free trade may even be proved force for both development poverty reductions. But unfortunately enough, most trade is neither free nor fair. The WTO, rule-based, predictable and democratic (one country, one vote and decision by common consensus) multilateral organization, was designed to correct the skews. But for years, rich nations browbeat aid-dependent poor ones to work out deals that favoured the former. It was during the Seattle meet in 1999 that for the first time outsiders demanded a say in the deal making process and talks collapsed. In Cancun, the African nations and others, heat by low global prices of agricultural products, ensured a repeat performance. The reason; the rich nations arrogantly told them that the problems relating to high subsidies given to their farmers would be tackled later. According to a study by the 'International Food Policy Research Institute', US farm policies deprive developing nation of $11 billion annually in lost export income. In case of the EU, the figure is $20 billion.

The Singapore issues are just mock thrown up by the West to disguise their own obstinacy over agriculture. Amitabh Mattoo, Leading Economist of World Bank explains: 'many developing countries would have been willing to pay the price of negotiating these issues if there had been a sufficient commitment by the EU and others to eliminate subsidies'. Rich countries may also have over played their hand and misjudged the strength of filling in the developing world. The World Bank estimates that there had been a deal gone through at Cancun, 144 million people in developing countries would have been out of poverty. And there is also the danger that formation of regional trading blocks and country-to-country deals will gain further momentum now, forcing the poorest to yield more. Arvind Panagriya, Professor, University of Maryland says: 'some large developing countries like China, India and Brazil already face discrimination in the European and US market. This will get worse'. Cancun is a semi-colon, not a full stop. India must act quickly to shape its post-Cancun agenda as it has a bigger stake in a multilateral trading system. For instance, it must carefully assess its farm strategy: What concerns prevent its overall comparative advantage in agriculture from translating into a more aggressive negotiating position. Further, there should be coercion of the effective role of developing countries in the international trade. The developing nations should express their views before countries with full solidarity and strongly for achieving economic and commercial concessions (facilities) in agriculture and other sectors too in WTO in future as well. The developing nations should have very effective role in the determination of the infrastructures of different monetary and financial organization (WB, IMF etc.) too in addition to commercial organization (WTO). FAO has opined: "open and free unilateral trade system is in the social and economic interest of all countries–either it may be rich or poor." Broadly observing, it seems that WTO is such a weapon in the hands of developed countries by which they can hold over the markets of developing nations anyhow in the name of liberalization and globalization. It is not in the interest of India at all that less then 20 per cent people of the world are consuming more than 80 per cent wealth and assets. India and other developing countries should not worry from it, but they should shape its rules and regulations in favour of their interest with full solidarity. There should be equal and justice able distribution of the benefits of liberalization and globalization between rich and poor countries under the system of the WTO.

After cold war, developing countries were kept fully isolated and on the periphery. After that the first time the developing countries recognized themselves as 'developing countries'. They established their identification as a part to the developing world in the WTO at Cancun, after all the differences divisions within themselves. The perversity of developed world to keep the developing world deprived of from the benefits of world trade is solely responsible for the failure of 'Cancun meet'. The attitudes and activities of the developed nations proved a question mark on the democratic and legal framework (setup) of WTO as 'One nation-One vote' and 'uniform and unanimous decision system' as well as 'rule-based world trade system', etc. Developing countries remained successful in thwarting the developed nations in propelling their own agenda on WTO. But it should be continued ahead via Geneva talk also Arun Jaitly said: "the result of Cancun is on its own place, now the 'balance of power between rich poor nations' has changed". But WTO has become the medieval organization now. The promises made during the 'Uruguay Round of Talks' are now no more. The agricultural export of India could not maintain its former level even before the constitution of WTO.

India has opposed the joint proposal of USA EU on the 'International Trade Issue of Agricultural Products' on 20th of August, 2003 itself in the WTO headquarter, Geneva by its another joint proposal supported by China, Thailand, Argentina, Bolivia, Mexico, Chile, Brazil, Columbia, Guatemala, Costa Rica, Peru, Paraguay and South Africa. The economy of the major countries included in those 14 countries is based on agriculture to great extent. Sixty per cent population depended on agriculture live in those 14 countries. Such 14 countries produce 60 per cent of world rice production, 35 per cent of wheat and 57 per cent of sugarcane.

WTO represents a new International economic order with significant polarization of production and trade. It is a unipoler system, which hardly bears the unique system of production, consumption, creative ingenuity of independent states. Liberal trade of comparative advantage of individual state based on factor endowment, which has been the kingpin of classical free trade doctrine, degenerated into the Italic control of the productive system of the different states. High tariffs quotes, controls and regulations of the advanced countries has practically reduced the spirit of mutual trade among the nations into hard battle of bargain between the rich and the poor nations. Production and trade of agricultural are going to be hit severely by the difference agreements. General Agreements on Trade in Services (GATS) is an encroachment in the decision-making process of states regarding health, education and environment and other social-sector services, (GATS cover 161 service activities in 12 classified sectors). The serious implications of the services sector agreement is that the corporate take over of these services will make the services scarce and costly and hence, beyond the reach of majority of poor people.

India's economic reform, about one and half decade old is gradually spreading over different spheres of activities. Liberalization process started in industry, has not yet yielded any spectacular result. Usual moderate growth of industry has not made leap forward with foreign capital inflow. India's foreign exchange reserves have increased with NRI deposit inflow and portfolio investment. Foreign direct investment, however, has not been spectacular, compared with major South, East and South-East Asian countries like China, Malaysia, Singapore and Indonesia. Foreign direct investment flow in India has been very low. In 2001, China's FDI flow was $ 46846 million while India and Singapore's flows were $ 2403 million and $ 8609 million respectively.

Nor did India have any significant boost in respect of export. WTO regulations have strictly limited Indian export in the advanced countries. Trade Policy Review Mechanism of WTO made third review of India's trade policy in June 2002. According to the report, India's tariff regime continues to be complex. It is observed that restricted import policy, export subsidies, greater competitiveness of Indian export in the international market. The report pointed out that protection through high tariff and small-scale reservation has been impediment to India's export.

India, however, maintained that her trade partners in advanced countries imposed restrictions, which have to be reduced following the negotiations in the Doha work programme.

India has to formulate her own policy in order to reap the benefits from global trade relations. Neither China nor USA is really competitive. They maintain their own interest by imposing restrictions, which are trade distortionary. In international investment trade and agreement on services both the countries strictly guard their national interest of output and employment. In textile, pharmaceutical, agriculture and any other sectors India should not succumb to the WTO pressure. With only a limited growth of industries, India can ill afford to allow foreign multinationals to crowed out domestic investment and immiserize her new industrial structure. Like many other countries, India should restrict the scope of FDI only to development areas, which encourage export and contribute to growth. Foreign investment should add to the development process of the country a clear reflection of which is the contribution to growth and employment. India must protect against encroachment on multinationals in small-scale sector and agriculture.

However, the WTO regime offers advantage to have technological upgradation of Indian industries. There are distinct areas where foreign companies will bring improved technology and our products will have competitive edge in the international market. China has reaped advantage from this classification of technology application and export opportunities. This will encourage domestic competition and improve efficiency.

The WTO forum is undoubtedly the biggest international trading organization at the global level. It helps in implementing the past negotiations, making new arguments for future and settling the trade disputes among the countries. Therefore, India can make future trade negotiations for augmenting export and inflow of foreign direct investment. In addition, WTO provides an opportunity to negotiate with the advanced countries on issues like labour standards and environmental standards. These negations are for the better improvement of production system of developing countries and India can open multilateral and bilateral negotiations on these issues. India and other developing countries would have to make hard bargain, as they did in Uruguay Round, Doha and Cancun on IPR and services. The game of trade negotiations will continue and India and developing countries will have to mobilize strength. On the other hand they will have to improve their own structure of production.

Given the intransigence of the advanced countries in the trade negotiations under the WTO, the developing countries like India will have to cultivate bilateral platforms of trade. Along with GATT, one European Union has developed as an epicene of trade negotiations. ASEAN has now become a powerful trading block at our doorstep and those blocks are bilaterally and multilaterally making trade negotiations. NAFTA is equally strong trading block. In our case, SAARC although two decade old, is scuttled by political squabble between India and Pakistan and BIMSTEC also.

For India, it is more essential to enter into and make strong the regional trade association. South Asia is, therefore, a very good potential area where India's trade relation has to be strengthened vigorously. It is through these regional blocks that India can improve in the game of trade negations. G-17 in the Cancun Ministerial meeting is a pointer to this effect. Close to our border, India should have stronger trade relations with Myanmar, Bangladesh and China. Bilateral open trade arguments will be more beneficial than the multilateral trade. While we have duty free entry of Bhutan, the same can be reached with Bangladesh and Myanmar. This form of bilateral trade is not the dissociation from WTO; rather these bilateral trade arguments with countries of mutual interest with make it easier to have strong position in the multilateral trading forum like WTO.

During the November 2001 WTO meet in Doha Qatar, the WTO member state agreed to place development issues at the forefront of the new round of trade liberalization negotiations. The decision to focus on development, properly known as the 'Doha Development Agenda' was premised on the consensus that removing global barriers to trade is the best manner to promote worldwide growth and foster prosperity in developing countries. The Doha agenda offers the world once in a generation opportunity to remove barriers to trade and thereby stimulate economic growth in developed countries alike. The core of the

Doha Development Agenda is market access, agricultural reforms reduction and elimination of trade barriers on consumer and industrial goods and liberalization of trade in services. The round of trade talks launched in Doha marked the first time that developing countries interest were placed at the centre of multilateral trade negotiations. A good pro-poor Doha agreement that lowers tariff peaks and averages in both rich and developing countries did not gained because negotiations have been dead locked over issues of fundamental importance to developing countries market access in agriculture and labour intensive products, intellectual property in medicines and the nature of special differential treatment for developing countries. But realizing the gains will not be possible unless the trade ministers find a way to break the dead lines. Yet many rich countries continue jealously guard trade-distorting policies, especially in agriculture. In absence of meaningful steps by the rich countries, developing countries are reluctant to further open their markets which will reduce the price of imports, increase productivity and help expand exports. Having already taken great strides to open their markets, poor countries want to first see reciprocal action by developed countries. Trade is, therefore, two way street and the fate of the Doha agenda does not rest solely in the hands of rich countries. A success of Doha deal will benefit rich and poor countries alike and all will have to shoulder their respective responsibilities to deliver on their part of the development bargain. Doha agreement was only one step towards a world more supportive of development but it was an important one.

From September 10-14, 2003 Trade Ministers gathered in Cancun, Mexico for the WTO ministerial meeting to review progress and negotiate the next stages in the Doha Development Agenda. Developing counties were watching to see if the so-called Doha agreement agenda will live up to its promise of using global trade and investments to address the persistent poverty that overwhelms many in developing world. The Cancun meet was an opportunity for removing trade barriers and stimulating growth in developed and developing countries against which to access whether the outcomes of Cancun represent a move towards a true development round.

(i) **Agriculture:** Most people in the developing world live in the rural sector, which is why free and fair trade in agriculture matters. It is not just a question of providing access, but of eliminating the subsidies that encourage production in rich countries and harm farmers in poor countries.

(ii) **Drugs and Intellectual Property:** TRIPS intellectual property regime adopted in the last round of trade negotiations, deprived millions in the developing world of access to life saving drugs. Developing countries also continue to worry about bio-piracy the patenting by western firms of traditional foods and drugs.

(iii) **Textiles:** The Uruguay round promised the elimination of quotas in 2004 enabling many developing countries to exploit another area of comparative advantages. But many developing countries worry that trade restrictions will remain and the west will remain some way top wiggle out of its commitments.

(iv) **A More Balanced Liberalization Agenda:** with services compromising an increasing share of production in developed countries attention has shifted to liberalization of trade in services.

(v) **Competition:** Everyone advocates fair competition. But discussions about competition and fair trade demonstrate the intellectual property and inequity of trade negotiations. Developing countries worry that efforts to introduce competition within trade negotiations will only made life even more difficult.

In the Cancun again, EU and US insistence on the four Singapore issues on investment, transparency in procurement, competition and trade facilitation. These issues basically favour the developed world. Indian Commerce Minister Arun Jaitly made a presentation against Singapore issues, especially investment issue. Ultimately, the investment issue was dropped from the WTO agenda. The developed countries failed to force their agenda on the developing countries. It was a decisive moment in the war between the rich and poor. About 80 countries from Africa, the Carribean and others protested against Singapore issues. They felt that the development agenda of Doha is only rhetoric now: development for the developed countries. They indicate that a draft would have to address the developing nations concerns on agriculture. Ultimately, the Cancun meet closed without a declaration, saying that talks had collapsed.

Hence, Cancun was not Doha: whereas a collapse at Doha would have cost the member nations the new round it self, with some luck, the damage from the collapse at Cancun will be limited to a delay in the conclusion of the ongoing round. While virtually all WTO members share the responsibility for the collapse in Cancun, the first finger must be pointed at the misguided leadership at some of the international institutions. Joined by many Western NGO's these leaders have recently bombard the media airwaves with the assertions that the current trading system is unfair to the poor countries, that rich country protection now exceeds poor country protection and that it is unfair to ask poor countries to liberalize when rich countries remain protected. Developed countries also cannot escape from the responsibility for the collapse. The US approach to negotiations in agriculture is especially puzzling.

The subsidy has become one of the weapons in the hands of the rich countries. The vast agriculture subsidies of the prosperous nations harm the economies of the poor countries in many ways. It is evident that all developed nations grant subsidies to their farmers on very large level. According to a document prepared by United Nations Development Programme (UNDP), the developed nations grant $ 311 million per year that is $ 100 crore (Rs. 5,000 crore) per day to their farmers. The USA alone grants $3 million per year to its farmers. The agriculture subsidies granted by the developed nations to their farmer is six times more developing countries and there became 25 per cent increase in it after 1997. The USA particularly is great orthodox and dual player in the field of agriculture subsidy. In Doha (14 September 2001) and in Cancun, Mexico (10-14 September, 2003) along with its other agriculture exporter countries, it has been campaigning for abolishing agriculture subsidy and criticized European Union also for it. But USA, in spite of reducing the subsidy on agriculture, it has passed the act for large expansion in the amount of subsidy on agriculture by promulgating 'United Nation Agriculture Act' in 2000. In this act the proposal of 80 per cent increase in agriculture subsidy has been made. There is provision of $ 10,000 crores increase in further six years and $ 18,000 crores increase in further 10 years in this Act.

In this respect the subsidy of Indian farmers is not more. The subsidies given by the developed countries in their agriculture-section effect adversely to the agriculture economy of the developing nations. Indian Commerce Minister, Arun Jaitly appealed US to reduce the amount of $3 million per year subsidies given to its agriculture sector, in the Ministers level meet of WTO at Cancun, Mexico (September 10-14, 2003). The developed countries should abolish their high rate of subsidies given to their agricultural sectors. Otherwise, it will be very damaging and harmful for the economies of poor countries.

It is evident that developed nations had reduced duties on their agriculture import. But it is set so wisely that the apparent duties on the import made from developing countries become high. The proof of it is that there is 350 to 900 per cent import duties on sugar, rice and dairy products. But developing countries like India are compelled to reduce their import duties under conditions of taking loan from World Bank and International Monetary Fund. If India opens its door, its market will be full of the agricultural products of developed countries and the peasants will come near stable miseries. It is evident that there become many episodes of suicides by the Indian farmer in Andhra Pradesh, Karnataka and other parts of the country. The coconut growers became impoverished due to the import of the palm oil. The developed countries want privatization of health, education, water, electricity and all such services so that they may make their grip and may penetrate their hands in those sectors under the globalization policy. The health and education in the countries like India will be beyond access of the poor persons. Education will be possible only for the progenies of rich people. So, it is essential for the countries like India that these sectors should remain out of the circle of WTO.

Europe, USA and Japan do not really want any reduction in agriculture subsidy in their countries. The poor countries become unable to export $4,004 crore of agricultural products due to the vast agriculture subsidy of the prosperous nations. At the same time becomes deficit of the income of $ 2,600 crore from the agriculture and agricultural industries. The gigantic as well as in justification of the agriculture subsidy of developed nations can be reviewed from these examples:

1. European Union grants subsidy of $ 2 per 9 $ 730 per year = Rs. 34,710 per year approx.) for every cow (farming) of the country, when a large parts of the world lead their lives on less than $ 1 a day.
2. Japan government grants subsidy of $ 2,700 (Rs. 1,28,000 approx.) per cow per year. Indian farmers can buy at least 50 cows at this cost.
3. USA sells its wheat in the world market at 46 per cent lesser price, and maize at 20 per cent lesser price due to the large amount of subsidy given on these products.
4. Developed nations subscribe 311 Arab dollar (i.e. Rs, 5,000 crore daily or six times the level of assistance provided by rich nations to poor) agriculture subsidies to their farmers.
5. The US spends $4 Billion ($1,60,000 per farmer) subsidy on cotton farming alone.
6. EU spends $803 per cow (dairy farming) per year.

Due to this huge amount of subsidy in each product of agriculture in the world market, certain countries have their supremacy. There is no question of competition with them to the farmers of poor countries. In this situation opening of world market of agricultural goods on one side there is decay of agriculture, animal husbandry and dairy farming of the poor nations. This is the real agenda of World Trade Organization (WTO). If the rate of agriculture subsidy becomes low or it is reduced by the developed countries, in that position also poor countries like India have rare chance to benefit from it. More benefits will go in the share of high and middle nations whose agricultural productivity is more and who are main exporters of agriculture. These countries are known as CAIRNS Group. The main countries of this are USA, Canada, Australia, New Zealand, Argentina, Malaysia, Thailand and South Africa, etc. Remaining majority poor countries of Asia, Africa and South America have little chance to get benefited from it. To the contrary, if the poor countries will have to reduce their import duty in place of reducing agriculture subsidy, they have to face both sided strokes.

Agriculture accounts for nearly a third of its gross domestic product but agricultural products constitute just about one-eight of its total exports Worse, the share of agricultural and allied products in total exports has been falling steadily over the years - down from as much as 20.5 per cent in 1996-97 to 12.3 per cent in 2002-03. In actual terms the export of agricultural products has declined by an annual compound rate of 1.1 per cent from $6.42 billion during the same period. In contrast, the imports of agricultural products have grown by a massive 11.6 per cent annually compounded, from $1.37 billion in 1996-97 to $2.64 billion in 2002-03. India's total imports during the same period grew by an annual compound rate of 7.8 per cent agriculture's share in total imports as results, rose from 3.5 per cent to 4.3 per cent during the same period. The share of the agriculture in total imports declined is not surprising. For, India's agriculture export's to most of the developed countries expect the US has been falling of late. Export to Japan has declined by an annual compound rater of 8.1 per cent. Similarly agricultural exports to Russia, Germany and U.K, India's main trading partners, have fallen by an annual compound rate of 12.75 per cent, 2.14 per cent and 1.5 per cent respectively during the period. In contrast, import of agricultural products from the developed countries has grown steadily during this period. And if their shares in India's total agricultural imports are not very significant, the magnitude of growth has been very high. Import from Denmark, Germany, Russia and France grew by an annual compound rate of 50.42 per cent, 6.2 per cent, 25 per cent and 78.8 per cent respectively, between 1996-97 and 2000-2003 (GOI: Economic Survey, 2004).

The breach of commitments by the developed world in the field of agriculture, industry and services is the biggest concern of India. India is worried that if in the process of opening up, the floodgates are opened, it will hurt agriculture-based industries. There are already complaints about dumping by the developed nations from certain countries like China. India's fears are not totally unfounded. The manufactured goods have suffered acutely from heavy imports is now well accepted and even ardent supports of liberalization have to concede that the domestic industry, used to a sheltered market for so many years, can not be exposed to foreign competition, so suddenly and at least for some period of time.

The most serious disadvantages to India are likely to flow from the agreement pertaining to Trade Related Aspects of Intellectual Property Rights (TRIPs), Trade Related Investment Measures (TRIMs) and Services. TRIPs agreement would badly affect the economy of India because it goes against the Patent Act of India 1970. Under this Patent Act, only the process patents are granted in food, chemicals and medicines, whereas in TRIPs Agreement product patents are granted in all these areas. The extension of intellectual property rights to agriculture has serious consequences for India. The Agreement on Agriculture would harm the interests of farmers. The TRIMs agreement is also unfavorable for developing countries like India. The developed countries are benefited much more from the TRIMs Agreement. So, far Service sector is concerned there is a vast level of difference on this issue between developing and developed countries. Inclusion of trade in services is bound to benefit the developed countries than developing countries like India. These are the main concerns of India. It has to observe the agreement on the one hand and Safeguard the agriculture, industry and service sectors from the cutthroat competitions of developed countries on the other.

'Might is Right' and 'Buffalo belongs to Bludgeon' are two popular proverbs and these two proverbs seem to be true even in the arena of WTO, Since the very inception of WTO there has been a fight between the mighty developed countries and the feeble developing countries. It is a fact that the feeble developing countries can never match the mighty ones. No matter how impartial the referee is, and how equally the rules apply to both the boxers in a contest between Mohammad Ali and Biplab Dasgupta, the former would always win (Biplab Dasgupta, 2001). Gandhi once said very aptly that there couldn't be any equality between the giant and the dwarf. The fact is that the referee is far from being neutral and the rules are far form non-discriminatory. Under the present prevailing situation, it would be futile to make hope for justice.

Thus, there are both positive and negative views on WTO and Indian agriculture. There are gains and losses for every member nations. It is not a wise step for India to get out of WTO, but it should think of an alternative. India must exhaust the bilateral option just as China did, and become powerful enough to handle the WTO circuit. Bilateral trade gives India the option of giving concession to one country and taking concession from it. In multinational trade, whatever India gives to one country, India has to give to all. And, when India has less to give, India gets loss. This kind of alternative thinking is not very common in India.

There is no one 'fit-all' size. Each country has to devise its own model, its own pace and its own institutions. There is a clear conflict between forces of localization and forces of globalization. Ordinary peasants do not know any things about WTO.

We cannot analyse anything independent of the west. We accept the prescriptions of the west – their principles, their models, their institutions, and their languages. What we lack in India is originally an Indian model which evolves mass peasants in the developmental process because of the ordinary peasants in India do not know anything about WTO.

Thus, to move into the WTO cautiously and surely the following suggestions could be looked into the most from all the US EU has gained multilateral WTO negotiations.

1. India should think like China on bilateral trade option instead of multilateral trade options.
2. India should develop its own model, which involves mass peasants in the developmental process.
3. India should be careful about the US-EU efforts to split the alliance among the developing countries and least developed countries.
4. India should stand firmly on the issue of subsidies till complete abolition of farm subsidies given by the US-EU alliance.

The WTO agricultural agreement provides a vast opportunity for the Indian agricultural sector, but for the realization of those benefits, India has to be alert and has to catch up in numerous directions. In the liberalized trade scenario, backed by WTO regime, Indian agriculture would be fully integrated with the global trading system. Aggregate measurement of support and sanitary and photo-sanitary measures, patenting of seeds and technology and food security etc. are the areas of real concern. WTO regime has many safeguards, relaxations and exemptions for the developing countries, which India must exploit to its favour. The new regime would have far-reaching implications for Indian agriculture-both positives and negative. India should try to maximize its gains and minimize its losses in the changing world environment. The Government of India should take advantage of the safeguards laid down within the WTO framework to protect Indian agriculture and promote its global competitiveness. It is heartening to note that India has a great potential to increase its agricultural production by raising productivity, improving quality, providing irrigation facilities, developing rural infrastructure, spending liberally on agricultural research and strengthening marketing network. Besides, India should organize developing countries to get WTO agreement on agriculture suitably amended to their benefit. Especially it should exert pressure for inclusion of food security clause allowing developing countries to adopt a suitable policy regime required to create and maintain food security. Shifting of a sizeable proportion of workforce to non-agricultural sectors, diversification of agriculture, rising per hectare yield to the global level, protecting dairy and poultry sectors from the onslaught of foreign competition are some of the challenges to be met for increasing the global competitiveness of India agriculture.

In order to meet the above challenges, the Government of India will have to take serious and bold steps at the policy level. One serious problem has been lack of preparedness for negotiations. Obviously, the process of preparedness requires a high level of professional expertise with analytical and practical wisdom. There has to be a close nexus between the negotiators of the Government on the one-hand and industry, business circles and academic and research bodies on the other.

One serious problem in increasing exports of agricultural products is that despite commitments to reduce subsidies, the countries in EU are continuing their agricultural subsidies programme in some form or another. To meet this challenge India will have to form a block of developing countries to safeguard their interests. It is hearting to not that at the recently concluded WTO ministerial conference at Cancun, India has emerged as a leader of the developing nations of the world. The Indian team was able to argue for the interests of 650 million

Indian farmers, the highly successful and growing software sector etc.

While all that India might have wanted was not fully achieved, some lessons have emerged for the agricultural sector. The increased market access of the rest of the world to our markets would become a reality to be dealt with by strong action on the ground of land reforms, irrigation, agricultural modernization, and better grain storage. The big opportunity is there for India to become a top agri-export country. All support on free movement, rapid rural road building, clean and reliable power and provision of other technical and infrastructure support to facilitate global trade will become mandatory and urgent.

REFERENCES

Bhalla, G.S. and Gurmail Singh (1996), "Impact of GATT on Punjab Agriculture, Ajanta Book International, Delhi.

Dasgupta, Biplab (2001), "WTO and India's Reform Agenda: One Step Forward and Two Step Backward" (ed), G.K. Chadha in "W.T.O. and the Indian Economy", Deep and Deep Publication Pvt. Ltd., New Delhi.

Datt, Rudra (2001), "Second Generation Economic Reforms in India", Deep and Deep Publication, New Delhi.

Government of India (2003), Economic Survey, 2002-03.

Government of India (2004), Economic Survey, 2003-04.

Gulati, Ashok (2000), "Indian Agriculture and the WTO: Preparing for the New Millenium", Indian Economic Association, 83rd Conference Volume, Jammu.

Kumar Nagesh (2003), Investment on WTO Agenda, Economic and Political Weekly, July 26.

Narasaiah, M. Lakshmi, World Trade Organization and Agriculture, Sonali Publications, New Delhi.

Planning Commission, Government of India (1999), Ninth Five Year Plan, 1997-2002, Vol. I, New Delhi.

Planning Commission (2003), Tenth Five Year Plan.

RBI, (2002-03), Annual Report.

Suman Ranjit Singh (2001), W.T.O. Regime: Some Challenges to India Agriculture (ed), G.K. Chadha in "W.T.O. and the Indian Economy", Deep and Deep Publication Pvt. Ltd., New Delhi.

The Indian Economic Journal, January-March, 2002-03.

WTO AND ITS IMPACT ON INDIAN AGRICULTURE

Alakh Deo Prasad and Vijay Mistry

INTRODUCTION

World Trade Organisation is a multilateral institution. It has come to replace General Agreement on Trade and Tariffs (GATT), which was in existence from 1948 to 1994. So, WTO is also called 'New GATT'. Along with the IMF and the World Bank, the GATT happened to be the third pillar of the 'Bretton Wood' System, which was used to govern world trade in goods only while the WTO has now acquired much wider and ever-increasing scope and coverage.

India is one of the founding members of WTO which came into existence on January 01, 1995 replacing GATT (General Agreement on Tariffs and Trade) and promising the herald of a new era in the rule based system of governing and promoting international trade concomitant with the needs of the ongoing process of globalisation. WTO provisions related to international trade are now similarly applicable to agriculture, which was brought within the fold of GATT in the Uruguay Round (1986–93) of Multilateral Trade Negotiations (MTNs). Application of WTO provisions on agriculture involves many contentious issues and is an area of serious concern for India, which is primarily an agrarian economy. Moreover the world despite growing interdependence and integration is highly heterogeneous with regard to levels of development. This heterogeneity is very noticeable when we compare the agriculture sector of developed countries and India. There are vast differences between developed countries and India with regard to the extent, economic condition and application of modern technology, skill and literacy levels of the farmers and farm size in the agriculture sector. The developed countries are highly competitive and efficient. Agriculture is much more mechanised there. Support infrastructure like storage, processing, finance, marketing, transport and R&D facilities are much more advanced and organised. In sharp contrast for millions of farmers in India who derive their livelihood from agriculture, it is still a way of life and not an occupation they have chosen for themselves. Indian farmers are mostly involved in subsistence farming with very little or no marketable surplus. On the other hand, there have been instances where in the USA farmers have been given subsidies worth millions of dollar to keep their farmland uncultivated (abundance of farm production led to dumping of foodstuff into the sea). In India, 70 per cent of the land holding are not of the economic size making application of modern technology difficult and unaffordable for the farmers.

The developed countries like USA, Japan and EU countries heavily subsidize their agriculture. With high qualify standards and aggressive marketing practices, these countries hold 72 per cent share of world trade in agricultural products and keep the developing countries virtually at the periphery of world market. International trade in agricultural products is not competitive. UNCTAD study (1983) cited by Gill and Brar (1996) estimates that half a dozen or fewer transnational corporations account for 60 per cent of internationally traded sugar, 70 per cent of rice and more than 85 per cent of wheat, cotton and maize. It is noteworthy that India is a miniscule player in the world market though in some staple commodities like rice great possibilities do exist through proper marketing and required tariff changes.

AGRICULTURE UNDER WTO

WTO provides free and market oriented trading system in agriculture. WTO is based on the principle of non-discrimination, free trade and promotion of fair competition among the member countries. Presently about 95 per cent of world trade is governed by the rules and regulation of WTO. The Quad countries (USA, EU, Canada and Japan) with their major share is 80 per cent of the global trade, dominate the decision-making of WTO. At present, 149 countries including India and China have accepted the membership of WTO. The main features of WTO under AoA are opening up to world market for agricultural products. This agreement provides for abolishing non-tariff barriers and restrictions, reduction in import duty, significant reduction in subsidies, price support and other measures of protection of domestic agriculture and rationalization of export subsidies and assistance.

Agreement on agriculture conditions provisions in mainly three broad areas of trade and agricultural policy is (1) market access (2) domestic support and (3) export subsidies. This can be studied under the following heads:

Market Access

Market access for agricultural products is to be governed by a tariffs only regime. The agreement states that there can be no restrictions on farm trade except through tariffs. This means that non-tariff barriers such as quantitative restrictions on imports (i.e. quota, import restrictions through permits, import licensing, etc.) as were in existence before the agreement came into force, were to be replaced by tariffs on imports to provide the same level of protection and then were to be followed by progressive reduction of tariff levels. However, India had not converted their quantitative restricting into tariffs, were allowed to have ceiling reductions commitments.

The provision of market access may be divided into two parts. The first part is related to 'minimum access' and the other part is related to 'current access'.

(a) **Minimum Access:** Minimum access requirement is implemented on the basis of the "Tariff Rate Quota" (TRQ) whereby a certain quota at below the normal tariff rate or at a nominal rate according to most favoured nation principle (MFN).

(b) **Current Access:** Current access may be defined as the amount of exports to a particular country under bilateral trade agreement at preferential tariff rates. We can say that the intention of such agreement is also to protect the current access (i.e. exports of existing exporters to other countries at preferential tariff rates). It has been clearly mentioned in the agreement that the two provisions are not cumulative, rather they exist side by side.

It is important to discuss that where tariff bindings are either too high or incomplete tariffication, current access provisions do not prevail, minimum access provision are sufficient for imports which is equal to 3 per cent of 1986-88 TE base level consumption and rising to 5 per cent till 2000 by the developed countries and one per cent of 1986-88 TE base level consumption, rising to 2 per cent in 1999 and 4 per cent in the year 2005 by the developing nations. It is also important to note that the provision of market access do not apply when the commodity in question is a traditional staple in diet of any developing country. For instance, wheat and rice are staple foods in India and so, these imports can be restricted.

Domestic Support

Domestic support may be considered as the economic help to the member countries. But the domestic support has now become a threat to the developing countries. This support is intended to bring competitiveness and to cherish the weak in domestic market. But the developed countries are providing heavy subsidies to the agriculture in the name of domestic support under different boxes. The extent of subsidies is calculated through aggregate measure of support (AMS) at 13.3 per cent of the proceed value including all supports to years.

(i) Aggregate Measure of Support (AMS): Agreement on agriculture has clearly defined aggregate measure of support (AMS) as consisting of all such subsidies which have a distortion affect on trade or production. Further, the agreement on agriculture has classified all types of subsidies provided by different countries of the world into three separate boxes and the base period for calculating total AMS could either be taken as the year 1986 only or the same as in other case i.e. 1986-1988.

In short, AMS is the annual level of support in monetary terms extended to agriculture sector. It is the non-exempted support of following two types:

(a) Product Specific Support/Subsidies (SS): It is the market price support/subsidies to be provided to the producer of specific crop. This kind of subsidy cover the support to at least 22 products such as rice, wheat maize, cotton, soya, etc.

(b) Non-Products Specific Support (NPS): This support includes sum total of subsidies on inputs such as power, irrigation, fertilizer, pesticides, credit and other inputs. The AMS to Indian agriculture is still below 10 per cent in terms of WTO stipulations the product-specific support provided to Indian agriculture under AMS during reference period (i.e. 1986-88) T.E. on an average was 21.6 per cent of agricultural GDP. Again it reduced to 38.6 per cent during 1995-96, which now might have increased due to recent face in the international agricultural prices in, rises in MSPS for wheat and rice while the product specific support accounted to 4.04 per cent of agricultural GDP during 1986-88. It increased to 7.52 per cent during 1995-96 and again declined to 5.27 per cent during 1997-98. We can understand the status of AMS in some countries with the help of Table 1.

Table 1
Status of AMS in Some Countries (per cent)

Countries	*1986*	*1994*	*1997*
New Zealand	15	18	3
Australia	10	10	9
USA	30	21	160
Canada	42	31	20
E.U.	48	48	42
Japan	73	74	69
India	(-) 34	(-) 40	(-) 28

Source: IEA, Conference Volume, 2001, p. 103.

The AMS is calculated by subtracting the domestic price from the international price and multiplied by quantities of production. The AMS in India was (-) 59 per cent in 1991, (i) 52 per cent in 1992 and (-) 52 per cent upto 1998. The table also shows the clear picture of AMS in India as well as other countries. It is negatively lower in India while in other countries AMS remained positively higher during the same period as shown in Table 1.

(ii) Amber Box Subsidies/Support: Amber box subsidies include policies that provide support and considered to have a substantial impact on production of agricultural commodities and flow of trade. Under Amber box subsidies, such domestic support is included which is meant to encourage farmers to produce more. Such subsidies are considered trade distorting as they obstruct the free working of market mechanism. A market price support mechanism, which sets no limit on production, would fall into this box.

(iii) Green Box Subsidies: It constitutes those measures that provide domestic support, which have minimal impact on trade and production. These domestic supports are therefore, exempted from the estimation of aggregate measures of support (AMS). Hence, subsidies/support under green box is provided for general services like research programme, pest and disease control measures, training facilities, advisory services, marketing and promotional services, infrastructure service, food security, buffer stock operations, domestic food aid relief from natural disasters resource retirement programme and environmental protection programmes. In fact, green box subsidies include direct income support for European, US and Japanese farmers, which is formally decoupled from production levels and prices. It also includes subsidies granted in the name of environment protection and preservation, and for agricultural research and development. In reality, it is a kind to heavy support to the agriculture of developed countries.

(iv) Blue Box Subsidies/Supports: This support is exempted from reduction commitment under WTO and is related mainly to the developed countries. It is a product-limiting subsidy and covers the fixed costs of the farmers indirectly. Agreement on agriculture has simply mentioned that all such policies, which provide domestic support/subsidies, that fall in between the amber box and green box measures are mainly the direct payments made to farmers for production restricting programme.

(v) Special and Differential (S&D) Treatment Box Support: Developing countries are related to this kind of support and this support is exempted from reduction commitment under WTO. This support includes the following:

(a) Agricultural input services to low income or resource poor farmers.

(b) Investment subsidy to agricultural sector on farm development work e.g. channels, field, land leveling, shallow wells, etc.

Table 2
Import Duties on Agricultural Products in India

Country	*T.E. 1986-88 (WTO's Base Period)*			*1999*		
	Per Farmer	*Per Hectare*	*Total Subsidies (UIS $ in mn)*	*Per Farmer*	*Per Hectare*	*Total Subsidies (US $ in mn)*
Canada	12000	75	5645	9000	52	3093
EC	11000	707	95214	17000	831	114450
Japan	15000	10048	53637	26000	11792	58885
USA	17000	98	41890	21000	129	54009
OECD	11000	187	246226	11000	218	282780
India	11	8	1058	66	53	7247

T.E. = Triennium Ending Average per annum
Source: Government of India, Agricultural Statistics At A Glance, 2002, Ministry of Agriculture.

It is also important to mention here that the developed countries have their commitments in full spirit for reducing domestic support. Rather subsidies have been increased to the agriculture sector during the post WTO period. We can understand the status of agricultural subsidies to be provided by the developed countries in selected OECD countries.

The table clearly depicts that the annual subsidies for agriculture in OECD Countries have increased from US $ 246.2 billion during 1986-88 (WTO's base period) to US $ 282.78 billion in 1999 while the agricultural subsidies for India were only US$ 1.6 billion and 7.25 billion during the said respective period. It is also necessary to note here that per farmer subsidy provided in USA increased very fast from US $ 17000 in 1986-88 to US $ 21000 in 1999 while in India, it increased from US $ 11 to US $ 66 only during this respective period.

In India, agricultural subsidies stand at about 3 to 6 per cent of the total output as compared to 72 per cent of Japan, 27 per cent of USA and 37 per cent of EU. In fact, OECD countries are providing heavy subsidies to agriculture sector through green and blue boxes. During the period of 1995, green box support accounted for 33.11 per cent of agricultural GDP in USA as compared to only 2.34 per cent of India.

Export Subsidies

In India, agricultural goods received no export subsidies other than specified in a member's lists of commitments. On the other hand the developed countries are providing as high as 90 to 100 per cent export subsidies. Some indirect incentives are provided for agricultural item for exports. Developed countries have agreed to cut the value of export subsidies by 36 per cent over a period of six years from 1995-2000 and the developing countries have to cut the same by 24 per cent over a period of ten years. The developed countries have to reduce 21 per cent in quantities of subsidised exports and developing countries have to reduce 14 per cent of the same during the same period as stated above. Developed countries are allowed to reduce the cost of marketing and transporting exports under certain conditions.

The developed countries such as UK, France, Germany, etc. provide an average export subsidies of 265 per cent, Brazil 60 per cent, Thailand 40 per cent and even Pakistan 30 per cent. This has created a panic in the agricultural economy of India. Besides, imposition of import duties is neglected; QRs have been withdrawn; no direct export subsidy is given to the exporters of agricultural commodities. On this background, India has to oppose such hike in export subsidies in the forthcoming Agricultural Round.

FUTURE VISION

With rapid changing global economic environment, it is now necessary to shift the focus from self-sufficiency to export orientation. In order to accomplish the vision and achieve the targets set for Indian agriculture by the year 2025, a carefully designed strategy of increasing total factor productivity growth in agriculture and simultaneously raising the growth of factor supplies to agriculture should be followed.

- High rate of technological progress in agriculture;
- High rates of public and private investment in agriculture;
- Significant growth in total cropped area, which can be achieved by increasing the area under irrigation; and

- Increasing the effective applications of high yielding variety of seeds in dry-land farming.

The policy initiative required for this purpose should focus on the utilisation of the created irrigation capacity by putting in place a comprehensive irrigation management system. Further, there is an urgent need to involve the corporate sector formally in the cultivation of high value, capital intensive and modern technology based crops with potential for exports. Corporatisation of farming will not only facilitate technological upgradation but would also ensure rapid growth of private investment in Indian agriculture. Corporatisation of the farm sector would also result in a significant quality upgradation and growth of value added products and in the process, it would significantly enhance the export orientation of Indian agricultural sector.

CONCLUSION

With the advent of WTO regime, we need to prepare our agriculture and allied activities for the global competition with cost effective production and efficient management. It is obvious that benefits to developing countries like India, in terms of increasing their exports will occur only after the elimination of export subsidies and substantial adoption in domestic support in the developed countries has been effected. The opening up of agricultural trade should be looked at as a major opportunity for raising the overall economic growth rate by exploiting india's competitive as well as comparative advantage in agriculture for improving the efficiency of resource use in agriculture and for technologically upgrading the rural sector, we need to devise a multi pronged strategy to face the emerging challenges under the WTO regime and make Indian agriculture a sustainable and internationally competitive.

REFERENCES

Awasthi, Arvind and Roli Misra (2001), "Agreement on Agriculture: A Need for Review of Provisions and India's Food Policy", Indian Economic Association, Conference Volume.

Dholakia, Bakul H. (2002), "Source of India's Accelerated Growth and the Vision of Indian Economy in 2020", Indian Economic Journal, Vol. 49, April-Jun, 2001-02.

Rao, C.H. Hanumanta (1994), "Agriculture Growth, Rural Poverty and Environmental Degradation in India", Oxford University, New Delhi.

Madaan, D.K. (2003), "WTO and Indian Agricultural Development: A Case Study of Punjab", *Indian Economic Journal*, Jan-March, 2002-03.

Naik, S.D. (2003), "WTO and Agriculture: Will It Be Advantage to India", The Hindu Business Line, New Delhi, July 22.

OECD (2004), "Agricultural Policies in OECD Country: Monitoring and Evaluation".

Balakrishnan Vijaylakshmi (2003), "Pyrrhic Victory at Cancun", The Hindu Business Line, New Delhi, September 27.

International Institute of Food Policy Research, quoted by Balakrishnan Vijaylakshmi, *ibid.*

A COMPARATIVE STUDY ON AGRICULTURAL REFORMS AND WTO IN INDIA AND CHINA

Deepak Bishoyi and Santosh Kumar Sahu

India and China account for 40 per cent of world's population and they are almost one half of the worlds poor that survive on less than one dollar a day. The two nations face similar challenges on how to further reform their economies for future growth and make the resulting gains more equitable both countries implemented a series of economic reforms in the past few decades. China initiated this process at the end of 1970s, while India began in the early 1990s. These reforms led to rapid economic growth rates of 8 to 9 per cent per annum in China, and 5 to 6 per cent per annum in India. Both India and China, as participants in the Uruguay Round, have had the Agreement on Agriculture (URAA) before them as they continued to reform their agricultural and trade policies over recent years. China did not join the WTO until December 2001, but it has nonetheless been undertaking reforms and has entered into substantial commitments to further reform its farm sector by the end of 2004, when all other countries UR commitments are due to be fully implemented. The paper reviews the progress expected to be made over the ten years since 1995 in two populous developing countries India and China, some comparative study on reforms and policy changes affecting agriculture in India and China and finally, analysis of WTO with their agricultural trade. If there is information flow between the India and China on comparative advantages and transparency in marketing, trade volumes can go up several folds, benefiting millions of poor in these two countries.

China's high economic growth since 1978 has been a hot topic of discussion in economic development and economic reform literature for the last few years. Her 10 per cent annual average growth rate plus her largest population has made China the largest and the most attractive market in the world for business and investment for several years. India, the second largest country in terms of population, initiated her reforms in 1991 and has achieved some satisfactory results so far. If India can replicate China in terms of economic growth and development, not only will Indians benefit from the rise in living standards, but also, like China, India will become a sought after market that will provide numerous business and investment opportunities. The boom will mostly have a positive effect on other countries.

The Chinese and Indian economies put together make up two-fifths of the human race. These continental size nations have a lot in common and hence a comparative study of their reform strategies can be helpful for both to learn from each other experiences. While China has been the focus of world attention for some time now, India has only recently begun to be noticed. Of course, this is largely because China has had a thirteen-year ahead start over India in consolidating economic gains after launching her program of economic reforms in 1978 (Bajpai, 2002).

Table 1
GDP Growth

	1950-1980	*1980-1990*	*1990-2000*
CHINA	4.40	10.1	10.3
INDIA	3.75	5.8	6.0

Source: World Bank (2002).

However, although both economics experienced acceleration in growth during 1980-2000 compared to the previous three decades (Table 1), given China's slower rate of growth of population, China's average growth rate of per capita income, at nearly 9 per cent per year, far exceeded India's 4 per cent per year, so that China's per capita income was nearly 70 per cent higher than India's by 2000.

China and India pursued similar state-directed and state-controlled industrialization strategies with emphasis on heavy industry until their recent reforms. However in China, state control was direct and total: agriculture was collectivized, almost all industries were state-owned and most services were supplied by the state. India had a mixed economy with agriculture, all of small scale and a significant part of large scale industries being in the private sector. Although, China grew faster than India before reforms, most of the difference is attributed to China's greater savings and investment rates.

The sequencing of reforms was also somewhat different in the two countries. China reformed its agriculture first by abolishing collectives, introducing the household responsibility system and reducing mandatory deliveries of output to the state by farmers and thereby enabling farmers to produce for the market. India's agriculture, while always in the private sector, was insulated from world markets, riddled with government interventions, the domestic market for agricultural inputs and outputs, whose net effect was to disprotect agriculture. Indian reform process is still to be extended to agriculture. Clearly, the fact that China reformed agriculture first and achieved spectacular results for several years not only provided credibility to its reform process, but also increased incomes of the poorer segments of the Chinese economy. In India, agriculture in particular, and the rural economy in general, are yet to be reformed systematically (Srinivasan, 2003).

China and India are the world's biggest food producers after the USA and neither country will want to rely too much on world markets to feed their large populations. China is almost self-sufficient in grain supply, and may even become a net exporter if population growth slows. Efficiency of food use rather than access to supplies is likely to become the main factor shaping Chinese markets, while infrastructure will have to be improved to ensure that storage and distribution facilities can cope with demand. Analysis for India is similar to those for China. Demand for meat and dairy products will grow as the economy expands, with a spectacular increase in demand for feed grain. The so called Green Revolution has now run its course, so improvements will come from better use of inputs and techniques and products derived from biotechnology. The government is aware of the advantages of "GMO" crops given the need to conserve land and water resources, but there is significant political opposition against foreign multinationals to control Indian agriculture. However, the Indian agro-food system is extremely inefficient, e.g. food production is only two-thirds of that of China, although India has more arable land. Improved farming techniques will help but the entire system needs to be modernized. Given the absence of any coherent production and distribution infrastructure, the best hope may be large, vertically integrated firms who can control their own supply, transport and storage and retailing. Potential market leaders may be reluctant to abandon their niche markets and invest the sums required but if economic growth continues, lifestyle and income changes could make this option more attractive.

CHINA

The unilateral decision in December 1978 to open up the Chinese economy was a major stimulus to economic growth: the pre-reform rate of per capita GDP growth of 3.1 per cent per year more than doubled and has remained above 7 per cent for the past two decades (final row of Table 2). Rapid economic growth is normally accompanied by a relative decline in the farm sector, but in China that was initially tempered by the introduction of the farm household responsibility system (which led to the replacement of collective farms with individually managed holdings), and by the raising of prices received by farmers.

Agriculture grew nearly as rapidly as industry from 1979 to 1984. However, the one-off efficiency effects of moving to the household responsibility system and raising relative prices for farm products were mostly reaped by the mid-1980s, after which agriculture grew at only one third the pace of industry and less than half that of the service sector as industrialization boomed on the eastern seaboard (Table 2).

Employment, output and exports of rural township and village enterprises, meanwhile, boomed (Table 3). Despite that migration of farm workers to rural industrial and service activities (not to mention the temporary migration to urban jobs such as in construction), the average farm size and the share of farm household income from farming have fallen steadily since the late 1970s.

Table 2
Growth Rates of China's Economy (1970 to 2000)

	Pre-Reform 1970-78	*1979-84*	*1985 - 95*	*1996-00*
Gross domestic product	4.9	8.5	9.7	8.2
Agriculture	2.7	7.1	4.0	3.4
Industry	6.8	8.2	12.8	9.6
Service	Na	11.6	9.7	8.2
Food production volume				
Grain	2.8	4.7	1.7	0.03
Oilseed crops	2.1	14.9	4.4	5.6
Fruit	6.6	7.2	12.7	8.6
Red meat	4.4	9.1	8.8	6.5
Fish	5.0	7.9	13.7	10.2
Value of output of non-farm rural enterprises	Na	12.3	24.1	14.0
Population	1.80	1.40	1.37	0.90
Per capita GDP	3.1	7.1	8.3	7.1

Note: Figures for GDP in 1970-78 are the growth rate of national income in real terms. Growth rates are computed using the regression method. Growth rates of individual and group of commodities are based on volume of production data, while sectoral rates refer to value added in real terms.

Source: SSB Statistical Yearbook of China, various issues; MOA, Agricultural Yearbook of China, Various issues.

Table 3 shows the initial slowdown in the decline in agriculture's shares of GDP and employment in the 1980s, but then its subsequent acceleration from the latter 1980s. That share was greater than 30 per cent pre-1980s but by 2000 was down to 16 per cent. Similarly, the agriculture's contribution to employment has fallen from more than 70 per cent pre-1980s to less than 50 per cent now. And its share of exports also has fallen, from more than 30 per cent pre-1980s (greater than twice the average of other countries) to just 6 per cent in 2001 (or less than two-thirds that of the rest of the world).

Income growth has boosted the demand for foods that are high in protein and nutrients relative to those high in carbohydrates, which has stimulated major structural changes within agriculture as farmers responded to changes in domestic demand. For example, livestock and fish increased their share of agricultural output from less than one-fifth in the late 1970s to two-fifth by the late 1990s (Table 3), while within the crop sub-sector, fruit and vegetable production grew two to three times as fast as grain output (Table 2). The prices and marketing of grain and oilseed products have continued to be highly regulated, whereas markets for horticultural, livestock and fish products have been greatly liberalized. This has accentuated the growth in output of the latter group relative to grain and oilseed output since the mid-1980s (Table 2).

Table 3
Changing Structure of China's Economy
(1970 to 2000)

	1970	*1980*	*1985*	*1990*	*1995*	*2000*
Share of GDP						
Agriculture	40	30	28	27	20	16
Industry	46	49	43	42	49	51
Services	13	21	29	31	31	33
Share of Employment						
Agriculture	81	69	62	60	52	50
Industry	10	18	21	21	23	23
Services	9	13	17	19	25	27
Share of Agriculture Output						
Crops	82	76	69	65	58	56
Livestock	14	18	22	26	30	30
Fish	2	2	3	5	8	10
Forestry	2	4	5	4	3	4
Share of Population that is rural 83	81	76	72	71	64	

Source: State Statistical Bureau, China Statistical Yearbook, various issues; and China Rural Statistical Yearbook, various issues.

POLICY CHANGES AFFECTING AGRICULTURE

As in most developing countries, agriculture in China was squeezed at early stages of Industrialization with gross fiscal contributions to the sector being more than outweighed by implicit taxation in the form of depressed prices for farm products, neglect of public infrastructure in rural relative to urban areas and capital outflows via the financial system (Huang and Ma 1998). Then price and other market reforms associated with China's policy shift from a socialist to a market-oriented economy began to be introduced, starting with non-strategic commodities such as vegetables, fruit, fish, livestock and oil and sugar crops. The aims of the early reforms were to raise farm level prices and gradually deregulate the market. As the right to private trading was extended to include surplus output of all categories of agricultural products after contractual obligations to the state were fulfilled, the foundations of the state marketing system began to be undermined (Rozelle et al. 1997). Despite periodic stop-go cycles in the reform process, the proportion of retail commodities sold at market prices has kept rising. According to Lardy (2001), the share for agriculture was just 6 per cent in 1978 but had risen to 40 per cent by 1985, 79 per cent by 1995 and 83 per cent by 1999.

What have these policies meant for nominal rates of agricultural protection in China (the percentage by which domestic prices exceed prices at the country's border)? Table 4 shows new estimates based on quota and negotiated procurement prices and on wholesale market prices for key agricultural commodities for some recent years. It suggests rice, meat, fish and fruit and vegetables have been priced at less than border prices while other grains, oil seeds, sugar, cotton and milk have been priced at one-fifth to two-fifths above border prices. Maize and cotton also enjoyed export subsidies in 2001 (amounting to one-third and one-tenth of f.o.b. prices, respectively).

Table 4 also shows what China has committed to in its WTO Protocol of Accession: tariff rate quota will apply to grains, sugar and cotton for which out-of-quota tariffs are quite high but otherwise, after the phase-in period, the tariffs range between just 1 and 15 per cent–representing substantial liberalizations over 2001 level. As well, producers of major crops may continue to be affected by commodity-specific policies of government procurement of a portion of the crop at lower than market prices as in the past–(Sicular 1988) or at higher than market prices as in 1998–(Huang 1998 and Lu 1999). They are likely to continue to be subjected also to charges/levies by local governments too–charges that became more regressive over the 1990s as local governments sought to meet central government demands in the face of inadequate transfers from Beijing. According to Lin et al. (2002), they have amounted to as much as one-quarter of the net income of poorer farmers in the hinterland.

Table 4
Nominal Rates of Protection (Tariff Equivalent), Agricultural Products, China (1978 to 2000)

(per cent)

	1995	*1997*	*2001*	*2007 in-quota tariff*	*2007 out-of-quota tariff*	*Assumed NRP in 2007*
Rice	-5	-5	-3	1	65	-3
Wheat	25	17	12	1	65	12
Coarse grains	20	28	20	1	65	32
Vegetables and fruits	-10	-8	-4	11	11	-4
Oilseeds	30	28	32	3	3	3
Sugar	44	42	40	15	50	20
Cotton	20	17	17	1	40	20
Meats	-20	-19	-15	12	12	-15
Milk	30	30	30	11	11	11

Source: Based on research subsequently reported in summary form in Huang and Rozelle (2002).

What will those reforms mean for agricultural trade? Many analysts have been expecting China to become even more dependent on agricultural imports in the course of the economy's rapid industrialization over the past two-plus decades. Some extremists (e.g., Brown 1995) have even suggested that China could seriously deprive other developing countries of food. Yet net food import growth has not yet happened, at least not in a sustained way and China has continued to be a net exporter of meat, fish, fruit and vegetables. Indeed on occasions in the latter 1990s, China also was a net exporter of grain and cotton. How much of that is due to government policies that constrained domestic demand including occasional export subsidies is a moot point.

In its WTO Protocol of Accession, China has agreed to have no agricultural export subsidies and to limit its domestic support to farmers to 8.5 per cent of the value of production (compared with 10 per cent for other developing countries). The import market access commitments China has made to WTO members look substantial on paper. Tariff rate quotas will be retained only on wheat, rice, maize, edible oils, sugar, cotton and wool, domestic production of which in aggregate comprises only about one-sixth of China's agricultural GDP. The quota volumes are to grow over the next three years at annual rates ranging from 5 to 19 per cent. A further commitment by China is that state trading monopolies will disappear (except for tobacco): even though some state trading enterprises will continue to operate, there will be competition from private firms in the importing and exporting of farm products, at least within the tariff-rate-quotas.

Farmers and the rural sector more broadly will also be affected by China's commitment to provide improved and WTO-bound market access for industrial products. Mineral and manufacturing tariffs will be bound and generally reduced on a broad basis, with many tariffs falling to 10 per cent or less. Tariffs will be cut on accession and further cuts will be phased in by 2005 (with just a few exceptions). Furthermore, for industrial products, China will reduce significantly its non-tariff measures and eliminate all quotas, tendering and import licensing on non-farm merchandise not later than by 2005. Quotas on Chinese imports of automobiles and parts will grow by 15 per cent annually from a level of around US$ 6 billion in 2000 and these quotas will be eliminated by 2005. For textiles and clothing, however, the current 'voluntary' export restraints will not be completely phased out until the end of 2008. Substantial commitments to open up services markets in China have also been made.

Over the 1990s, the average scheduled tariff rates for manufacturing initially exceeded but declined for agriculture and by 2005, the manufacturing average will be well below for agriculture (a simple average of 7 per cent versus 17 per cent for agriculture). That does not give a true indication of the extent of change in protection that is taking place, though many manufactures have been entering China at reduced or zero tariffs via duty drawbacks in 1990s to encourage foreign investment in processing of imported intermediate goods for subsequent export. Some agricultural products also have entered at less than the scheduled rate including through smuggling.

INDIA

How do China's recent and prospective developments compare with India? India too began to reform its economy in the 1980s, at least tentatively but the growth it generated was largely a result of building up external debt that was unsustainable. A balance of payments crisis in 1991 was followed by a more concerted effort at opening up of the economy and that caused the growth of GDP to accelerate to 6.7 per cent per year between 1992-93 and 1996-97. After then implementation of reforms slowed down and the binding constraints became inflexible labor markets and inadequate infrastructure. Hence, GDP growth slowed to 5.4 per cent over the subsequent five years with a halving in both the agricultural and industrial growth rates (Table 5).

Table 5
GDP Growth Rates in India (1970-71 to 2001-02)

(Per cent p.a.)

	TOTAL	*Agriculture*	*Industry*	*Services*
1970-71 to 1980-81	3.2	2.0	4.0	7.2
1981-82 to 1990-91	5.7	3.8	7.0	6.7
1992-93 to 1996-97	6.37	4.6	8.0	7.6
1997-98 to 2001-02	5.4	2.3	4.5	7.8

Source: Ahluwalia (2002).

While much lower than China's, India's GDP growth rate has been much higher than in the past and well above that for other low-income countries including on per capita basis. Agricultural GDP growth in India in the 1990s was nearly as fast as in China (3.4 per cent compared with 4.3 per cent p.a.) and China remains nearly as agrarian as India in terms of the rural sector's share of population and agriculture's share of employment, even though China is now classified as a lower middle-income country. However, India has not had the dramatic decline in the share of GDP from agriculture that China has seen in the 1990s (Table 6). This is showing up in the trade statistics: the index of 'revealed' comparative advantage in agricultural products has hardly changed for India since 1990, whereas it has halved for China; and agricultural net exports are still 30 per cent of agricultural exports plus imports for India but index of trade specialization has gone from 0.12 per cent to 0.09 per cent for China (bottom of Table 7). That is, China is now a net importer of farm products in aggregate (though still a net exporter of food), while India remains a net agricultural exporter by a considerable margin.

Table 6
Basic Economic Indicators, India and China

	India	*China*
GDP,1999 (USS billion)	447	989
Population, 1999 (million)	998	1,254
GDP per capita,1999(US $)	450	790
GDP growth, real (% p.a), 1980-901990-99	5.86.0	10.110.7
GDP per capita growth, real (% p.a), 1980-901990-99	3.74.5	8.79.5
Agricultural GDP growth, real (% p.a), 1980-901990-99	3.13.4	5.94.3
GDP in agric, as % of total, 19901999	3128	2718
Employment in agric, as % of total, 19701999	70na	6947
Rural population as % of total, 19701999	8072	8368
Life expectancy, 1999 (years)	63	70
Adult literacy, 1999(%)	56	83
Land per capita, total,1999(ha)	0.230	0.75
Land per capita, arable,1999(ha)	0.17	0.10

Source: World Bank (2001).

That slower pace of industrialization in India is only partly due to India having considerably more arable land per capita than China (0.17 compared with 0.10 hectare). Also contributing has been a slower pace of deregulation and especially of opening the economy to foreign trade and investment. India's export growth has been only 60 per cent as fast as China's since 1990, and its share of GDP that is exported is barely half that of China's now. India also is still attracting only a small fraction (3 per cent) of its investment from foreign sources, in contrast to China's 13 per cent. And as recently as 1999, trade duties comprised as much as 28 per cent of total tax revenue in India, compared with just 7 per cent in China (Table 7).

POLICY CHANGES AFFECTING AGRICULTURE

The past decade of policy reforms in India have altered the incentives of farmers and affected agriculture more than other sectors of the economy. For example, the switch over from a

Table 7
Basic Trade Indicators, India and China

	India	*China*
Exports of Goods & Services, 1999 (US$ billion)	54	219
Import of Goods & Services,1999 (US$ billion)	67	197
Growth of Merchandise Exports, 1990-2001 (% p.a)	450	790
Exports /GDP,%, 19801999	12	822
Import/GDP, 1999(%)	15	19
Inward Foreign Investment Stock, 1998(% of GDP)	3	28
Foreign Direct Investment Flow, 1998 (% of Gross Capital Formation)	3	13
Trade Duties as % of Total Tax Revenue, 1999	28	7
Agriculture's Share of Merchandise Exports, %, 19902001	2015	166
Tactile/Clothing sare of Merch.Export, %, 19902001	2628	2720
Revealed Comparative Advantage in Agriculture, 19902001	1.601.66	1.320.68
Agricultural Net Export Index, 19902001	0.340.31	0.12-0.09

Source: World Bank (2001), UNCTAD (2001) and WTO (2002).

fixed to a flexible exchange rate regime in 1993 enabled the abolition of restrictive import licensing on capital and intermediate goods. The government was reluctant to remove quantitative restrictions on imports of final consumer goods because those measures protected many small producers but they too were abolished in 2001 following a WTO dispute settlement case brought by the United States. The long list of industries also reserved solely for production by the public sector has been reduced to just three. Even the list of items (some 800) reserved for production by the small-scale sector has begun to shrink in 2001 and 2002, 64 of them were removed from the list including such crucial ones as garments, shoes, toys and motor vehicle parts. In addition, tariffs on imports have been coming down. The weighted average import duty declined from 72 per cent in 1991-92 to 25 per cent by 1996-97. The average increased in the latter 1990s to 36 per cent but in February 2002 the government signaled further cuts and so it declined to 29 per cent in 2002-03 and potentially 15 per cent by 2004-05.

That is still high by the standards of many other developing countries including China whose commitment is to be down to 9 per cent by 2005. Nonetheless, it reflects a significant reduction in protection provided to the industrial sector, the flipside of which is a reduction in the disincentive to farming.

According to Ahluwalia (2002), the domestic index of agricultural prices relative to those of manufactures increased by almost 30 per cent in the past ten years. To what extent have agricultural policy reforms themselves contributed to that increase? Ostensibly for the sake of food security, exports of farm products from India had been restricted by numerous controls such as ban, licenses, quotas, marketing controls and minimum export prices. The reform of those export measures began with the opening up of rice exports in 1994 but the process of reform is far from completion. For example, export licenses are generally still required for such products as cattle, milk, cereals, edible oils and pulses and yet export subsidies also have been provided from time to time. For example, the fall in cereal prices in 1999 coincided with increases in support prices for wheat and rice that led to rapid growth in India's food grain stocks. A decision was taken in November 2000 to subsidize wheat exports and the following year to do the same for rice. As a result, grain exports rose to 2 MMT in 2000-01 to 6 MMT in 2001-02 and even more in the current year. (The government justified them under Article 9.4 of the URAA).

On the import side, the removal of quantitative restrictions led to little initial growth in imports because international food prices were at historical hights in the mid-1990s. However, as international food prices fell from 1999, imports began to rise for wheat, maize, pulses, edible oils and milk. The government responded by reversing earlier tariff cuts, as it was able to give its very high ceiling bindings. For example, the government lowered the import duties on edible oils from 65 per cent in 1994 to 15 per cent by end-1999. Then when the international price fell in the late 1990s, imports surged to 4 or 5 MMT in each of 1999, 2000 and 2001, causing India's self-sufficiency to plummet from 97 per cent in 1993 to 55 per cent by 2001. In response, the Government raised the tariff to 25 per cent and then 75 per cent before lowering it in October 2001 to 65 per cent (Gulati and Mullen 2003).

In the case of rice, the lifting of the export ban in 1994 caused India's rice exports to soar from less than 1 MMT to around 5 MMT but when international prices fell in the late 1999s exports more than halved and some rice was imported. Wheat exports were allowed in 1995 but as domestic prices rose, the government banned their export again in 1996. More than that, it allowed wheat to be imported duty free. The fall in international prices caused imports to jump, despite the bumper domestic crop, thereby contributing to the surge in stocks that had to be disposed of with an export subsidy.

What role did the Uruguay Round Agreement on Agriculture (URAA) commitments made by India have on this reform process? It probably had very little overall liberalizing effect, as those commitments involved ceiling bindings of 100 per cent for primary commodities, 150 per cent for processed products and 300 per cent for edible oils or an average bound rate of 115 per cent. This is well above applied rates, which in April 2002 averaged 35 per cent, according to Gulati and Mullen (2003). So while the URAA probably encouraged India to tariff its agricultural QRs, it brought no effective discipline to the level of tariffs chosen by the government. The high bindings allowed, for example, the above-mentioned reversal of the 1990s' tariff cuts in more-recent years.

Bearing all this in mind and the fact that farmers still enjoy subsidies for fertilizer and under pricing of water and electricity, Gulati and Mullen (2003) conclude that Indian agriculture may have had on average a small positive producer subsidy equivalent during the past three years but prior to that, the PSE was negative. That current direct assistance to agriculture is almost certainly more than offset by the indirect taxation of farmers caused by manufacturing protection, however, much less now than in earlier decades, when overvalued exchange rates also discouraged farming.

In short, the net effect on agricultural output and exports of the decrease in disincentives to farmers since the 1980s clearly has been positive. Production grew rapidly, particularly in the early years of the reform (Table 5), and India's share of world agricultural exports rose from 0.8 per cent to 1.2 per cent over the 1990s. Table 7 shows that the importance of farm products in India's exports has fallen but by much less than for China. Indeed, the share has fallen in agriculture's share in global exports, such that India's index of revealed comparative advantage in farm products rose slightly over the period from 1990 to 2001–whereas for China that index halved over those years, from 1.32 per cent to 0.68 per cent (bottom of Table 7). Further, reforms to 2005 are scheduled for India but they are not being driven by India's commitments to WTO. Rather, they continue to be in response to domestic pressures for unilateral market liberalization domestically and at the country's border –and will continue to be constrained by traditional protectionist forces. It will take more than a two-third reduction in India's ceiling bindings on agricultural tariffs before WTO would restrain the Indian government's capacity to intervene at the border in response to gyrations in international and/or domestic food markets. Even then, SPS measures rather than tariffs may kick in as the binding constraint on food import growth (Anderson, 2003).

Finally, there were great expectations at signing the various agreements in 1995 under the auspices of WTO but India has much to learn from China in the field of economic and social policy. In a liberalized trading environment for agriculture, tariff and non-tariff barriers would come down and fair trading opportunities would open up for all countries including India. Based on this assumption of substantial reductions in tariff and non-tariff barriers, some studies predicted enormous gains to developing countries including India. These macro models assumed perfectly comparative markets for agricultural commodities. Unfortunately even after seven years of signing the WTO agreement, an imperfectly comparative export market persists.

Thus, in conclusion, globalization of the economy including agriculture, offers an opportunity to correct for the "anti-agriculture" bias in Indian trade policy since 1950s. With this, the hidden "impact taxation" on agriculture would go down, and the agriculture sector would get on opportunity to respond favourably to these signals. Agriculture can move on to a higher growth trajectory if supply side bottlenecks are freed and a protective cover is accorded to the poor, at least for some time. If this happens, agriculture can propel growth in other sectors too on sustainable basis while promoting intersectoral and interpersonal equity.

REFERENCES

Ahluwalia, M.S. (2002), "Economic Reform in India Since 1991: Has Gradualism Worked?" *Journal of Economic Perspectives* 16(3): 67-88, Summer.

Anderson, K. (2003a), "Agriculture and Agricultural Incentive in China and India, Post Uruguay Round"www.ecostat.uncial.it/2003 agtradeconf/invited%20papers/Anderson.pdf.

Bajpai, N. (2002), "Reform Strategies of China and India: Suggestions for Future Actions" www.cid.harvard.edu/hied/564.pdf

Brown, L.R. (1995), *Who Will Feed China? Wake-up Call for a Small Planet,* New York: W.W.Norton.

Fan, S., P. Hazell and S. Thorat (2000), "Government Spending, Growth and Poverty in Rural India", *American Journal of Agricultural Economics* 82(4): 1038-51, November.

Gulati, A. and K. Mullen (2003), "Responding to Policy Reform: Indian Agriculture During the1990s and After", Paper for the 4th Annual Conference on Indian Economic Policy Reform, Stanford University, 5-7 June.

Hazell, P. and L. Haddad (2001), "Agricultural Research and Poverty Reduction", Food, Agriculture, and the Environment Discussion Paper 34, IFPRI, Washington, D.C., August.

Huang, J. (1998), "Evaluation of Current Three-Grain-Policy", CCAP's Working Paper WP-00-C01, Center for Chinese Agricultural Policy, Chinese Academy of Agricultural Sciences, Beijing.

Huang, J. (2001), "Agricultural Policy and Food Security in China", mimeo, Center for Chinese Agricultural Policy, Chinese Academy of Sciences, Beijing.

Huang, J. and H. Ma (1998.), "The 20-Year Reform and the Role of Agriculture in China: Capital Flow from Rural to Urban and from Agriculture to Industry," *Reform* 5: 56-63.

Huang, J. and S. Rozelle (2002), "The Nature of Distortions to Agricultural Incentives in China and Implications of WTO Accession", revision (2 April) following its presentation at the second project meeting on WTO Accession and Poverty Reduction in China, World Bank Resident Mission, Beijing, 26-27 October 2001.

Lardy, N. (2001), *Integrating China in the Global Economy*, Washington, D.C., Brookings Institution.

Lin, Y.F., R. Tao, M. Liu and Q. Zhang (2002), "Rural Direct Taxation and Government Regulation in China: Economic Analysis and Policy Implications", Working Paper, China Center for Economic Research, Beijing University, August.

Lu, F. (1999), "Three Grain Surpluses: Evolution of China's Grain Price and Marketing Policies, 1978-1999", paper presented to the Symposium on China's Agricultural Trade and Policy: Issues, Analysis and Global Consequences, San Francisco, June 25-26, 1999 (http://aic.ucdavis.edu/research/).

Martin, W. (2002), "Implication of Reform and WTO Accession for China's Agricultural Policies", *Economies in Transition*.

Rozelle, S., A. Park, J. Huang and H. Jin (1997), "Liberalization and Rural Market Integration in China," *American Journal of Agricultural Economics* 79(2): 635-642, May.

Sicular, T. (1988), "Plan and Market in China's Agricultural Commerce", *Journal of Political Economy* 96(2): 383-87, April.

Srivanasan, T.N. (2003), "China and India: Growth and Poverty, 1980 2000", www.scid.Stanford.edu/pdf.

UNCTAD (2001), *World Investment Report 2001,* Geneva: UNCTAD.

World Bank (2001), *World Development Indicators 2001*, Washington, DC: World Bank.

WTO (2002), *International Trade Statistics 2002*, Geneva: World Trade Organization.

Yu, W. and S.E. Frandsen (2002), "China's WTO Commitments in Agriculture: Does the Impact Depend on OECD Agricultural Policies?" paper presented at the 5th Conference on Global Economic Analysis, Taipei, 5-7 June.

IMPACT OF WTO ON INDIAN AGRICULTURAL TRADE

B.N. Pandey and N.K. Mishra

The establishment of World Trade Organization is an important landmark in the history of International Trade. The WTO Agreement on Agriculture is stipulated to bring agriculture effectively for the first time under the discipline of a multilateral trading system. The WTO formally came into existence on January 1, 1995 in India and the implementation on the Uruguay Round resulted from the same date (Kumar: 2005) and the developing countries including India have almost surely benefited from it. What is needed is cautious optimism, rather than euphoria, in evaluating its potential benefits and knowing its drawbacks. However, it has completed a decade of existence during which it has evoked the entire spectrum of opinion from being the saviour of the global economy to the destroyer of less developed countries including India. During this period of ten years, much has been already written and said about the World Trade Organization (WTO) and Indian agriculture. Many concerns have been voiced about the fact that Agreement on Agriculture (AoA) of WTO is disadvantageous for developing countries like India. Now, what needs to be ascertained and determined is that, whether these concerns are genuine, based on a cogent analysis of the provisions and arguments, or, is it mere rhetoric uttered for the sake of negating the role of WTO. The purpose of it is to liberalize agricultural production and trade. This will go a long-way in fighting against world poverty. The commitments under AoA may broadly be categorized into (1) market access commitments, (2) domestic support commitments and (3) export subsidy commitments (Kallur and Rasure: 2005).

AGREEMENT ON AGRICULTURE (AoA)

The Agreement on Agriculture (AoA) is the name given to the agreement reached at the end of the negotiations on trade in agriculture under the Uruguay Round of Negotiations of the erstwhile GATT, the forerunner to WTO. The general idea of the AoA is to open up trade in agricultural products as far as possible.

The commitments under the AoA can be divided into three broad areas, commonly referred to as the "three pillars" of the agreements; these are (a) Market Access, (b) Export Competition and (c) Domestic Support. All WTO members were required to make commitments in each of these areas, though the extent of the commitments varies.

Market Access

Under the market access conditions, both developed and developing nations were to convert all non-tariff barriers into tariffs (a process known as tariffication). The tariffs also had to be bound i.e. each country had to commit itself to ceilings on its tariffs. As far as the maximum limit of tariff is concerned, no country is permitted to impose tariff beyond a certain limit. All industrialized developed countries are to reduce tariff by 36 per cent across the board within six years and ensure a minimum tariff reduction of 15 per cent on any product. Developing countries like India have to reduce tariff by 24 per cent across the board within 10 years. On any individual agro product, tariff cut has to be at least by 10 per cent.

Export Competition

Under the export competition commitments the developed countries were to reduce the value of direct export subsidies by 36 per cent over a period of six years and in volume terms by 24 per cent. The base period for these cuts is 1986–1990 or 1991–1992 if exports were higher in that period. Over the same period the developing countries are to reduce the value of direct export subsidies by 24 per cent and in volume terms by 10 per cent.

Domestic Support

The key area of commitments was domestic support. This issue is linked with providing state support to farmers in farm production. Under AoA (Agreement on Agriculture), developed countries were to cut AMBER BOX subsidies within 6 years by 20 per cent starting from 1995 with 1986–1988 period as base. The same has to be reduced by 13 per cent within 10 years by developing countries.

AoA has classified all subsidies given to farmers into three categories–AMBER BOX subsidies, BLUE BOX subsidies and GREEN BOX subsidies. Under AMBER box subsidies such domestic support is included which is meant to encourage farmers to produce more. Such subsidies are considered trade distorting as they obstruct the free working of the market mechanism. A market price support mechanism–minimum support prices to help the farmers when the prices are falling–that sets no limit on production would fall into the AMBER BOX. BLUE BOX subsidies are related to quantum of output hence are considered minimally trade distorting. They directly link production to subsidies, they also sets limits on production by way of quotas. Such subsidy is provided only up to certain limit of production. GREEN BOX subsidies produce no adverse effects either on production or on trade. Direct income support schemes unlinked to production would be typical example of GREEN BOX subsidies.

The commitments to reducing subsidies made under the AoA were restricted to AMBER BOX subsidies alone. This has led to serious anomalies that have effectively undermined the spirit of the AoA. Developed countries have used provisions of AoA to further reduce the interest of their farmers. For example they have remodeled AMBER BOX subsidies in such a way that these qualify to be put into BLUE or GREEN BOX subsidies. These countries are consistently pressurizing developing countries for greater market access for agricultural products but are not willing to bring down the level of support that they provide to their own farmers. According to a Monitoring and Assessment Report of WTO there has been no change in the domestic support provided by members of OECD to their farmers since the year 2000.

In fact, India expected that market access for her agricultural products would expand after the reduction of subsidies by the developed countries under WTO agreement. But the developed countries have not implemented fully their WTO commitments for reducing agricultural subsidies. Rather, their agricultural subsidies have been increased during post WTO period due to increased support under green and blues boxes of WTO agreement. But due to high farm subsidies by the developed countries, the share of farm products in the global exports of the developing countries like India stands at one per cent only, and has not been increased during the post WTO period. The globalization of agriculture has posed new challenges to Indian agriculture.

INDIA'S FOREIGN TRADE

At present, the provisions of AoA do not appear to have threatening impact on Indian agriculture. So India need not lose its sleep over the stipulations to reduce domestic support and export subsidy under AoA. The non-product specific support amounts to 7.5 per cent of the value of agricultural production in India. Since product specific support is negative, the aggregate measure of support to Indian agriculture is still below the deminimise of 10 per cent in terms of the Uruguay Round stipulations. India has already suggested that AMS be calculated as the sum of the product specific and non-product specific support. As it is input subsidies to resource-poor farmers are exempt from reduction commitments under WTO (these come under non product specific support), so the overall level of support given to Indian agriculture is less than the minimum of 10 per cent as set by under WTO stipulations.

Agriculture sector in India has responded sluggishly to the launching of macro-economic reforms in 1991. With liberalization of exchange rate, the terms of trade for agriculture have shown a little improvement. Private investment in agriculture registered a steep rise in the post-reform period (GOI, Planning Commission, 2000). At 1993-94 prices, private investment in agriculture was over 50 per cent higher in 1999-2000 when compared to 1993-94 (GOI, Planning Commission, 2001). As per the commitments to WTO, all types of quantitative restrictions on imports have been lifted since April 2000. As a sequel to this, India has already negotiated tariff bindings at the level of 100 per cent for raw commodities, 150 per cent for processed agro commodities and 300 per cent for most edible oils. These are sufficient to protect the relevant commodities against cheaper imports, which are made possible due to high domestic support in countries of their origin. India is also free to impose countervailing tariff on imports from countries having high export subsidy.

Data on foreign trade in agriculture reveal a different picture of so called gains of WTO initiated trade liberalization across the world. The value of India's export in US dollar terms has increased considerably from $ 33470 million in 1996-97 to $ 63843 million in 2003-04 registering a growth of 97 per cent. However, the growth of agri-exports remained somewhat dismal. Agri-exports registered declining trend from 1996-97 to 1999-2000. Agri-exports decreased from $ 6828 million in 1996-97 to $ 5608 million in 1999-2000 registering a cumulative decrease of 18.99 per cent. Agri-exports increased to $ 6004 million in 2000-01 (7.06% increase) but again declined by 2.21 per cent in 2001-02. Year 2002-03 and 2003-04 have registered an impressive growth of Indian agricultural products. As a result, the value of agri-exports stood at $ 7533 million in 2003-04. Cumulatively agri-exports are higher by merely 10.3 per cent during the period 1996-97 to 2003-04. This figure is much lower than an impressive increase of 97 per cent in total exports. It is clear from the Tables 1, 2 and 3 that India could not gain from the trade liberalization era of WTO.

Table 1
Growth Rates of India's Foreign Trade

(Value in Millions US dollar)

Year	*Exports*				*Imports*			
	Total Exports		*Agri-Exports*		*Total Imports*		*Agri-Imports*	
	Value	*% increase*	*Value*	*% increase*	*Value*	*% increase*	*Value*	*% increase*
1996-97	33470	–	6878	–	39137	–	1428	–
1997-98	35006	4.58	6594	(-)3.43	41485	6.00	1847	29.34
1998-99	33218	(-)5.11	6037	(-)8.45	42389	2.18	2919	58.04
1999-00	36822	10.81	5608	(-)7.11	47212	11.38	2624	(-)10.10
2000-01	44560	21.01	6004	7.06	50536	7.04	1858	(-)29.19
2001-02	43827	(-)1.64	5871	(-)2.21	51413	1.74	2294	23.47
2002-03	52719	20.29	6734	14.67	61412	19.45	2803	22.19
2003-04	63843	21.10	7533	11.86	78149	27.25	3568	27.29

Source: GOI, Economic Survey (Various Issues), Ministry of Finance, New Delhi.

Table 2
India's Agricultural Exports

(Millions US dollar)

Items	*1996-97*	*1997-98*	*1998-99*	*1999-00*	*2000-01*	*2001-02*	*2002-02*	*2003-04*
Tea	292.0	505.0	538.0	412.0	432.6	360.5	343.6	356.3
Coffee	402.0	456.0	411.0	331.0	259.4	229.6	205.5	236.3
Rice	1104.0*	910.0*	1495.0*	724.0*	644.3	665.5	1218.1	907.0
Wheat					90.9	278.9	363.6	520.4
Sugar & Molasses	..	..	..	..	111.9	373.6	375.1	269.0
Tobacco	213.0	288.0	181.0	233.0	190.6	169.3	212.5	238.6
Spices	339.0	379.0	388.0	408.0	354.4	313.9	342.8	336.1
Cashew	362.0	377.0	387.0	567.0	411.4	354.4	424.2	370.0
Sesames & Niger seeds	78.0	81.0	78.0	86.0	130.9	127.0	93.2	164.2
Guar gum Meal	100.0	147.0	173.0	188.0	132.0	84.5	100.6	110.0
Oil Meals	985.0	924.0	462.0	378.0	447.6	474.5	308.8	728.7
Fruits & Vegetables	208.0	204.0	184.0	209.0	248.4	262.8	300.2	453.2
Processed Fruits & Vegetables	59.0	73.0	69.0	86.1	122.1	107.5	118.8	74.8
Meat & Meat preparations	200.0	217.0	187.0	189.0	321.7	250.2	284.6	373.1
Marine Products	1129.0	1207.0	1038.0	1183.0	1393.8	1236.4	1431.6	1328.7
Others	1359.0	824.0	446.0	614.0	712.1	590.6	611.1	1066.1
Total Agri- Exports	6828.0	6594.0	6037.0	5608.0	6004.0	5871.1	6734.0	7533.1
Total Exports	33470.0	35006.0	33218.0	36822.0	44560.2	43826.7	52719.4	63843.0
Agri-Exports as per cent of Total Exports	20.4	18.8	18.2	15.2	13.5	13.4	12.8	11.8

* Includes value of export of Rice and Wheat together.

Source: GOI, Economic Survey (Various Issues), Ministry of Finance, New Delhi

Table 3
India's Agricultural Imports

(Millions US dollar)

Items	*1996-97*	*1997-98*	*1998-99*	*1999-00*	*2000-01*	*2001-02*	*2002-02*	*2003-04*
Cereals	137.2	291.5	287.7	133.6	19.4	18.2	24.5	19.4
Pulses	250.8	321.4	168.5	63.2	109.2	662.6	565.6	497.2
Milk & Cream	0.7	1.4	2.9	22.4	1.6	1.8	2.0	19.5
Cashew Nuts	193.7	206.4	230.3	220.0	210.6	90.4	255.4	298.5
Fruits & Nuts excluding Cashew Nuts	18.3	154.7	159.3	84.2	175.2	158.7	132.6	174.4
Sugar	0.9	126.5	264.1	255.0	7.0	6.8	6.8	13.6
Oil seeds	1.3	0.8	-	2.0	1.7	0.3	2.4	3.0
Vegetable Oils fixed (edible)	825.1	743.0	1803.9	1842.5	1333.7	1355.6	1814.2	2542.5
Total Agri-Imports	1428.0	1846.7	2918.8	2624.1	1858.4	2294.0	2803.4	3568.2
Total Imports	39132.9	41484.5	42388.7	47212.1	50536.3	51413.3	61412.1	78149.1
Agri Imports as per cent of Total Imports	3.7	4.5	6.9	5.6	3.7	4.5	4.6	4.6

Source: GOI, Economic Survey (Various Issues), Ministry of Finance, New Delhi.

On the import front the picture is rather grime. The value of Indian import increased from $ 39137 million in 1996-97 to $ 78149 million in 2003-04. The cumulative increase is 99.5 per cent. But the value of agri-imports increased from $ 1428 million to $ 3568 million, net increase of 149.8 per cent. However, this increase is attributed to the increase of edible oils, which had shown an increase of more than three times during the same period.

But on reaching the Cancun Meeting, it was clear to the developing countries that in actual the developed countries are neither reducing subsidy on agricultural exports to the desired level as per WTO Agreement on Agriculture nor reducing domestic support and further levying very high tariffs on imports so as to restrict the entry of the agricultural products of developing countries. As a result of this, Cancun Summit had failed where India has played a significant role. It is clearly found that the developed countries are levying heavy tariffs on India's agricultural exports and same is the position with the other developing countries. It is so because the developed countries have not implemented WTO Agreement on Agriculture in proper manner. Thus, the US and EU have got the excess to markets in developing countries and they are making the agricultural produce cheaper with the help of subsidies while the developing countries are not in position to subsidize the agricultural produce to the level of developed countries. Developing countries must remain united under the leadership of India in WTO to fight for their interests.

Though there is clearly a need to be constantly vigilant and work in league with other developing countries like China and Brazil for greater market access into developed countries and removal of tariff and non-tariff barriers, the major challenges to Indian agriculture come from within. To counter the cleverly crafted strategy of the developed countries at WTO, we need to take measures, which make Indian agriculture more competitive.

STEPS FOR FUTURE

(i) Yield improvement where greater attention needs to be paid to pulses, edible oils and coarse cereals.

(ii) Creation of more exportable surplus.

(iii) Making agriculture more efficient and competitive so that it can withstand the impact of the fluid world economic environment and greater integration with the world economy.

(iv) Strengthening and upgrading rural infrastructure, greater product diversification and more research on resource management and varietal improvement.

(v) To carry forward agricultural marketing reforms. In this respect, the 'Agricultural Product Marketing Regulation Act' needs to be amended to allow for easier movement of goods.

Moreover professionally managed and organized marketing facilities need to be developed. Initiative from the private sector should be encouraged.

(vi) To increase the flow of institutional credit to agricultural sector.

(vii) Improvement in rain fed agriculture and water management.

(viii) Step up real public investment in agriculture. Public investment in agriculture has been on a constant decline due to fiscal exigencies. This has led to lower allocations for infrastructure like irrigation, rural roads, electrification and markets (Chauhan and Singh: 2005).

SUGGESTIONS

Equally important is the need to restructure, modify and revamp our agriculture sector so that it can rise up to the challenges thrown by growing integration with the rest of the world. The need of the time is to make it more efficient, modern, diversified and competitive. The fortunes of Indian agriculture which now accounts for about 22 per cent of the GDP and provides employment to about 60 per cent of labour force crucially depend upon greater investment, both private and public, in irrigation, power, roads and the ability of agriculturists to access the modern technology specially the yield augmenting technology. Conditions need to be created for widespread diffusion and application of this technology by the farm sector. Initiatives should be taken up to educate the farming community of the country to face the challenges and avail the opportunities in WTO regime. Farmers should be encouraged to adopt diversification of crops and larger investment should be encouraged in production where they can have comparative advantage. For achieving international achievements, farmers should improve the qualities of their agriculture produce. Such agricultural commodities should be produced in larger quantities, which are in good demand in the international market. In this way not only will India's agricultural exports increase but also it will leave a multi-dimensional effect on improving the socio-economic environment of rural India.

REFERENCES

Chauhan, S.S.S. and S. Singh (2005), "WTO and Indian Agriculture", The Indian Economic Association, 88th Annual Conference, Vishakhapatanam, Andhra Pradesh.

Government of India (2001), Planning Commission.

Government of India (2004-05), Economic Survey, Ministry of Finance, New Delhi.

Kallur, M.S. and K.A. Rasure (2005), "Impact of WTO on Indian Agriculture", The Indian Economic Association, 88th Annual Conference, Vishakhapatanam, Andhra Pradesh.

Kumar, R. (2005), "WTO and Its Impact on Tamil Nadu Agriculture", The Indian Economic Association, 88th Annual Conference, Vishakhapatanam, Andhra Pradesh.

REVIEW AND POTENTIALS OF AGRO–PRODUCTS EXPORTS OF INDIA UNDER WTO REGIME

Reeta Kumari Bhagat and S.K. Upadhaya

INTRODUCTION

Agriculture is still the major sector of India contributing near about one fourth to the GNP and providing employment to about more than 50 per cent of the total working force. This sector provides not only livelihood to the people but also supplies bulk of wage–goods and raw materials required by non–agriculture sectors. Thus, India in agriculture constitutes a significant component of world market. It has become the pride of the national economy even after decades of planned economic development. It is also the bedrock of Indian economic activities. In order to reduce external-debt and improve the foreign exchange position, agricultural trade must be strengthened.

Today, Indian economy is facing many challenges of the new economic scenario. The most critical factor to meet this challenge will be exporting capability of the country in a highly competitive environment, when every country is desperately struggling to export something or to other. The establishment of world trade organization (WTO) on January 1, 1995 is tended towards globalization of world economy. The agreement on agriculture (AoA) of WTO recognizes free and market oriented trading system in agriculture.

But agricultural trade was an exception to liberalization before the WTO agreement. It was highly protected sector in the developed countries using several trade and non- trade barriers like technical standards, environmental and social controls, high tariff, quantitative restricting quota, strict hygienic restrictions, package standards, labeling requirements etc. which have been discouraging our exports e.g. floriculture products, marine products and basmati rice to European Union, mushroom exports to USA are the order of the day. As a result, the agricultural exports of the developing country like India suffered a lot. The trade experience of India in the recent years also reveals that the share of agro-products in world- market has declined to a considerable extent.

The reasons for such a decline cannot be attributed to the only trade policies of the developed countries alone, but also our own domestic policies which includes the high cost–structure, the policy of over-valued exchange rate, low producer prices, export taxation, infrastructure and quality problems. These reasons are also responsible for our poor agricultural performance, which declined export of our country.

India being a founder member of the World Trade Organization (WTO) has been following the WTO decisions. It was expected that under WTO, the entry of the agricultural products from India in the world market would be without much restrictions owing to market predictability, reduction in AMS (Aggregate Measure Support) and export subsidies, undoubtedly there are significant improvements in the structure of India's balance of payments after the adoption of new EXIM Policy in 1991. From the available facts shows that after WTO has come into existence, the level of net export jumped to a good position i.e. form $ 3119 million in 1995-1996 to $ 4565 million in 1996-1997, but this position can not be maintained for a long time, i.e. after 1996-1997, the level is declining continuously. So, India's share in global agricultural exports before WTO witnessed an increase but experienced a decline in the past WTO period.

Before examining the future prospects and potentials of agro products of India, it would be important to look at the existing status of its export trade, India's share in the world agricultural exports remained very low. In order to assess the possibility as well as direction required export–trade, it is important to study the existing pattern and structure of exports of India.

PERFORMANCE AND REVIEW OF AGRO-PRODUCTS EXPORTS UNDER WTO REGIME

The performance of exports of major agro–products of India in terms of quantity and value during the period of 1980-81 to 2003-2004 has been appreciable after economic reforms. Though the economic reforms of 1991 created favorable conditions to agriculture through the trade policy reforms and devaluation of rupee. The Table 1 shows the aggregate agricultural exports, which rose from $2.6 billion in 1980–81 to $6.3billion in 1995–96, declined to $ 6.1 billion 2001-2002 and again registered an increase to the tune to $7.8 billion in 2003-2004. The country's export basket in the past was heavily dependent upon items like tea, mates and coffee, which in recent years has widened including commodities like rice, marine products, fruits and vegetable etc. (Table 1). Some of these commodities such as rice, other cereal preparation, fruits and vegetables and processed fruits and vegetables have high potential for exports.

India has dramatically increased its rice exports in the last decade. During 2002-2003, it exported around 5 million tonnes of rice accounting for nearly 1/5 of the world rice trade. However, large fluctuations have characterized rice export as is evident from Table 1. The tremendous increase was due to devaluation of Indian rupee in 1991, abolition of quota system and quantitative restrictions on export of rice in 1992 burgeoning stocks and export subsidy.

India has been able to raise its coffee exports form less than one lakh tonnes (0.87) lakh tonnes in 1980-81 to 1.88 lakh tonnes in 2003-2004. The export earning increased form $290.9 million in 1980-1981 to $449 million in 1995-1996 but registered a decline after that band reached to $236 million during 2003-2004. During the period 2000-2001 to 2003-2004, despite of increase in the volume of coffee export; India's export earrings from coffee followed a steep decline due to a crash in global coffee prices, which was put coffee industry in serious trouble.

The quantity of tea exported by India followed a "U' curve during this period. For instance, its export first declined substantially from 299 thousand tonnes in 1980-81 to 158.7 thousand tones till 1995-96 and again registered growth. After that the unit value realization from export of tea and mate also

Table 1
Composition of Indian Agricultural of Exports (Qty. in thousand tones, Value in 000 US$)

Commodity	*1980-81*		*1990-91*		*1995-96*		*2000-01*		*2001-02*		*2002-03*		*2003-04*	
	Qty.	*Value*	*Qty.*	*Value*	*Qty.*	*Value*	*Qty.*	*Value*	*Qty.*	*Value*	*Qty.*	*Value*	*Qty.*	*Value*
Coffee	87.3	270.9	86.5	141	156.1	449	184.9	259	176.3	230	184.9	205	188	236
Tea & mate	229.2	538	199.1	596	158.7	350	202.4	433	180.1	360	184.4	344	178	356
Oil cakes	886	158	2447.8	339	433.1	702	2417.8	448	278.2	474	177.6	382	325	729
Tobacco	91.3	178.7	87.1	147	87.1	134	108.3	191	97.9	169	100.5	211	121	238
Cashew kernels	32.3	177.2	55.5	249	70.8	370	244.9	412	92.4	346	1219.4	424	99.7	370
Spices	84.2	140.8	1033	133	204.1	237	83.8	354	239.3	314	278	343	267	336
Sugar & molasses	97	50.4	191	21	734.4	151	769	112	1677.5	374	1870.2	375	1299.2	269
Raw cotton	131.6	208.6	374.4	471	33.3	61	30.2	49	82	9	11.7	10	179.6	205
Rice	726.7	283.2	505	257	4914	1366	1534.45	644	2208.4	666	4967.8	1205	3412.1	1025
Fish & Fish preparations	69.4	269.2	158.9	535	3101	1011	502.6	1394	—	1236	—	1432	—	1329
Meat & meat preparations	—	70.81	—	78	—	187	—	322	—	250	—	284	—	373
Pulses, fruits vegetable's	—	277.8	—	12	—	240	—	239	—	327	—	350	—	513
Others	—	101	—	11	—	223	—	906	—	259	—	307	—	305
Total	—	2601	—	35	—	6320	—	6256	—	6146	—	6962	—	7888

Source: Directorate General of Commercial Intelligence & Statistics, Kolkata.

exhibited a considerable year-to-year variation and were close to $ 3.5 billion in 2003-2004, which is clear from Table 2.

Table 2
Growth Trends in the Export of Agricultural Products (1986-87 to 2003-04)
(Compound Average Rate CAGR in per cent)

Commodities	*Period I (1986-87 to 1994-95)*		*Period II (1995-96 to 2003-04)*		*Period III (1986-87 to 2003-04)*	
	Qty	*Value*	*Qty*	*Value*	*Qty*	*Value*
Coffee	5.8		3.07	-10.14	6.65	3.05
Tea & Mate	-3.4	-0.49	6.33	-0.69	-0.70	-1.48
Oil Cakes	14.14	-4.87	-13.76	-6.66	7.24	5.44
Tobacco	0.34	18.86	3.26	2.02	4.03	4.6
Cashew	9.34	0.51	4.68	0.50	6.18	4.28
Spices	8.04	5.97	1.16	1.51	7.65	5.23
Sugar & Molasses	45.43	-3.72	-20.42	16.18	21.7	22.14
Raw Cotton	6.08	3.87	-24.97	-19.74	-5.12	-6.85
Rice	15.49	1.40	-30.95	-3.63	14.37	11.51
Fish & Fish Preparations	15.75	10.29	6.35	3.56	12.38	8.65
Meat & Meat Preparation	—	9.41	—	8.65	—	11.62
Fruits &Vegetables	—	4.28	—	-1.68	—	8.22
Agricultural & Allied Products	—	7.78	—	0.81	—	7.35

Source: Directorate General of Commercial Intelligence & Statistics, Kolkata.

Sugar used to be a significant export commodity from India. During the last decade, export of sugar has shown fluctuation due to sharp rise in its domestic demand; even marginal decline in its production has led to occasional import of large size. The reason for which seems to be mismanagement of supply and lack of clear policy regarding pricing of sugar.

Spice export have shown a steady increase from 84 thousand tones in 1980-81 to 278 thousand tones in 2002-2003 and then declined to 267 thousand tones in 2003-2004. In value terms, the export earrings forms spices have been shown about a 2.5 time increase

The annual compound growth rates for the agro exports during the period (1986-87 to 2003-2004), shows that export earning from India's agro and allied products grow at the rate of 7.78 per cent per annum in the pre WTO period and plummeted to 0.81 per cent in post–WTO period. Growth rate in the overall WTO period was, however, 7.35 per cent. Appreciable increase in export has come about mainly due to the devaluation of the Indian rupee and opening up of the economy due to significant reduction in the import duties. The decline in agricultural exports in the latter half of the nineties is probably due to sharp reduction in the international prices of agricultural commodities.

Among the various agricultural export groups the growth rates registered by fish and fish preparations were significant both in volume and value in all the three periods followed by cashew kernels and meat and meat preparation.

The results reported in Table 2 showed that during period I, the quantity exported coffee rose at the 5.50 per cent per annum while in terms of value, it registered a negative growth rate to the tune of 0.49 per cent. Similar trends were recorded for the period II too. Tea and mate witnessed a negative growth rate both in volume and value in period III. During period I, the export of tea (in quantity terms) declined at an annual rate of 3.4 per cent, while it recorded a positive growth rate of 6.33 per cent in period II.

India's share of agricultural exports in different years is presented in Table 3. It reveals that India's share of some of the traditional items in world exports has been declining rapidly in the post-WTO Period. In the case of tea and mate, India's share in world exports declined from 26.2 per cent in 1985 to 12.6 per cent in 2003. Earlier India enjoyed a respectable place in spices exports with its share in world export around 19.3 per cent in 1985, but it came down to 8.5 per cent in 2003. A mixed trend was observed in the case of tobacco. India has had a reasonable presence in the world market of rice with her share around 5.1 per cent in 1985. It further increased to 18.1 per cent in 2003-04, which is really commendable.

On the other hand, India's share in the world fisheries export remained around 2.5 per cent in value terms during the period under study. India thus, does not have a substantial presence in the world exports of fisheries products. But India's output is the largest and it is the seventh largest producer and on opening up her large fisheries sector to the world trade may have considerable effect on the nature of the world equilibrium in terms of price and subsequently outputs. India's share in world coffee export increased from 1.9 per cent in 1985 to 2.8 per cent in 1995 and remained close to it the subsequent period.

Table 3
India's Share in Worlds Exports of Selected Agricultural Products

(in per cent)

Commodity	*1985*	*1990*	*1995*	*2000*	*2001*	*2003*
Coffee	1.9	1.7	2.8	2.3	2.6	2.3
Tea and mate	26.2	22.1	14.3	14	13.3	12.6
Cereals & cereal prep	0.6	0.6	2.7	1.5	-1.8	2.8
Tobacco & Tobacco manufacture	1.8	0.8	0.5	0.7	0.6	0.7
Unmanufactured tobacco	3	2.1	2.1	2.7	2.1	2.9
Spices	19.3	7.7	9.5	10.3	9.2	8.5
Sugar and molasses	0	0.1	0.8	0.9	2.42	2.4
Rice	5.6	6.4	18.6	10.2	9.7	18.1
Meat & fish preparations	2.4	1.6	2.1	2.7	2.4	2.6
Meat & meat preparations	0.4	0.2	0.4	0.7	0.5	0.6
Fruits & vegetables	1.4	0.8	1	1.3	1.1	1.1

Source: Directorate General of Commercial Intelligence & Statistics, Kolkata.

The forgoing discussion highlights many significance aspects of agricultural trade. The share of Indian agriculture in global agro-trade has been diminished to about 9 per cent over the period .The average annual growth rate of Indian agricultural GDP has decreased from 3.5 per cent during pre WTO period to 2.57 per cent during the post WTO period. Liberalization under WTO has not increased the share of agricultural products in India's global exports.

The overall impact of WTO on agriculture is positive as well as negative. There are some positive impacts in some area like floriculture, horticulture, diary, etc. due to opening up of the agricultural trade. The proportion of fruits, vegetables and processed products has increased; it shows the constantly

Table 4

Share of Agricultural Products in India's Global Trade (1990-2004)

Sl. No.	*Item*	*1990-91*	*1991-92*	*1992-93*	*1993-94*	*1994-95*		*1995-96*	*1996-97*	*1997-98*	*1998-99*	*1999-00*	*2000-01*	*2001-02*	*2002-03*	*2003-04*	
	Share in India's Exports	*Pre WTO Period*					*Average 1990-95*	*Post WTO Period*									*Average 1995-2004*
1.	Pulses	0.0	0.0	0.1	0.1	0.1	0.1	0.1	0.1	0.3	0.2	0.3	0.3	0.2	0.1	0.1	0.2
2.	Rice Basmati	1.4	1.1	1.5	1.5	1.0	1.3	0.8	1.1	1.3	1.3	1.1	1.1	0.9	0.8	0.7	1.0
3.	Rice Other than Basmati	0.0	0.6	0.3	0.3	0.4	0.3	3.5	1.6	1.3	3.2	0.8	0.4	0.6	1.5	0.7	1.5
4.	Wheat	0.1	0.3	0.0	0.0	0.1	0.1	0.3	0.6	0.0	0.0	0.0	0.2	0.6	0.7	0.8	0.4
5.	Other Cereals	0.0	0.0	0.0	0.0	0.0	0.0	0.0	0.0	1.4	0.0	0.0	0.0	0.1	0.0	0.1	0.0
6.	Tea	3.3	2.8	1.8	1.5	1.2	2.1	1.1	0.9	1.3	1.6	1.1	1.0	0.8	0.6	0.5	1.0
7.	Coffee	0.8	0.8	0.7	0.8	1.3	0.9	1.4	1.2	0.7	1.2	0.9	0.6	0.5	0.4	0.4	0.9
8.	Tobacco Unmanufactured	0.6	0.7	0.7	0.5	0.2	0.5	0.4	0.6	0.1	0.4	0.5	0.3	0.3	0.3	0.3	0.4
9.	Tobacco Manufacturd	0.2	0.1	0.2	0.1	0.1	0.2	0.1	0.1	0.1	0.1	0.1	0.1	0.1	0.0	0.0	0.1
10.	Spices	0.7	0.8	0.7	0.8	0.7	0.8	0.7	1.0	1.1	1.2	1.1	0.8	0.7	0.6	0.5	0.9
11.	Cashewnut shell Liquid	0.0	0.0	0.0	0.0	0.0	0.0	0.0	0.0	0.0	0.0	0.0	0.0	0.0	0.0	0.0	0.0
12.	Cashew	1.4	1.5	1.4	1.5	1.5	1.5	1.2	1.1	1.1	1.2	1.5	0.9	0.9	0.8	0.6	1.0
13.	Sesamum Seed	0.3	0.2	0.2	0.1	0.2	0.2	0.2	0.2	0.2	0.2	0.2	0.3	0.3	0.1	0.2	0.2
14.	Groundnut	0.2	0.0	0.0	0.2	0.1	0.1	0.2	0.3	0.4	0.1	0.2	0.2	0.1	0.1	0.2	0.2
15.	Guargum Meal	0.0	0.2	0.2	0.2	0.2	0.2	0.2	0.3	0.4	0.5	0.5	0.3	0.2	0.2	0.2	0.3

Sl. No.	Item	1990-91	1991-92	1992-93	1993-94	1994-95		1995-96	1996-97	1997-98	1998-99	1999-00	2000-01	2001-02	2002-03	2003-04	
	Share in India's Exports	Pre WTO Period					Average 1990-95	Post WTO Period									Average 1995-2004
16.	Oil Meals	1.9	2.1	2.9	3.3	2.2	2.5	2.2	2.9	2.6	1.4	1.0	1.0	1.1	0.6	1.1	1.6
17.	Castor Oil	0.2	0.3	0.2	0.4	0.5	0.3	0.7	0.5	0.4	0.5	0.7	0.5	0.3	0.2	0.2	0.4
18.	Shellac	0.0	0.1	0.1	0.1	0.1	0.1	0.1	0.0	0.0	0.0	0.0	0.1	0.0	0.0	0.1	0.0
19.	Sugar Incl. Mollases	0.1	0.4	0.7	0.3	0.1	0.3	0.5	0.9	0.2	0.0	0.0	0.2	0.9	0.7	0.4	0.4
20.	Fruits/Vegeta-ble & Seeds	0.7	0.8	0.6	0.6	0.6	0.6	0.5	0.5	0.5	0.4	0.5	0.4	0.6	0.0	0.0	0.4
21.	Marine Products	3.0	3.3	3.2	3.7	4.3	3.5	3.2	3.4	3.4	3.1	3.2	3.1	2.8	2.7	2.1	3.0
22.	Cotton Raw incl. Waste	2.6	0.7	0.3	0.9	0.2	1.0	0.2	1.3	0.6	0.1	0.0	0.1	0.0	0.0	0.3	0.3
	Total (including others)	18.5	17.8	16.8	18.0	16.0	17.4	19.2	20.3	19.1	18.3	15.9	14.3	14.2	13.6	12.7	16.4

Source: Govt. of India, Agricultural Statistics at a Glance 2004, Ministry of Agricultural & Economic Survey, 2003-04, Ministry of Finance, New Delhi.

upgrading trade. It is clear that the exports share of Indian fruits, fruit products, fish and fish preparation, meat and meat preparation is increasing rapidly. In horticultural crops like fresh fruits, fresh vegetables and fruits and vegetables seeds have achieved the annual growth of 9.85 per cent. 13.32 per cent and 8.52 per cent respectively. The exports of processed product had achieved 18.34 per cent annual growth rate. The exports of individual item like processed fruits and processed vegetable grew at 20.06 per cent and 14.73 per cent respectively annually. Among other items, meat preparations and spices have also achieved appreciable growth at 21.04 per cent and 20.04 per cent respectively.

But the over all desired results in agricultural exports and improving the production and productivity have not yielded under WTO regime. The two major factors are responsible for the present downfall of Indian agriculture. First, in its eagerness to reduce fiscal deficit, the government has substantially reduced the development expenditure sector. Secondly, import liberalization has contributed in a big way to reduction in prices of agricultural products.

The causes of decline and slow growth of export of India's agro-products is attributable to numerous reasons, some are domestic while some are external. The major causes are lower prices of agricultural commodities in foreign markets, economic crisis in South East Asian Countries and Japan and the decrease in exports to some of India's trade partners such as Indonesia and Bangladesh. There is also a gradual reduction in subsidies in developing country like India as against the high level of subsidies provided by developed countries, result in high cost of production for comparable agricultural crops and affects adversely the growth of agriculture and allied exports in India. All these causes have adversely affected export of agricultural products from India during post WTO regime. But it may be stimulated that India undertakes steps both at the domestic as well as international level. The formation of the WTO was the right step at the international level. It has provided both the challenges and opportunities to all countries particularly the developing countries.

The focus of Sixth WTO Ministerial Conference of Hong Kong from December 13-18, 2005 focused on Agriculture, as it has been for most part of the Doha Round. The ongoing Agricultural Negotiations have witnessed a stand off on agriculture between the developing countries led by the G-20 and the G-33, on the one hand and US-EU on the other. Developing countries have insisted that the developed countries should undertake comprehensive policy reforms involving their agriculture sectors by reducing subsides and tariffs.

Viewed form this perspective, the Hong Kong Ministerial Conference did make some progress. An agreement was reached with the EU [the largest user of agriculture export subsidies] an end date for the removal of subsidies while most countries wanted to eliminate the subsidies by the end of the decade, the EU sought out a longer period. The agreed end date of 2013 gives the EU (European Union) its level of comfort by phasing out its agricultural export subsidies as a part of the next phase of reform its common agricultural policy (CAP). For country wanting to see the EU ending these subsidies, the agreement on the end-date means that they have finally been able to push the EU away from its earlier held position.

POTENTIALS OF AGRO-PRODUCTS

India has a unique opportunity to capture a large share of world market to substantially increase its exports of agricultural products, particularly in the free trade regime under World Trade Organization (WTO) because of highly diversified nature pf agricultural products are like cereals, pulses, oilseeds, fruits, vegetables, floriculture, water based products, animal products, fiber products, condiments, spices plantation crops like tea, coffee and so on.

At present, India's share in world export of processed fruits and vegetables is about 4 to 5 per cent. All this, however, indicates tremendous potential for growth of processed fruits and vegetables sectors in India. The major players in world export of processed fruits and vegetables are Brazil, USA, Netherlands, Italy and Germany. Despite adverse balance of trade position, floriculture is a sector in which India has unlimited opportunities because of its liberal policies towards horticultural trade and most places of India have ample sunshine during winter, which does not require artificial lighting or heating in winter. India is centrally situated in compression with major important flower consumption centers in European and South Asian countries. Another advantage is that of auction, market for floricultural product is likely to be established in Singapore. Also, there is a possibility of making use of Dutch trading channels to the rest of the European markets. Apart from this; Japan, Hong Kong and Singapore are also expected to be important. The flower seeds exports also have tremendous possibilities especially to US, similarly tissues cultural plants and protected cultivated plants have good potentials in Europe. The new economic environment during post WTO periods proving several incentives to India like reduction in export tariff and tax advantage, market access, domestic support, financial assistance setting up for new processing unit to bolster up the export of agriculture commodities.

The share of agricultural export of India in world marker is declining but due to the favorable scenario under WTO regime in net trade, it has got significant position. The long-term battle can be won only through the field of agriculture.

The increasing share of processed items in total agricultural export is a sign of boom. Food processing industry is vital for India's prosperity as it contributes about 18% of agricultural GDP. India is the second largest producer of fruits and vegetables with annual production of 140 million tonnes but it hardly processes 1.5% to 2% and living huge wastage and value destruction up to 20% to 40% of the total produce. The performance of exports of agricultural products and processed products has shown tremendous results in the last decade, which have potential of further growth in the future. Due to increasing importance of food processing sector after economic liberalization in the country and WTO, Foreign Direct Investment in this sector has also increased substantially.

The recently released "Government of India, Economic Survey, 2005-06" has also concern over the low productivity growth in agriculture and allied sectors in India. However, it projects a rosier view about the sectors like horticulture, floriculture, fishery, poultry and animal husbandry. These account for 30 per cent of production in agriculture and allied sectors and are expected to grow at a rate of 6 per cent from 2005-06 onwards. The desired growth of the agriculture sector in general and economic prosperity of rural farmers in particular are achievable only with and effective integration and synergy between agriculture and agro–based industries. Out of various agro-industries, processed and packaged food article industries ensure a substantial value addition to the primary agricultural products.

During the last two five year plans (i.e. 9th and 10th Plans), attempts were made to plan, develop and promote various processes food sector like fruits and vegetables, meat, poultry, milk, egg, fish, grain processing, etc. Besides, provision of grants-in-aid to prospective entrepreneurs for setting up and modernization of the processed food plants, extensive research and development assignment are being initiated to match the shift in consumer demand in the globalised era. The potentials and constraints of a few emerging processed food sectors are mentioned below.

(a) Fruits and Vegetables Processing

India varied agro-climates favour her farmers to grow a large number of horticulture crops such as fruits, vegetables including rood tuber and ornamental crops, medical and aromatic plants, spices and plantation crops like coconut, cashew, cocoa. Presently, 8.5 per cent of country's gross cropped area is under horticulture crops. The total horticulture production is 145.78 million tones. India is the second largest producer of fruits and vegetables and produces fruits around 57.6 million tones from 5.2 million hectares. Vegetables are raised in an estimated area of 6.3 million hectares with a production of 99.4 million tones. This indicates India's share in world fruit and vegetable production is 10 per cent and 13.28 per cent respectively. Table 5 shows the pattern of production of fruits and vegetables during years 2002-03 to 2005-06.

The increase in production of fruits and vegetables indicates that there is a crying need for development of appropriate process technology and manufacturing of quality processed food items. The overall installed capacity of fruits and vegetables processing industry, in 2005 marked an increase of 73 per cent over that in 1993. The capacity of this sector was estimated at 11.08 lakh tonnes as in 01.01.1993 and 19.24 lakh tonnes as on 01st January 2005. The utilization of fruits and vegetable for processing in the organized and unorganized sectors is estimated to be around 2 per cent of the total production. There has been a positive growth in "ready to serve" beverages, fruit juices and pulps, dehydrated and frozen fruits and vegetable products, tomato products, pickles, processed mushrooms and curried vegetables.

Table 5
Production of Fruits and Vegetables (2002-03 to 2005-06)
(in million tonnes)

Crops	*2002-03*	*2003-04*	*2004-05*	*2005-06*
Fruits	45.2 (3.8)	49.2 (4.8)	53.1 (5.0)	57.6 (5.2)
Vegetables	84.8 (6.1)	84.8 (5.9)	91.6 (6.1)	99.4 (6.3)

*Source:*Government of India, Economic Survey, 2005-06.

(b) Cereal Based Consumer Food Industry

Cereal based consumer food industry includes pasta, breads, cakes, pastries, rusks, buns, rolls, noodles, rice flakes, corn flakes, biscuits, ready to eat and ready to cook products constitute the largest segments of consumer foods in India. With the opening up of the economy, many overseas companies are coming to India to exploit the market potential of these food items and increasing their investment in plants and machinery for requisite modernization and expansion.

(c) Meat and Meat Processing Industries

Meat and meat products are highly perishable commodities and can be a medium for transmission of disease from animals to human beings. Thus, processing of meat and meat products ensures availability of safe, disease-free and wholesome meat products. These sectors can evolve as a promising sector if the relevant statute i.e. Meat Food Products Order (MFPO), could effectively be used for regulating production, storage transportation and marketing of meat products in the country.

(d) Dairy Processing Industries

In the livestock sector, the production of milk has gone up more than five fold since independence. This results in near doubling of per capita milk availability.

The above table indicates production and per capita availability of milk in India. Though 90.7 million tonnes of milk is produced in India by 2004-05, milk organized dairy industry accounts for less than 15 per cent of total production. The rest of the milk is either consumed at farm level or is sold as fresh, non–pasteurized milk through unorganized channel. The present shift in consumption pattern of the Indian consumers from milk to innovative milk products brings in a large scope for dairy processing in the country. The rise in the market for dairy products is likely to witness a growth rate of over 20.3 per cent per annum. Many international dairy companies are now viewing India as a perfect investment destination in order to tap India's vast growing market for dairy products.

Table 6
Production and Per Capita Availability of Milk

Year	*Milk Production*	*Per Capita Availability (Grams per day)*
1950-51	17.0	124
1960-61	20.0	124
1970-71	22.0	112
1980-81	31.6	128
1990-91	53.9	176
2000-01	80.6	220
2001-02	84.4	225
2002-03	86.2	230
2003-04	88.1	231
2004-05	90.7	232

Sources: GOI, Department of Animal Husbandry, Dairy and Fisheries.

(e) Fish Processing

India is the third largest producer of fish and second largest producer of inland fish in the world. This sector is a source of livelihood for over 11 million people and one of the major foreign exchange earners through exports. During 2004-05, a total of 6.3 million tonnes of fish produced out of which 4.7 million tonnes were exported.

Considerable infrastructure facilities are needed for processing of marine products. At present their are over 369 freezing units with a daily processing capacity of 10,266 tonnes and 499 frozen storage with a capacity of 1,34,767 tonnes. Considering India‘s vast coastline and rich but under exploited marine resources efforts should be made3 to increase various infrastructure facilities required for this sector's growth viz., setting up of improved and qualitative canneries pre–processing units and dry fish storages, freezing units etc.

Export of marine products from India at present is valued at about Rs. 6,188 crore. Indian marine products are exported o over 64 countries. Japan is by far the most important market for our marine products in terms of value followed by USA, South East Asia and European Union. Non–compliance to the international quality standards has restricted production of exportable mariner products in India.

So, these are the above highly potential areas and constraints of agro-food processing sectors of India. The government therefore, should take necessary initiative in the policy, programme, legal and other constraints relating to export of agro-products.

The proportion of agricultural export to total exports of India was 10.2 per cent in 2004-05. The major exports during 2005 (April to October) included marine products (Rs. 33,264.8 million), meat and meat products (Rs. 12534.5 million),. This shows the potential of processed food sector. This aspect has, therefore, attracted many multinational investors to invest in India. Food processing industries have attracted a cumulative amount of (Rs 50439 million) foreign direct investment (FDI) in India during 2002-03 and 2005-06 (April–November).

The Union Budget (2005-06) allowed hundred per cent income tax rebate on profit for first five years and 25 per cent for another five years for new upcoming fruit and vegetables processing units. The food-processing sector in India can ensure enormous benefit by way of value addition of primary products.

The Union Budget (2006-07) has proposed to treat food–processing sector as a priority sector for extension of bank credit. NABARD has been instructed to create a separate window with a corpus of Rs. 1000 crore for refinancing loans to the sector, especially for agro–processing infrastructure and market development. Government has also proposed to setup the National Institute of Food Technology Entrepreneurship and Management (NIFTEM) for promotion of processed food products. The Budget has also proposed to reduce customs duty on packaging machines from excising 15 percentage to 5 per cent, which will boost the packaging industry in general and packaged food-processing units in particular. Various processed and packaged foods like condensed milk, ice cream, meat preparations, fish and poultry products, pectin; pasta and yeast will now be fully exempted from central excise duties. The excise duty on ready–to–eat packaged food and instant food mixes like dosa, idli mixes, etc. This initiative will give a fillip to the food processing industries as a consumer demand for the packaged and processed food items are expected to rise.

CONCLUSION

The WTO (World Trade Organization) agreements have created excellent opportunities for Indian food industries to increase their exports. To utilize the WTO benefits, India has to improve the quality of products upto 'International Standards' set by the WTO agreement. The two important agreement measures, SPS (Sanitary and Phytosanitary Standard) and TBT (Technical Barriers to Trade) address the food quality standards to follow the member country. To utilize the WTO benefits, India has to comply with the SPS and TBT agreement, other wise she has to face the problem of non-tariff barriers in the form of 'food quality standards'. It become obvious that India will have to improve her quality norms to face the WTO challenges. India has to take some serious steps in the coming years. One of the important steps is to adopt HACCP (Hazard Analysis and Critical Control Point) for 'food quality management system' in their food processing units. But the adoption of HACCP requires huge amount of investment. Hence, it is not possible for all the Indian firms to adopt HACCP for management of food quality system.

Therefore, the government should act as a catalyst for bringing in greater investment into this sector, guiding and helping the industry in the proper direction, encouraging exports and creating a conductive environment for healthy growth of food processing industry. It should come forward to give subsidy for the 'initial costs associate' with its implementation and the 'recurring costs' can be borne by the respective enterprises.

A strong and dynamic food-processing sector could play a vital role in diversifying agricultural activities, improving value addition opportunities and creating surplus for export of agro-food products. This would however, require policies and plan for improvement of food processing infra-structure including up-gradation of technology and enforcement of quality standards, promoting investment in food processing and activating domestic market with focus on exports.

But is not denying the fact that the future of food-processing sector seems bright with growing potential for domestic as well as export market. Therefore, to minimize huge wastage in this field, steps should be taken by the government for development of agro-processing sector through creation of infra-structure, cold storage, proper post harvest handling techniques, standardization, packing, costly wooden boxes, colour, size and grading the availability of quality raw materials for agro-processing industries, which is one of the major issues affecting the performance and viability of processing industries. So, there are vast potentials with us to lead our traditional agriculture to value added agricultural economy under WTO regime.

REFERENCES

Datt, R. and K.P.M. Sundharam (2005), Indian Economy, S. Chand & Company, New Delhi.

Singh, Manmohan, India's Export Trends, Chapter –10.

Government of India (2005–06), Economy Survey, Ministry of Finance, New Delhi.

Government of India, Union Budget (2006-06 and 2006-07), Budget at a Glance.

World Bank Report (Various Issues).

Economic and political Weekly (various Issues)

Government of India, Five Year Plans (Various Issues), Planning Commission.

Government of India (2006), Yojna, Ministry of Information and Broadcasting, New Delhi.

Government of India (2003-04), Agricultural Statistics, Ministry of Agriculture and Economic Survey, New Delhi.

Government of India, Department of animal Husbandry, Dairy and Fisheries, New Delhi.

Directorate General of Commercial Intelligence and Statistics, Kolkata.

AGRI-EXPORT BUSINESS AND ROLE OF BANKS UNDER WTO REGIME

Rashmi Akhoury and R.C. Choudhary

BACKGROUND

The global agri-business, governed by the WTO-regime, would have far-reaching implications for Indian agriculture. Its full effect would be realised from January 2005 when GATT Agreements 1994 would stand fully implemented. In fact, this Agreement has brought, for the first time, agricultural sector and international trade of agricultural commodities within the purview of GATT and WTO, thus, integrating agriculture fully with the global market. The Agreement on Agriculture (AoA) under WTO, pertaining to subsidies, market access, and sanitary and phytosanitary measures would have a direct bearing on Indian agriculture. The bringing of intellectual property right (TRIPS) in the purview of WTO would also have serious effects of Indian agriculture through patenting of seeds and the upcoming sui-generis system. Changing the period of patent from 7 (as per India's Patent Act, 1970) to 20 (under WTO) years would make the situation from bad to worse. There is, thus, an urgent need to evolve appropriate policy measures and undertake a serious research so that ways and means could be found to prepare Indian agriculture for the fast changing domestic and global scenario. We would have to devise a multi-pronged strategy to face the emerging challenges and make Indian agriculture sustainable and internationally competitive.

Indian agro-tech culture has undergone remarkable transformations during the second half of the 20th century as a result of a series of successful agricultural revolutions: the green, the white, the blue and the yellow. The country is now poised for a series of next revolutions: "gene", "agricultural diversification" and "food-processing". It is a known fact that India possesses many outstanding competitive advantages in several commodities for agricultural export and has the potential to become a global leader in agriculture.

However, the share of our agricultural exports in the total export basket has been fluctuating over the years. In certain items, our agro-exports are much less than what the competitive potential warrants. The export of agricultural commodities is dependent on a number of factors, such as domestic production and consumption, exportable surpluses, quality, domestic and international prices and availability of necessary infrastructure for quality production, handling and storage.

The accelerated diversification and modernization of Indian agriculture envisaged will require substantial/radical policy changes, a renewed thrust on agricultural research, extension and a new climate that encourages much greater investment in both the public and private sectors. The National Agricultural Policy announced recently by the Government of India is a major step in this direction.

The most important objectives of agricultural sector reforms in India are to: (i) enhance productivity, (ii) raise the levels of domestic production of basic food commodities to their potential, (iii) improve the quality and standards of products and (iv) diversify production and export by promoting the development of new crops and processing primary products.

Achieving these objectives would require building up of our farming capacity, attracting new investment, promoting R & D and providing needed infrastructure, farm inputs and adequate/timely credit to all the producers, processors and exporters. Providing credit to farmer-entrepreneurs and exporters is one of the several inputs/services needed for promoting agro-exports from India. This paper is an attempt made to identify the areas where commercial banks and financial institutions could play an important role in promoting agro-exports, besides playing their catalytic role in providing short-and /or long- term credit to rural and agricultural sector under the priority sector credit.

INDIA'S AGRICULTURE TRADE IN POST REFORMS AND POST WTO PERIOD

Economic reforms initiated in the year 1991 gave a big boost to agricultural exports. The main factor for this impressive export growth was that international prices of several agricultural commodities were well above the domestic prices and liberalisation provided the opportunity to exploit this advantage. These achievements in farm exports led to the belief that Indian agriculture was highly export competitive and generated favourable environment for freeing agricultural trade. This happened at a time when new multilateral General Agreement on Trade and Tariff (GATT) was being finalised. It was anticipated that implementation of the new agreement would benefit developing countries like India. Thus, global liberalisation of agriculture trade was further seen as a great opportunity for promoting farm exports.

So, the decade of 1990s witnessed two significant developments that have profound impact on agricultural trade. The first development relates to liberalisation of economic policy as part of the economic reform programmes initiated in 1991. The second development concerns the new international trade regime following Uruguay Round agreement and formation of WTO, performance of agricultural exports and imports in relation to these two developments i.e. after the start of economic reforms and in the post WTO period can be seen from the data presented in Table 1.

The last column of Table 1 shows the percentage volume of the foreign trade in terms of GDP. These data shows fluctuating trends in the foreign trade volumes. There is a declining trend from 1995-96, after signing the WTO declaration. This column shows the exports for the year 1995-96, it is 7.37 per cent and for 1996-97, it is 7.30 per cent, for 1997-98, 1998-99, 1999-00 they are 6.99 per cent, 5.92 per cent, 5.30per cent respectively. Over all, these data show declining trend in trade per cent of GDP agriculture even from 2003 to 2006.

From the available facts showed in the Fig. 1, it is to be concluded that after WTO has come into existence, the level of net export jumped to a good position i.e. from $ 3119 million in 1995-96 to $ 4565 million in 1996-97 but this position cannot be maintained for a long time i.e. after 1996-97, the level is declining continuously. Again in 2003-04 and 2004-05, net export has increased and in 2005-06, it has decreased.

Table 1
India's Agriculture Trade in Post Reforms and Post WTO Period

Year	*Export*	*Import*	*Net Export*	*Trade as per cent of GDP Agriculture*		
	$ million	*$ million*	*$ million*	*Exports*	*Imports*	*Total*
1992-93	3028	1618	1410	5.22	2.79	8.00
1993-94	4023	1317	2706	5.69	1.86	7.55
1994-95	4227	2544	1683	5.20	3.13	8.33
1995-96	6120	3001	3119	7.37	3.61	10.98
1996-97	6868	2303	4565	7.30	2.45	9.75
1997-98	6634	2893	3741	6.99	3.05	10.04
1998-99	6633	4012	2021	5.92	3.94	9.86
1999-00	5615	4402	1213	5.30	4.00	9.30
2000-01	6013	2638	2275	–	–	–
2003-04	7532.0	3708	3824	11.9	4.7	7.2
2004-05	8001	3811	4190	10.2	3.5	6.7
2005-06	4885.5	2203.8	2681. 7	9.6	2.8	6.8

Source: Economic Survey, Ministry of Finance, GOI, Various issues.

Figure 1
India's Agricultural Trade in Post Reform and Post WTO Period.

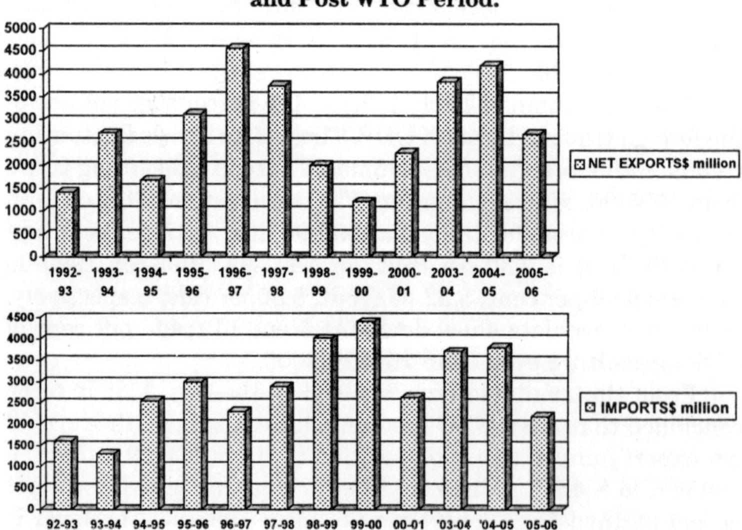

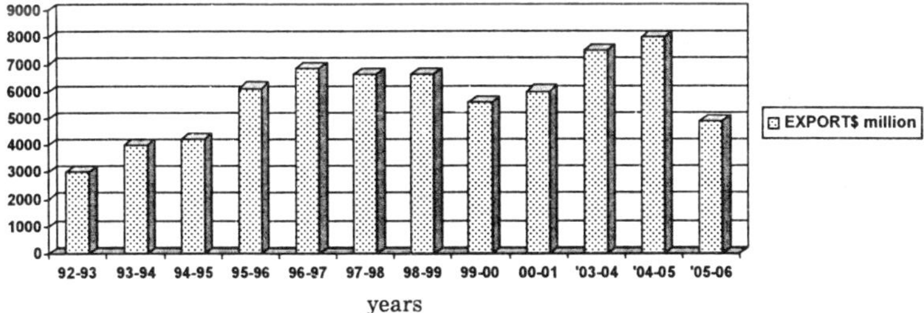

However, contrary to the expectations and anticipations, the price situation changed dramatically after implementation of Uruguay Round Agreement. International prices of agricultural commodities have dropped to a very low level, even in rupee terms and domestic prices have turned higher than the international prices. This has rendered Indian market attractive for import of several agricultural commodities. Even with moderate to high tariffs, imports are giving tough time to domestic produce. On the other hand, exports have witnessed sharp decline from 1996. Such adverse developments have renewed fear and apprehensions about the implication of trade liberalisations.

Several analysts had predicted that implementation of AOA would lead to increase in international prices and would improve export prospects for Indian agriculture. However, such predictions have failed to materialise and international agriculture prices witnessed a steep fall after 1997. After that feeling emerged that decline in agricultural prices in post WTO period, which is posing threat to domestic production, is the result of implementation of WTO agreement. There is also a lot of anxiety about the future behaviour of international prices.

In the post WTO period global agricultural exports have declined in value terms, where as quantity of export has grown. Thus, global trade in post WTO period has turned out to be favourable to consumers of agricultural producers. Similarly WTO has been favourable to net importing countries and unfavourable to net exporters of agricultural products. The decline in value of agricultural exports has been seen in the case of developing countries.

Though after WTO agreement, agricultural exports have not shown any dynamism even after liberalization as is evident

Table 2
Indian Agriculture Exports

(Rs. Crores)

Year	*Total Exports*	*Agriculture Export*	*Col. 3 as per cent of Col.2*
1980-81	6711	2057	30.65
1981-82	7806	2221	28.45
1982-83	8803	2258	25.65
1983-84	9771	2622	26.83
1984-85	11744	2997	25.52
1985-86	10895	3018	27.70
1986-87	12452	3422	27.48
1987-88	15674	3504	22.35
1988-89	20232	3723	18.40
1989-90	27681	4879	17.63
1990-91	32553	6317	19.40
1991-92	44042	7878	17.88
1992-93	53688	9457	17.61
1993-94	69751	13021	18.67
1994-95	82674	13712	16.58
1995-96	106352	21138	19.88
1996-97	118817	25040	21.07
1997-98	130107	25419	19.53
1998-99	139753	26104	18.68
1999-00	162955	24576	15.09
2003-04	63049.0	7532	11.9
2004-05	78205.3	8001.7	10.2
2005-06	51114.4	4885.5	9.6

Source: Economic Survey (Various Issues).

from Table 2. As it is observed from the table, while the share of agriculture in exports was 30.65 per cent is 1980-81, the highest even share during the two decades the share declined to the lowest share of 15.09 per cent in the year 1999-2000. Though Indian agricultural export share prior to liberalisation period has been fluctuating on and ultimately decline to 17.63 per cent in the year 1989-90 and again rose to 19.40 per cent in 1990-91. It further declined in post liberalisation period with marginal fluctuation and has fallen at the level of 15.09 per cent. The range of agriculture export falling in the decade 80-90s has been approx 11 per cent points while the range of agriculture exports falling in between the year 1991-92 to 1999-

00 has been 2.77 per cent approximately. During 2003-04, 2004-05 and 2005 -06, the share of agricultural exports in total exports is 11.9%, 10.2% and 9.6% respectively which shows declining trend.

AGRICULTURAL EXPORTS UNDER WTO REGIME

It was expected that under WTO, the entry of the agricultural products from India in the world market would be without much restrictions owing to market predictability, reduction in AMS and export subsidies. Undoubtedly, there are significant improvements in the structure of India's BOPs after the adoption of new EXIM Policy in 1991. The annual average growth of exports increased only up to 7.61 per cent over the period 1980-81 to 1991-92. The export cover of imports stood 74 per cent and 64 per cent over the period respectively (Economic Survey, 2000-01). The pertinent question is that how far has the WTO regime been simulative to the growth of exports of India's agricultural and allied products. Agriculture provides employment to large number of our people and occupies an important place in India's economic structure.

The response of agro-exports from India in the post WTO period is dismal. The share of these products in India's total export declined from 19.2 per cent in 1995-96 to 14.6 per cent in 1999-00 (Table 3). The agro-products constituting about 74 per cent of total exports of agriculture and allied products are marine products, cashew, tea, basmati rice, spices, oil meals, coffee, non-basmati rice and castor oil. The exports of these items declined about 3 per cent on average during 1996-2000. The three of these products that is non-basmati rice, oil meals and coffee have recorded the decline from 8.5 per cent to 2.7 per cent.

In Table 3, the share of various agro products like marine products, cashew, tea etc. in total exports has been shown. The table clearly indicates the tremendous changes that occurred between the periods 1995-96 to 1999-00. The agricultural products whose exports decreased in the post WTO period are marine products, oil meals, coffee, non-basmati rice, while the exports of two products (tea, castor oil) have been stagnant. The agricultural products, which showed increasing exports performance, are cashew, basmati rice and spices. After analysing data, it is to be concluded that overall exports of agro products is showing a declining trend.

Table 3
Export Response of India's Agro-Products (in per cent)

	Share in Total Exports		*Exports*
	1995-96	*1999-2000*	*D Exports**
Marine Products	3.2	3.1	-0.1
Cashew	1.2	1.5	+0.3
Tea	1.1	1.1	0.0
Basmati Rice	0.8	1.1	+0.3
Spices	0.7	1.0	+0.3
Oil meals	2.2	1.0	-1.2
Coffee	1.4	0.8	-0.6
Non Basmati Rice	3.5	0.8	-2.7
Castor Oil	0.7	0.7	0.0
Total of the above	14.8	11.2	-3.6
Total Agro Products	19.2	14.6	-4.6
Total Exports	–	–	–

* Changes exist in India's agro products exports between 1995-96 and 1999-00.

Source: Center for Monitoring Indian Economy (CMIE), July 2000, p. 2.

Figure 2
Export Response of India's Agro Product.

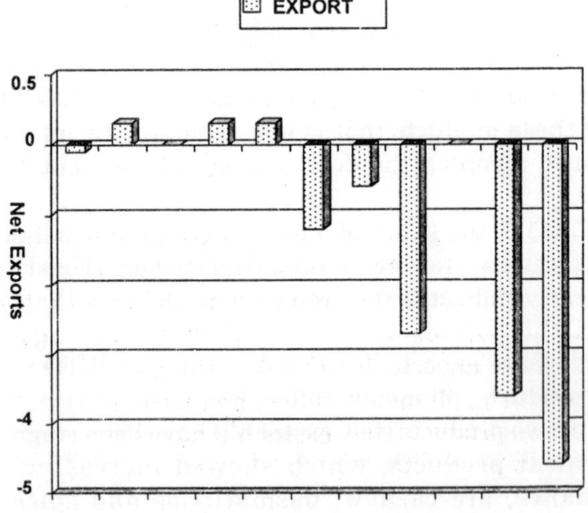

The analysis makes the support of the hypothesis that the basket of traditional agro products item in exports is rapidly changing. If however we want to survive and revive our agro exports, we should pay attention on the production of processed agro products namely fruits, vegetables, marine products and floriculture.

No doubt, the volume of agricultural exports in rupee terms has been increasing, but in terms of dollar it has shown a declining trend in recent years. After having the share of 20.4 per cent in total export during 1996-97, it came down to 18.8 per cent in 1997-98, 18.1 per cent 1998-99 and only 14.6 per cent in 1999-2002

CAUSES OF SLOW EXPORTS OF AGRO-PRODUCTS

The slow growth of India's agro-exports is attributable to numerous reasons. The major causes are lower prices of agricultural commodities in foreign markets, economic crisis in South East Asian Countries and Japan and the decrease in exports to some of India's trade partners such as Indonesia and Bangladesh. The developed countries continued subsidizing exports of farm products in the interest of food security, maintaining farm incomes and preserving the farming population (Gulati, Ashok, 2000) distorting agriculture trade unfavourable to the developing countries. The market access was thwarted by these countries restarting to Tariff Rate Quota (TRQ) i.e. importing certain amount of the product at low rate of tariff duty and the successive import of the same products at higher rate of tariff making the imports from the developing countries costly in their market.

India has followed low tariff rates compared to the negotiated tariff rates so far as imports of several agricultural products is concerned from abroad. In the year 2000-01 the average basis duty rate was 34.9 per cent as compared to UR Bound Tariff Rate 114.9 per cent. After the lifting of QRs on the remaining 715 items as part of WTO commitment, India's agriculture sector is likely to have far reaching impact.

Some of the far-reaching implications on agriculture are highlighted below:

1. The Indian market has faced with the problem of low cost import of most of the agricultural commodities from several

countries, which has caused considerable anxiety among the domestic producers.

2. The gradual reduction in subsidies in developing country like India result in high cost of production for comparable agricultural crops and affects adversely the growth of agriculture and allied exports in India.
3. Liberal import of agricultural commodities may create difficulties for supply-demand balance for essential commodities, especially food grains, in a developing country like India in the event of natural calamities like flood and drought.
4. Finally, increased investment in modernized and export-oriented agriculture would require re-allocation of financial resources.

INDUSTRY OVERVIEW

The Food Processing Sector in India is one of the largest in terms of employment production, consumption, export and growth prospects. Important sub-sectors in the food processing industry are Fruit and Vegetable Processing, Fish Processing, Milk Processing, Meat and Poultry Processing, Packaged and Convenience Foods, Alcoholic Beverages & Soft Drinks and Grain Processing. Primary food processing is a major industry with a large number of rice mills, flourmills, pulse mills and oil seed mills. There are several thousands of bakeries, traditional food units and processing units in the unorganized sector. In the organized sector, there are over 820 flour mills, 418 fish processing units, 5198 fruit and vegetable processing units, 171 meat processing units.

The turn over of the total food market is approximately Rs. 250,000 crores (US$ 69.4 billion) out of which value–added food products comprise Rs. 80,000 crores (US$ 22.2 billion). India is the world's second largest producer of fruits and vegetables, but hardly 2 per cent of the produce is processed. India is the land of spices producing all varieties worth over Rs.3500 crores (US$ 900 million) amounting to 28 per cent of world production, which is processed for value-addition and export. It grows 22 million tonnes of oilseeds covering most of the varieties. Other important plantation products include tea, coffee, cocoa and cashew. It has large marine product and processing potential with varied fish resources along the 8041 km. long coastline, 28000 km. of rivers and millions of hectares of reservoirs and brackish water. India's livestock population is the largest in the world with 50% of world's buffaloes and 20 per cent of cattle, but only about 1% of total meat production is converted to value added products. India is the largest milk producer in the world and about 15 per cent of the total milk production is processed through the organized sector. The size of the semi-processed and ready to eat packaged food industry is over Rs.4000 crores (US$ 1 billion) and is growing at over 20 per cent.

Table 4
Key Statistics: The Indian Food Processing Sector

Size of the Industry	Rs. 250,000 crores
No of Units	Approximately 6607
Investments	Rs. 20097 crores
FDI as on 31/2/04	Rs. 3500 crores
Contribution in GDP	5 per cent
Direct Employment	Approximately 2.77 lakh
Exports (2004)	Rs. 14500 crores
Growth	15 per cent per annum
Contribution in Total Exports	10 per cent

Source: Indian Development Foundation Report.

India is the second largest producer of fruit and also of vegetables in the world yet the commercial processing of fruit and vegetables is less than 2.0 per cent. The main reason being that domestic consumption of processed items is quite meagre because of economic reasons and also as a matter of habit. The Indian consumers by and large very much prefer fresh fruit and vegetables. The high cost of packaging pushes up the cost of the processed items and thereby makes them out of reach of the common man. Because of the varied agro climatic conditions, some fresh fruit and vegetable are available throughout the year. The fruits like bananas are non seasonal and apples, oranges, and potatoes etc. are put in the cold stores thus prolonging their self life and making them available even in the off season. Some fruits like guavas, oranges have two seasons so they are available in fresh form for four to five months in a year.

There are a little over 5198 units registered under the Fruit Products. Most of the units fall in the cottage and or small-scale sector. A few modern processing plants have, now come up and many more are in the pipeline. The installed capacity, which was 11.08 lakh tonnes in December 1993, increased to 25.00 lakh tonnes at the end of the year 2004.

ROLE OF BANKS IN AGRO-EXPORTS

The policy interventions initiated by the Government of India/ RBI providing favourable climate for increasing India's agro exports are given below:

- RBI has always been in the forefront to initiate appropriate policy interventions to facilitate flow of credit to agricultural and allied sectors. Exports have always been accorded national priority both in terms of providing credit access to the needy exporters and also extending finance at concessional rates. Even today, there are policy prescriptions on foreign banks to achieve 12 per cent of their net bank credit for export sector as a sub-target within their overall priority sector lending of 32 per cent and also in respect of domestic commercial banks there is an exclusive target of 12 per cent of net bank credit for export sector, besides the priority sector target of 40 per cent.
- In the mid-90s, RBI advised all scheduled commercial banks to have at least one specialized hi-tech agricultural branch in each state. As a result, 15 commercial banks opened such branches. Upto January 1997, over 70 high–tech (agricultural) branches have been operating in the country. Canara Bank and Union Bank of India had more than 12 such branches each.
- NABARD also came out with several innovative schemes with potential for agricultural export requiring bank credit, such as, floriculture, tissue culture and mushrooms.
- APEDA has over the years formulated many schemes for promoting agro-exports. Some of the important schemes of APEDA are: (i) feasibility studies, surveys, consultancy and database upgradation, (ii) infrastructure development, (iii) export-promotion and market development, (iv) packaging development, (v) assistance to promote quality and quality

control, (vi) upgradation of meat plant, (vii) organization building and HRD and (viii) generating relevant research and development through research institutions for common benefits of trade and industry.

- The Department of Commerce, Government of India is operating numerous schemes to promote exports, including agro-products. Schemes like Market Development Assistance, India Brand Equity Fund Trust and the Market Access Initiatives are open to all exporters including agro-exporters.
- APEDA and Airport Authority of India have been working together to strengthen the airport infrastructure facilities by establishing integrated cold storage and agro-handing facilities for perishable agricultural products for exports. There is also a scheme to set up walk-in cold storage facilities and integrated cargo handling centers at different airports, which will greatly help in improving the infrastructure requirements of export of agri products, such as, fruits, vegetables and flowers.
- The Ministry of Food Processing Industries is implementing a scheme for setting up of food processing industrial estates as food parks. An assistance upto Rs. 4 crore is available for the common facilities created in the food parks. So far, 22 food parks have been approved in the country.
- The EXIM Policy (2001) introduced the concept of Agri-Export Zones (AEZs) to give primacy to promotion of agricultural exports and effect a reorganization of agro-export efforts on the basis of specific products and specific geographical areas. A to Z of agri-export will be available to the entrepreneurs at these zones.
- In January 2002, RBI devised a new scheme of export credit to processors/exporters in the Agri-Export Zones. Earlier, the facility of pre-shipment packing credit at concessional interest was not available for supplying inputs to the farmers for producing a particular crop, which is finally procured by the processor/exporter for export. Under the new scheme, banks have been advised to treat the inputs supplied to farmers by exporters as raw material for export and consider sanctioning the lines of credit/export credit to

processors/exporters to cover the cost of such inputs required by the farmers to cultivate such crops to promote export of agro-products. Accordingly, the processor unit should be able to effect bulk purchases/import of inputs with the advantage of economies of scale and supply the same to the farmer as per pre-determined arrangement.

- In order to encourage investment, improve export performance and develop non-traditional product, the Government of India has identified biotechnology, floriculture, tissue culture, mushroom production, seed production, bio-pesticides, agro-processing and other agro-based industries as focus areas. Banks have been providing financial assistance to some of these projects.

PARTICIPATION OF BANKS IN PROMOTING AGRO-EXPORTS

Agricultural sector policy reforms remain high on the agenda of planning process of banks. The changes under the WTO regime in future are likely to be more radical. Against this scenario, the role of commercial banks in promoting agro-export is indicated briefly in the following paragraphs:

- During the past few years, many export-oriented "hi-tech agricultural projects" have come up in various parts of the country. Some of these are: high density farming, greenhouse cultivation of cut flowers, controlled environment livestock farming, bio-technology, tissue culture, bio-pesticides, bio-fertilizers, white button mushroom production/processing, aquaculture, food processing, etc. These projects were financed by the term lending institution and commercial banks. The specialized hi-tech agricultural branches of the commercial banks financed some of these projects. Corporates, mid-corporates technocrats have entered into this business and a majority of the hi-tech agriculture projects came up in Maharashtra. Andhra Pradesh, Karnataka and Tamil Nadu. However, the experience of some of the above projects financed by banks and FIs were not all that satisfactory. The projects relating to seed production, hi-tech poultry, broiler processing, cold storage linked pre-cooling, food processing are doing well. Sectors like aquaculture, floriculture, mushroom and tissue culture had faced problems at the initial stages. Some units, mostly floriculture and aquaculture, have also become NPAs due to many reasons. At one time, these hi-tech agri-projects were considered as agri-industry or 'sunrise industry', but now it is surrounded by "dark clouds". Because, as of date, the number of entrepreneurs including corporates venturing into this field is reducing. Some of the existing units as stated above are not doing well as projected. Added to this, fresh disbursements from the commercial banks have come down substantially. Some of the commercial banks are thinking of closing down their specialised hi-tech agriculture branches, exclusively created for financing these projects. The head/controlling offices of the commercial banks seem not much enthusiastic about these specialised outlets as well as hi-tech agriculture projects financed by them because they perceive that the units are likely to become NPAs. Added to this, the initial interest and enthusiasm shown by development financial institutions like NABARD for hi-tech agri-projects have also diminished over the period.

From the analysis of the performance of these projects, the study shows that the problems faced and are being faced now by the hi-tech agro-exports units are viewed differently by financial institutions, commercial banks, supporting/promoting agencies like APEDA/NHB and the entrepreneurs/promoters. A lot of conclusion and mistrust has also been created among these partners. The problems of hi-tech agro-export projects financed by banks are varied and project specific. However, the most common problems experienced by the units are given below as illustration:

(i) Start-up problems related to first generation promoters, their background and financial status lack of sources of funds, failure to obtain clearance from the Government, lack of market information or foreign collaboration, completion of mortgage formalities.

(ii) Technology and production problems like non-availability of technical know-how, problems of acclimatization of imported technology to Indian conditions, non-availability of quality inputs including planting materials, high–cost of imported inputs, lack of follow-up services by the consultants.

(iii) Infrastructure bottlenecks like poor approach roads, lack of cargo/airport cold chain at airports, non-availability of adequate utilities, lack of research and development support, problems pertaining to transit insurance for perishable goods, non–suitable location of unit and effect of environment, etc.

(iv) Marketing and distribution problems pertain to less realisation of price than projected, limited scope for domestic market, heavy cost of marketing/publicity, absence of brand equity of the products, failure of buy back arrangements and non-existence of direct link or outlets with the foreign markets.

(v) Financial problems mostly relate to non-availability of credit in time, inadequate own contribution of promoters, lack of collateral, risk perception, novelty of activity both for banks of promoters and stringent income recognition and asset classification norms, prescribed by RBI.

Dr. N.B. Shete of NIBM, Pune had conducted a survey of 40 EOUs regarding specific problems of hi-tech agro-exports covering floriculture, greenhouse production technologies, mushroom production/processing and aquaculture. Some of the important observations emerging from the survey are given below:

- Most of the entrepreneurs felt that imported "greenhouses" are very expensive and is a fad. During the recent years, a large number of firms from Israel had collaborated with the Indian firms and designed appropriate greenhouses suitable to Indian conditions. The cost of locally designed greenhouses are only Rs.200 per sq. mtr, as against Rs.1,100 for an imported one. Three factors, viz., low cost of production, high quality and low cost of transportation should be the guidelines for adoption of greenhouses by the promoters in future.
- The selection of suitable location, technology and foreign collaboration, financial and marketing are the important problems faced by the floriculture units. It was found that floriculture units having low production cost, better realisation, strict adherence to quality and nearness to airports are doing better. The units having more than three-hectare greenhouse with more varieties are working well.

- Intensive shrimp aquaculture has led to environment degradation, threatening the long-term sustainability, outbreak of diseases, poor productivity, etc. The environment concern should not be used as justification for limiting financing aquaculture and its exports. It is surprising that banks claim that almost all shrimp aquacultural units have become NPAs and closed down, but export of shrimp is increasing over all these years.

FUTURE PROSPECTS OF FINANCING EXPORT-ORIENTED PROJECTS IN AGRICULTURE

The views of the motivated entrepreneurs and development oriented bankers regarding the future of hi-tech agro-export projects, as given below, show that there is a ray of hope for enhancing the scope for lending to these sectors as we have vast untapped potential which should be explored.

- A group of development-oriented bankers and motivated entrepreneurs (mostly technocrats) are of the view that "no one has been able to foresee these problems and various risks (credit, technology, market, foreign exchange, etc.) associated with these units". The hi-tech agri-export industry is very young in India (just 7 to 8 years old) and for an agro-based industry of this kind; this gestation/ stabilization period is too short. "The problems faced by these units and banks are common to any industry, particularly during the formative stages". All these suggest that this period could be taken as an investment for future. These positive attitudes need to be developed by the other partners of this venture. A joint task force should be able to do this task. Some of the partners of agro-exports projects, particularly hi-tech have now realised that some of these problems are common to any budding industry. Today, it is easier to finance such hi-tech agri-export projects than 6-7 years ago. Now promoters have learnt many aspects and facts based on their experiences and it is easier for the banks to finance such projects. Added to this, locally developed technology is also available in India. A group of domestic consultants has also emerged during the recent years for hi-tech agro-exports projects.

POSSIBLE AGRO-EXPORT AREAS FOR FINANCING BY BANKS

- Agricultural biotechnology has been advancing rapidly and it is rewriting the rules in several key areas like agriculture, horticulture, pharmaceutical industry, food processing, etc. New emerging areas based on biotechnology in production, processing and distribution in the above areas will provide ample scope for financing since these projects are scientifically developed and have thus become economically and technically sound.
- The Agricultural Exports Zones (AEZs) are now treated on par with 100% EOUs. Adequate infrastructural facilities of international standards particularly testing and quality control would be created at the AEZs so that confidence and credibility is created in the international market. Synergy is also being established between the food parks and AEZs are being set up by APEDA so that the food processing industries being set up in AEZs could take advantages of the common infrastructural facilities being developed in the food parks. Banks can provide financial assistance to these AEZs with little or no risk related to credit, technology and market.
- Protected cultivation of vegetables in India has shown an annual growth rate of 30% vegetable production under appropriate greenhouse conditions has shown encouraging results so far as yield and quality of capsicum and cucumber are concerned. This practice can ensure a regular supply in the export markets. The asparagus, broccoli and other exotic vegetables which have been in great demand in the USA and the European markets can be successfully grown in India under greenhouse conditions. The commercial banks and financial institutions can provide financial assistance for such projects coming from technocrats. To start with one such project in each district (Lead District) should be started by commercial banks as an experiment. The success stories can be repeated in non-lead districts also. The market for such vegetables is unlimited and growing at a rapid pace.
- Fruit juices and pulps have 27% share in the total export of processed products of fruits and vegetables in India. India

has been exporting pulps and juices of mango, guava, papayas, etc., to develop and developing countries. Now production, processing and distribution technologies are indigenously made available for processing of other fruits, which will enhance the scope for export of pulp and juices. New fruits like custard apple for preparing pulp, whose delicacy and pleasing flavour is acknowledged worldwide, could be explored. Many corporates and mid-corporates are venturing into this field in a big way, which is evident from the data of direct foreign investment in food processing sector.

- At present, India is exporting "oleoresins" of black and white pepper only. The scope of exporting this extract from spices like chillies and garlic are being explored. The processing and extraction technologies have been indigenously developed and tested in various research institutions and have been found suitable. Oleoresins are mostly used as colouring agents in the preparation of meat, salad dressing and flavoring of snack foods in developed countries. Banks can enter into this area at least in southern States like Tamil Nadu and Kerala.
- Development of cold chains by packaging houses with pre-cooling facilities at potential places, for export as well as maintenance of international quality of fruits like grape, mango and other perishables with the "export-hub" has had helped in regular supply of fresh fruits and vegetables. The grape growers of Maharashtra have reaped good profit by adopting this post-harvest technology. Banks can provide credit to individuals and groups of farmers for growing fruits, crops and for construction of pre-cooling–cum-cold storages in potential areas where such fruits/vegetables are grown on a large scale. The subsidy from APEDA and NHB is also available for this post-harvest infrastructural development. Some of the State Governments also had subsidy schemes for pre-cooling cold storages.
- The major organic food products include dried fruits and nuts, processed fruits and vegetables, spices, herbs, meat, dairy products, tea, etc. It is estimated that by 2010, the organic food market size would be around $46 billion in the

European Union, $45 billion in the USA and $11 billion in Japan. The corporates are venturing into this market on a large scale. During the years, the private sector banks and foreign banks have entered into this business. The commercial banks can provide financial assistance to the corporates, directly or indirectly through "contract farming" right from the farming stage only.

- Branded rice is becoming popular in its consumption Significant corporate presence is visible in the domestic as well as export markets. During the last 3-4 years, a large number of modern milling units have come up in different parts of the country. Till date, 94 foreign investments with 100% EOU proposals have materialised with a total investment of about Rs. 949 crores. Similarly, eight pulse milling units as 100% EOUs have been approved by the Ministry of Food Processing Industries. Banks can take advantages of these changed developments, as demand for such products is likely to go up steadily. "Contract Farming" operating in India particularly for growing vegetables like gherkins has shown positive results. Banks can venture into such types of projects by financing corporate or group of farmers for growing crops like rice, wheat, pulses and oilseeds.
- The commercial banks should take advantage of the numerous schemes/projects/assistance which are available from the Ministries of Food Processing, Commerce and Agriculture, etc. Banks should identify, educate and encourage emerging entrepreneurs to take up such projects in their operational areas. The efforts made by Canara Bank and Indian Overseas Bank in establishing agricultural consultancy services at their head offices for promoting high-value, hi-tech, agro-exports projects are worth emulating by other banks. Bank of Maharashtra is bringing out a publication "Agro-Export News", which is well received. Recently, the State Bank of India started a novel programme of helping the grape growers of Maharashtra to increase their earnings by exporting seedless grapes to developed and developing countries.
- The Exim Bank is now acting as a pace-setter in promoting agri-export in the country. The bank organized a national

level seminar on "Prospects and Challenges in Agri-Exports", in Pune during January 21-22, 2002, which was well attended. The Exim Bank has also established an "agri-business cell" at its head office (Mumbai) and has started Agri-Export Advantage, a bi-monthly publication, though agri-export is only a fraction in its total business.

- NABARD, though was the initiator of hi-tech agro-exports projects, may have to play a leadership role in promoting agro-exports particularly in the non-traditional activities/ projects located in rural areas. It has both technical and organizational capabilities and entrepreneurs are looking for such leadership role from NABARD.
- Experiences of Rabobank in India in financing EOUs in agriculture are worth mentioning here. This bank had developed a business model; Agri Service Centres, which facilitate bank financing by integrating inputs providers, farmers and processors. The bank also provides advisory services in facilitating Agri-Service Centre concept in India. Similarly, Indian bankers can learn from Israel, a small country with poor natural resources, which has made her presence felt in the agricultural world map. For example, "Agrexco" is the leading agricultural export company in Israel, which exports 80 to 90% of the country's flowers, fruits and vegetables. This is the first and the foremost farmers' company acting for and on their behalf. Farmers and government own this Company. The company guides and educates the farmers, starting with the decision on which crop to grow the production process and post-harvest treatment. It also helps in marketing of the products through its branches operating in Europe and USA. Banks can depute their concerned officers to Israel for training. If properly co-ordinated, funds from APEDA, NABARD meant for HRD could be used for such visits.

Finally, let me conclude by quoting an entrepreneur of floriculture unit located near Pune. "All NPAs and sick hi-tech agricultural projects can become viable, provided all the concerned, including financial institutions, banks, APEDA, NHB, Government of India, etc., work as a team to harvest the untapped potential........ Holland and Israel have succeeded beyond success, why can't we?" Let us meet the challenge and prove that liberalization of trade in agriculture is a boon and not a bane.

CONCLUSION

All these suggest that in order to infuse a sense of dynamism into the export sector and maximize the export earnings on a sustainable basis in future, an effective export strategy will have to be evolved. This strategy should aim at increasing competitiveness of Indian exports by removing constraints on the supply side. On the demand side, India should continue giving priority in the negotiation on agriculture under the WTO to removal of numerous trade distortions and market excess barriers that are still present in the developed countries. In Industrial goods, the emphasis should be on the issue of tariff peaks and tariff escalation in developed countries. This will enable India to gain access to the markets in developed countries on an increased and continuous basis.

REFERENCES

Shete, N.B. (1999), "Financing of Hi-tech Agro-Export Projects: Banker's Experiences". *Journal of Foreign Exchange and International Finance*, Vol. XI (3) pp. 233-247, NIBM, Pune.

Shete, N.B. (2000), "Financing Agri-Business: A Technical Manual"; NIBM, Pune, January.

Shete, N.B. (2001), "Sectoral Study of Export Oriented Units in Agriculture," Research Paper, NIBM, Pune, April.

Shete, N.B. (2002), " Problems and Prospects of Agro-Exports" a paper presented at the National Seminar on "Export of Agriculture Produce; Prospects and Challenges," jointly organised by the EXIM Bank of India and Bank of Maharashtra, Pune, January 21-22.

Agro and Processed Foods: A Sectoral Study, Occasional Paper, EXIM Bank of India, Mumbai, January 2002.

Proceedings of National Seminar on Export of Agricultural Produce Prospects and Challenge jointly organised by EXIM Bank of India and Bank of Maharashtra, Pune, January 21-22, 2002.

Tripathi, D.P. (2002), Valedictory Address at the National Seminar on Export of Agricultural Products; Prospects and Challenges, Jointly organised by EXIM Bank of India and Bank of Maharashtra, Pune, January 21-22.

Government of India (1999-2000), Economic Survey, p. 146 and S. 88.

Government of India, Economic Survey, 2000-01.

Bhattacharya, B. (2000), "Food Security in India in the Context of Agreement on Agriculture." Paper presented at the Seminar on Consultation on Agreement on Agriculture, Ahmedabad, 31st January.

Roopali Srivastawa and J.N. Purwar (2005), "A Review of India Agricultural Export Scenario. The context of W.T.O. Regulations", published in 88th IEA Annual Conference Volume, Vishakhapatnam, Andhra Pradesh.

Alagh, K. Yoginder (1998-99), "Agricultural Trade and Policies", The Indian Economic Journal, Vol. 46, No. 3, January, March, p. 56.

Acharya, S.S. (2000), "Subsidies in Indian Agriculture and Their Beneficiaries", Agriculture Situation in India, August, pp. 251-260.

Goyal S.K., Pandey, R.N. and J.P. Singh (2000), "India's Agricultural Exports; Growth and Instability", Foreign Trade Review, Vol. XXXV, No. 1, April, June, pp. 32-46.

Salam, Abdus (2003), "Problems and Prospects of India's Export under WTO Regime: A Study of Agricultural Commodity" in Alagh, Y.K.(eds) Globalisation and Agricultural Crisis in India, Deep and Deep Publication Pvt. Ltd., New Delhi, p. 101.

State Bank of India (2003), Monthly Review, April.

WTO: SOME OPPORTUNITIES AND CHALLENGES TO INDIAN AGRICULTURE

Punam

INTRODUCTION

Agriculture occupies a very significant position in Indian economy. It plays a very vital role in the sphere of national income, employment, capital formation, food supply, industry, trade, transport, export, government budget and so on. But apart from this Indian agriculture is facing some difficulties and challenges, both internal and external. It is characterized by stagnating yield at a low level, a very large proportion of marginal, small and semi–medium holdings, burdened with high proportion of labor force, highly concentrated cropping pattern, very low income, lack of finance and credit. Over the period of time, the share of agriculture in GDP decreased to 26.2 per cent in 2001-02 from 59.1 per cent in 1950-51. So far as the labor force is concerned, 60 per cent of the total labor force is still employed in Agriculture. So, 60 per cent of population contributes only 26 per cent in national income. It is not justifiable whereas in developed countries only two or three per cent of total work force is employed in agriculture and the contribution of agriculture in GDP is also two or three per cent.

To shift the excess burden of labour force from agriculture to other sector, it is essential to create employment opportunities. These employment opportunities generate the purchasing power and increase the rate of saving of population and they can invest in agriculture to boost up the productivity and output with special preference to export oriented

Agriculture Groups. Besides this investment, the foreign investment is also essential in this direction because the rate of saving and investment is low in India. This gap would be filled by foreign investment. But one point is remarkable - foreign investment should not mainly be in consumer goods but in infrastructural facilities and in industries too. As agriculture forms the core sector of the Indian economy so it is necessary to develop agriculture. In the light of above description, an attempt has been made to analyze the role of WTO in the field of Indian agriculture.

Under the process of globalisation, the Indian economy, a leading member of the WTO, cannot live in isolation. On one hand, WTO gives some opportunities to Indian agriculture whereas on the other hand, it gives some challenges to Indian agriculture also. The main aim of the WTO is to facilitate free trade with rule based system. Free trade leads to better resource allocation and the economic system gets long run benefits in the form of adjustment of the system to technological innovation, new production structure and changing pattern of competition. Free trade provides competition among producers and sellers; it provides new technology of production. This competition and enhanced technology lead to efficiency of producers, which further lead to reduce the cost of production. It also improves the quality of production. Trade liberalization in agriculture would increase farmers' welfare as well as economic welfare but on the other hand consumers' welfare would be adversely affected because of rise in food grain prices.

But in the regime of WTO, Indian agriculture has to face some challenges. Domestic industry will be facing competition from cheap imported goods flowing freely from other countries due to lower tariff. The non-tariff barriers like environment, health, safety, prohibition of child labor and technical standard requirement, etc. are the main restricting factors in the direction of export. So, in the field of Indian agriculture WTO has to perform a great and positive role.

World trade organization (WTO) was established on 1st January 1995 by replacing General Agreement on Tariffs and Trade (GATT), which was in existence from 1948–1994. The 8th Round of Multilateral Trade Negotiations (September, 1986–1994), popularly known as Uruguay Round led to the birth of

WTO. GATT was not an organization but a multilateral treaty, governing trade in goods only. Agriculture is out of its purview whereas the WTO has acquired a much wider scope and coverage. Its scope includes trade in goods, services as well as protection of intellectual property rights (TRIPS), trade related investment measures (TRIMs). At present, 146 countries are its members including India and China. Under the Uruguay Round, all member nations committed themselves to a widespread reduction in tariffs, removal of quantitative restriction and opening up their economies to international competition in most fields of economic activities. So, WTO is based on the principles of non–discrimination, free trade, and promotion of fair competition among the member countries.

REASONS BEHIND THE EMERGENCE OF WTO

WTO was also established for the benefit of the developed countries. World trade had undergone a structural change during the four decades since the establishment of GATT in 1948. The share of agriculture in world merchandise trade, which was 46 per cent in 1950, had declined to 13 per cent in 1987. Simultaneously, the structure of employment and the contribution of various sectors to GDP of developed countries had undergone a qualitative change. The share of this service sector in the GDP of developed countries was rapidly increasing. It ranged between 50 to 70 per cent of the GDP by 1986. The share of employment in the service sector was also increasing. For example, in USA, services represented two-third of GDP and employed over 70 per cent of work force. In the commodity sector, the competitive cost advantages that moved in favor of Japan and several others newly industrialized nations. These factors impelled developed countries under the leadership of USA to take the initiative of bringing service sector into trade negotiations.

Thus, The Uruguay Round (UR) contained the mandate to have negotiations in following areas:

1. Tariff,
2. Non-tariff measures,
3. Tropical products,
4. Natural resources based products,
5. Textile and clothing,

6. Agriculture,
7. GATT articles,
8. Safeguards,
9. Multinational Trade Negotiations (MTN) agreements and arrangements,
10. Subsidies and countervailing measures,
11. Dispute settlement,
12. Trade Related Aspects of Intellectual Property Rights (TRIPS),
13. Trade Related Investment Measures (TRIMs),
14. Functioning of GATT System (FOGS)

Thus, for the benefit of the developed countries, besides the traditional GATT subjects such as tariff and non-tariff barriers and improvement in GATT rules and disciplines on subsidies, anti-duping measures, etc. certain new steps and areas such as Trade Related Aspects of Intellectual Property Rights (TRIPs), Trade Related Investment Measures (TRIMs) and trade in services were included for the first time for negotiations.

These negotiations were expected to be concluded in four years but on account of differences in participating countries or it may be said that the difference between developed and developing countries on certain critical issues, such as agriculture, textile, TRIPS and anti-dumping measures, agreement could not be signed. To break this deadlock, Mr. Arthur Dunkel, Director General of GATT compiled a very detailed document, popularly known as Dunkle Proposals and presented it before the member countries as a compromise document. The broad objectives of these proposals were:

1. To open up the world market to agriculture, manufactured goods and services,
2. To reduce the existing tariffs by at least one –third and
3. To improve the productivity in the industrial as well as the farming sector by making use of the ongoing improvements in technology and seeds.

The Dunkle Proposal changed into the final act on December 15, 1993 and India signed the agreement along with hundred and seventeen nations on April, 1994.

The developed countries dominate WTO. About 95 per cent of the global trade income is governed by the rules and regulations of WTO. The Quad countries (USA, European Union, Canada and Japan) with their share of 80 per cent of the global trade, dominate the decision making of WTO. There is negligence of developing countries in the decision-making procedure. So through the WTO, Quad countries want to maximize the use of their resources through the huge market of developing countries and to become more and more strong.

OBJECTIVES OF WTO

As far as the objectives of WTO are concerned, there are three main objectives of WTO:

1. To help trade flow as freely as possible and remove all the conditions which distort trade.
2. To work as a forum for trade negotiation.
3. To settle the disputes.

Besides, there are also some objectives such as–expansion of trade and services, making optimum use of world resources, expansion of production and trade of goods, protection and security of environment, etc.

FUNCTIONS OF WTO

The main functions of WTO are as follows:

1. Administering WTO agreements,
2. Work as a forum of trade negotiation,
3. Handling trade disputes,
4. Monitoring national trade policies,
5. Technical assistance and training for developing countries,
6. Corporation with other international organizations.

There is a Ministerial Conference that meets at least once every two years and directs WTO. In general, ministerial conferences are the WTO's highest decision-making body, providing political direction for the organization. After the establishment of WTO that is 1st January 1995, six Ministerial Conferences took place:

1. Singapore, 1996,
2. Geneva, 1998,

3. Seattle (USA), 1999,
4. Doha (Qatar), 2001,
5. Cancun (Mexico), 2003.
6. Hong Kong (China), 2005

INTERNAL AND EXTERNAL CHALLENGES OF INDIAN AGRICULTURE

India faces some internal and external challenges and problems regarding agriculture. Farmers not only face problems in international market but they also face problems in domestic market. The increase in the food grain production has been more than the increase in population since early 1950s. So, there is a problem of excess supply over demand. During the last few years the international prices of most agro-products were more than the domestic prices. So here India was in a position of gain and expected international prices to remain stable due to reduction of subsidies by the developed countries under WTO commitments. But the result was different. The international prices have declined except paddy and now domestic prices of India are more than international prices. For instance, during 1986–1988, India's domestic price of wheat was Rs. 174 per quintal as compared with the international price of Rs. 354 per quintal. But during 2002-2003, the economic cost of India for wheat was Rs.879.16 per quintal (including Rs. 620 per quintal as MSP) as compared to the international price of Rs. 415 per quintal.

The reason behind this was that the developed countries gave earlier a planned high level of subsidies to agriculture and after containment of subsidies according to the commitment of WTO a large part of subsidies still remained and so the prices of agricultural products in the international market came down. In this regard, increase in Minimum Support Prices (MSP) of Indian agriculture also plays a vital role. Thus domestic prices of India are more than international prices. "This resulted in a threat to India's domestic market from cheap imports."[1]

As procurement prices continue an upward trend so India's competitiveness in the agro export markets has been lost. During post WTO period, the share of India's agro exports in her global exports has declined from 19.2 per cent in 1995- 1996 to 13.4 per cent in 2001-2002.[2] India's food stock of wheat and rice had increased from 30.3 million tones in January, 1995 to 58 million tones in January, 2002 against the minimum norm of 16.8 million tones.[3] As a result; WTO has become a serious challenge to several food surplus states of India.

States are still not ready to open up their boundary of internal trade in agricultural commodities that leads into considerable variations in prices between surplus states (low prices) and deficit states [high prices] but there should be price equalization among regions. The current situation is that the government is forced to mop up the surplus at the procurement price. But there is a lack of time efficiency in this policy and this forced the small poor farmers to sell their produce at low prices to traders who then resell the produce elsewhere at procurement price. So here small farmers are losers. This is the picture of one angle, which relates to person. As far as states are concerned, the developed states dominate on PDS and they sell their surplus produce at procurement rate or Minimum Support Price and the backward states remain far behind in this race.

Besides, a transport infrastructure is also not so efficient. The cost of transporting grains from Punjab to Mumbai by road is twice the cost of shipping grains from Australia and four times the cost from Bangkok.

The scope to increase agricultural production and crops is very limited. In terms of wheat and rice the possibilities of expanding production through increase in irrigation and other factors in existing areas is limited. Productivity is more or less stagnant. With the increase in input intensity and fall of water table, the growth of total factor productivity also declined resulting in to the poor condition of farmers.

The problem is compounded with the fact that export oriented farming also tends to a large gap between larger producers and smaller farmers because the small farmers who try to cultivate crops with which they are unfamiliar, are not in a position to produce such a large volume of agricultural commodities demanded by exporting companies. There is thus increased use of plantation farming or contract growing to supply exports market, and a corresponding displacement of small farmers. However, food security is affected as the one-time rural producers migrate to swell the ranks of the urban poor."[4]

AGREEMENT OF AGRICULTURE (AoA) OF WTO

From the beginning, agriculture keeps an important place in the international trade. Under GATT Act, 1947, agriculture was the highly protected sector in the developed countries. US and the nations of European Union (EU) subscribe heavy subsidies to their farmers for agriculture. So the price of grains and other agricultural products becomes lower than its real cost. But on the other hand the economic condition of developing countries is not that much strong, so they cannot provide so many subsidies to their farmers resulting in higher prices of agricultural produce in comparison to developed countries. So their products have not been competed with the products of U.S. and EU in the international market. As a result, the agricultural exports of the developing countries suffered a lot. In this condition, developing nations impose heavy import duties on their import to save their farmers from international competition. But AoA of WTO recognizes free and market oriented trading system in agriculture. The developed world have been putting pressure on the developing and the third world countries to liberalize their agriculture field that is to reduce subsidies and to reduce tariffs, etc. whereas in practice the subsidies on agriculture are even much higher in USA and EU than in developing countries.

It is really strange that the developed countries want to protect the interest of their farmers who account for 4 to 6 per cent of their total working population, while they insist that developing countries should not protect the interest of their farmers who account for 40 to 60 per cent of their working population. Such logical inconsistency was vehemently opposed by developing countries. So agriculture has turned out to be the most difficult to negotiate on. The developing countries are against any rapid liberalization of trade in agricultural product because sudden reduction in tariff would flood the domestic market with foreign goods, which will only lead to large-scale resentment. The fear of India and other developing countries is linked to food security and the livelihood security of the vast number of people who depend on agriculture. The developed countries hold supremacy in WTO. The voice of developing countries is suppressed in this great organization. But in recent years the third world countries such as India, China, Brazil, South Africa, Argentina, Mexico are united on agriculture issue and that is also a main cause due to which Cancun Conference (2003) of WTO has not achieved success. It was decided at Doha (Qatar) that the USA and EU should stop subsidies to their farmers and vice versa developing countries should reduce import duties in their country. But in practice instead of reducing subsidies the developed countries had been increasing their subsidies continuously by one way or another. In view of the intransigent attitude of the European Union and USA, the Cancun Conference ended without any progress on the Doha Deceleration.

The agricultural negotiations are difficult because of the wide range of views and interests among member governments, the large number of active participants and the complexity of many issues. The aim is to contribute to further liberalization of agricultural trade, allowing countries to compete on quality and price rather than on the size of their subsides. That is particularly the case for many developing countries whose economy depends on an increasingly diverse range of primary and processed agricultural products, exported to an increasing variety of markets, including to other developing countries.

In this concern, there are three important pillars–

1. Market Access

Cutting tariffs, expanding tariff–quotas and various flexibility for these, the main aim of WTO is to provide a big market through free trade. As far as market access is concerned, Agreement on Agriculture requires that the existing non-tariff barriers in agriculture, which are considered trade distorting, are to be abolished and converted into tariff so as to provide same level of protection and subsequently, they are to be progressively reduced. In cases where tariff bindings are either very high or tariffication was not done completely, current market access has to be maintained as the amount of export to other countries at preferential tariff rate. The Market Access has been fixed at 5 per cent for developed countries and 4 per cent for developing countries. Thus, developed countries will have to import five per cent of product of domestic consumption whereas in the context of developing countries it is 4 per cent. But this process is not applied in this sphere of traditional staple food of developing countries. In case of India, wheat and rice are staple foods so their import can be restricted.

Tariffication

Tariffication means conversion of all non-tariff barriers on trade such as quantitative trade restriction (Quota) into tariff. Tariff bindings are also to be reduced under this agreement. Developed countries were to reduce their tariff bindings by at least 15 per cent for each tariff line and by 36 per cent on simple unweighted average over 6 year period (1995-2000) whereas developing countries were to reduce their tariff binding by at least 10 per cent on all tariff lines and by 24 per cent on simple unweighted average over 10 year period (1995-2004). Least developed countries are exempted from tariff reductions.

India has indicated tariff binding of 100 per cent on primary agricultural goods and raw commodities such as wheat, rice, milk and cream, etc.150 per cent on processed agro commodities like cotton, etc. and 300 per cent on most edible oils. But in practice, import duty imposed by India is as per Table 1.

Table 1
Import Duties on Agricultural Products in India

(As on 2001) (Per cent)

Sl. No.	*Commodity*	*WTO's Bound Rate*	*Applied Rate*
1.	Wheat	100	50
2.	Spelt wheat	80	50
3.	Rice	70 & 80	70 & 80
4.	Pulse	100	5
5.	Maize	60 & 70	50
6.	Sugar	150	60
7.	Oilseeds	75	75
8.	Raw cotton	100	10
9.	Crude palm oil	300	65
10.	Refined palm oil	300	92.4

Source: Government of India, Economic Survey, 2001-2002.

Due to the reduction of tariff and also due to drought, the import of edible oil has increased to a great extent. India is now the world's biggest importer of edible oils, importing 44 per cent that is 4.4 million tons of the total requirements, of which the per cent of palm product is the highest. It occupies 61 per cent of total import requirement of edible oils." Edible oils have emerged as the second largest item in India's import bill after petroleum products and by 2014-15, its demand is likely to increase to 26,000,000tn (26 million tones)."[5] Thus, due to this tariffication our import bill has risen but on the other hand our exports have also risen. The cotton industry and the readymade garment industry have been increasing in the field of export at a large extent.

2. Reducing Domestic Support/Subsidies

Cutting supports that distort trade (by stimulating overproduction and artificially raising or lowering prices) and disciplining form of support that could distort trade. Subsidies are powerful weapons for developed countries. The vast agricultural subsidies of the developed and prosperous nations harm the economies of the poor countries in many ways. The domestic support/subsidies to agriculture were quantified through a measure called the Aggregate Measure of Support. These supports are divided into two categories–Exempted Support (non-trade distorting domestic support) and Non Exempted Support (traded distorting support).

AMS is the annual level of support/subsidies in monetary terms extended to agricultural sector. The Non-exempted support/subsidies are divided into two parts:

1. **Product Specific Support:** It is the market price support/ subsidies given to the producer of specific crops.
2. **Non–Product Specific Support:** These subsidies are imposed on import like power, irrigation, fertilizer, and credit.

In the case of developed countries if AMS exceeds 5 per cent of the total value of agricultural production the country is committed to reduce domestic support by 20 per cent over six years. In the case of developing countries if AMS exceeds 10 per cent of the total value of agricultural production the country is committed to reduce domestic support by 13.3 per cent over ten years. The AMS to Indian agriculture is still below 10 per cent in terms of WTO stipulation. Thus, trade-distorting support for farmers will be reduced by 20 per cent over six years for the developed countries and 13.3 per cent for the developing countries.

As far as the Exempted subsidies on non- trade distorting the domestic support measures are concerned, they have been divided into three parts:

1. **Green Box:** The Green Box Measures for subsidies on exempted from any reduction commitment which have minimal impact on trade Like research, training, pest and disease control, market intelligence, information, infrastructural services, food security, buffer stock operation, relief from natural disasters, etc. This subsidy has no upper limit. It is related to environment assistance programs.
2. **Blue Box Support:** This Blue Box subsidy is also exempted from any reduction commitment, but it has an upper limit. These types of subsidies related mainly to the developed countries. It is product-limiting subsidy and covers the fixed cost of the farmers indirectly. Subsidies under Blue Box include direct payment given to farmers in the form of deficiency payment that is the difference between the government minimum support price and market price is paid directly to the farmers.
3. **Special and Differential Box Support/Subsidy:** This support is related to the developing countries and is exempted from reduction commitment under WTO. This subsidy includes two things:
   - (i) Investment subsidy to agricultural sector on farm development work such as land leveling, shallow wells, etc.
   - (ii) Agricultural input services to low income and resource poor producers or farmers.

As regards to subsidy the developed countries have not implemented fully these things. So, it is worthwhile to mention that the developed countries have not implemented fully their commitments for reducing domestic support; rather agricultural subsidies have been increased during the post- WTO period.[6]

It is evident that all developed countries grant subsidies to their farmers on a very large level and in fact developing countries cannot afford that high level subsidy. Europe, USA and Japan do not really want any reduction in agricultural subsidies in their countries. According to a document prepared by United Nations Development Programme (UNDP) the developed countries grant $311.00 million per year [Rs. 5000 crore] per day to their farmers. The agricultural subsidies granted by the developed countries to their farmers are six times more than the developing countries. The U.S. spends $4 billion ($1,60,000 per farmer) on cotton subsidies alone. In spite of reducing the subsidies on agriculture the developed countries have been increasing it day by day. USA has even passed the act for large expansion in the amount of subsidy on agriculture by promulgating "United Nation Agriculture Act" in 2000. In this act the proposal of 80 per cent increase in agricultural subsidy has been made. In the recent Ministerial level meet of WTO at Cancun, the Indian Commerce Minister appealed to US Government (USA-$3 million per year) and also to developed countries to reduce their high level subsidies given to their agricultural sector. The high level subsidies given by developed countries should be abolished otherwise it will be very damaging and harmful for the economy of developing countries. In this situation if third world countries open their market of agricultural goods for free trade; there is decay of agriculture, animal husbandry and dairy farming of these countries.

3. Export Subsidies

Eliminating these and disciplining export credit, food aid and state trading enterprises to eliminate hidden export subsides. Export subsidies that need to be reduced as per provision of WTO are not provided in India. Regarding the prohibition of export subsidies, GATT agreement stipulates that countries like India with per capita less than $ 1000 are exempted from the removal of such subsidies for products where their share in world trade is less than 3.25 per cent.

Under the commitments of WTO, developed countries are to reduce the volume of subsidized agricultural exports by 21 per cent and the value of direct export subsidies by 36 per cent of the average base period 1986-88 within six years whereas;

developing countries are to reduce the same by 14 per cent and 24 per cent respectively within 10 years.

Table 2
Indian Exports Share

(US$ Million)

Commodity	*World*	*India*	*India's Share (Per cent)*
Rice	6,975	836	12.0
Tea & Mate	2,095	232	11.1
Spices	1,932	216	11.2
Iron ore	9,401	730	7.8
Leather manufacturers	23,124	806	3.5
Gems and Jewellery	44,470	4,815	10.8
Total	5,082,220	33,470	0.7

Source: Compiled from Economic Survey (1998-99).

CANCUN SUMMIT (MEXICO)

In this fifth Ministerial summit of the WTO in Cancun, 2003, the third world countries had united against the farm subsidies given by EU and US who are also restricting the import from developing countries through different methods. The US-EU continued their effort to split the alliance of G-21 that has mounted pressure for phasing out farm subsidies. USA announces a $750 million technical assistance package to least developed countries towards agriculture, capacity building and infrastructural development. Besides they also announced some other facilities for least developed countries and in this way, the US-EU had tried to divert the poor countries away from the alliance led by India–China–Brazil. But finally at Cancun the developing countries started to raise their voice against the dual policy of developed countries and refused to accept the dictatorship of developed nations.

HONG KONG SUBMIT (CHINA)

The sixth WTO Ministerial Conference was held in Hong Kong, China, 13-18 December 2005. 149 members were participated in the conference. In the Hong Kong conference a number of issues have been settled or partly settled.

1. Market Access

- In this direction the tariff reduction formula, 'bound' tariffs will be sorted into tiers according to how high they are so that higher tariffs can be cut more steeply.
- All countries will be given flexibility for sensitive products, details are still being negotiated.
- Developing countries are given further flexibility for 'special products' and can use a 'special safeguard mechanism' still to be developed. Delegations advocating greater flexibility for developing countries, special products have been preparing proposed indicators to be used so that these products comply with the criteria of the 2004 frame work, food security, lively hood security and rural development needs.

2. Domestic Support

- All developed countries will make substantial reduction in distorting supports and those with higher levels are to make deeper cuts from bound rates.
- As for 'Green Box' supports, currently unlimited criteria for defining supports eligible for this category will be reviewed and clarified to ensure that the supports really do not distort trade or do so minimally.
- The Blue Box supports (distorting but less so because of production limits or other criteria) will be capped; at the moment blue box has no limit. The fine print contains details but also stresses that these have to meet the long-term objective of 'substantial reductions'. On top of that in the first year each country's ceiling of permitted overall support will be cut by 20 per cent.

3. Export Subsides

- In this conference the most important agreement aimed at ending export subsides in agriculture by 2013.
- Loopholes have to be plugged to avoid hidden export subsides i.e. elimination of subsides in government supported export credit, food aid and state-sanctioned exporting enterprises.

- All forms of export subsidies for cotton will be eliminated developed countries, in 2006.
- Cotton exports from 32 less developed countries will be allowed into developed countries without duty or quotas from the commencement of the implementation period.
- In agriculture and NAMA (Non Agricultural Market Access) the ministerial conference has fleshed a significant framework for full modalities.

Thus, then Hong Kong conference ended in a healthy environment and there has been a rebalancing in favour of developing countries. Almost all of the members described the agreement as not fully meeting their expectation but most urged fellow-members to accept it as a good basis foe making progress in the negotiations. The 'bottom up' approach that is inputs coming directly from members rather than from above was praised more for contributing to the success of the conference. WTO Director-General Pascal Lamy said about the result: 'There has been a rebalancing in favour of developing countries whose interests have now been placed at the heart of our negotiations as we launched this round. And more importantly we have built the political energy necessary to advance technically during 2006, and believe me, there will be plenty to do next year. We now have enough fuel in the tank to cruise at the right negotiating attitude now.' He further added 'we have managed to put the Round back on track after a period of hibernation.'

IMPACT OF WTO ON INDIAN AGRICULTURE

The impact of WTO on Indian agriculture is positive. The market opportunity for agricultural products has been increasing. Developed countries are reducing their subsidies so their price of agricultural goods is rising. Further domestic subsidies to Indian agriculture will not be reduced. Rather more subsidies can be given because Aggregate Measure of Support (AMS) under WTO is below the upper limit of 10 per cent of agricultural product in India. The export subsidies will not affect the Indian agricultural export because Indian agriculture is out of its range. India will restrict their import in regard to their traditional staple food production. Further, during the regime of WTO the nature of Indian agriculture has also been changing so as to acquire a commercial outlook. The Protection of Plant Varieties and Farmer's Right Act, 2001, save the patent right of Indian farmers. A former can save, use, resow, exchange, share or sell his farm produce including seeds of protected variety in the same manner as before except "branded seed."[7]

On the other hand, India has to face some challenges also or it maybe said that there are some negative impacts of WTO on Indian agriculture. The high domestic subsidies, export subsidies and different tariff and non–tariff barriers in the developed countries have resulted in to a fall in global agricultural commodity price in the post-WTO period, which affect agricultural export of Indian agriculture and it has been falling down. Further, international quality standards should be maintained to survive in the global market. It is very difficult for Indian farmers. Very few big farmers will achieve this goal and this will lead to inequality.

CONCLUSION AND SUGGESTIONS

Indian agriculture has been facing large opportunities and serious challenges under WTO. But during this global era, no one remains indifferent to WTO. India is the founder member of GATT so it is not a wise step for India to go out of WTO but it is the time for India to think about alternative steps so that India can exist in global trade.

India is a predominant agricultural country, so firstly it has to give great priority to agriculture, then to agro-based industries, light and heavy industries and lastly on service sector. Raising the cropping intensity of our existing agricultural land is extremely requisite. Agricultural productivity of India can be improved by increasing public investment in irrigation, power, roads and agricultural research. India's must increase its irrigation potential through scientific watershed development that is rainwater harvesting.

It is essential for India to diversify its agricultural product. Alternative crops like oilseeds, pulses, horticulture, fruits and vegetables, which give higher returns, should be promoted. Besides, food-processing industries should also be developed. Further, special emphasis may be given for diversification of non-food crops such as dairying and poultry, etc. As far as food-processing industry is concerned, Agricultural Export Zones (AEZs) may be created under the new EXIM Policy of Central Government. On one hand, this exaggerates our agricultural export and on the other hand it also generates employment.

India should develop its marketing network so that our farmers get good market facilities and efficient levels of price.

India can increase its domestic subsidies to agriculture under Green, Blue and S and D Boxes of WTO because they are exempted from subsidies reduction.

The storage facilities should be developed so that farmers get profitable price.

Indian government should promote the use of Information Technology in agricultural sector by giving computer training to farmers due to which they can know about the latest technique of agricultural operation, latest information on agricultural commodity prices in different countries, advanced weather report, etc.

India should stand firmly on the issue of subsidies till complete abolition of farm subsidies given by U.S.-EU alliance.

India should develop a particular type of growth model through which a large percentage of workforces, which are engaged in agriculture but contributes comparatively a small part in national income (GDP) should be diverted from agriculture to other sectors.

India should develop its research work. It should develop a culture for registration of patent of their agricultural products. Due to such patent policies India may receive a lot of royalty for these plant species and medicinal plants like turmeric and neem. India should think like China on bilateral trade option instead of multilateral trade options.

Thus, with these steps and measures India can establish itself in a strong position in the sphere of agriculture as well as in global market. To develop economy on a strong base it is essential to strengthen economic foundation, which can be achieved through the right process of development. India should adopt the right strategy for development. So, India will have to accept the challenges of WTO and also benefit from its opportunities and facilities. The third world countries can unite together in order to protect and promote their interests as seen in the Cancun Ministerial Conference as well as in Hong Kong

Ministerial Conference of WTO where the rebalancing has occurred in favour of developing countries.

NOTES AND REFERENCES

1. Dhar, Biswajit (2002), "A Crop of Distortion", Economic Times, January 11.
2. Government of India (2003), Economic Survey, 2002-2003, p. 173.
3. Ibid, p. 92
4. Jaiswal, Rajesh (2003), "Implication of WTO on Various Sectors", Bihar Economic Journal.
5. The Financial Express Newsline (2000), December.
6. Paul, Ved (2000), "WTO–Challenges on Opportunities for India" The Indian Economic Association, Conference Volume.
7. Anitha, Ramanna (2001), "India's Policy on IPRS and Agriculture," Economic and Political Weekly, Volume -XXXVI, No. 51, December 22 -28, p. 4689.

WTO AGREEMENT ON AGRICULTURE–OPPORTUNITIES AND CHALLENGES

R.U. Singh and R.P. Gupta

INTRODUCTION

The birth of World Trade Organisation (WTO) is indeed a major turning point in the history of world trading system and is a trend towards globalisation of the world economy. Indian agricultural trade has been facing serious challenges under the globalisation (Madaan, 2005). In the emerging global environment, the Indian agriculture is becoming weak and getting further marginalized. Due to decline in infrastructure and withdrawal of various types of incentives being provided to the Indian agriculture sector, the Indian agriculture sector is becoming incapable of international competition in the global environment. There is also increased threat of dumping of agricultural goods in the country.

WTO: AGREEMENT ON AGRICULTURE

The Agreement on Agriculture contains provision in three broad areas of trade and agriculture policies viz. (i) market access, (ii) export subsidies and (iii) domestic support.

(i) Market Access

Market access or agricultural products is to be governed by a 'tariffs only' regime. That is to say, the agreement states that there can be no restrictions on farm trade except through tariffs. This means that non-tariff barriers such as quantitative restrictions on imports (i.e., quotas, import restrictions through permits, import licensing, etc.) as were in existence before the Agreement came into being, were to be replaced by tariffs on imports to provide the same level of protection and then were to be followed by progressive reduction of tariff level. Tariffs resulting from this "tariffication process" as well as other tariffs are to be reduced by a simple average of 36 per cent over 10 years in the case of developing countries. However, developing countries like India who had not converted their quantitative restrictions into tariffs, were allowed to have ceiling bindings which were not subjected to these reduction commitments.

Indian had bound its tariffs at 100 per cent for primary products, 150 per cent for processed products and 300 per cent for edible oils, except for certain items (comprising about 119 tariff lines), which were historically bound at a lower level in the earlier negotiations. Out of these low bound tariff lines, binding on 15 tariff lines which included skimmed milk powder, spelt wheat, corn, paddy, rice maize, millet, sorghum, rape, colza and mustard oil, fresh grapes etc. were successfully negotiated under GATT Article XXVIII in December 1999 and the binding levels were suitable revised upward to provide adequate protection to the domestic products. India has also not taken any commitment to provide minimum market access opportunities, which other countries that had terrified their QRs had to undertake to the extent of 3 per cent of its domestic consumption going upto 5 per cent at the end of the implementation period. Though India is not entitled to use the Special Safeguard Mechanism of the agreement, which can be used only by countries which had ratified, yet it can take safeguard action under the WTO agreement on safeguards if there is a surge in imports causing serious injury or if there is a threat of serious injury or if there is a threat of serious injury to the domestic products.

(ii) Exports Subsidy

Disciplines in the area of Export Subsidies required developing countries to reduce, over a period of 10 years the base period (1986-90) volume of subsidized exports by 14 per cent in volume terms and 24 per cent in budgetary outlays.

Export subsidies of the kind listed in the Agreement on Agriculture, which attract reduction commitments, are not extended in India. Also, developing countries are free to provide certain subsidies such as subsidising of exports marketing costs, internal and international transport and freight charges, etc. India is making use of these subsidies in certain schemes of Agricultural and Processed Food Products Export Development Authority (APEADA) especially for facilitating export of horticulture products.

(iii) Domestic Support

Domestic support measures, according to the agreement, are meant to identify acceptable measures of support of farmers. These measures are targeted largely at developed countries where the levels of domestic agricultural support have risen to extremely high levels. Domestic support is divided into two categories viz. (a) support with no, or minimal, distort effect on trade (often referred to as "Green Box" and "Blue Box" measures) and (b) trade distorting support (often referred to as "Amber Box" measures).

The trade distorting domestic support is measured in terms of what is called the "Total Aggregate Measurement of Support (total AMS), which is expressed as a part of percentage of the total value of agricultural output and includes both products specific and non-product specific support. Domestic support given to the agricultural sector upto 10 per cent of the total value of agricultural produce in developing countries is allowed. In other words, AMS within this limit is not subject to any reduction commitment. Obligation to Indian agriculture is not under any effect on cut in subsidies.

In India, the product-specific support is negative, while the non-products specific support i.e., subsidies on agricultural inputs, such as power, irrigation, fertilizers etc., is well below the permissible level of 10 per cent of the value of agricultural output. Therefore, India is under no obligation to reduce domestic support currently extended to the agricultural sector.

Tariff escalation (increase in tariff with successive stages of processing) block exports of value –added products from developing to the developed countries. Stringent Sanitary and Phytosanitary (SPS) measures continue to be a major barrier in diversifying exports in horticulture and meat items. Fresh commitments have therefore, to be negotiated to substantially improve market access for products of particular interest to developing countries. Since entry of new comers is difficult in the existing tariff quota (TRQ). TRQ is a trading mechanism that provides for the application of a customs duty at a certain lower rate of imports of a particular good up to a specified quantity (in quota quantity) and at a higher rate on imports of that good when it exceeds in (in-quota quantity) regime, India is demanding substantial expansion of TRQs pending their eventual abolition. It is also essential that administration of tariff quotas should become more transparent and equitable. Finally, the expectations about reductions in domestic support subsidies prevailing in the developed countries at the time of conclusion of AoA have not materialized. Market access has thus been effectives denied to developing countries.

OPPORTUNITIES FOR AGRICULTURAL EXPORTS

Though the problems for our agri-exports are numerous, but we have opportunities too and, therefore, in the light of these opportunities, we have to adopt proper policy measures so that we can reap the benefits from the process of globalisation. Our agricultural exports even within the aforementioned conditions have some interesting features, which can enable us to have better results. They are:

(i) Despite some fluctuations, a sizeable and growing demand stands for basmati rice. In recent years, the spectacular production advancement and favourable buffer stock and growing demand for basmati rice in international market enabled India increased from 5.05 lakh tons in 1990-91 to 23.98 lakh tons in 1997-98 and 49.64 lakh tons in 1998-99. But the export declined to 18.23 lakhs tons in 1999-2000, the major reasons being the protectionist policies of the developed world and rising competition from the developing countries. However, with some efforts like qualitative and processing improvement as well as proper price management we can boost up our export of basmati rice.

(ii) There exists a good demand for durum type of wheat in Egypt and West Asian markets.

(iii) In cotton, India can boost up the export of varieties of staple length. It can produce that best quality cotton. With sound change in export policy, we may be able to export at least 25 lakh bales of cotton every year.

(iv) Spices play a vital role in export of agricultural commodities. The export earning of spices increased from Rs.239 crores in 1990-91 to Rs.794 crores in 1995-96, Rs.1633 crores in 1998-99 and Rs.1702 crores in 1999-2000. Even in terms of dollars the increase has been recorded from $ 339 million in 1997-98 to $ 393 million in 1999-2000, accounting for 7.2 per cent of our total agri-exports. In future also, they can be an important source of export promotion.

(v) India is the second largest producer of fruits and vegetables in the world. It has a comparative advantages in growing a variety fruits and vegetables throughout the year because of diverse agro-climate conditions and availability of skilled cheap labour, while in many growing fruits and vegetables is a costly affair for the. The export of fruits and vegetables increased from Rs. 2.16 crores in 1990-91 to Rs. 1067 crores in 1997-98 and Rs. 1212 crores in 1999-2000. However, the trend has been fluctuating and the export of these commodities amounted to only Rs. 931 crores in 1998-99. Which invites proper policy measures, quality control and proper processing and packing activities.

CHALLENGES FOR AGRICULTURAL EXPORT

Despite these opportunities or the features of our agricultural exports, a smooth trend of export growth of agricultural and allied products is still not visible. On the one side, we have fluctuating trend of agricultural production and exportable surplus and on the other, changes in the world market situations have a definite impact on our exports. Being tagged with the global market, our exports have also to bear the brunt of international market situation. The slow down in the world economy has led to a declining trend in our exports in recent years.

As far as India is concerned, it has been possible to maintain without any hindrance the domestic policy instruments for promotion of agriculture or for subsidized targeted supply of food grains. The domestic policy measures like the operation of the Minimum Support Price (MSP), the Public Distribution

System (PDS) as well as provision of input subsidies to agriculture have not in any way been constrained by the Agreement. In fact, certain provisions contained in Annex-2 of the Agreement (popularly known as the 'Green Box') give us the flexibility to provide support for research and extension services, pest and disease control, marketing and promotion services, infrastructure development, payments made for relief from natural disasters payments under regional assistance programme for disadvantaged regions and payments under environmental programmes.

In the recent announcements, a tax holiday for five years and 30% deduction of profits income for the next five years to the enterprises engaged in the integrated business of handling, transportation and storage of food grains has been given.

As agriculture constitutes a vital segment of the Indian economy, finding greater market access for India's agricultural products, especially in the developed country markets, is one of protection of the interests of domestic farmers and their livelihood as well as the need for export maximization is the guiding principles for the ongoing negotiations. But several clauses of the WTO itself and especially the provision related to Intellectual Property Rights (IPR) provides enough scope to these countries to hamper the agriculture in developing countries like India. The entry of multinational into agricultural sector with IPR would mean a substantial control over entire range of seeds, fertilizers, pesticides and research. They will not only control important inputs and research but also have command on investment, production distribution and marketing. By this command, they can also command, control and regulate the agro-based industrial sector, agro-trade sector and agro-services. In other words, in the name of trade liberalisation and globalisation, we are moving towards monopolisation and our commanding heights are gradually being reduced.

The Transnational Corporations (TNCs) have also strong hold food items like coffee, cocoa, tobacco, banana, sugar, wheat and rice etc. and they influence not only the international exports but also the domestic markets. The globalisation of agri-business will lead them to enter the domestic market and their free entry will provide more challenges than opportunities to the domestic companies in the competitive market environment. Challenges in the sense that these companies have strong financial, technical, market information and administrative network, which is easily compete with our domestic companies and throw them away from the native market. For example, improved and hybrid seed producing MNCs can complete and drive out domestic seed producing companies like National Seeds Corporation etc. and thus can capture the domestic market too. However, despite such challenges, they also provide good opportunities for the domestic companies in improving the quality of production, in setting up of agro-based industries, in providing employment opportunities and spreading new technology etc. All these opportunities must be taken timely and utilised by domestic companies so that they can compete well in global trade, otherwise they will fail to reap the benefit.

Development in the field of biotechnology that is being developed by the West may also pose a serious threat to agriculture, live stock breeding, forestry etc. Some of the large industry have purchased bio-technology farms and are carrying out research in the field of tissue culture, monoclonal antibodies any hybriodomas and gene splicing (recombinant DNA Transfer) to innovate new products and process. Knowledge concerning developments in the field of bio-technology is kept as exclusive preserve of the western countries which may cause a lot of harm to export of farm products of developing nations like India.

Thus, there are several challenges, posed by the free flow of goods and services under the policy of globalisation adopted by the new GATT accords and the formation of WTO. But even after such possibilities the process of globalisation is irreversible. In the contemporary world situation, there is no alternative but to adjust to the realities. We have to search the better opportunities and ways for the export promotion of agricultural commodities where we can have better chances with little efforts.

SUGGESTIONS

In order to reap the benefit of globalisation and move into the international marketing arena cautiously and surely, the following suggestion can be looked into:

(i) Huge investment in agriculture is needed to boost up the productivity and production in general and in particular special emphasis needs to be given on the promotion of production and productivity of the selected export-oriented agriculture crops.

(ii) The Government should assume a more dynamic role in the field of agri-marketing.

(iii) Encouragements to the exports of agricultural commodities are unique in the world (due to geographical features) and identification of the commodities where there is a real surplus for exports is also essential.

(iv) Setting up of export-oriented farms for selected agricultural crops and spices by offering incentives to small farmers. Pooling of their operational holdings is also necessary.

(v) Promotion of value-added products is also the need of the hour. Deliberate planned efforts are necessary to bring away from the traditional form of exporting in bulk. Production and promotion of value-added products would help in earning more foreign exchange while at the same time; efforts should be made to tackle the problem of increasing production and productivity beyond certain levels.

(vi) Special encouragements should also be given to the 100 per cent export-oriented units. For setting up such units, the Government can offer duty free import of capital goods and other requirements.

(vii) Emphasis must be given to value addition by growing thrust to agro-processing industries.

(viii) Air-cargo transportation facilities need to be stepped up to meet the delivery of scheduled products with speed.

(ix) A common brand name for export promotion of all agricultural products and individual logo for specific commodity/product is highly necessary.

(x) Facilities for the testing of packages, etc. should also be provided to the exports. Stringent measures should be adopted to see that he material being exported is of desired quality. It would do more damage to export in the long run if poor quality is exported. Here, Export Inspection Council of India should be involved closely and the organisation needs to be further strengthened.

(xi) Surveys and analytical studies on agricultural marketing should be conducted, so that appropriate policy adjustments and refinements could be made for better integration with international market forces.

(xii) Systematic planning is essential for agricultural exports. Product-wise policy is essential to bring out the necessary consistency in export policy over a long-term period. An effective system of market intelligence and research on agricultural exports needs to be developed.

Besides these recommendations, greater co-operation is needed between Central and State Governments to plan agricultural production in a proper way for domestic production and export promotion. We must move on the path of market-friendly export-oriented growth strategy. And finally we can say that the nature of markets and institutions, industrial organisation and structures and social relations of production as well as the principle and policy of international trade have been transformed dramatically and India's role to the new world order is going to be decided by its response to these changes particularly to the increasing globalisation of economic process.

REFERENCES

Bhattacharya, B. (2001), "Exim Policy–2001-02: India Comes to Age", *Yojana,* Vol. 45, May, p. 7.

Government of India (1999-2000), Economic Survey, Ministry of Finance, p. 146 and S. 88.

Government of India (2000-01), Economic Survey, Ministry of Finance, p. 107.

Nasurudeen, P. and Balkrishnan (1996), "Agricultural Exports: Prospects and Problems", The Bihar Journal of Agricultural Marketing, October–December, p. 326.

Government of India (1997-2000), Ninth Five-Year Plan Vol. 1, p. 5.

Rao, C. Hanumantha (1994), Agricultural Growth, Rural Poverty and Environment Degradation in India, Oxford University Press, New Delhi.

Ravi Kumar, K.N. Raja, V.T. and Krishnan Kumar, K.V. (1997): "Globalisation and Liberalisation of Indian Agricultural Marketing System- A Critical Note", BJAM, Vol. V, No. 3, September, p. 346.

Panchmukhi, V.R. (2000), "World Trade Organization, India's Challenge and Perspective," *Indian Economic Association*, Conference Volume, pp. 7-8.

Chadha, G.K. (2000), "Indian Economy under the WTO Regime, Happenings, Non-Happenings and Missing Links," *Indian Economic Association*, Conference Volume, pp. 13-15.

Madaan, D.K. (2005), Indian Economic Association, Conference Volume, Vishakhapatnam.

EXPERIENCES ON IMPLEMENTATION OF AGREEMENT ON AGRICULTURE UNDER WTO: IMPLICATIONS AND CONCERNS FOR INDIA

Lokbardhan Gupta and K.B. Gupta

INTRODUCTION

The General Agreement on Trade and Tariff (GATT) and World Trade Organization (WTO) are considered to be extremely successful over the last 58 years at reducing tariff and other trade barriers among countries. GATT started it journey in 1947 with only 23 members on board and the number of member countries has increased continuously over the years. After the establishment of WTO in 1995, the number of member countries further increased and at present has reached to 149, accounting for more than 97 per cent of global trade. The WTO is not only an organization for liberalizing international trade but also a negotiating forum where the member countries sort out the trade related problems that they face with each other. WTO covers a set of rules (in terms of various agreements), negotiated and signed by a large number of trading nations, which provide legal ground-rules for international commerce. WTO also helps to settle disputes among the nations arising out of their conflicting interests.

The present paper is divided into eight sections. Section 2 of this paper discusses the basic principles of WTO, followed by a listing of major agreements under WTO in Section 3. The evolving scenario in WTO era and the objectives of the present study are presented in Section 4. Section 5 discusses the major provisions of Agreement on Agriculture (AoA) while Section 6 analyzes the implementation related issues of AoA. The learning from the Sixth Ministerial Conference of WTO and its implications for Indian agriculture are highlighted in Section 7. The lessons learnt through the present study are presented in the final section.

BASIC PRINCIPLES OF WTO

The main principles of the WTO are discussed below:

A. Trade Without Discrimination

- Most-Favoured Nation Treatment: Under this, a country cannot normally discriminate between its trading partners. If a member country offers a benefit or a tariff concession to another WTO member (for example, a reduction in its import tariff for agricultural implements), it will have to offer the same tariff concession to all the other WTO members as well. However, countries are free to give developing and least developed countries special access to their markets or restrict trade of certain commodities from certain countries, if it is found that the specific country is trading certain products unfairly.
- National Treatment: Under WTO system, the imported products (and services) should be treated at par with locally produced products after it enters the domestic market.

B. Achieving Freer Trade Through Negotiation

WTO strives to achieve freer trade gradually through negotiation. Since the creation of GATT in 1947, eight rounds of trade negotiation have taken place and a ninth round, under Doha Development Agenda (DDA), is currently under progress.

C. Predictability Through Binding and Transparency

Under WTO, countries have agreed to bind their tariff rates for different products. This binding tariff rate is essentially the maximum limit for a product beyond which the country will not charge custom duty for import. The bound rate of tariff provides the predictability and transparency to the other countries, encouraging investment in the domestic country. This may result in more job creation and consumers may also get the benefits of competition in terms of larger available choices for products and lower prices.

D. Promoting Fair Competition

WTO rules on non-discrimination (MFN and national treatment), dumping (when a company exports at below its cost of production for gaining market share in other country) and various types of subsidies basically promote open, fair and undistorted competition.

E. Encouraging Development and Economic Reforms in Countries

To encourage development and economic reforms, developing and least developing countries have been given greater flexibility in terms of time to implement various WTO agreements. Based on a ministerial decision at the end of Uruguay Round, many developed countries have started to allow duty-free and quota-free imports for almost all products from least-developed countries (like Bangladesh, Nepal, etc.).

MAJOR AGREEMENTS UNDER WTO

The major agreements under WTO are listed below:

- Agreement on Agriculture (AoA)
- Agreement on Application of Sanitary and Phytosanitary Measures (SPS)
- Agreement on Technical Barriers to Trade (TBT)
- Agreement on Textiles and Clothing (ATC)
- Agreement on Anti-dumping Measures
- Agreement on Pre-shipment Inspection
- Agreement on Rules of Origin
- Agreement on Subsidies and Countervailing Measures (SCM)
- Agreement of Safeguards
- Agreement on Trade Related Investment Measures (TRIMS)
- Agreement on Import Licensing Procedures
- Customs Valuation Methods
- Agreement on Trade-Related Aspects of Intellectual Property Rights (TRIPS)

- General Agreement on Trade in Services (GATS)
- Understanding Rules and Procedures Governing the Settlement of Disputes.

There is no pick and choose policy under WTO. Any country, which is a member of WTO or wants to become member of WTO, has to accept all the above agreements. However, there are two plurilateral agreements in existence, which basically cover the issues in which only a small group of countries are interested. The two plurilateral agreements (not signed by all the members) are given below:

- Agreement on Trade in Civil Aircraft (30 members)
- Agreement on Government Procurement (28 members)

EVOLVING SCENARIO AND OBJECTIVES OF THE STUDY

The rule based approach on principles of trade without discrimination, freer trade through negotiation, predictability through binding and transparency, promoting fair competition and encouraging development and economic reform schemes of WTO has resulted in increased trade and lower level of import tariff in the world. Tariff on manufactured products has fallen from a trade-weighted average of 35 per cent before GATT came into existence in 1947 to about 6.4 per cent at the start of Uruguay Round. The volume of trade among WTO members in 2000 has reached about 25 times its 1950 volume. It has been proved by researchers that growth in international trade although increased more slowly than world GDP in the early years of the GATT; it has outpaced world GDP growth in recent years since middle of the decade 1990s (Crowley, 2003). However, its impact on different sectors of economy has been a widely debated issue. The different stakeholders like policy makers, industry, farmers, researchers and general public are not unanimous on types and scale of impact on specific sectors because many times their opinions are based on mere perception and partial information.

The objective of the present study is to analyze the various provisions of Agreement on Agriculture, which is of prime importance for the country like India. Based on the experiences with the implementation of Agreement on Agriculture so far under WTO, implications and concerns for India have also been presented in the paper.

AGREEMENT ON AGRICULTURE (AoA)

Agreement on Agriculture mainly addresses three issues, namely market access, domestic support, and export subsidies. Important provisions under AoA are discussed below:

A. Market Access

Market access is the extent to which a country allows the import of foreign products. Countries have traditionally used both tariffs and non-tariff measures to regulate imports of agricultural goods. The market access provisions aim to regulate and lower protectionist barriers to trade. The three major provisions of market access in WTO, relevant to agricultural trade are:

- *Tariffication, Tariff Bindings and Reductions*
  - (i) All non-tariff barriers (NTBs such as quantitative restrictions, canalization, licensing etc.) had to be replaced by equivalent tariffs and all tariffs are to be bound. The tariffs should work out to be equivalent to the barriers that were in place in the base reference period of 1986-88.
  - (ii) Tariffs had to be reduced by 36 per cent with a minimum reduction of 15 per cent per tariff line on average over six years for developed countries. The developing countries had to reduce the tariff by 24 per cent with a minimum reduction of 10 per cent per tariff line on average over ten years. The least developed countries did not have any commitment to reduce the tariff level.
- *Minimum and Current Access*

  The countries had to maintain minimum market access commitments as a share of domestic consumption (1-4% for developing and 3-5% for developed countries) for products subject to tariffication.
- *Special Safeguards (SSG) Provision*

  AoA established rules for application of additional duties (special safeguards) up to 1/3rd of normal duties if imports surge or the prices fall below trigger price levels for products subject to tariffication.

B. Domestic Support

Domestic support is the annual monetary support given by the government to agricultural producers either for the production of specific agricultural products, or in more general forms such as in infrastructure and research. The AoA classifies supports into three main categories as shown in Table 1.

Table 1
Various Categories of Domestic Support under AoA

- 'Green Box' supports are deemed to be minimally trade distorting. They are acceptable within the AoA and are not subject to any reduction commitments.
- 'Blue Box' supports are a special category created to house the EU's and US' production limiting programmes. These include EU's land-set aside programmes and the US' deficiency payments. They too are not subject to reductions.
- 'Amber Box' supports are deemed to be trade distorting and are subject to reduction commitments. These supports are measured by the Aggregate Measure of Support (AMS) index.

AoA also includes 'De minimis' clause, which allows countries to maintain a certain level of AMS. These come in two forms, product specific de minimis-related support and non-product specific de minimis support. Special and differential treatment allows developing country governments to provide input and investment subsidies.

C. Export Subsidy

The agreement establishes a ceiling on both the value and the volume of subsidized exports of agricultural products over the base period 1986-90. Export credit guarantee and export promotion programmes are not included as export subsidies. The agreement requires developed countries to cut the value of export subsidies by 36% and to reduce volume of subsidized exports by 21% over the period of 6 years. The base period is 1986-90. Countries may keep their existing export support programmes but may not introduce new programmes. Developing countries must reduce the value of subsidies by 24%

and volume of subsidized exports by 14% over 10 years with no reduction applying to the LDC's.

EXPERIENCES WITH IMPLEMENTATION OF AoA

A. Market Access

Despite commitments made under AoA, tariffs on farm products continue to remain very high. The use of 1986-88 as base period for conversion of non-tariff barriers resulted in much higher tariff equivalents. Although, there are bound tariff levels for all the agricultural products, the binding rate is too often quite high and hence do not result in any significant decrease in import tariff for agricultural products. In fact, for most of the developing countries, the applied rate of import tariff (actual tariff rate applicable) is much lower than the binding rate. The average maximum allowed tariff under WTO for countries in certain regions are shown in Figure 1, which reaches as high as about 130 per cent for Non-EU Western European Countries.

Figure 1
Region-wise World bound Agricultural Tariff Averages,

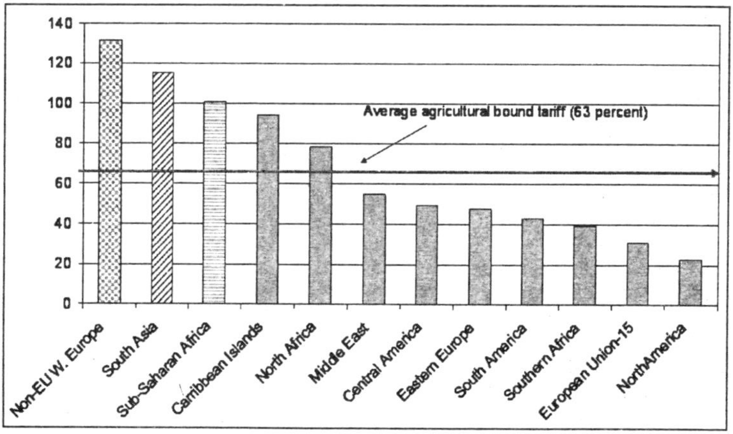

Source: Sharma, V.P. (2004)

The average bound tariffs for EU, Japan, Korea and India for agricultural products are 31, 51, 66 and 114 per cent respectively. Average binding rate on certain commodities such as dairy, meat, sugar, and certain grains are quite high. Applied tariff rate are although lower than binding rate, they are quite high for many products, affecting the free trade. There is also no clear indication about which formula to be used for reduction in tariff rate over the years. Different formulae have been proposed by certain countries.

B. Domestic Support

Domestic support is the most difficult issue to handle under AoA. There are so many exceptions and possibility of manipulations on domestic support front, which may give undue advantage to domestic producers in many countries. 89 per cent of domestic support is concentrated in three countries, EU (44 per cent), USA (24 per cent) and Japan (21 per cent).

The idea behind categorization of domestic support into green, blue and amber boxes was to identify what types of domestic supports have minimal or maximum distortion effect on international trade. Supports under Green and Blue Boxes were allowed to continue as they have less trade-distortion effect. However, lately many countries are devising innovative ways to shift their domestic support from Amber Box to Green Box, resulting in either little or no decrease, or sometimes even increase in total volume of domestic support given to farmers compared to base period level. The shift in domestic support from one box to others in two major countries EU and USA are shown in Figure 2.

It can be seen in Figure 2, that domestic support under green box was non-existent in the base period in EU, but has gone up to US $ 25 billion. The overall domestic support in case of USA has increased over the years. Although based on WTO guidelines, there is no problem in increasing the domestic support under green box but ultimately the purpose of the free trade gets defeated through these manipulations. Supports under green box, although are less trade distorting compared to amber box, they cannot be said to be completely free from trade distortion effect.

C. Export Subsidies

Export subsidies given in agricultural products are of the order of US $ 4020.2 Million. 90.3 per cent of export subsidy in

Figure 2
Shift of Domestic Support from One Box to Others

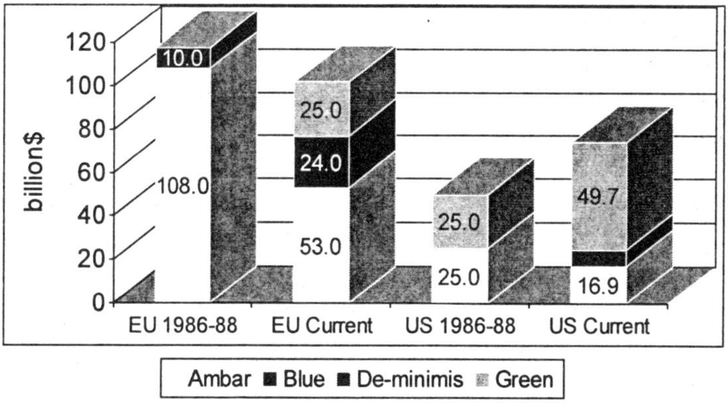

Source: Sharma, V.P. (2004)

agricultural products is concentrated in EU. The shares of Switzerland, USA and Norway in export subsidy are 4.4, 2.2 and 1.2 per cent respectively. The export subsidies are mainly going to the products like dairy products, bovine meat and wheat. The shares of commodities in global expenditure on export subsidies are shown in Table 2.

Table 2
Share of Commodities in Global Expenditure on Export Subsidies

Dairy products	33
Bovine meat	21
Wheat	11
Other coarse grain	2
Fruit and Vegetables	2
Others	31

Source: OECD, 2001

HONG KONG MINISTERIAL DECLARATION (2005) AND IMPLICATIONS FOR INDIAN AGRICULTURE

The topmost decision-making body of the WTO is the Ministerial Conference, which has to meet at least every two years. The Sixth WTO Ministerial Conference was held in Hong Kong, China during 13–18 December 2005. Some of the major issues covered under this conference related to AoA and their implications for Indian agriculture are presented below.

A. Market Access

Developing country members will have the flexibility to self-designate an appropriate number of tariff lines as Special Products (SP) guided by indicators based on the criteria of food security, livelihood security and rural development. Developing country members will also have the right to have recourse to a Special Safeguard Mechanism based on import quantity and price triggers, with precise arrangements to be further defined. Special Products and the Special Safeguard Mechanism will be an integral part of the modalities and the outcome of negotiations in agriculture.

India being among the countries having highest average applied tariff, any negotiation that has impact on applied tariff is going to be serious issue for agriculture sector. Selection of Special Products and Safeguard Mechanism for various products are very crucial. However, in India there are more than hundred agricultural products, which are candidates for Special Product category based on the criteria of food security, livelihood security and rural development. A suitable mechanism will have to be developed to designate certain Special Products, where India wants to have more cushion, keeping in view of several important issues such as existing socio-political situation in the areas where these products are produced, cost of production, substitutes available, value addition, investment requirement, market structure including price fluctuation, consumer perception, etc.

B. Domestic Support

On domestic support front, Hong Kong declaration agreed to have three bands for reductions in final bound total AMS and in the overall cut in trade-distorting domestic support, with higher linear cuts in higher bands. In both cases, the member with the highest level of permitted support will be in the top band, the two members with the second and third highest levels of support will be in the middle band and all other members, including all developing countries, will be in the bottom band. In addition, developed countries in the lower bands with high relative levels of final bound total AMS will make an additional effort in AMS reduction.

However, it may take a long time for achieving the positive impact of liberalization on domestic support front because the formula for reduction of domestic support is yet to be finalized and the implementation schedule is also not yet decided. To achieve the potential of increase in trade after reduction of domestic support in developed countries, India will have to investigate her strengths in agricultural competitiveness at different sub-sector level vis-à-vis the same for other developing countries. It is not unlikely that in future the developed countries may insist on linking the reduction in their domestic support to reduction in tariff and non-tariff barriers in other developing countries, presently existing in the name of food safety and environment protection. India will have to see whether it can withstand a lower tariff rate regime. Public investment in India is just about 0.3 per cent of national GDP for agriculture (Sardana, 2005). For Indian agriculture to survive in free trade regime, these numbers will have to be revised considerably upward so as to maintain the necessary infrastructure for supporting agriculture and maintaining/ enhancing its competitiveness.

There has been some convergence concerning the reductions in Final Bound Total AMS, the overall cut in trade-distorting domestic support and in both product-specific and non product-specific de minimis limits. It is good development provided the blue box and other indirect subsidies are transparent in nature and calculated properly. India will have to ensure that fertilizer, irrigation, power, pesticides, procurement and marketing related subsidies are monitored closely in these markets and they should not affect prices of agriculture inputs in their domestic markets.

C. Export Subsidies

Hong Kong declaration agreed to ensure the parallel elimination of all forms of export subsidies and to discipline all export measures with equivalent effect, to be completed by the end of 2013. This will be achieved in a progressive and parallel manner, to be specified in the modalities so that the end of the first half of the implementation period itself realizes a substantial part.

The words "progressive and parallel manner" raise some doubts about the likely intentions. It may mean that the export subsidies will not go unless developing countries also offer something in return. India needs to be ready with its negotiation strategy in terms of "progressive and parallel manner".

LESSONS LEARNT

The Agreement on Agriculture (AoA) with its three pillars (market access, domestic support and export subsidy) was an historic achievement of WTO and did help in reducing the tariff levels in different parts of the world. But many countries have devised new ways of non-tariff barriers that are hampering the free and fair trade in agricultural products. Export subsidies are mainly limited to very few countries especially EU, Switzerland, USA and Norway in products like dairy products, bovine meat, wheat, coarse grain, etc. It is heartening that EU has agreed to remove the export subsidies by 2013 progressively. But the term 'parallel manner' is little disturbing and needs to be clarified and strategy should be prepared at the national level accordingly. Not much progress has been made so far at domestic support front, which is the most contentious issue under AoA. The aggregate level of domestic support in many countries has not come down. In fact, it has even increased in many countries as pointed out earlier. There are many loose ends on domestic support front, which need to be tackled suitably, if countries are really serious about long term success of AoA. Support under green box should also be capped at certain level, otherwise the member countries will continue to manipulate the domestic support from amber box to green box, resulting in no significant decrease in aggregate level of domestic support at the respective countries level. This will seriously affect the free and fair trade as envisaged in basic principles of WTO.

There is a serious need to strengthen the AoA discipline by addressing their weaknesses. Non-trade concerns about agriculture should also be given due care so as to achieve societal objectives like rural development, food security, poverty alleviation, etc. But it should be done in such a way that it is well targeted, transparent and minimally trade distorting. It is a great solace that Hong Kong Ministerial Conference has tried to touch some of these issues in its final declaration. Let us hope for a better environment for international trade of agricultural product, based on free and fair trade rules, where efficiency is rewarded but at the same time, its human face is also not lost.

REFERENCES

Crowley, Meredith A. (2003), "An Introduction to the WTO and GATT", Economic Perspectives, 4Q/2003, Federal Reserve Bank of Chicago.

International Trade Centre, Geneva. Various International Trade Statistics.

Sardana, Vijay (2005), Hong Kong WTO Ministerial Declaration and its Implications for Indian Agriculture, New Delhi: CITA.

Sharma, V.P. (2004), "Notes on WTO", presented in a Management Development Programme at IIM, Ahmedabad.

World Trade Organization (2005), "Understanding the WTO", book available at www.wto.org.

SECTION - II

WTO AND GLOBAL MARKET

WTO REGULATIONS, EMPLOYMENT AND EXPORTS FROM INDIA'S IT SECTOR: PROBLEMS AND PROSPECTS

Vikram Chadha and Neeru Chadha

The world is much tenuously integrated now since 1990s than during 1970s and 80s. There is much freer trade transactions, capital and factors movement and technology trade and transfer all across the globe. World exports of goods and services, which averaged $2.3 billion a year during 1983-92, more than tripled to an estimated $7.6 billion in 2001. Thus demand for cross border finance and financial liberalization facilitated inter-country capital movements. Global gross capital flows in 2000 amounted to $7.5 trillion, representing a four-fold increase over that in 1990 (Hausler, 2002).

Globalisation and integration has resulted in integration of factor and commodity markets, making factor and commodity prices to largely converge internationally. The WTO norms and regulations made it mandatory for the member countries to dilute and finally eliminate tariff and non-tariff trade barriers. By forcing the lowering and liquidating of tariff levels to the binding tariff levels of 5 per cent, most of the member countries have witnessed trade explosion. Though in countries like India, the average weighted rates of tariff are still higher than the binding tariff levels, yet the peak custom rates has been brought down to 15 per cent from a high of 300 per cent in 1990, which is a no mean reform.

Besides, the globalisation of services in the health, insurance, banking, transport and financial services, the developments in the field of information technology (IT) including computers, telecommunications and the consequent development of the knowledge economy, has further accentuated the global integration of the modernizing economies (Freeman and Soete, 1997). It is in this context of the increasing global integration and trade, this paper aims at analyzing India's export performance and employment trends in its IT sectors.

KNOWLEDGE ECONOMIES AND INTANGIBLE SOURCES OF GROWTH

Modern developed societies have increasingly become information based knowledge societies, where products and services have become progressively information intensive and investments have become predominantly intangible-dependent upon the competencies of diverse kinds. This knowledge and information accumulation has been taking place through sustained investment in science and technology (S&T), research and development (R&D) and in the process of learning and spread of information and knowledge. Affluent and industrialized countries, which possess a monolithic stock of knowledge and specialized human capital, have far outpaced other countries on the development path. They have entered the stage of intellectual capitalism where knowledge and information lead to higher generation and accumulation of material capital. Their sources of growth have become more intangible and immaterial, and that's why the modern growth theory incorporates human capital, information, knowledge, know-how, S & T and R & D, as explicitly endogenous factors in economic growth, unlike the neo-classical theory, which treated them at best, exogenously determined (Rivera-Batiz and Romer, 1991).

INDIA AS A FAST EMERGING KNOWLEDGE AND INFORMATION ECONOMY

In order to achieve economic and technological self-reliance, the Indian Government has been spending huge amounts on R&D and S&T activities since Independence. Besides this, a vast chain of engineering, scientific and research institutes has been set up to groom home trained S&T manpower.

The national R&D expenditure was merely Rs. 139.64 crore in 1970-71, i.e. 0.33 per cent of GNP, which increased to about

Rs.18 thousand crore in 2001, i.e. 0.88 per cent of GNP. Whereas the Ministry of Information Technology apportioned 1 per cent of the national R&D expenditure; Department of Biotechnology spent 1.3 per cent; Department of S&T spent over 4 per cent and the Council of Scientific and Industrial Research shared about 10 per cent of the national R&D expenditure in 1999 (Government of India, 2002).

Among the most knowledge intensive industries, Rs. 520.26 crore were spent on R&D in the biotechnology industry in 1999, Rs. 377.50 crore in drugs and pharmaceutical industry, Rs. 200 crore in electrical and electronics industries and Rs. 85.96 crore in telecommunication industry, while the IT industry spent only Rs. 38.35 crore on R&D.

A knowledge economy has to be built around the development of knowledge, training and skill formation, instructions and education, particularly scientific and technical education at higher levels. To strengthen the knowledge base of the Indian economy, expenditure on education has been spontaneously scaling up since the beginning of planning era. Whereas national education expenditure zoomed up from Rs. 114.4 crore in 1950, to a whopping Rs. 61148.8 crore in 1999, the expenditure on university and higher education spiraled up from Rs. 1106.9 crore in 1985, to Rs. 6771.19 crore in 1999, i.e. 14 per cent of the total education expenditure. As a result of the increasing education expenditure, particularly in sciences, the commercially active stock of S&T personnel in the country expanded from 62.25 lakh in 1996 to 72.04 lakh in 1999, out of which 11.5 lakh were engineering personnel (Government of India, 2002).

With growing investment in S&T, education and research and development and in grooming domestically trained and skill S&T manpower, India is strongly emerging as an impeccable knowledge economy. The massive stock of S&T manpower, which is applying scientific and technical knowledge and innovation in all spheres of the productive sectors, is the backbone of the knowledge base of the country. Ostensibly, perceptible developments in the field of information and communication technologies (ICT), software and telecommunications and their application in growth steering sectors have revolutionized the value added growth of various sectors.

ICT INDICATORS IN THE INDIAN ECONOMY

India's prowess in the field of ICT testifies India's inimitable stake as a fast emerging knowledge and information economy, which is reflected in its ICT indicators. Total number of cellular subscribers in India increased from 76.7 thousand in 1995 to 64.32 lakh in 2001. Number of telephone subscribers escalated from 2.84 crore to 4.50 crore during 1999-01. Number of Internet users bolstered up from 28 lakh to 70 lakh and the number of PCs from 33 lakh to 60 lakh during the same period.

That's why the recent World Bank Report, 2005 on India's development as a knowledge economy acknowledges the potential of India's knowledge base in terms of innovativeness, ICT growth and education. It accepts India as the impending hub of IT and R&D, and about 100 MNCs have recently set up their R&D units in the areas of biotechnology, electronics and computer software (World Bank, 2005).

EXPORTS FROM THE INDIAN IT SECTOR

With the strengthening of the scientific and technical knowledge, the spectacular growth of the IT sector in India was a natural outcome. The IT industry grew at an incredible rate of 50 per cent per annum during the 1990s and established India as an exporter of knowledge intensive services. From a modest revenue of $195 million in 1990, it generated a mind-blowing revenue of $8.3 billion by 2001, out of which 75 per cent, i.e. $6.2 billion were earned by way of exports. In 2003, it generated a total revenue of Rs. 79337 crore.

The Indian software industry may be just 2 per cent of the $400 billion global software industry but India's share in the global market for customized software, i.e. outsourced software development, is around 18.5 per cent in 1999. That's why the National Taskforce in IT and Software Development (NTITSD) project the Indian software industry's growth to $85 billion by 2008, out of which $50 billion would come by exports of IT products.

About 44 per cent of the software development in India is on offshore basis. Indian software companies are developing high-end packaged software including financial and accounting software for banks and marketing industries including petrochemicals, steel, chemicals and refineries, etc. However, in spite of the efforts to collaborate with foreign companies and governments for packaged software development, the share of products and packages in Indian exports of software is still low at 7.9 per cent in 2000. This is due to high entry barriers and brand loyalties of the established foreign MNCs. Nevertheless, as the image and credibility of the Indian software firms exacerbates, their global reach would elongate.

Due to the bright prospects of IT exports, the number of IT companies increased from 38 in 1988 to 850 in 2001, besides innumerable small and informal sector enterprises in this sector. According to Nasscom, in 2001, top 5 companies accounted for 29 per cent share in exports of software. In 1999, there were 79 foreign subsidiaries of the MNEs and 94 per cent of their earnings came from exports. But their overall share in the India's exports of software was just 19 per cent.

India's software exporting companies are sufficiently globally oriented. About 212 Indian software companies have set up 509 overseas offices or subsidiaries, mainly in North America with 266 offices; 122 in Europe and 25 in Australia and so on. Most of these companies have obtained international quality certification ISO 9000. Indian companies are exporting 62 per cent of their software to North America, mainly to the US and 24 per cent to Europe.

Thus, the share of software exports in India's total exports of goods and services has risen from a negligible figure in 1990 to nearly 8 per cent in 2001. In value terms, the exports of software industry in India increased from $60.07 billion in 1998, to $79.76 billion in 2001. It is projected by a Nasscom Report that by 2008, software and services exports would account for 35 per cent of India's exports (Chadha, 2006).

Thus, the IT industry is emerging as an export oriented sector with a global reach and has become India' leading growth steering sector.

EMPLOYMENT AND JOB POTENTIAL IN THE IT SECTOR

According to Nasscom survey, the Indian software industry employed some 3.40 lakh professionals in 2000, as compared with 1.60 lakh in 1996, which gives a compound annual growth of 28.51 per cent. In 2003, the number of workers in India's IT sector has gone up to 6.50 lakh. It is projected that by 2008, the software industry would employ 2.2 million workers including 1 million jobs in the IT enabled services, (while in 1999 there were 23 thousand professionals in IT enabled services), and about 5.60 lakh jobs will be in the back office operations, such as data entry operations and maintenance and repairs, etc. Besides this, a huge employment potential exists in small and informal micro enterprises in the customization, data entry and Internet bureau, etc. In all, 60-70 per cent of the IT professionals employed are in the software development segment, while 10-15 per cent are in the software marketing and consultancy work and 32 per cent are employed in the BPO activities including data processing and data bases creation etc.

About 75 per cent of those employed in the software industry are IT degree holders. The proportion of women IT professionals increased from 19 per cent in 1996 to35 per cent in 2005. But in the IT enabled services, women workers account for 37 per cent of the employed therein, e.g. as call center operators, medical transcriptions, Internet operators, data entry operators, accountants and cellular services, etc. Overall in 2003, 1.60 lakh IT specialists were engaged in the IT enabled services (Kumar, 2001).

POLICY IMPLICATIONS AND CONCLUSIONS

With the onset of the forces of globalisation, the possibilities of trade across geographical boundaries of countries have increased enormously with the dilution of tariff and non-tariff barriers. The provisions of TRIPS under the WTO regime have enabled firms and governments to seek patent rights on software development. This has opened opportunities for the companies in the West, particularly the US, to get offshore development of software without running the risk of these being pirated or imitated. This has exacerbated export activities from the Indian IT sectors. The above analysis highlights that exports of both goods and services from India's IT sectors have increased tremendously over the last decade.

A number of factors have helped in bolstering up the Indian IT industry, such as the availability of a large stock of skilled manpower at low wages, strong tradition in science and technology, bourgeoning investments in scientific and innovative research systems and the building of an inimitable capability in computing and networking technologies, availability of infrastructure and communication links, favourable policy regime, network of expatriate Indian technical and managerial personnel and so on.

However, the gains have to be consolidated and improved for a sustained development of the IT sector:

(i) Due to the rising demand for specialized and skilled manpower all across the globe, a shortage of IT professionals has started to be felt in India, particularly the exodus of large number of these in response to the lucrative opportunities in the western countries. Thus a major challenge for the policy makers is to increase the supply of the trained manpower by training these specialist knowledge workers on specific skills.

(ii) Rising demand for IT specialists, particularly from affluent developed countries, is inducing unprecedented rise in wages and salaries of these knowledge workers by about 20 per cent. This is eroding the cost advantage for the Indian IT industry, as competition from other emerging low wage countries is stiffening. Thus, Indian enterprises will have to deal with this by moving up the value chain as salaries rise and will have to increase the overall efficiency of utilization of human resources or increase productivity faster than the wage cost to become increasingly competitive.

(iii) Infrastructural development to support an expanding IT sector has to be further augment. Thus, adequate bandwidth for data transfer has to be fabricated and the built up space for software development has to be extended.

(iv) The R&D spending and employment in the Indian IT sector have so far not been consistent with the pace of growth of this sector. R&D spending in the IT industry increased from barely Rs. 31.38 crore to Rs.38.35 crore during 1996-99, hovering around 1.50 per cent of the aggregate national R&D expenditure. By 2001, this proportion increased to 4 per cent but the R&D intensity of this industry remains low at 1.40 per cent. Though some of the leading IT companies individually spend about 14-19 per cent of their turnover on R&D, yet this has to go up further to enhance the competitiveness of India's IT industry.

Besides this, the IT industry employed barely 882 personnel on R&D, out of a total employment of 21.65 thousand in 1998. Hence a small R&D effort compared to the scale of operations and the impending competition from foreign IT companies.

Keeping these problems in view, the state has started to play a proactive role in reorienting the education system with a greater stress on its vocationalisation, especially in the area of IT. Intake in IITs has been enhanced, RECs have been upgraded into NIITs, setting up technology parks, tax incentives for IT investments, trade liberalization in IT equipment and software, checking software piracy, steps to augment bandwidth, easy availability of venture capital, facilitating the internationalization of Indian IT firms. Firms are also taking strategic management decisions to recruit, train and retain talent by focusing on high value consultancy and packaged software and emphasizing geographical diversification.

REFERENCES

Chadha, V. (2006), "Globalisation, Technology Intensive Exports and R&D Effort in an Emerging Knowledge Economy Like India: The Case of Some Selected Science Intensive Sectors", a paper presented at the *ISA XVI World Congress of Sociology*, held at Durban, South Africa, during July 23-29.

Freeman, C. and L. Soete (1997), *The Economics of Industrial Innovation,* London: Pinter.

Government of India (2002), *Research and Development Statistics,* New Delhi: Ministry of Science and Technology, Department of Science and Technology.

Housler, G. (2002), "The Globalisation of Finance", *Finance and Development*, March, pp. 10-12.

Kumar, N. (2001), "Indian Software Industry Development: International and National Perspective", *Economic and Political Weekly*, Vol. XXXVI, No. 45, pp. 4288-89.

Rivera-Batiz, L. and P.M. Romer (1991), "Economic Integration and Endogenous Growth", *Quarterly Journal of Economics,* Vol. 106, No. 2, pp. 531-55.

World Bank (2005), *India and the Knowledge Economy: Leveraging Strengths and Opportunities,* Washington D.C.: World Bank Publication Department.

WTO AND INFORMATION TECHNOLOGY

Asha Singh and Tapan Kumar Shandilya

INTRODUCTION

India has come a long way since GATT (General Agreement on Tariff and Trade) was initially established in 1947. During the last 59 years, we have striven progressively to lower barriers to trade all over the world. As a successor to the historical GATT, which was a temporary legal agreement and not a proper organization, the World Trade Organization, better known by its acronym WTO, is only 10 years old, having crossed that threshold on 1st January 1995. Its establishment has created a forum for continuous negotiations to reconcile the sometimes conflicting interest of trading partners. The importance of the WTO within a global trade regime and the overall unprecedented growth in trade and global capital flows in the 1990s is of great interest, not only in terms of facilitating economic growth but also in alleviating intra-state conflict. The role of WTO in influencing greater trade openness is well established. It is perhaps the only multilateral body based in Geneva that has the ability to globally influence the lives of people cutting across the different strata in society. The all-encompassing ability of the WTO has made it a serious topic for deliberation the world over.

DOHA MEET, 2001

Since its establishment in 1995 it has been a roller coaster ride for this trade negotiating body. In ten years, the WTO has seen several debates, protests, failures and revivals. No other multilateral body would have had such turbulent formative years as the WTO. During this period, WTO in spite of two major failures (Seattle and Cancun Ministerial Conferences), has shown tremendous resilience. The Doha Ministerial, which followed the Seattle Ministerial, launched a new "Round" of negotiations. A "Framework Agreement" signed at Geneva has put the Doha Round of negotiations back on track and has negated the collapse of the ministerial conference at Cancun. The failure of the ministerial conference at Seattle led people to the conclusion that the WTO had lost its significance. But the Doha Ministerial, which followed the 9/11 terrorist attacks on the US, ended with the launch of a "Development Agenda" rekindling hopes that the WTO may eventually become an instrument for development and poverty alleviation across the globe.

At Doha (Qatar) in 2001, while the broad support for the successful anti-subsidy position in agriculture seemed a developing country achievement, the developing countries were a visible part of the alliance. A clear victory in agriculture and other areas was forthcoming. For India, safeguarding the interest of farming sector is a matter related to the very survival and sustenance of their population. Moreover in a representative democracy like ours, it would be a political hara-kiri if the government ignores the interests of farmers and agriculture under international compulsions. In the Doha round of negotiations while the developed countries were mainly concerned about issues like market access and IPR, the developing countries voiced concern over food security, poverty elimination and economic growth with respect to the process of globalization. It is alleged by developing countries that the developed world shows only hypocritical concern about these issues.

The issues of least-developed countries complying with subsidy and intellectual property rules were accepted at Doha in spite of initial strong opposition by developed countries, indicating that the developing countries were a necessary part of any bargain. The meeting accepted that special and differential treatment (allowing different policies by developing countries and requiring different policies towards them) would be "an integral part" of any final settlement, potentially better than the Uruguay Round, which had offered only minor adjustments to policy and non-obligatory concessions. The Doha Round is widely acknowledged as a 'development round' that promises to place development at the heart of trade negotiations and focus on issues of direct interest to developing countries.

CANCUN MEET, 2003

The Cancun meet was focused on agriculture. G-5 group countries with India, China, Brazil, Argentina and South Africa as its members emphasized the urgency of the need to reduce farm subsidy in developed countries especially in USA and EU countries. India played a proactive role in this initiative. Even Australia and New Zealand supported the stand taken by the G-21 group of developing countries.

At Cancun, the developed countries did not yield much to the long-standing demands of the developing world but cleverly included issues like investment, competition, trade facility and government procurement to build pressure on the developing countries. In the ministerial conference, the developing countries recorded their objections in many issues for the interest of the developing countries economic development hence, the new alliance so called G-21 united and countered the traditionally huge weight that the US and the EU towards the rich states with call for more understanding of the problems of the world's poor people. If we look the results of the ministerial conference there is no a remarkable outcome to favor of the trade disputes settlement, therefore trade related disputes settlement has not any impressive to reduce cases i.e. reduced from 22 in 1995 to 20 in 2004.

The revised draft presented for negotiations on the third day was heavily and unfairly titled towards the West. It proposed, for instance, that while developing countries like India would reduce agricultural subsidy by 70 per cent, the EU reduce it by 41 per cent and US would cut it merely 36 per cent. In short, there was actually an effort to have a differential treatment for the affluent. More than that, it brought up all the Singapore issue in forefront. The revised draft was a big blow to the heightened expectations of the developing countries. India's representative and the then Commerce and Industry Minister Arun Jaitley commented pointing the American negotiator Rober Zoellick and EU Trade Commissioner Pascal Lamy that they have buried the development rhetoric of Doha and now appeared "interested only in the development of the developed countries."

The Cancun Meet collapsed due to confrontation between developed and developing countries on long-standing issues of developing countries. The "Framework Agreement" on 1 August 2004 reached among Five Interested Parties (FIPs) comprising of EU, US, Australia, Brazil and India, resolved the divergent positions on key aspects of each of the three pillars in the agriculture negotiations. The Framework Agreement explicitly agrees to eliminate export subsidies by a credible end date. It imposes a down payment of 20 per cent on overall trade-distorting domestic support in the first year of implementation besides containing a combination of cuts, disciplines and monitoring requirements in various elements of the domestic support pillar, and a tiered formula for tariff reductions based on proportionately lower commitments by developing countries than by developed countries. The FA also recognizes the critical importance of agriculture to the economic development of developing countries and the need to enable them to pursue agricultural policies that are supportive of their development goals, poverty reduction strategies, food security and livelihood concerns, including through instruments such as special products and a new special safeguard mechanism against likely import surges. Although the WTO's dispute mechanism has so far worked well, there are many important issues need to be addressed in order to improve the ways in which disputes are settled and to remove some of the structural causes of dispute.

HONG KONG MEET, 2005–SOME ISSUES

Wild swings took the WTO to the brink on several occasions, but in Hong Kong, trade ministers of 149 nations made a dramatic comeback to hammer out a 'compromise deal' holding a lot of promise for the developing countries like India on future market access gains for agriculture products as farm export subsidies of rich nations would be phased out in stages by 2013. Regarding market access, the Hong Kong Declaration mandates the adoption of four bands for effecting tariff cuts. This mandate is based on a proposal submitted by the G-20 countries, which argued for progressive tariff cuts, which would ensure that higher tariffs are subjected to deeper cuts. But the more important component of the market access mandate given by the ministers in Hong Kong for countries like India is the inclusion of the special products (SPs) and special safeguard mechanism (SSM).

For the past several years, developing countries have argued that tariffs on products vital for ensuring food security and livelihoods should not be subjected to either minimum or no reduction. The Hong Kong Declaration provides that the developing countries would have the flexibility to designate an appropriate number of tariff lines as SPs "guided by indicators based on the criteria of food security, livelihood security and rural development". As regards SSM, the declaration provides that this mechanism would apply both in the event of sudden surges in imports and sudden drop in international prices. India and other developing countries would find that the price-based triggers particularly useful since they can help them to take advance action for preventing a flood of cheap imports from entering their markets.

In return for committing a deadline for ending farm export subsidies; the industrialized world had managed to force developing countries to accept the 'Swiss' formula for import duty reduction bindings for industrial goods. With not much progress in services, the 'compromise' deal tries to balance a trade off between developing countries and enhanced market access in industrial goods to appease rich nations.

The developing countries have waited for nearly ten years for trade super powers that dominate the WTO to show sensitivity to their efforts to change global trade from being an instrument of their domination to serving as a mechanism to advance their economic development.

The focus of the current round of negotiations on issues concerning the developing countries has had a salutary effect on the coalitions involving these countries, which have gathered momentum over time. Hong Kong saw the culmination of this process as the "grand alliance" involving the G-90, G-33 and the G-20 countries took shape. While this 'grand alliance' has already taken the momentum of trade negotiations away from the developed countries, its influence on the outcome of the current round of negotiations may not be long in coming.

INDIA AND WTO

India is proud to have been a founder member both of GATT and WTO. Over the years, our negotiations have played a prominent role in shaping the contours of the multilateral trading system as it exists today and has contributed significantly to the successful conclusion of all trade negotiations. India's unilateral trade liberalization occurred simultaneously with the Uruguay Round agreement. Major commitments in the area of trade liberalization of the traditional goods sector became a part of reforms and were already under way in the form of the liberalized trade policy announced in 1992. As is well known that India had adopted al liberal import policy in 1992 by allowing imports of raw materials, technology and capital goods. The trade policies announced thereafter, of course have been in line with India's commitments to the WTO. According to Julian Morris, Executive Director, International Policy Network and a Visiting Professor at the University of Bukingham, "Trade liberalization does create winners and losers: The biggest winners are poor consumers, who will benefit from lower cost goods, greater opportunities for employment and greater freedoms as entrepreneurs. Meanwhile, the losers will be the members of the elite in both rich and poor countries, who have been the main beneficiaries of trade restrictions."

The Hong Kong ministerial declaration holds a mixed bag for India. On the one hand is acceptance of the 'Swiss' formula on reduction in industrial tariffs, which was vehemently opposed till the last moment. Since multiple 'coefficients' are to be applied, the level of customs duty reduction will be lower than what industrialized countries would face.

The impact of trade liberalization would be dramatic also. Morris observes, "The removal of all tariffs and quotas on goods and services could increase World GDP by over $ 1 trillion (USD) annually. Approximately 36% of this increase would go to India, China and Africa, with average income in those places rising by over $ 100 per person per year. Over 10 years, average incomes of the poorest could rise by $ 1000 per capita or more–potentially eliminating absolute poverty."

The Indian economy grew at a rate of 8.1 per cent in 2005, following the 7 per cent and 8.6 per cent growth experienced in 2004 and 2003 respectively. The growth momentum was sustained despite an insufficient monsoon, increasing global oil and steel prices and reduced growth rate in the agriculture and allied services.

IT UNDER WTO

The Indian economy has moved from being dependent on agriculture to services, which are now the key driver of the Indian economy. Information Technology (IT) and IT enabled services (outsourcing) have been a key contributor in making India a global services destination, a trend that is expected to continue and grow at a rapid rate.

India's main strengths in software technology have been, large talent pool, exports and global outsourcing and rapidly improving infrastructure. For knowledge workers, information and knowledge are both raw material as well as product. This form of intangible asset varies from industry to industry but all of them subscribe to common commands like research and development, patents, proprietary, technology, databases and their ability to fulfill societal needs.

In recent years, a large number of initiatives have been taken for strengthening indigenous capability including super computers, Java Competency Centre of India, programme, ATM test bed. "Government of India consider IT as an agent of transformation of every facet of human life that bring about a knowledge-based society in twenty first century" said A.K. Chakravarti, Adviser, Information Technologies, Government of India.

Recently, some research centers have been established in India. Motorola's two research and development facilities in India helped produce a sub-$40 cellular phone for emerging Intel has 800 India-based engineers working on software and hardware designs for its communication and semiconductor product lines. But what is more required is to establish and strengthen our own infrastructure bases with strong R & D supports capable of innovations and developing appropriate technologies compatible with societal needs. Klaus Schwab, Founder Executive Chairman of World Economic Forum remarked, "It is not enough of companies to have developed great technology these days. Timing is intrinsically important in deciding which technologies are successfully integrated into society. History shows us that successful technologies fulfilled an empty but important niche."

India's software industry earns a lot of foreign exchange. In a decade behind, it has forged ahead with impressive growth rate. It is one of the fastest growing industries in India. The share of IT software and services in GDP has been 401 per cent of the GDP in 2004-05. Its national economic output has rose from 102 per cent in 1997-98 to 3.5 per cent in 2003-04. Indian 17.3 billion (expected) from the growth of 33 per cent with revenue US $ 12.8 billion in financial year 2003-04. Total number of IT and ITES-BPO professionals employed in India has grown from 284,000 in financial year 1999-2000 to over 1 million in financial year 2004-05. Tables 1 and 2 exhibit impressive growth of IT and software industries.

Table 1
Electronics and IT Production (Rs. in Crore)

Year	*Hardware*	*Software*	*Total*	*Growth%*
1999-2000	28,100	24,350	52,450	7.5
2000-01	31,100	37,750	68,850	31.3
2001-02	32,750	47,374	80,124	16.4
2002-03	37,500	59,500	97,000	21.0
2003-04	43,800	70,850	118,290	18.2
2004-05	49,750	97,860	147,610	24.8

Source: NASSCOM (DIT Annual Report–2005).

Main factors behind this phenomenal growth are new emerging service lines R & D Services and BPO, low operating costs, large human resources with requisite skill, exports and global outsourcing rapidly improving infrastructure, MNC customers and government incentives. High quality IT knowledge workers in large numbers has played a pivotal role in India's IT industries growth.

Legal and regulatory framework has also contributed to the growth. Information Technology Act, 2000 provide a legal framework for electronic transactions in form of E-commerce. It covers electronic contracts prevention of computer crimes, electronic filling of documents, etc. It provides a legal base for conduct of business in cyber-space. Besides it, Indian regulator frame in from of IPRS offer requisite protection in forms of patents, design registration, trademark registration and copyrights.

Table 2
Electronics and IT Exports (Rs. in Crore)

Year	*Hardware*	*Software*	*Total*	*Growth%*
1999-2000	1,400	17,150	18,550	45.6
2000-01	4,788	28,350	33,138	78.6
2001-02	5,800	36,500	42,300	27.6
2002-03	5,600	46,100	51,700	22.2
2003-04	7,700	58,240	65,940	22.0
2004-05	8,750	78,230	86,980	32.0

Source: NASSCOM (DIT Annual Report–2005).

CASE OF INDIAN SOFTWARE INDUSTRY

In terms of number of patents, Indian industry in general (Table 3) and the software industry in particular is a too low profile but in terms of performance and piracy the software segment is quite significant. According to Heeks, un-branded assembled computers loaded with pirated software still form a significant segment of the Indian market. Thus, software includes operating systems and other general-purpose software. In the decade of 1990s when Indian software industry was preparing itself for the boom, assembled computers coupled with pirated software acted as a catalyst in providing training to masses at a low cost.

Table 3
Number of Applications and Patents Granted for Selected Countries

Country	*Applications filed (p.a.)*	*Patents granted (p.a.)*
Japan	400000	250000
United States of America	90000	35000
United Kingdom	70000	30000
India	10000	2000

Source: www.wipo.com

India was able to generate such a specialized skill formation in a very short span. This lead to both R & D and production in large quantum at a low cost that finally gave a comparative cost advantage to the Indian software industry. Being primarily an export oriented industry, the gains of its low cost production dissipated to importing countries (USA and EU). In turn over time, India due to specialization became the hub for some of the future technologies like that of IT enabled services. The benefits of such a specialization are again meant for advanced world. Thus, piracy and unbranded hardware has acted as catalyst in developing the hubs for the future technologies of the world.

If a strict IPR regime had been there in the early nineties, Indian software industry, the giant source of software products and services for USA and EU, would have not come into existence at all. If the pioneer institutions and firms in earlier developments in both hardware and software had gone in for strict IPR in the decades of 1960s and 1970s, the giant firms like Microsoft would have not been on the world map today. All big forms and leading nations in the software industry are reaping the benefits of past liberal IPR regimes. The tighter IPRs will, no doubt help the few countries and firms to earn more but will raise the costs and hinder the future technology development at lower end. The whole process of skill formation and specialization generation will be affected adversely.

CONCLUSION

Discussion on WTO brings out mixed reactions from people across India. It is, by many, viewed as a forum where the developed world hammers the developing countries into accepting agreements that takes them nowhere near the institution's professed philosophy of improving the living standards of poor people across nations. The developing countries are still not at a very mature stage to understand the agreements and their full implications. Faith in the multi-lateral trading system will increase manifold if people perceive that it is sensitive to their needs and concerns. The developing countries are a highly diverse group often with very different views and concerns. The WTO's new rules for global trade present both opportunities and challenges to Asian developing countries.

Trade must contribute to poverty reduction. Pro-poor trade measures have a direct impact on poverty reduction while pro-growth measures have indirect effects. Since trade liberalization policies may adversely affect the poor in the short run, a cautious approach is necessary so that existing socio-economic and institutional structures respond in a pro-poor manner to the structural adjustments in the post WTO period.

Deeper regional integration is necessary. It requires various kinds of regional co-operation arrangements, areas and methods of co-operation, institutional arrangements to facilitate co-operation like Asia Development Bank, Central Asia Regional Economic Co-operation, Asia Pacific Economic Co-operation, South Asian Association for Regional Co-operation, bilateral and regional trade arrangements, relationship of these to WTO, etc. Institutions like ADB can play a significant role in training and preparing the Asian developing members to understand and actively participate in the WTO negotiations.

India is, however, deeply committed to the success of multilateral trading system (MTS). The WTO and the MTS must be effective instruments for serving the needs of the weakest section of the society in all parts of the world. No single pattern, no single package of measures can be considered to be universally applicable. We would be deluding ourselves by thinking that a single remedy can be applied across the board. What we should strive to achieve is the amelioration of the living conditions of all people, particularly the poorest. In the words of Mahatma Gandhi, "I neither believe in the 'greatest' good of the greatest number, nor can I agree that might is right. For human beings, the object in view should be the good of all, with the weak being served first".

One of the arguments of diehard opponents of the new liberal regime is that India should opt out of the WTO. We must give a thought to this statement at this juncture. India can anytime opt out of the WTO if the Government so wishes. But imagine what will happen once we are out of the WTO. All the other 148 members will find themselves free to impose all sorts of barriers on exports from India-tariff, conventional and non-conventional. More than 95 per cent of world trade takes place among the members of the WTO. We are aware that China was knocking at the doors of GATT ever since the Uruguay Round commenced in 1984 and finally accessed the WTO, so that the other members will no longer be able to discriminate against China in matters of trade. And if they do, WTO is the platform available for China since December 2001, to fight it out. One more advantage is that, unlike the IMF, each member of the WTO has one vote. Going by the numbers, the developing countries are in majority. So, if united, they will stand the conspiracies of developed countries.

Since WTO decisions and actions have far reaching effects on the lives of billions of people and the environment upon which they depend, it should make the multilateral trading system more open and friendly to developing countries. Its operations and decision-making procedures have to be more transparent, participatory and democratic.

India has done remarkably well in software technology. The growth of IT sector in India is exemplary. Over a period of time, there have been significant technological innovations and developments of knowledge and concept of intellectual property is being recognized world-over with the strengthening of technological capability in India coupled with urgency for integrating the IP system consistent with international practices and IPR, it has become important that Patent Act be harmonized in such a manner that it becomes user-friendly and adequately equipped to protect national and public interests while simultaneously meeting India's obligations under the TRIPS Agreement. It should be kept in mind that with tighter IPR regime, large MNC would get the benefit while small entities will suffer. Cheaper processes can be used to compete with more expensive products, as no reverse engineering will be possible.

REFERENCES

Amendment to Indian Patent Act-Free Software Foundation of India, March 27, 2005. Available at http://fsf.org.in/presss/press.html.

Economic Intelligence Unit, 2004.

Hanna, N. (1994), Exploiting Information Technology for Development, W.B., Washington D.C.

Heeks, R. (1999), India's Software Industry, IDPM, University of Manchester, UK.

Kurukshetra (Various Issues).

Mehta, Vinnie (2001), "Glimpses of Indian IT Industry", an address by the director of MAIT on Independence Day (August 14).

NASSCOM, (DIT, Annual Report), 2005.

Narendra Nath K.G. (2005), "Software Patents under Ordinance Face Reversal," March 29.

Nightingale, P. (2000), "Knowledge, Technology and Organisation: Understanding the Dynamics of Pharmaceutical Innovation Process", Science Policy Research Unit, University of Sussex, available at http://www.druid.dk/summer2000/conf-papers/Nightingale.pdf.

The Hindu Business Line (2004), "Changes in Bill to Give Patents for Software," Dec. 27.

TIFAC (2003), Technology Information, Forecasting and Assessment Council, IPR Bulletin Vol. 7, No. 7-9.

World Bank Report, 2005.

GATS AND HIGHER EDUCATION IN INDIA: PROSPECTS AND PROBLEMS

Talwar Sabanna

INTRODUCTION

Education shapes the destiny of mankind. The quality of life in depth cannot be achieved unless the human society is empowered with input of knowledge and progress of the mind, spirit through developmental process of science and technology. Education also plays a very important role for character building and developments. This can be achieved well through contacts with universal faces. Education does not teach to accept humans as negative tools of hammering upon disastrous conditions of mankind. But a forceful component that inspires human to promote vision to liberate the society from curse of poverty and slavery to the dictates of ruthless concept of mankind (Varma, 2003). An illiterate person can hardly be expected to enter into a rational economic transaction on the basis of calculation of cost, price and profit. Literacy and education help to improve the skill of a person. They have a large and significant impact on growth of productivity. Modern technology is easily adopted by the educated. Spread of technology depends on the earning potential and motivation that are linked to the development of formal schooling. Educational attainment and literacy have another important role in the society as they positively affect efficiency in resource allocation, leading to higher income and more equal distribution of such income (Kishor, 2003). Actually, economic reforms and educational reforms should go hand in hand. Whether we can provide facilities so that the poor can exercise this right should be the primary responsibility of all economic and educational reforms.

There are more critical positions on globalization and its impact on Indian educational system. Over the years, there have been two kinds of flows of human capital from India. The first took place prior to globalization and led to emigration of knowledge workers to feed the western market (Patel, 2004). The second occurred after the inauguration of the new trade regime of WTO and GATS and involves new strata of students who are now being trained by western educational institutions based in India or established through a system of franchising. Therefore, the objective of the present paper attempts to point out the various issues of higher education of India in the light of Globalization and GATS.

I

HIGHER EDUCATION IN INDIA

This section deals with the education system and status of Higher Education in India.

THE INDIAN EDUCATION SYSTEM

The Indian Education System has undergone a tremendous transformation from elite system, nurtured by colonial roots to a mass system attempt to meet the demands of a vibrant democracy. But it is still continued to be considered as a social service rather than a trade service. Learning is considered to be an excellence of wealth that none can destroy and cannot be attained by chance. The educational system in India passed through three main eras viz., Gurukul era, British era and Independence era. In the 'Gurukuls' the main objective was to provide overall personality development of the pupil. This concept of education still prevails in India. During the British era emphasis was on training a class of people qualified by their intelligence and morality for employment in the civil administration of India. Efforts were made to make natives of the country thoroughly good English Scholars. The promotion of European literature and science amongst the people of India was emphasized during British era. The whole education system was tailored to suit the needs of the British regime, making the system more or less elitist in nature.

The independent India had started its journey on a social philosophical base of education with the Nehruvian approach. The rapid course of globalization has started transforming that to an individualized philosophical base. On account of that the national objective has now shifted from the establishment of an egalitarian social order to the encouragement of technological innovation, increased efficiency and maximization of profits. Public investment in areas like health and education has been drastically cut to hand them over to the private parties. Hence, the state sponsored education is being fetched out and replaced by privatized education. Education under globalization is no more a social product for social consumption rather it is a private product for private consumption (Pathy, 2003). It is argued that elementary and mass education is the first condition for a healthy global economy and thus this sector of education warrants larger share of investment than the other two viz., secondary and higher education.

TRENDS IN HIGHER EDUCATION

Every Nation around the world provides higher education for human resource development to man about its industry, science and technology and socio-economic development. In this regard, India is no exception to such provision; higher education institutions in the country have rapidly expanded after Independence. Today there are 254 university level institutions and 7929 colleges (Table 1). Further, there are 86 lakh students in degree colleges and 36 lakh students in Professional Courses (Table 2). This system is considered for India as one of the largest in the world's higher education.

GENDER DISPARITY IN HIGHER EDUCATION

There is an increasing awareness of and concern about the issue of women's development. Several efforts are being made to understand issues pertaining to this subject, including the role of women in contributing to development, and the role of education and other aspects in women's development. Till recently, women have been considered as either victims of social practices or targets for development but not as participants in development. Now there is a rethinking on the role of women in society. Further, the UNDP Human Development Report of

1995 dedicated the entire volume to gender issues. The report says: "Investing in women's capabilities and empowering them to exercise their choices is not only valuable in itself but is also the surest way to contribute to economic growth and overall development". As long as women are excluded from the development process, development will remain weak and lopsided (Indiresan, 2002).

Table 1
Number of Educational Institutions in India

Type of Educational Institutions	*1971*	*1981*	*1991*	*2000*
Primary	5,17,804	6,23,339	7,28,268	8,82,295
Secondary	36,738	51006	79,796	1,26,047
Degree and above General Educational Institutions	2,285	3,421	4,862	7,929
Universities/Institutions of National Importance	100	132	184	254
Technical Institutions	134	171	351	880

Source: Manpower Profile India Year Book 2002, Institute of Applied Manpower Research, New Delhi, 2002, page no. 43.

Table 2
Enrolment by Level of Education in India

(In thousand)

Level of Education	*1971*	*1981*	*1991*	*2000*
1. Primary	70713 (87.10)	95656 (85.69)	133036 (84.63)	159254 (79.47)
2. Secondary	6580 (8.10)	8807 (7.89)	14365 (9.14)	18993 (9.48)
3. Pre-University	1040 (1.28)	3079 (2.76)	3658 (2.33)	8626 (4.30)
4. Degree and above	1647 (2.03)	2320 (2.08)	3672 (2.33)	8626 (4.30)
5. Professional	1204 (1.48)	1765 (1.58)	2468 (1.57)	3661 (1.83)
Total	81189 (100.00)	111627 (100.00)	157199 (100.00)	200385 (100.00)

Source: Manpower Power Profile of India-2002, Institute of Applied Manpower Research, New Delhi, 2002, p. 49.

Note: Figures in brackets denotes percentages.

There has been a phenomenal growth in the number of women enrolled in higher education since 1980's. The number of women enrolled per hundred men registered a rapid increase between 1971 and 2000. A caparison can be drawn between the male and female rates at various levels of education in India during the time period 1971 and 2000. For this purpose the number of females per hundred males at primary, secondary and various disciplines of higher education is presented in Table 3. During the period between 1971 and 2000, the number of girls per hundred boys has increased from 63.10 to 76.27 in primary education; in case of secondary education it has increased from 35.06 to 63.41 and in case of degree and above we witness remarkable increase from 28.04 to 62.12 and unsatisfactory increase from 15.60 to 39.42 in Professional Courses.

Table 3
Number of Girls per 100 Boys Enrolled in Different Education Level in India

Type of Education	*1971*	*1981*	*1991*	*2000*
Primary	63.10	64.67	70.86	76.27
Secondary	35.06	43.04	50.09	63.41
Pre-university	28.04	37.15	46.97	62.12
Degree and above	31.65	42.24	52.49	58.45
Professional Education	15.60	21.44	23.76	39.42

Source: Manpower Power Profile of India-2002, Institute of Applied Manpower Research, New Delhi, 2002.

Through an inter-discipline study (Table 4), it is observed that Faculties of Arts and Medicine have been quite popular among women in India. The discipline-wise break-up of University education shows that in the year 1980-81, the Arts discipline was most popular among Indian women followed by Medical and Science disciplines. A change is noticed in the recent years- maximum women enrolment is concentrated in Medicine, followed by Arts and the lowest percentage goes for the Engineering stream. It is noticed that percentage of females in the Faculty of Arts accounts 38.00 in 2000-01, while in case of Professional Courses; it is the Medicine discipline where females have good participation (i.e., 40.6 per cent during 2000-01). We do witness an appreciable increase in the number of females going for higher education but still not as high as the number of males. Some disciplines show a dismal record concerning female enrolments namely, Engineering where female enrolment is 22.3 per cent during 2000-01 while in Science and Commerce streams, the share of females is around 38.0 per cent and 35.6 per cent respectively during the same period.

Table 4
Faculty-wise Enrolment of Girls as per cent of Total Enrolment in University Education

Year	*Arts*	*Science*	*Commerce*	*Education*	*Engineering / Technology*	*Medicine*
1980-81	37.5	27.9	15.2	46.7	4.6	23.8
1985-86	37.9	29.8	20.9	43.9	5.9	29.5
1990-91	39.8	36.8	24.0	44.2	10.9	34.3
1991-92	39.8	31.5	25.4	45.4	9.1	34.8
1992-93	39.4	32.4	26.5	43.8	10.6	34.4
1993-94	39.4	32.9	26.7	44.6	11.1	36.5
1994-95	39.8	33.3	28.0	43.2	13.1	33.9
1995-96	41.5	35.5	29.0	41.2	14.2	34.5
1996-97	41.9	34.6	29.7	43.1	14.8	35.4
1997-98	41.5	35.6	30.6	43.1	16.9	36.1
1998-99	44.7	35.6	31.6	42.5	14.9	33.7
1999-2000	44.9	37.4	34.0	42.6	22.1	37.8
2000-01	38.0	38.0	35.6	42.8	22.3	40.6

Source: Manpower Power Profile of India-2002, Institute of Applied Manpower Research, New Delhi, 2002, Page No. 59.

EDUCATIONAL EXPENDITURE IN INDIA

Table 5 provides data for educational expenditure in India. By the year 1980-81, educational expenditure had risen to a level of 2.80 per cent of GDP as against 0.68 per cent in 1950-51 and 2.41 per cent in 1970-71. During 1980-81 to 1990-91, a gradual increase in educational expenditure was witnessed and it reached a peak level of 4.06 per cent of GDP in 1990-91. Thereafter, this percentage has shown a gradual decline from 4.06per cent in 1990-91 to 3.93 per cent in 2000-01. Further, it is witnessed from Table 6 that of the budget expenditure, Government of India spent 14.6 per cent on University and Other Higher Education and 3.9 per cent on Technical Education during 2000-01 whereas, expenditure on primary and secondary

Table 5
Educational Expenditure as percentage of GDP
(At Current Prices)

Year	*GDP (Rs. Crores)*	*Total Expenditure on Education (In Crores)*	*Education Expenditure as Percentage of GDP*	*Percentage Change in Educational Expenditure*
1950-51	9445	64	0.68	-
1960-61	15999	260	1.63	0.95
1970-71	41957	1011	2.41	0.78
1980-81	130176	3645	2.80	0.39
1985-86	249547	7457	2.99	0.19
1990-91	510954	20761	4.06	1.07
1991-92	589086	22639	3.84	-0.22
1992-93	673221	25303	3.76	-0.08
1993-94	781345	28599	3.66	-0.10
1994-95	917058	32875	3.58	-0.08
1995-96	1073271	38769	3.61	0.03
1996-97	1243546	44216	3.56	-0.05
1997-98	1390042	52305	3.76	-0.20
1998-99	1616033	62020	3.84	0.08
1999-2000	1786459	77546	4.34	0.50
2000-01	1989480	78237	3.93	-0.41

Source: Manpower Power Profile of India-2002, Institute of Applied Manpower Research, New Delhi, 2002, Page No. 87.

Table 6
Percentage Distribution of Budgeted Expenditure by Stage of Education

Stage	*1980-81*	*1991-92*	*1995-96*	*2000-01*
Elementary Education	46.3	43.8	48.3	48.6
Secondary Education	30.8	30.5	32.8	30.1
University & Other Higher Education	14.0	13.2	12.3	14.6
Technical Education	4.6	4.8	4.1	3.9
Others	4.3	7.7	2.5	2.9
Total	100.00	100.00	100.00	100.00

Source: Manpower Power Profile of India-2002, Institute of Applied Manpower Research, New Delhi, 2002, Page No. 90.

education accounts 48.6 per cent and 30.1 per cent respectively during the same period. This indicates a lower priority given to education in the post-reform period (1991-2001) as compared with the pre-reform (1981-90), despite the fact that the Government has been proclaiming that it intends to increase it to 6 per cent of GDP.

Dr. V.R. Panchamukhi has calculated the average annual growth rate of per pupil expenditure in education in the pre-reform and post-reform period. Table 7 indicates that there has been a serious deterioration in per pupil expenditure in education in all sectors of education. In the sphere of elementary education, the annual average growth rate of expenditure slumped from 6.9 per cent during 1985-90 to merely 1.2 per cent during 1990-96. In secondary education, there was zero growth rate of per pupil expenditures and in university education; this growth rate became negative to the extent of 4.4 per cent in the post-reform period.

Table 7
Average Annual Growth Rate of Per Pupil Expenditure in Education

(In per cent)

Level of Education	*Pre-Reform Period (1985-90)*	*Reform Period (1990-96)*
Elementary Education	6.9	1.2
Secondary Education	5.0	0.0
University Education	0.2	-4.4

Source: EPW, March 4-10, 2000, p. 839.

Higher education institutions in India faced financial crises due to escalating costs and increasing needs on the one hand and shrinking budgetary resources on the other. Although higher education in India is characterized by massive public investment, this investment is still regarded as much below the optimum. Recently major efforts have been mounted for mobilization of resources and it has been recommended that while the Government should make a firm commitment to higher education, institutions of higher education should make efforts to raise their own resources by raising fee levels, encouraging donations and by generating revenues through consultancy and other activities.

Further, the reasons for this declining trend of expenditure on education are the policy measures of both state and central governments. Further, economy in expenditure is achieved by withdrawal of subsidies. In India, education, particularly higher education, is a highly subsidized sector (Cyril, 2003). During reform period, subsidies are withdrawn and fees are raised in higher education. The fee rates in schools and colleges/ universities have been raised during the past one-decade not only in the institutions run by the private management but also in the institutions owned and managed by government.

Now the system of higher education is taking a new turn. The youth of India has started preferring technology and employment-oriented courses. As a consequence more and more engineering and other technical institutions have started coming up. In order to meet the growing demand for such technical and employment-oriented courses, the Government started permitting the private institutions to come into education sector and encouraged more private investment in education. As a result, commercialization of higher education started and self-financed private universities started developing in India since last decade. The thrust of the new developments is on market-oriented economic policies.

II

GATS AND HIGHER EDUCATION

The recent process of globalization has changed not only the territorialisation aspects of human endeavors but also the focus on competitive compression and efficiency in many sectors, its growth being beset with varying phases of transformation depending on the pace of globalization as measured by openness in trade finance and commodity and service markets (Giriappa, 2003). The General Agreement on Trade Services (GATS 1995) was one of the agreements signed under the purview of WTO in 1995. The perception of GATS is that progressive liberalization of trade in commercial services would promote economic growth in WTO member countries. The commercial services cover diversified fields like entertainment, e-commerce, education, etc.

Trade in education is organized into five categories or sub-sector services viz., (i) Primary education services, (ii) Secondary education services, (iii) Higher education services; (iv) Adult education services and (v) Other education services. Presently, only higher education is under negotiation though primary and secondary would also feature subsequently. Progress of negotiations in the area of education is, in fact, the slowest among services.

The GATS provides an international as well as multilaterally accepted legal framework for the promotion of liberalization of trade in services. Trade in services has been defined under the GATS in terms of four modes of delivery viz.,

- Cross border supply (e.g., international telephony),
- Consumption abroad (e.g., tourism),
- Commercial presence (e.g., opening of a consultancy firm on foreign soil), and
- Movement of natural persons (MNP) (e.g., persons working on foreign soil on a contract and time bound basis) (Aggarwal, 2003).

Most Favoured Nation Treatment (MFN) clause has been the fundamental principle first of GATT and then of WTO. The principle, however, has a number of exemptions. To begin with, there are exceptions granted under 'economic integration' of a regional grouping. The regional groupings in the world, which have been freeing trade and capital movements, have been maintaining trade barriers against the rest of the world. In fact, higher the integration within the customs union, the more difficult it is to achieve the MFN clause with the rest of the world.

From India's point of view, since it is not a member of any trading customs union, it does not realize the benefits of an MFN treatment. To consider possibilities, if India is given an MFN status by the US/EU, there could be a bilateral liberalization of education. This would enhance the existing comparative advantages of both parties involved (Shani and Kale, 2004).

ADVANTAGES FROM GATS

- India with its rich cultural, spiritual and philosophical heritage can offer to impart education in all fields of arts, linguistics, philosophy and culture. India, with strong national agricultural research and education system can offer tailor suit courses in agriculture and allied subjects to all developing and under developed countries.

- India is emerging as a nuclear and space science power in the world. In Indian Institutes of Technology (IITs) and Indian Institutes of Management (IIMs), training can be imparted in different disciplines of technology.
- With a vast geographical variability, India can shelter the foreign students comfortably at their suitable climate and environmental regions.
- India can broaden general education to prepare students with attitudes and capabilities for life-long learning. It will create better socio-ethical awareness and motivation.

India's entrance into GATS would help to promote Indian educational institutions in countries where the Indian diaspora is substantial and thereby help the Indian diaspora to create stronger bonds between them and the mother country. " The Indian universities have, in recent year, commenced offering degree and diploma programmes through distance education mode in countries having a large Indian diaspora" (Khajapeer, 2003).

Given the growing importance of services in promoting economic development, competitiveness and productivity, the GATS is of great significance. Trade liberalization in services can result in increased competition, lower prices, more innovation technology transfer, employment creation and greater transparency and predictability in trade and investment flows. The GATS can help in facilitating these benefits (Dadibhavi, 2003).

THRUST AREAS UNDER GATS

With liberalization of higher education, universities in all countries are trying to attract overseas students to pursue their higher education in their respective universities. For attracting overseas students, the course curriculum should be well tailored not only to suit their needs but also to develop scope at international arena.

In countries like India with an added advantage of English as a medium of education, there is a tremendous scope for liberalization of higher education, time to identify the thrust areas in higher education, which are needed to support the Indian Government to enable it to meet the challenges of rapid globalization. However, the fields of education on these aspects are so wide and it is difficult to identify the thrust areas in all fields of specialization. The efforts of WTO to include education in the GATS agreement should be seen as significant contribution to enhance further total factor productivity leading to a higher growth-rate in GDP. Therefore, India has to pay serious attention to the GATS agreement as applicable to educational services, identify opportunities and competitiveness in various sub sectors and negotiate WTO commitments accordingly.

But at the same time, we must remember that, being a global citizen does not necessarily mean having to part with one's indigenous identity. True globalization is not about discarding one's own culture, but about facilitating a free flow and exchange of thoughts, ideas and knowledge. But unfortunately, what we are having now is global eating and dressing and not thinking. This is true in the sphere of education too.

The globalization of economy has led to internationalization of higher education, not merely for economic benefits, but also for increased social interaction and promotion of international understanding. We have reached a stage in which the higher education is not at all different from any other commodity or a commercial product, which can be bought and sold at the market place. It is considered by WTO that the process of export and import of higher education will be covered under its complex rules and legal arrangements. If WTO and similar organizations at national level come in the picture, higher education will be subjected to free trade. With many more countries waiting to tap this vital sector, India has to take a lead on behalf of the developing countries by using WTO as the forum to utilize education as the weapon to demand its due share in the education market.

GLOBALISATION AND HIGHER EDUCATION

Globalization, liberalization, privatization and marketization are synonymous terminologies. If we accept one, it would be presumed that we accept the rest. Few years back education was widely considered to be a public good and free good like air and water. It was unthinkable that on the Indian soil education could be sold or purchased like any other goods. But not it is a reality. As air and water (once considered free goods) have been converted into trade goods, so has been education. What is said is true and for that purpose education is increasingly being accepted as a private good than a public good that too without much protest from deprived class. But while considering the issue in the context of developing nation like India, one would hesitate to accept the argument without being critical (Pathy, 2003). Meriless Grindle, Professor of International Development, speaking on the impact of globalization on the developing world aptly remarks, "Many developing countries are at competitive disadvantage in the context of rapid globalization. In almost all countries of course, there are elites who are benefiting significantly from globalization. They stand in great contrast to most of the rest of the population in countries whose low levels of education, health and economic security put them in particular disadvantage in the knowledge driven era of globalization".

With privatization of higher education in recent years, it is felt that India can now open up the trade in higher education with other nations. But there are various inherent social and economic problems, which may come in the way of globalization of higher education in India. In many countries, the fee structure for higher education is cost-effective. The major objective of such fee structure in those colleges and universities is self-reliance and self-sufficiency. The universities raise funds in those countries with a missionary zeal. But in India the policy of higher education is that it should not be privilege of those who can afford it financially. In other words, the higher education in India goes by merit not by money. To ensure that every one can afford higher education and it is not constrained by poverty, the fees are fixed by government at a very low level. But in order to support the universities to sustain this, the government provides grants to the universities. In other words, the government subsidizes education through grants. In fact, the subsidies can be paid to the student by allowing cost-effective fees structure in the universities. But by paying to the universities through grants the subsidies are channeled. Now, the self-financed institutions are asked to enhance the fee structure so that these universities/institutions become self-reliant and self-sufficient.

PRIVATISATION AND HIGHER EDUCATION

One of the major impacts of globalization seen today is the involvement of the private sector in education. Privatization of higher education is being strongly advocated. It entered the Indian higher education scenario in the 1970s. Private education has grown due to excess demand and differentiated demand for higher education. The concern here is of institutions, which are totally private i.e. colleges and universities which are being managed and funded by the private sector with no government intervention. These are purely unaided private institutions and provide major financial relief to the government at the present times of financial crunch. The proponents of privatization of higher education favor it on the grounds that not only it would relieve the financial burden of the government but also it would provide enhanced levels of internal and external efficiency and raise the quality of higher education. It is also believed that it provides a more relevant type of education responding more quickly to the market needs.

However, self-financed and unaided private institutions charge a high tuition fees and 'capitation fees' or donations. In higher education, there has been a mushroom growth of private engineering and medical colleges, which charge either capitation fees or a considerably higher tuition fees than the colleges run by the government.

Within Indian academia, there have been two contradictory positions on the issue of privatization. The first not only accept but also promotes the policy of private control of education on the ground that the state has no longer any funds for higher education and that is through private initiatives alone. There could be an improvement in accountability and efficiency in the management of colleges and universities, which are in a state of complete decay. Some commentators have, instead, argues that one part of the contention is wrong–the state has funds for public institutions, but has no political will to mobilize and utilize them in the best interest of the public (Patel, 2004).

III

CHALLENGES FOR HIGHER EDUCATION

GATS and Globalization has thrown new challenges to the Indian educational institutions. The Indian education system needs to adopt the emerging technologies in order to face the challenges. The challenges faced by the Indian educational institutions are multi-dimensional. Some of them are as follows:

- The major risk in the globalize world is country risk, arising out of intrusion and investment characterized by political, financial and economic uncertainties. The already widening global inequality will be further fuelled by educational inequality in appropriating opportunities.
- Where the role of market becomes paramount and rural development turns out to be the kingpin of development of India.
- Globalization of education has a potential danger for developing country like India, as inequalities are likely to be accentuated with the developed countries becoming stronger and dominant.
- Higher education will become commercialized and the values of the market place will dominate university campuses.

The globalization of education under GATS is thus posing serious threats before the conventional system of higher education in India.

SUGGESTIONS

The institutes of higher education in India, till now, have not set any clear goals in higher education. Now, under the fast globalization of higher education under GATS (General Agreement on Trade Services) there is a need to review the present dimensions of higher education and provide directions with clear goals for achievements. In different areas of higher education, we have strengths as well as weaknesses. How much of our higher education should be committed to GATS depends on our strengths, the level of preparedness of higher education in different branches of higher education. In this connection, following suggestions may be helpful:

- Produce a large number of technocrats so that no field of activity should suffer from lack of manpower.
- Develop higher education and human resources in order to pave way for economic development.
- Create a level of high quality in students that should be directly reflected in their achievements so that there is more demand for them in India and abroad.
- Mobilize resources in the universities towards financial self-sufficiency through consultancy, patenting and other contractual services.
- The share of expenditure on education must be raised to the recommended level of 6 per cent from the present level of around 3 per cent.
- The quality of higher education is very poor as assessed by the NAAC. So, all steps should be taken to improve the quality of education by replacing outmoded methods of teaching and material with modern methods and materials.
- To prevent inequalities from increasing, the government should provide liberal scholarships and loans to deserving poor students.
- With respect to foreign education provided in India the government should give permission to educational institutions only when they meet certain requirements for maintenance of a minimum standard.
- Creation of global environment on campuses so that our students may have international outlook to deal with issues of their concern.
- Our own social-cultural heritage should be preserved along with the acceptance of international exposure and technological advancement.

CONCLUSION

Globalization has a multi-dimensional impact on the system of education. It has underlined the need for reforms in the educational system with particular reference to the wider utilization of information technology; giving productivity dimension to the educational system and emphasis on research and development. It has advocated privatization of higher education without realizing the dangerous possibility of making the system a commercial enterprise. Once India makes commitments for trade in higher education under WTO policy regime and allows market access, commercial presence mode will be further strengthened. Thus, India must realize the impending threats of trade in education and try to convert these into opportunities.

REFERENCES

Khajapeer, M. (2003), "GATS in Hihger Education in India: Some Implications" in Dadibhavi R.V. and Bagalkoti S.T. (Ed): 'World Trade Organisation: Implications on India', Department of Studies in Economics, Karnatak University, Dharwad.

Dadibhavi, R.V. (2003), "General Agreement in Trade in Services (GATS)-Some Implications" in Dadibhavi R.V. and Bagalkoti S.T. (Ed): 'World Trade Organisation: Implications on India', Department of Studies in Economics, Karnatak University, Dharwad.

Shani, Rohini and Sumita Kale (2004), "GATS and Higher Education: Some Reflections", Economic and Political Weekly, Vol. 39, No. 21, May 22-28, pp. 2174-2180.

Patel, Sujata (2004), "Higher Education at the Crossroads", Economic and Political Weekly, Vol.39, No.21, May 22-28, pp.2151-2154.

Bhushan, Sudhanshu (2004), "Trade in Education Services Under GATS", Economic and Political Weekly, Vol. 39, No. 23, June 5-11, pp. 2395-2402.

Varma, P.L. (2003), "Globalisation and Impact on Human Development with a Focus on Education: An Experiment in Tagore's Land" in NIEPA (Ed) 'Globalisation and Challenges for Education', Shipra Publications, Delhi.

Giriappa, S. (2003), "Globalised Education and Human Development: A Risk Analysis" in NIEPA (Ed) 'Globalisation and Challenges for Education', Shipra Publications, Delhi.

Cyril, Kanmony J. (2003), "Impact of Globalisation on Human Development and Education" in NIEPA (Ed) 'Globalisation and Challenges for Education', Shipra Publications, Delhi.

Pathy, M.K. (2003), "Globalisation: The Threat Perceptions to Equality of Educational Opportunities" in NIEPA (Ed) 'Globalisation and Challenges for Education', Shipra Publications, Delhi.

Kishor, C. Samal (2003), "Equity and Financing Education" in NIEPA (Ed) 'Globalisation and Challenges for Education', Shipra Publications, Delhi.

Aggarwal, Raj (2003), "A New WTO Paradigm: Equity and Equality in Higher Education" in NIEPA (Ed) 'Globalisation and Challenges for Education', Shipra Publications, Delhi.

Ushadevi, M.D. (2001), "Poverty Database in Education", Economic and Political Weekly, Vol. 36, No. 29, July 21-27, pp. 2779-2783.

Paliwal, K. Dinesh (2002), "Globalisation of Indian Education", University News, Vol. 40, No. 39, September 30-October 6.

Grindle Merilee, www.ksgharvardedu.com.

The World Bank (2000), Higher Education in Developing Countries, Peril and Promise, The Task Force on Higher Education Society, Washington.

World Bank (1994), Higher Education: The Lessons of Experience. Development in Practice Series. Washington, D.C.

Manpower Profile of India (2002), New Delhi.

Gandhar, Harsh (2005), Gender Disparity in Higher Education in Independent India, University News, Vol. 43, No. 42, 17-23rd October.

Indiresan, Jaya (2002), Education for Women's Empowerment, Konark Publishers Pvt. Ltd., New Delhi.

Tilak, Jandhyala (2005), Higher Education in 'Trishanku', Economic and Political Weekly, Vol. XL, No. 37, 10-16th September.

WTO-GATS AND INDIA: AN OVERVIEW

Dinesh Kumar Sharma and
Vikas Kumar

INTRODUCTION

Services are simply defined as diverse group of economic activities distinct from manufacturing, mining and agriculture. The term encompasses a broad range of industries that provide the basic economic infrastructure (communications, transport, distribution, energy-related services, construction, water supply, sanitation and sewerage services, waste collection and disposal), financial infrastructure (banking, insurance, financial markets), support to business (advertising, marketing, computer services, professional services), or needed social infrastructure (education, health and social services).

In the beginning of the 21st Century, the global economy shows significant structural changes with a swing of services sector's contribution. In the process of economic development, the high growth of services sector is phenomenal in recent decades rather than simultaneous growth of primary, secondary and tertiary sectors. This is directly due to the development of sophistication in the information technology. Since 1980s, the share of services sector in the real GDP in India has also surpassed that of agriculture and industry. It is also reflected in the state-level developmental growth. No doubt, the dynamics of the services sector infuses new growth impulses stimulating investment, income, consumption and employment. But there seems to be some conflict between the growth of employment and growth of output in the Indian context.

The technological advancements and globalisation have created immense scope for trade in services. The growth of trade in services is expected to lead to the following benefits:

Economic Performance: Presence of an efficient services infrastructure is a precondition for economic success. Services such as telecommunications, banking, insurance and transport, supply strategically important inputs for all sectors, both in goods and services.

Development: Access to world-class services help exporters and producers in developing countries to capitalize on their competitive strength.

Employment Opportunities: Growth in trade in services promotes employment within the country and growth in opportunities for professionals overseas.

Consumer Choice: There is strong evidence in many services, e.g. Telecom that liberalization leads to lower prices, better quality and wider choice for consumers.

Technology Transfer: Services liberalization encourages foreign direct investment (FDI). Such FDI generally brings with it new skills and technologies that spill over into the wider economy in various ways.

The Services Sector constitutes a large part of the Indian economy both in terms of employment potential and its contribution to national income. This Sector has been the most dynamic sector of the Indian economy, especially over the last ten years. Table-1 shows the changes that have been taking place in the Services Sector over the last few decades. From a low level of 27.52 per cent of GDP in 1950-51, the share of services increased to 47.88 per cent in 1999-2000. Between 1950-51 and 1990-91, the share of Services Sector in GDP rose by only 13.07 percentage points, which is an increase of about 0.33 percentage points per annum. However, between 1990-91 and 1999-2000, the share had increased by 7.29 percentage points, which is an increase of 0.81 percentage points per annum. Clearly, the rate of growth is significantly higher in the 1990s.

The Table 1 also shows the contribution of various sectors of economy in GDP. In this classification, Services includes (a) transport, communication and trade; (b) banking and insurance, real estate, dwellings and business services; and (c) public administration, defence and other services. Agriculture includes forestry and logging, fishing, mining and quarrying while manufacturing includes construction, electricity, gas and water supply.

Table 1
Sectoral Shares in GDP

(in per cent)

Year	*Services*	*Agriculture*	*Manufacturing*
1950-51	27.52	59.19	13.29
1960-61	28.65	54.74	16.61
1970-71	31.97	48.12	19.91
1980-81	36.59	41.82	21.59
1990-91	40.59	34.92	24.49
1991-92	41.99	34.08	23.93
1992-93	42.09	34.17	23.74
1993-94	42.77	33.54	23.69
1994-95	42.71	32.94	24.35
1995-96	43.95	30.58	25.47
1996-97	43.69	30.86	25.45
1997-98	45.77	29.03	25.20
1998-99	46.46	29.03	24.51
1999-2000	47.88	27.49	24.63

Source: Economic Survey 2000-2001.

World Trade Organisation (WTO) which is the outcome of GATT especially Uruguay Round of negotiations which was elongated for the period of about eight years that is, from 1986 to 1994. It took birth on January 1, 1995. General Agreement on Tariffs and Trade (GATT) as the title itself suggests was mainly concerned with trade and tariff but WTO is related to worldwide trade and trade is not only confined to commodities but also to services.

Prior to the Uruguay Round, services were considered to have less scope for trade expansion than goods due to existence of technical, institutional and regulatory barriers. With the development of new transmission technologies facilitating the supply of services (e.g. satellite communication, electronic banking, tele-education), the opening of monopolies in various countries (e.g. telecommunication) and gradual liberalization of sectors which were earlier state regulated like transport, banking and insurance and simultaneous changes in consumer preferences, enhanced the "tradability" of services. These developments increased international services flows and created a similar need for multilateral disciplines - as in the area of goods. Thus, there was a need to create a credible and reliable system of international trade rules, which ensured fair and equitable treatment of all countries on the principles of non-discrimination.

The General Agreement on Trade in Services (GATS) came into existence and enforced on 1 January 1995 with the establishment of the WTO as a result of the Uruguay Round of negotiations. The multilateral legal instruments resulting from the Uruguay Round were treated as a single undertaking. India also signed all the WTO agreements under the single undertaking rule and GATS is a part of this whole package. It aims at stimulating trade and development by seeking to create a predictable policy environment wherein the member countries voluntarily undertake to bind their policy-regimes relating to trade in services.

The GATS covers all internationally traded services with two exceptions: services provided to the public in the exercise of governmental authority and in the air transport sector, traffic rights and all services directly related to the exercise of traffic rights. The WTO Secretariat has divided all services into the following 12 sectors.

1. Business services (including professional and computer services)
2. Communication services
3. Construction and Engineering services
4. Distribution services (e.g. agents, wholesale & retail trade and franchising)
5. Education services
6. Environment services
7. Finance (including insurance and banking) services
8. Health services
9. Tourism and Travel services
10. Recreation, Cultural and Sporting Services
11. Transportation Services, and
12. Other services not elsewhere classified.

GATS give the flexibility to each member country to decide the service sectors in which it will undertake and schedule commitments. It allows the member countries to indicate measures that will be kept in place for that sector, which will act as limitation to market access and national treatment, as well as the Modes in which commitments are to be taken. These commitments are specified by modes of supply.

MODE 1: Cross-border supply refers to a situation where the service flows from the territory of one Member country into the territory of another Member country. For example, an architect can send his architectural plan through electronic means; a teacher can send teaching material to students in any other country; a doctor sitting in Germany can advise his patient in India through electronic means. In all these cases, trade in services takes place and this is equivalent to cross-border movement of goods.

MODE 2: Consumption abroad refers to a situation where consumer of a service moves into the territory of another Member country to obtain the service. For example, a tourist using hotel or restaurant services abroad; a ship or aircraft undergoing repair or maintenance services abroad.

MODE 3: Commercial presence implies that service suppliers of a Member country establish a territorial presence (a legal presence) in another Member country with a view to providing their services. In this case, the service supplier establishes a legal presence in the form of a joint venture/ subsidiary/representative/branch office in the host country and starts supplying services.

MODE 4: Presence or movement of natural persons (this only refers to export of manpower) covers situations in which a service is delivered through persons of a Member country temporarily entering the territory of another Member country. Examples include independent service suppliers (e.g. doctors, engineers, individual consultants, accountants, etc.) However, GATS covers only temporary movement and not citizenship, residence or employment on a permanent basis in the foreign country.

The scope of study covers the policy position of services and their impact on India's trade in services. The scope of the commercial and public services is bound to vary overtime and between countries. However, there is a common denominator across nations that the availability of certain services is in the general economic interest or even more broadly in the general interest of the country.

The status of public services is one of the highly debated issues surrounding the GATS. There are two approaches to distinguish such services from any other services: an institutional approach that focuses on the legal and institutional conditions governing supply (e.g. ownership status, market organization), and a functional approach based on the policy objectives that may be involved (e.g. distributional and quality-related considerations, concepts of universal access).

This study also focuses on the relevance of the GATS for different organisational settings - from government monopolies to regulate and/or subsidize private provision -that may be used by WTO Members to meet typical public service objectives. It turns out that virtually all forms of organization, the framework of the Agreement to fully exploit its opportunities and avoid unpleasant surprises, however, governments would need to thoroughly analyse the relevant provisions in the light of their own policy objectives.

Though, it is the concern of every nation to ensure the supply of some necessary services to all sections of society for the attainment of human welfare and economic growth. The nations also aim to attract as much foreign investments in as many sectors to harness maximum growth opportunities. The issue before is to set proper state policies regarding the services. Thus, there is a need to thoroughly analyse the nature, type, users and purpose of any service before deciding to undertake any commitment under GATS in any particular service area by India. On the basis of type, services can be broadly classified - public services and commercial services.

The organisation of this paper into various sections is as follows:

- **Public Services:** This section will briefly discuss the public services, their importance for development and the concerns of a developing country like India before making any commitment under GATS, regarding ensuring their adequate and timely supply at reasonable cost and quality.

- **Commercial Services:** This will analyse the scope of commercial services, the opportunities available to India for trade expansion in such services through various modes of service supply outlined under GATS.
- **India and GATS:** It will brief an account of India's negotiating positions under GATS, as evidenced by her negotiating proposals; requests made by India and made to India from WTO members under GATS; decision on initial offers, their scope and to the extent allowed; her participation in bilateral market access negotiations.
- **Conclusion:** The position and challenges before India in current scenario are described in the concluding section. India virtually finds herself at the crossroads of decision-making in journey to reach upto the destination of trade growth leading to sustainable economic development.

PUBLIC SERVICES

Services are essential for development, broadly understood as improvements to human welfare. Availability of essential services, such as water supply, sanitation, power supply, transportation, education or health, is associated with higher productivity and earnings. But services are often inaccessible, prohibitively expensive or even when accessible of low quality and unsuited to the needs of consumers (World Bank, 2003). Moreover, services sectors can be particularly important in terms of employment because many services are labour-intensive. In principle, the development of the labour-intensive sector can help reduce poverty by generating labour-intensive growth.

The scope of public services for the different countries and same country at different times tends to vary. There is no stable relationship between the measures that government might take in a particular sector and a particular set of GATS provisions. The legal and institutional arrangements ultimately govern the provision of a particular service at a particular point of time. One of the prime concerns is government continued ability to ensure adequate supplies of socially relevant services such as health and education. The GATS could sound the death knell, it is feared, for the free provision of core public services-to the detriment of less privileged users and ultimately, social cohesion.

From that perspective, it appears that the safest approach for a WTO Member is not to undertake any commitments in potentially sensitive areas. However, safety could come at a cost in terms of missed investment and growth opportunities. There are two options in principle to avoid such problems and facilitate the assumption of GATS commitments in public service sectors. One is country-specific and another consists of the conditioning of specific commitments in a manner that confines their scope to closely circumscribed segments of a sector.

Financial incentives and sanctions (taxes and subsidies): Governments have wide leeway under the GATS to use financial incentives and disincentives with a view to modifying market outcomes. The most-favoured-nation principle may operate as a potential constraint but as noted before, it is difficult to see why governments might want to discriminate between services or suppliers of different origin or nationality.

Again, the ensuing policy constraints do not appear to be substantial in many cases. Why would governments want to discriminate against foreign suppliers and their facilities (schools, hospitals, telecom operators, transport companies, etc.)? Are these less suited than their domestic counterparts to meet relevant sector objectives? As far as modes 3 and 4 are concerned, the answer can hardly be positive since all domestically established suppliers, regardless of nationality, are subject to the same regulations and controls. Although a number of Members nevertheless retained the option of operating discriminatory taxes and subsidies in particular under mode 3, it is interesting to note that many of these limitations are of a horizontal nature and specifically related to subsidies for research and development (R&D). They are thus more likely to reflect industrial policy considerations rather than, for instance, health-or education-specific concerns.

Protection in services (e.g. prohibitions of new entry into the market, or more restrictive operating conditions imposed solely on the new entrant, be it foreign or not) is, first of all, a tax on domestic consumers. The primary effect of protection is to reduce the supply of certain services and thereby force domestic demand towards more expensive, domestically produced services. Protection reduces supply and raises prices directly because of the higher costs of domestic producers. As such, protection becomes a tax on domestic consumers and leads to a redistribution of income from consumers to domestic producers. The effects of protection on prices to consumers can even be worse if the market is characterized by imperfect competition or a monopoly.

If the government intends to promote sector development via private participation in open segments, commitments may help to stabilize market expectations and enhance investors' confidence. Empirical research for the telecom sector confirms a significant positive relationship not only between openness, but also between GATS-committed access conditions and typical performance indicators in the sector. Absence of commitments might have impeded sector expansion.

Although experiences have varied considerably across countries and sectors, the introduction of competition has generally led to improvements in services performance, increases in infrastructure investment and service coverage, improvements in service quality and prices more closely aligned to underlying costs. The size of such changes depends enormously on the extent to which the market is liberalized and the effectiveness of regulation. In telecommunications, competition has boosted telecommunications coverage, lowered repair requests, raised call completion rates and reduce the time needed to receive a telephone line. In railroads, market reforms have increased locomotive availability. In ports, market reforms have shortened waiting times for vessels; while in electricity, they have lowered energy losses, outages per customer, and rates of plant unavailability.

To fully explore the impact of GATS on government's scope for action, it is also important to keep in mind certain conceptual limits. In contrast to the GATT, all substantive disciplines are exclusively 'import-related' the Agreement does not impose any constraints on Members' ability to promote or restrict own supplies under the four modes. In turn, this may enable or facilitate policies to promote the availability of public services. To give two examples:

- Obligations and commitments concerning mode 2 relate to government measures affecting the consumption of services by nationals who leave the country. Cases in point are prohibitively expensive tourist exit visas or the exclusion of university studies or medical treatment abroad from otherwise available domestic support schemes. Conversely, there are no constraints under whatever GATS provision that would diminish a government's ability to regulate the consumption of services by foreign tourists, students, patients, etc. within its own jurisdiction. The application of deterrents such as special taxes or quotas would not fall under the GATS; they may be used, for example, to ensure domestic consumers priority access to relevant facilities (hospitals, universities, etc.).

- The range of persons covered by obligations and commitments on mode 4 is confined essentially to foreigners seeking to supply services within another WTO Member's territory. Outbound movements of domestic doctors, teachers, nurses, etc. are not covered, however. There are thus no constraints on government initiatives to discourage such movements with a view, for example, to prevent losses of scarce skills and expertise.

In order to retain as many policy options as conceivable, a WTO Member might not want to undertake commitments in areas considered to be key governmental responsibilities. If monopolies are earmarked for gradual opening over time, there is the option of undertaking pre-commitments with a view to enhancing the credibility of the envisaged reforms and stabilize expectations.

Article VIII relates only to the supply of services by monopolies but not to their purchases of services for own consumption (example: a monopoly supplier of telecom services builds or buys new offices). Does this imply that the supplier is free-even in areas subject to specific commitments-to discriminate in favour of domestic companies? The answer may be in the affirmative. First, it might be argued that, in the absence of government interference, the GATS has no role to play in this context.

COMMERCIAL SERVICES

Cross-border trade in services is growing rapidly with both developed and developing countries among the most dynamic exporters. The importance of commercial services can be judged from the fact world trade in commercial services amounted to

US$ 1440 billion in the year 2001, which is 23 per cent of goods trade.

Despite the substantial global benefits from such trade, the adjustment pressures created in importing countries could provoke a protectionist backlash-some signs of which are already visible in procurement and regulatory restrictions.

Figure 1
Average Growth Rate of Exports of 'Business Services' for Selected Countries, 1995-2000

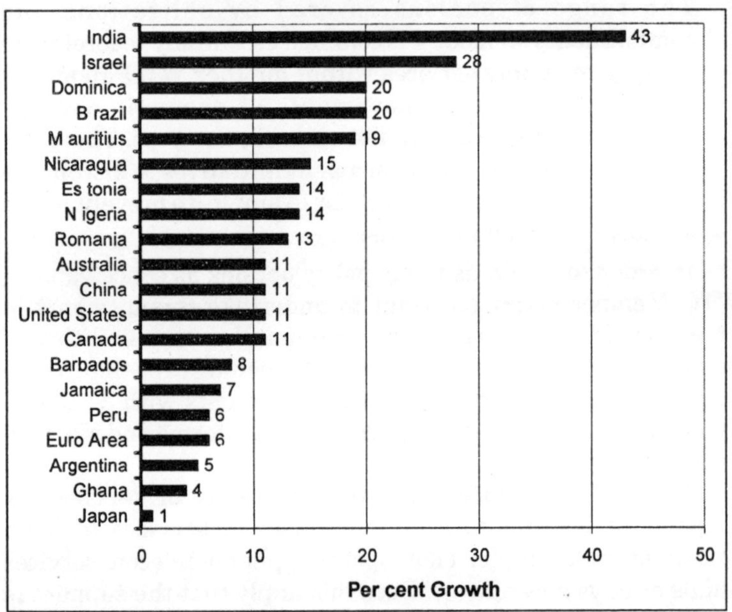

Source: IMF Balance of Payments Statistics.

No reliable estimates are available for trade in *business process outsourcing* services, but the IMF Balance of Payments category *business services* covers trade in all services other than *transport* and *travel* services.

ROLE OF INDIA AS COMMERCIAL SERVICES EXPORTER

The mode of supply of particular interest to India and other developing countries is Mode 4, i.e., the movement of natural persons. India, in particular, has a large pool of well-qualified professionals in the services sectors like computer and related services, education services, audiovisual services, accountancy services, architectural services, construction and engineering services, health services and consultancy services. India has fairly large comparative advantage over other member countries with regard to supply of professional services in these service sectors.

Table 2
Leading Exporters of Commercial Services, 2001

Exporters	*Values*		*Share Annual Percentage Change*		
			'90-'00	*2000*	*2001*
United States	262.9	18.3	7	9	-3
United Kingdom	108.3	7.5	8	3	-6
Germany	79.8	5.5	5	-3	-1
France	79.0	5.5	2	-1	-3
Japan	63.3	4.4	5	13	-7
Hong Kong, China	43.0	3.0	9	13	2
Canada	34.7	2.4	7	7	-5
China	31.0	2.2	18	15	3
Korea, Rep of	28.4	2.0	12	12	-2
India	20.1	1.4	14	26	14
Ireland	19.2	1.3	18	8	15
Malaysia	13.6	0.9	14	15	0
World	1440	100	6	6	-1

Source: Annual Report, 2002, World Trade Organisation.

Besides mode 4, modes 1 and 2 are also important for India. India can deliver professional services electronically via mode 1. Under mode 2, India can provide services such as medical, educational and tourism services to the foreign patients, students and tourists visiting India. India has competitive advantage in Business Process Outsourcing (BPO) services under mode 1. Typical BPO services include the following functional areas:

- Administration: tax processing, claims processing, asset management, document management, transcription and translation.

- Finance: billing services, accounting transactions, tax consulting and compliance, risk management, financial reporting, financial analysis.
- Human Resources: benefits administration, education and training, recruiting and staffing, hiring administration.
- Payroll Services: records management, payment services, credit/debit card services, cheque processing, transaction processing.
- Logistics and Distribution: materials management, distribution/warehouse management, logistics management and procurement.
- Customer Care: database marketing, customer analysis, telesales/telemarketing, inbound call centre.
- Content Development: engineering, design, animation, network consultancy and management, research and development.

ROLE OF INDIA AS COMMERCIAL SERVICES IMPORTER

Providing access to Foreign Service providers in Indian domestic market and undertaking commitments under GATS is another concern of trade in services. The experiences of liberalisation and allowing access of foreign banks, financial institutions, insurance companies and travel agencies in Indian market has revealed that market reforms and strengthened prudential regulation, has had a dynamic positive impact on the efficiency and competitiveness of local systems.

INDIA AND GATS

The General Agreement on Trade In Services (GATS) is the first set of international rules for the international trade in services. India has been a signatory to the Agreement since its entry into force in 1995. GATS sets out a framework of legally binding rules governing the conduct of world trade in services. It is supported by a number of schedules of specific commitments undertaken by individual WTO Members. These commitments bind Members not to introduce more restrictive rules, which could have an adverse effect on trade. India made initial commitments at the time of entry of GATS into force.

Table 3
Leading Importers of Commercial Services, 2001

(Billion Dollars and Percentage)

Exporters	*Values*		*Share Annual Percentage Change*		
			'90-'00	*2000*	*2001*
United States	187.6	13.1	7	16	-7
Germany	128.5	9	5	-3	-3
Japan	106.7	7.5	3	1	-8
United Kingdom	88.5	6.2	8	2	-5
France	60.0	4.2	2	-3	-2
Canada	39.6	2.8	4	7	-4
China	36.4	2.5	24	16	2
Ireland	33.6	2.4	19	8	17
Korea, Rep of	32.6	2.3	13	23	-1
India	23.7	1.7	13	15	21
Malaysia	16.3	1.1	12	13	-2
World	1430	100	6	6	-1

Source: Annual Report, 2002, World Trade Organisation.

The mandated negotiations under GATS to work out the rules and framework for further liberalisation of trade in services are underway. The main objective of the negotiations is to liberalise commitments in all the service sectors and all the modes of supply of services and to improve the multilateral rules for trade in services. The main method of negotiations under GATS is the Request and Offer process under which each country tables its demands from its trading partners and its offers to its trading partners sector-wise. Under successive rounds of negotiations aimed at progressive liberalisation, Members individually choose the sectors in which binding commitments are to be made and those in which commitments are not to be made. This is known as a "positive listing" or "bottoms-up" approach. Negotiations proceed on the basis of requests and offers; that is, countries request each other to consider liberalisation in particular sectors and respond with offers. Agreement to liberalise is not reached until all participating Members–including developing countries–are satisfied with the total package being offered.

It has been decided at the Doha Ministerial Conference that each member country must submit initial requests and initial offers. This request-offer process is underway. In formulating the offers, Members are not obliged to respond positively to any particular request. Nor is there any requirement for reciprocity. That is, a request made by India in one area/sector/ activity does not impose any obligation to accept a similar request made of it by other countries. Further, the Doha Ministerial Declaration reaffirms the rights of Members to regulate and to introduce new regulations on the supply of services.

India has to decide on the extent to which she can afford to meet the requests that have been made to her and also to identify the market access barriers that she faces and frame requests for liberalisation appropriately. This objective is to be achieved by providing the opportunity to all interested parties in India to participate in the formulation of India's offers in the negotiations with trading partners under GATS. In this direction, the requests made by India to member countries and vice-versa are summarised as:

Requests by India

- Take full commitments in respect of the category of independent professionals de-linked from commercial presence.
- Put in place a visa system to ensure the fulfillment of horizontal and sectoral commitments undertaken.
- Undertake to put in place a Visa system-ensuring grant of multiple entry visas for professionals.
- Allow inter-firm mobility to professionals.

Requests to India

India has been asked to take commitments with regard to transparency in domestic regulations, simplify procedures, eliminate differential treatment of Foreign Service suppliers and facilitate the movement of natural persons under Mode 4. The categories of professionals on which commitments have been sought include intra-corporate transferees, contractual service suppliers and specialists (tradespersons, associate professionals, professionals and managers).

India has submitted 'requests' to her trading partners in computer related services, architecture services, health services, audio-visual services, tourism services, maritime services and financial services. On the other hand, India has received requests from 22 countries and has to finalise her response to these requests through an "initial offer". The initial offer would point towards the direction in which a Member is willing to liberalise. However, the initial offer has no legal status and can be withdrawn or amended at any time if the Member feels that the trading partners' offers are not satisfactory or adequate.

India is a proponent of liberalisation of trade in services through Mode 4. In order to promote the liberalisation of mode 4, India has submitted a proposal at the special session of the Council for Trade in Services on "Liberalisation of Movement of Professionals". The salient features of the proposals are as follows:

(i) The Indian proposal notes that the developed member countries have taken limited commitments in Mode 4, which is of significant interest to developing countries. These commitments are further reduced in scope on account of various measures taken by developed member countries.

(ii) The Indian proposal suggests following strategy for improving trade in services through mode 4:

   (a) Economic Needs Test (ENT): In order to reduce the scope for discriminatory practices in use of ENT, multinational norms need to be established.

   (b) Social security contributions need not be required to be made for temporary movement, as contributors are not eligible for receiving benefits of such contributions. As it affects the comparative advantage of professionals, they should be exempted from such payments.

   (c) Administration of visa regimes may be made more transparent. Notion of a separate GATS visa for personnel covered by horizontal and sectoral commitments scheduled by a Member, different and less onerous from the normal immigration visa, may be considered.

   (d) Specific Sectoral commitments in line with requirements of developing countries need to be taken. For this purpose, more detailed sub classification of categories of personnel and their inclusion in sectoral/horizontal commitments may be required.

(e) Non-recognition of qualifications by developed countries often acts as a serious barrier to market entry. It would be necessary to work for the establishment of multilateral norms to facilitate Mutual Recognition Agreements (MRAs) among Member countries. There should be a mechanism to attend to specific problems being faced by developing countries regarding the mutual recognition of qualifications so as to ensure complete equity and fairness in recognition matters.

SEEKING ENHANCED ACCESS IN FOREIGN MARKETS: WHERE AND HOW?

As experienced, the principal beneficiary of trade reform is the reformer, particularly if it is a small country. Nevertheless, if other countries liberalize their markets in sectors of own export interest, the unilateral liberaliser benefits twice because a country cannot on its own improve access for its exports to foreign markets. The pertinent question raised therefore is not whether to seek more access in foreign markets but where (in what sectors or modes of supply) and how.

Services have been among the fastest growing components of world trade over the last two decades particularly in the 1980s. Indeed, over the period 1980-1990, the average annual growth rate of services exports was over 8 per cent compared to 5.7 per cent for merchandise exports. The performance of services trade was particularly impressive in the second half of the 1980s, with an average growth rate of 15.5 per cent per annum. However, thereafter the record is mixed. At the aggregate level, services and merchandise trade have evolved in a roughly similar way since 1990 (both growing at 6.6 per cent per annum), leaving the share of trade in services in international trade stagnant, at around a fifth of all cross-border trade.

INDIA REAPING THE BENEFITS OF THE OUTSOURCING TREND

Apart from the undeniable interest in supply through mode 4, India has a genuine interest in the expansion of commitments on cross-border trade (mode 1). Technological advances increasingly allow the spatial fragmentation of goods and services production, and off-shoring to operational units abroad and even outsourcing to a foreign third party service supplier has become common practice among multinational corporations. Developing countries are indeed becoming exporters of so-called Business Process Outsourcing (BPO) services. India is the most notable beneficiary case of this trend of BPO services but other countries (e.g. China, Malaysia, and Philippines) are also joining the business and posing new challenges. India enjoys competitive advantage in the form of low-labour costs, the availability of a well-educated pool of workers, and the improvement in the quality and price of international telecommunications.

For the moment, the vast majority of the services are the paper-based back-office ones that can be digitalized and communicated over telecommunications networks anywhere around the world. However, the more advanced developing countries are even moving from this type of services (data entry, etc.) to more integrated and higher-end service bundles in fields like customer care, human resource management and product development.

CONCLUSION

The share of services in GDP and employment tends to rise with income, but even for the poorest countries it is now significant. In 2001, service sectors accounted for 45 per cent of GDP in low-income economies; 57 per cent in middle-income and almost 71 per cent in high-income. Services activities in low and middle-income countries have been expanding faster than GDP for the last two decades and represent on average 5 to 10 per cent points more of GDP than in the early 1980s. An implication of this continuous shift toward services is that the overall growth of productivity in the economy will be increasingly determined by what happens in the service sector (IMF, 1997).

However, productivity gains–and therefore growth and poverty reduction-are often hampered by an inefficient allocation of resources as a consequence of trade protection. Although countries usually approach multilateral trade negotiations with the objective of seeking "concessions" or market access opportunities in other markets, while minimizing the export opportunities that they grant in their own markets–a crude but real mercantilist approach to negotiations-it is worth emphasizing that trade protection results first and foremost in a cost to the country that imposes it.

Liberalization of services sectors means not only the reduction or elimination of barriers that affect the services per se, but also those barriers that affect services firms, such as restrictions on entry, legally established monopolies or oligopolistic market structures, discriminatory taxation, limits on foreign investment. The liberalizing of trade in services ensures the improvement of resource allocation in line with social marginal costs and benefits (the traditional static gains from trade); a better access to better technologies, inputs and intermediate services; greater domestic competition; transfer of know-how and technology through investment and a shake-up of industry that may create an innovative and competitive environment which leads to growth. The GATS basically implies greater competition in the market and non-discrimination against foreign services and service suppliers, leads to a more economically rational market structure. Markets in protected economies are narrow and lack of competition from the rest of the world, whether actual or potential, fosters oligopoly and inefficiency. Protectionism creates market power for domestic firms; while trade openness exposes those same firms to greater competition, reducing monopoly rents, driving down margins and reducing prices for consumers. In a competitive environment, firms are forced to innovate, to introduce new products and to improve quality constantly; otherwise, they will be forced to exit the market.

However, trade liberalization and integration into the world economy is not an end in itself but a powerful means to achieve the objective of sustainable economic growth and development. Powerful as it may be, it is worth remembering that trade liberalization is a necessary but not a sufficient condition to attain economic development. Many other factors, such as geography, resource endowments, the protection of property rights in its largest sense, and the quality of the institutional and regulatory frameworks will be determinants of success. And it should be unfair to place all the expectations of success in only one aspect of any development policy –trade liberalisation and globalisation.

From the above discussion, it is established that GATS provides an international platform to India like all member countries to negotiate, make and receive offers regarding trading of services with probable and potent trading partners to achieve the business goals of the economy and to fulfill her developmental necessities. The situation can be better described as a crossroad rather than a final destination in the journey of economic empowerment and national development through the path of liberalisation and globalisation, where the era ahead is full of challenges and prudent decision making for India. In this context, India has to adopt dynamic and proactive approach in dealings under GATS, keeping in view her necessities, priorities, situations and global trade environment. The policies should be framed and appropriate positions should be taken timely to avoid any opportunity loss in the form of missed investment, capable of expansion and development of any service sector through proper allocation and utilisation of available resources and thus, enabling cost reduction and adequate supply of services. At the same time, India should be vigilant in ensuring essential public services supply both in terms of quality and quantity at appropriate time and competitive prices, hence safeguard the social development dimension of the nation.

REFERENCES

Adlung Rolf (2005), "Public Services and the GATS" WTO Working Paper ERSD-2003-05.

Adlung, Rudolf (2003), The GATS Negotiations: Implications for Health and Social Services, Intereconomics, Vol. 38, No. 3, pp. 147-155.

ASEAN Workshop on the GATS Agreement and its Impact on Health Services (2002), GATS, Trade, Health & Services, Jakarta. [www.who.or.id/download/eng/GATS,trade,health and services.zip]

Chaudhuri, Mattoo & Richard (2004), "Moving People To Deliver Services: How Can The Gats Help?" World Bank Policy Research Working Paper.

Fidler & David (2004), Legal Review of the General Agreement on Trade in Services (GATS) from a Health Policy Perspective, WHO: Globalization, Trade and Health Working Papers Series, Geneva.

Jansen M. & Keck A. (2004), "National Environmental Policies and Multilateral Trade Rules" WTO Staff Working Paper ERSD-2004-01.

Keck A. & Low P. (2004), "Special and Differential Treatment in the WTO: Why, When and How?" WTO Staff Working Paper ERSD-2003-04.

Marchetti Juan A. (2004), "Developing Countries In The WTO Services Negotiations" WTO Staff Working Paper ERSD-2004-06.

Mattoo, A. (2003), Shaping Future Rules for Trade in Services: Lessons from the GATS, in Ito, T. and Anne Krueger, eds, Trade in Services in the Asia-Pacific Region–NBER-EASE Volume 11, University of Chicago Press.

Mattoo, A., and S. Wunsch (2004c), "Pre-empting Protectionism in Services: The WTO and Outsourcing", World Bank Policy Research Working Paper 3237, March 2004.

Winters, Alan (2003), "The Economic Implications of Liberalising Mode 4 Trade." in Mattoo and Carzaniga.

WTO (2001), Market Access: Unfinished Business, Special Studies No. 6, Geneva.

WTO (2001), Market Access: Unfinished Business- Post Uruguay Round, Inventory and Issues; Geneva: WTO Staff Working Paper ERSD-2001-06.

WTO (2002a), "GATT/WTO Dispute Settlement Practice Relating to GATT Article XX, Paragraphs (b), (d) and (g)–Note by the WTO Secretariat", WT/CTE/W/203.

WTO REGIME AND INDIA: GLOBAL MARKET, COMPETITIVENESS, OPPORTUNITIES AND CHALLENGES

Shakeel Ahmad Khan and Md. Reyazuddin

INTRODUCTION

Great depression of 1930s and the horrors of Second World War adversely affected the world trading system and reluctantly many countries had to impose import restriction for safeguarding their economies. This led to sharp decline in international trade. Many proposals for extending international trade were put forwarded by USA in 1945. Later in view of the situation 23 countries at Geneva signed an agreement related to tariffs imposed on trade (known as GATT) on October 30, 1947 with the main objective to reform world trade, which was highly distorted due to direct and indirect subsidy on various sectors of the economy across the world. The Eighth Uruguay Round of GATT started in 1986 in Uruguay and ended in Geneva on December 15, 1993 covering new complex areas, especially agriculture and services, including banking insurance and telecommunication. After Dunkel Draft was signed by all the member nations on December 15, 1993 and the accord was approved and adopted on April 15, 1994 and came into effect from January 1, 1995 in the form of World Trade Organisation which act as a permanent watch dog on the international trade. It has a legal status and enjoys privileges and immunities on the same footing as the IMF and the World Bank. There were 148 member countries of the WTO as on September 2003. The principal mandate of the WTO is to promote an open, equitable and non-discriminatory multilateral trading system. The members themselves decides on the rules governing their trade relations, and periodically enter into rounds of negotiations aimed at further opening up of markets and reforming the agreements. Global free trade is the corner stone of the WTO creating a fair and equitable, rule based multilateral trading system. India joined WTO since its inception. The formation of WTO synchronizes the beginning of economic reforms in India. This paper is an attempt to analyse various aspects of WTO implications on vital sectors of Indian economy. It examines closely all possible challenges, opportunities, alternatives, missing links, development paradigms, strategic planning to face the onslaught of WTO.

WTO AND AGRICULTURE

Impact of WTO on agriculture is of paramount importance. The undercurrent among farmers seemed to be a fear of the unknown. Farmers need to worry about domestic issues rather than WTO. World agricultural prices have dipped below the Indian prices in the last few years. The volatility of world prices of agricultural goods has increased over the last few years and the cyclical pattern in prices has not been effected under WTO agreement. As procurement prices have upward trend Indian prices will exceed world prices and which leads to export decrease specially in case of wheat exports from India. Agriculture exports of basic commodities are subject to export restrictions. In terms of wheat and rice the possibilities of expanding production through increased irrigation in existing areas is limited and as result productivity is stagnant. Internal problem is that export-oriented farming also trends to favour larger producers over smaller farmers who cannot produce volumes demanded by exporting companies or who are trying to cultivate crop with which they are unfamiliar. There is thus increased use of plantation farming or contract growing to supply exports markets, and a corresponding displacement of small farmers leading to food security problem.

Environmental degradation for the use of pesticides and fertilizers will have also adverse effect on food security among the marginal section of society. The removal of QRs (quantitative restrictions) on 825 agriculture items would definitely create stiff competition for Indian agriculture market. To tide over the challenges of cheap foreign goods several effective measures need to be taken. As a measure India should impose tariff duties on the import of those items for which QRs have been removed. This would not go contrary to the spirit of WTO agreements. Secondly, India along with other developing countries should negotiate for more liberal trade environment in the rest of the world too. (Gulati, 1999) In fact, India has a reasonably strong comparative advantage in most of the agricultural products but she cannot enjoy this advantage because agricultural market in the developed countries is highly protected. For example in the European Union, products like meat, milk and cream, cheese, rice, wheat flour etc. continue to carry tariffs of over 120 per cent. Besides this, countries provide huge subsidies to farmers to enable them to compete in the world market. If these restrictions, which are contrary to WTO provisions, are removed, India would be able to compete successfully in the world agricultural markets even after withdrawal of QRs. Measures should be taken to prepare our agricultural and allied activities for global competition with cost-effective production and efficient management.

Table 1
Trend of Primary Commodity Prices in the Global Market (US $/MT)

Year	*Wheat*	*Rice*	*Sugar*	*Cotton*	*Tea*
1970	250	574	323	-	-
1980	240	571	877	2843	2305
1990	136	271	277	1819	2058
1995	149	269	246	1785	1249
1998	121	293	189	1389	1968

Source: World Bank, Word Development Indicators 1993-1999.

Table shows that between 1980 and 1998, the wheat price in global market declined from $240 to per ton to 121, while prices of rice declined from $571 to $293, of sugar from $877 to 189; of cotton from $2843 to $1389 and of Tea from $2058 to 1968. Thus, the declining trend in the global primary commodity prices may affect the global competitiveness of Indian agriculture. According to some studies (Parikh, 1998) due to India's intervention in global rice market, global export prices may decrease further and import prices may increase affecting India's position adversely. Some other studies (Bhattacharya, 2000) apprehend that the globalization of trade under WTO regime may lead to food insecurity in developing countries like India. However some other studies (Gulati, 1994, Bhalla, 1996) hope that in India would gain from its participation in liberalized trade in agriculture. But commitment to WTO, India is going on reducing the subsidy level regularly, paving way for the developed countries to enter into Indian agricultural market. As a matter of fact the WTO agreement itself provides enough loopholes to take advantage and the developed countries are fully exploiting these loopholes. Two types of exemption for subsidy reduction "Green Box Measures" and Blue Box Measures" are being used by developed countries substituting market price support by direct payment. Whereas India's policy of subsidy reduction in agriculture for few years is not the right step. Demand for abolition of such support measures must be raised very strongly by India in future round of ministerial conference of WTO.

The most adverse affect and huge losses to India, which are expected from the agreement of TRIPS (Trade Related Aspects of Intellectual Property Rights). Under our patent Act 1970 only the process patents are granted in food, chemicals and medicines, whereas in TRIPS agreements product patents are granted in all these areas. The extension of TRIPS to agriculture has thus serious implications for India harming the interests of farmers. The TRIMs (Trade Related Investment Measures and Services) agreement also goes against all developing countries including India. The free play of multinational seed companies and others are posing great threat to the Bio-wealth/ Bio-diversity and environment of India. In terms of WTO guidelines, the main concerns in agriculture are on domestic subsidies, public distribution system, access to Indian market to be given to foreign suppliers and patenting of seeds. The major issues that have controversies are Trade-Related Intellectual Property Rights (TRIPS) and Trade Related Investment Measures (TRIMs) and trade in services. The accord on TRIPS had raised a whole range of apprehensions in the country. In particular, the patenting of seeds and genes, generated a lot of controversy. Farmers were told that they would have to buy their seeds every year from the multinational seed companies like Pioneer, Sandoz, Cargill etc. The TRIPS agreement covered eight types of intellectual property, viz., patent, trade mark, copy rights, industrial designs, integrated circuits, geographical indication, protection of undisclosed information and control of anti-competition practices in contractual licenses. Of these, it is only in the area of patents that the most serious controversy is going around in India, that the advanced countries have a distinct advantage and a decisive lead over the developing and the least developed countries. A patent is given for an invention. To qualify for a patent, an inventive step's and satisfy three fundamental criteria, viz., it must be new, must involve an inventive steps and be useful in industry and agriculture. An invention would be regarded as new only if it is not known or used or made public anywhere in the world before the filling of the patent application. Anything existing or previously known or used, could not be given intellectual property protection. Protection by patent in agriculture threatens to deprive farmers of their rights to produce, reproduce, modify and sell seeds. Under this agreement now cannot use farm-saved seed unless he pays royalties to the patent holder. TRIPS ensure to promote measures and procedures so that intellectual property rights do not become barriers to legitimate trade. Although intellectual property regime covers pharmaceuticals, agriculture, chemicals, living organisms within the compass of patent laws, yet the fundamental apprehensions about TRIPS are caused by product protection through patents to all categories of inventions including drugs and pharmaceuticals and agriculture. Despite the grace period of ten years to implement products and process patent laws, there are clear indications that product protection for drugs and pharmaceuticals will produce adverse consequences on research work in developing alternative processes for the manufacture of essential drugs, which are currently marketed in India. The twenty years products patent, provided by TRIPS, injects an excessive monopoly power to multinational drug companies. Because a majority of patented drugs marked all over the world are under the jurisdiction of multinational companies. (BEJ, Conference Volume, 2003)

TRIPS to agriculture make no difference between subsidy to promote food security and self-reliance and those meant to increase exports of agriculture products. Subsidy only up to 10% of the value of production will cause difficulties for the government to give price support to particular agricultural products. Although it is not in case of input subsidy. Subsidies on fuel, electricity, fertilisers, transportation and seeds to the farmers may be curtailed in future due to increasing pressure on budget. In aggregate terms farmers will be the sufferers. In view of poor infrastructures on agriculture front and mass poverty integrated package of technologies, services and public policies should be provided to face the challenges of comparative disadvantages in world trade.

Developed countries engaged themselves in dirty tariffication, that is, they used data, which allowed tariffs to be bound as high as possible. These countries went in from higher reduction in low tariff sectors than in the high tariff ones. Reducing tariffs at an average rate of 36 per cent but average tariff levels were reduced by less than 18 per cent while on the other hand has agreed to tariff bindings of zero per cent in some commodities like milk powder, which are now being renegotiated to at least 50 per cent as the domestic market is witnessing the average effects. Punjab is facing the onslaught of imported milk products, prices of dairy products have crashed, and the state government has demanded that the Central Government should impose an anti-dumping duty of least at 60 per cent. During the period when India has been net importer of wheat, the extent of negative protection has been even greater. In recent years with declining international wheat prices and sustained increases in MSP (Minimum Support Price) for wheat, the price wedge has narrowed down. Therefore, MSPs for wheat is not expecting exceed the international prices in the near future, as any increase in MSP is likely to be offset by depreciation of the Indian Rupee. Even at the current wheat prices of around US$ 130 per tonne, India is not required to reduce product specific support for wheat, as MSP is lower than the import parity price. Non-product specific support in India has been positive and rising. Bhalla and Singh (1996) and Gulati and Sharma (1997) have estimated non-product specific support in the range of 5 to 7 per cent of value of agricultural production. India had bound its tariffs for wheat at 100 per cent and wheat flour at 150 per cent without giving any market access commitments on balance of payments considerations. Wheat import in India in the last five years on an average have been around one million tonnes. These imports have been affected by the Government on considerations of food security and not because of the AoA (Agreement on Agriculture). Removal of protective measures and reductions in farm support in EU and other developed countries would lead to elimination of exports of wheat from the EU; India was expected to become a net wheat exporter. Competitiveness of our wheat in the international market has been worked out by comparing the cost of Indian wheat and the US wheat for the period 1991-92 when wheat price was US 216 dollars per tone. In all other years, Indian wheat was not competitive in international market as it is clear from the table.

Table 2
Export Competitiveness of Indian Wheat

Year	*Wheat Cost ex-Kandla Rs. / Quintal*	*FOB Price (US$/ tonne)*	*Exchange Rate (Rs. / US$)*	*FOB Rupee Price (per quintal)*	*Ratio of Indian Wheat Coot of US Wheat Price*
1991-92	406.50	150	24.47	367.05	1.11
1992-93	535.08	143	30.65	438.30	1.22
1993-94	593.58	143	31.37	448.59	1.32
1994-95	615.31	157	31.40	492.98	1.25
1995-96	650.77	216	33.40	721.44	0.90
1996-97	718.86	181	33.50	606.35	1.19
1997-98	865.67	142	37.17	527.81	1.64
1998-99	879.35	121	42.35	514.25	1.71

Source: Computed from Commission on Agricultural Cost and Price Report (1999).

It is also very important that the higher procurement and handling costs of wheat due to inefficient operations of FCI also adversely affected wheat exports. An analysis was carried out to evaluate the economics of wheat exports with procurement costs and different levels of international wheat prices.

It is assumed in the above table that international trade in wheat is conducted in perfectly competitive markets without any major trade distortions. In de facto terms the international wheat market, is however, highly concentrated. Five transnational corporations control more than 70 per cent of worldwide wheat trade (Brown, 1993). These corporations are vertically integrated and can affect trading prospects of a country by transfer pricing mechanisms.

Table 3
Export Competitiveness of Wheat: Sensitivity Analysis
(Rs./Quintal)

Wheat Price FOB / US$ US Gulf)	*Rupee Price of US Wheat at Rs. 45 per US$*	*Wheat Cost Ex Kandla (FCI cost a 50 per cent of the Procurement Cost*	*Wheat Cost at Kandla with FCI Cost at 75 per cent of its Procurement Cost*	*Ratio of Indian Wheat to US Wheat at 50 per cent of FCI Cost*	*Ratio of Indian Wheat to US Wheat at 75 per cent of FCI Cost*
150	6750	738.46	808.90	1.09	1.20
175	7875	738.46	808.90	0.94	1.03
200	9000	738.46	808.90	0.82	0.90

Source: Computed from Commission on Agricultural Cost and Price Report (1999).

The adverse impact of Indian agriculture, which was feared by many in the country, seems to unfounded given the inherent competitiveness of Indian wheat. Greater attention needs to be devoted to the provision of inputs such as seeds, fertilizers and uninterrupted power supply to boost agricultural production. Non-tariff barriers have been replaced by tariffs, but effective measures can be used. In view of above integration of Indian agriculture in the global trade, a competitive trade scenario can be realized only by reducing domestic cost of production through measures, which increase productivity and control procurement and distribution costs. We can increase competitiveness of agriculture products including wheat, rice etc. by cost effective method at domestic level.

India was forced to either phase out or eliminate the quantitative restrictions (QRs) on agricultural commodities and products latest by April 1, 2001. India has therefore opened its market and in turn makes the farming community vulnerable to the imports of highly subsidised products. In Kerala, the prices of coconut, rubber, coffee and spices have crashed to the extent of 50% to 80%. In a competitive market the commodities are supplied and marketed, as determined by the cost of production. But if the imported commodities are highly subsidised this does not reflect a fair practice. The policy of WTO as enshrined in AoA is discriminatory, as it allows a number of relaxations in one form or the other to one-member countries, while it denied the same to another.

AGGREGATE MEASURE OF SUPPORT

Under AoA of developing countries, whose product specific and non-product specific Aggregate Measure of Support (AMS) does not exceed 10 per cent (5 per cent for a developed economy) of the total value of its agriculture product is not subject to any reduction commitment. The obligation is on total aggregate measure of support and within that a country enjoys flexibility of choosing products to be covered and extent of support measure to be extended. In India, the aggregate measure of support to agriculture has been found to be negative for each year of the 1990s. The quantitative difference between the official and non-official estimates notwithstanding (Gulati-Narayan, 1999). This position has been accepted by the WTO and Indian agriculture is therefore not under obligation to affect any cut in subsidies. But this is only one side of the picture. The developed countries are calculating their AMS on different basis, which are different from the criteria set by the WTO. The support of agriculture in EFTA countries during 1997-99 was as high 60 per cent. In EU, Turkey and OECD countries PSE ranges between 30 to 45 per cent. Subsidies are granted in many developed countries on the basis of per hectare cultivated, or per unit of output or per cultivating household. This does not qualify for the norms set by WTO adopted by the developed nations. Such practices are bound to hinder the market access of agricultural commodities produced by developing countries.

It is relevant to note that the procedure for estimating AMS is not full proof. It has a lot of inbuilt ambiguity. The estimates of AMS can very widely depending upon which reference prices and domestic prices one choose or multiplies the difference in these prices by production or only marketed surplus of the produce and so on.

In the U.S.A. subsidy in the forms of direct income support is given to farmers, which AoA considers to be non-market distorting and hence it is not required to be reduced as is the case with subsidies granted either on inputs or for extending market support, which are seen as market distorting. The USA has been relying heavily on direct income support, which is called decoupled income support, to take care of the uncertainties faced by its agriculture producers in recent years. This decoupled income support was introduced in the USA after the Federal Agricultural Improvement and Reform Act of 1996 had been enacted to bring about structural changes in the country's agriculture.

U.S. actually wants a drastic reduction in global farm tariff from an average of 62% to 15%. All these are expected to improve access of US farm products to the European Union and to the Developing Countries. The reason behind the situation is that the U.S., like all other countries has been giving priorities to domestic imperatives than to the future of global trade in agriculture.

Table 4
Agricultural Subsidies to the Farmers in Selected Developed Countries

Country	*Subsidy to Agriculture in Billion Dollars*	*No. of Full Time Farmers*	*Area under Arable & Permanent Crops (In Ha.)*	*Area Per Farmers ($)*	*Subsidy Per H.A. in Dollars*	*Subsidy Per Farmer in $*
Switzerland	6.2	178000	423000	2.38	146570	34831
Japan	56.8	3236000	4336000	1.34	13099.6	17552
U.S.A.	97.3	3174000	17700000	55.80	5457.0	30655
O.E.C.D.	334.6	20500000	1169300000	57.00	16322	-

Source: The Economist (London), Reproduced here from the Hindu Survey of Indian Agriculture, 2002.

On the other side developed countries are providing adequate support to their farmers trade tariff from the countries like U.S.A., E.U., Japan and Canada which ranges from 4.3 per cent in Japan to 8.3 per cent in Canada, but it is very strange that their tariff to keep out the export of developing countries in some cases are about 550 per cent. We also see that products with high tariffs in quad countries includes major agricultural stable food products, such as meat, sugar, mild dairy products, chocolate, tobacco, some alcoholic, beverages, fruits, vegetable, textiles clothing and footwear. These are the sectors in which the developing countries have a competitive and comparative advantage.

The table clearly shows that heavy amount of subsidies are paid to the farmers in developed countries. This is against the spirit of Doha Declaration (2001). Continuation of agricultural subsidies by the EU and US has been identified as a major factor of persisting poverty and unemployment adverse balance of trade in most of the countries.

EXPORT AND IMPORT TRENDS

(a) Export Trend

Performance of India's agricultural exports and imports in pre and post reforms period of WTO can been seen in the following table.

Table 5
India's Agricultural Trade in Post Reforms and Post WTO Period

Year	*Exports $ million*	*Imports $ million*	*Net exports $ million*	*Trade as %GDP Agriculture*		
				Export	*Import*	*Total*
1992-93	3028	1618	1410	5.22	2.79	8.00
1993-94	4032	1317	2706	5.69	1.86	7.55
1994-95	4227	2544	1638	5.20	3.13	8.33
1995-96	6120	3001	3119	7.37	3.61	10.98
1996-97	6868	2303	4556	7.30	2.45	9.75
1997-98	6634	2893	3741	6.99	3.05	10.04
1998-99	6033	4012	2021	5.92	3.94	9.86
1999-00	5615	4402	1213	5.30	4.00	9.30
2000-01	6013	2738	2275	-	-	-

Source: Economic Survey Ministry of Finance, GOI, Various Issues.

Table clearly indicates that India's agriculture exports increased to about $3.2 billion during 1990-91 to 1992-93 and again it went to $4 billion in 1993-94 and in the year 1995-96 it registered further jump of $6.1 billion, which continued till 1996-

97. Agriculture imports mainly included fertilizer showed mixed trend during the same period. Share of agriculture export in sectoral GDP increased from 5.2% in 1992-93 to 7.3% in 1996-97 and share of agricultural trade in GDP also witnessed impressive growth showing increased trade orientation of Indian agriculture.

During early 1990s marine products topped the list of agricultural export followed closely by export of oil meal. Other important items of export were tea, cashew nut, basmati rice, spices and tobacco with value ranging between $122 to $337 million. Liberalisation of export of non-basmati rice in mid 1990s provided impetus to its export. As a result, rice export figured at the top during 1995-96 and during 1998-99. Out of the two grades of rice basmati rice showed upward trend in its export but non-basmati rice showed violent year to year fluctuations. This is clear in from the following table.

India's export of non-basmati rice was not so much impressive till March 1991. We could export only 25 to 30 thousand tonnes between 1987 and 1990 entirely due to our export price being not competitive against the international market price of rice. Although due to some relaxation of export of common rice during 1992 quota system on export of rice was abolished which resulted in improvement of our export of rice. During 1995-96 a major boost to rice export was witnessed under the impact of major policy changes. India used to export basmati rice since 1995-96; export of non-basmati rice actually dominated the rice trading. Export of non-basmati rice constituted less than 10% of the total rice export during late 80s. But in recent time its share has increased above 75% of total export of rice. It is important to note here that export of non-basmati rice got a setback during 1999-2000 and 2000-01 mainly for two reasons-sharp decrease of price in International market and increase in domestic prices. It all resulted in huge stocks of rice in government warehouses. In order to tackle the situation FCI started selling raw rice at Rs. 5650 and half boiled rice at Rs. 60000 per tonne to traders for export. Although open market price in the country is about Rs. 9500 per tonne. Private traders responded well to this offer and booked export order at Rs. 8242 to Rs. 9891 but due to mismatching of prices FCI had to suffer huge loss as cost of acquisition of rice by FCI makes about Rs. 10230 per tonne.

Table 6
India's Export of Selected Agricultural Commodities Before and After WTO

(US $ million)

Item	*1992-93*	*1993-94*	*1994-95*	*1995-96*	*1996-97*	*1997-98*	*1998-99*	*1999-00*	*2000-01*
Agricultural & Allied Products	3028	4023	4227	6120	6868	6634	6033	5504	6013
Basmati Rice	276	338	276	255	352	454	446	411	470
Non Basmati Rice	60	72	108	1113	543	454	1046	316	172
Wheat	3.5	0.07	13.5	110	197	0.11	0.32	-	97
Cotton raw Inc. Waste	63	208	45	61	444	221	49	19	49
Pluses	18	23	29	39	37	97	53	94	118
Oil Meal	534	740	573	703	985	925	461	370	448
Sugar and Molases	122	57	20	152	304	69	6	9	110
Marine Products	602	813	1127	1912	1129	1207	1038	1180	1390
Groundnut	2.7	54.3	32.3	68.6	91.8	152.6	33.2	42.3	69.3
Spices	136	182	195	238	339	380	388	393	356
Tea	337	337	311	351	292	505	538	408	433
Coffee	130	174	335	450	402	457	411	315	260
Tobacco Mfd. & Unmfd.	164	147	81	134	213	288	181	229	191
Cashew	257	333	369	370	362	377	387	566	412
Castor Oil	40	92	141	222	177	155	160	245	208
Guargum Meal	36	45	68	100	147	173	189	129	47
Polutry and Dairy Products	-	-	16	18	35	32	23	28	322
Meat & Meat Prep.	89	110	128	188	200	218	187	180	29
Floriculture Product	5	6	10	18	18	23	25	21	34
Fresh Fruits	-	-	60	69	69	75	63	66	100
Fresh Vegetables	108	132	79	89	94	84	65	82	181
Processed Fruit/Vegetable	41	49	79	104	92	105	109	151	–

Source: Economic Survey, Ministry of Finance, GOI, various issues.

The US-EU block and developing countries led by India, China, Brazil, Argentina and others are two largest agriculture-trading blocks in world. The US-EU have light and illogical farm policies. The US-EU alliance on both agriculture as well as market access for non-agriculture issues has taken most developing countries by surprise. According to the latest report compiled by Research and Information System (RIS) for non-aligned and other developing countries, the huge subsidies doled out by the US-EU has resulted in other developing countries like India to tune of $40 billion. The US-EU subsidies are not limited to just the farm sector. For instance, in the US, about 28 per cent of industrial research conducted by American companies is funded through government subsidies.

(b) Import Trend

So far as our import trend is concerned, India depends no more upon rice imports, and import of cereal preparations has reduced to very low level as shown in the table ahead. Despite very high growth in production and claim of self-sufficiency in foodgrains, India occasionally imports large quantity of wheat. Besides production fluctuation, unplanned exports also result in import of wheat.

Table shows that import of pulses in the country was increasing till 1997-98 but it had decreasing trend in later period. Import of vegetable oils also recorded much more increase from the year 1993-94 onward.

India along with other developing countries like Brazil, China opposed strongly at Cancun Talk (2003) the stand and rigidities of developed nations regarding their proposals for labour and environment standards. Due to their strong opposition the conference ended without reaching any consensus. For this reason India's stand was highly appreciated by the developing world. Under this situation India must take this opportunities of leadership in hand and continue to oppose any exploitative proposals or such attempts by the developed countries. Being one of the fastest growing economies and heavily populated countries of world India should excel its bargaining power in the field of international trade. Because of very poor share (0.6%) of the world trade this can be achieved expectedly by India alone. European countries formed a Union in partnership with Canada and Mexico. ASEAN is also strong Union to fight against all types of exploitations. Many economic blocks such as Andean pact Caricom-Fragile have also emerged for the safeguard of their interest.

Table 7
India's Import of Selected Agricultural Commodities Before and After WTO

Commodity 1996-1997				*1991-1998*	*1992-1999*		*1993-2000*	*1994*		*1995*
	92	*93*	*94*	*95*	*96*	*97*	*98*	*99*	*00*	*01*
Rice	4	25	18	3	neg	neg	ng	1	6	4
Wheat	neg	245	40	neg	3	114	266	277	179	0.6
Cereal prep.	66	63	35	26	21	22	25	9	70	11
Pulses	121	117	186	199	212	265	322	168	82	108
Sugar	neg	neg	neg	727	65	1	127	264	256	7
Fruit & Nut	41	65	69	100	99	129	155	159	136	176
Milk/cream	3	15	5	2	11	1	1	3	25	2
Cashew nuts	108	130	154	220	227	194	207	230	276	211
Cotton raw		44	6	161	156	9	22	90	289	259
Vegetable oils	101	58	53	199	676	825	745	1803	1844	1301
Sub total agri.	444	762	566	1637	1470	1560	1870	3003	3118	3079
Crude fertilizer	185	159	124	153	157	132	178	198	204	219
Mfd. Fertilizer	645	699	633	767	1381	686	845	811	1080	440
Fertilizer total	830	557	756	916	1538	816	1023	1009	1284	659
Total: Agri.	1256	1618	1217	2544	3001	2303	2893	4012	4402	2738

Source: Economic Survey, Ministry of Finance, GOI, various issues.

SMALL ENTERPRISES IN INDIA AND WTO

Under WTO agreement there is no separate agreement, which directly deals with small-scale industries still WTO agreements directly affects that Indian small-scale industries. Under agreements it was decided to reduce tariffs, eliminate tariffs escalation and dismantling of non-tariff barriers including quantitative restrictions. As results, small-scale industries would face stiff competition not only from multinational companies but also from Indian large-scale companies. As for impact of WTO agreements the import of goods will be flooded.

Adverse affect is likely due to gap between small-scale industry in India and the multinational companies of developed countries. It for this reason that after WTO agreement the MNC products of wide range are capturing the Indian markets day-by-day. Not only this, the patent agreement of WTO secures rights to patent holders for the next twenty years. As it has already been discussed above that drugs, pharmaceuticals, agro-products, agro-chemicals are affected under this act and all these items are produced in small-scale industries. Because of MNC products in agro and dairy of high standards and having organised markets for their products, small-scale industries in India are loosing their home market. It is important to note here that 812 items where reserved for small-scale industries before WTO agreement had reached and presently there are only 58 items are reserved for SSIs industries.

The existing labour laws are not small-scale industries friendly and large numbers of small-scale industries are facing labour unrest. The government should make efforts to remove unfriendly laws. The banks are charging high rate of interest (16 to 18%), which results in higher total cost of products. RBI should make reasonable and affordable interest policy at par with other countries. Our Government should also arrange suitable training programmes for SSI for value added products of international standards to compete in the global market.

WTO AND FOREIGN DIRECT INVESTMENT

Foreign direct investment having prominent place in the global economy, is an important avenue through which investment takes place in country. One of the objectives of introducing globalisation was that it would attract foreign direct investment, which will generate employment, reduce income inequality and poverty. It would also allow free flow of human capital from one country to other. Data reveals that important sectors to attract FDI in India during 2002-2003 are power (27.4%) telecommunications (19.9%) electrical equipment including computer software (9.8%) and the transportation industry (7.4%). These four sectors accounted for roughly 50 per cent of FDI inflows. Electrical equipment including computer software and electronics are the sectors, which have attracted highest approval technology transfer. But here a very remarkable point is that the actual inflow of FDI in India is much less than the amount approved. It also deserve to mention here that the rising trend of the opposite trend of FDI was marked in the year 2001 though several countries made many favourable laws for attracting FDI in their countries. Further, the developed nations were the recipients of bulk of total FDI of the world. More than 60 per cent and in some years even more than 80 per cent FDI was received by the developed nations whereas developing nations require for FDI due to mass poverty, hunger, malnutrition, unemployment, lack of infrastructural facilities for education and health, etc. India also needs it urgently in its various sectors under given and rigid policy framework of WTO. It is also essential to enhance competitiveness efficiency of vital sectors at par with international standard and at the same time to build a strong and stable infrastructure for getting and impressive hold in global market in the years to come.

IMPACT ON VULNERABLE SECTIONS

WTO agreement and policy adversely affects the poor, the Dalits, the women causing entitlement failures and capability deprivation. Against this backdrop poverty ratio has increased and per capita availability of rice in the country has reduced from 80.9 kgs. to 73.8 kgs. in 1999. It has led to increase the rice import in the country. Food insecurity coupled with massive unemployment has afflicted such people in the country. About four million of work force in rural and about three million in urban areas are lost their job during 1998. Many sectors of the economy in India as well as in China face a crashing time because of duty free imports on hundreds of food and industrial items. Implications in terms of job opportunities large number of workers in both the countries will loose their jobs in the years to come. Moreover, much inflow of western agrarian products into these countries worsened the farmer's position as well as it has caused migration among poor and labourers.

In recent years the issue of child labour has become a trump card in hands of WTO and ILO to serve the interest of some developed countries. The WTO takes child labour in developing countries as an excuse to restrict of goods from these countries and thus it is hardly guided by any ethical or humanitarian motive. Malafied intention of USA, U.K. and EU is to protect their own industry, agriculture and trade. As result of WTO agreement, substantial cut in agricultural subsidies will adversely affects the farmers. As there is high incidence of child labour in agriculture sector due to subsistence farming and mass poverty, magnitude of child labour and marginalisation of their families will further increase. Industrial sector, which is a big employment provider, will also loose the employment potential under WTO promoting the practice of child labour. Due to structural adjustment programme of the government, social security, food security, health, literacy, poverty elimination activities will also be even worsened than before. Although WTO under its labour laws has restricted the use of children in manufacturing sector especially in export industries but on the other its unjust and hegemonies along with hidden agenda will pave the way for increasing such problems.

CONCLUDING OBSERVATIONS

There are both positive and negative views on WTO and Indian agriculture. There are gains and losses for every member nations. It is not a wise step for India to get out of WTO, but it should think of an alternative. Bilateral trade gives India the option of giving concession to one country and taking concession from it. India should think like China on bilateral trade option instead of multilateral trade option developing own model. Remaining careful about the US-EU efforts to split the alliance among the developing countries and least developed countries. We should stand firmly on the issue of subsidies till complete abolition of farm subsidies given by the US-EU alliance. Present global trade situation also demands that India should gear up the strategies in upgrading the quality of products, level of knowledge etc. as the competitiveness of our products seems to be poor. The impact of WTO on Indian export has not made a good shape in tangible term but it cannot be denied that it may leave its positive impact on our attitude in long run as under WTO regime. Now we are moving towards competitive market rather than protective.

WTO proposal for zero for zero tariff elimination in seven sectors which all are very important in terms of exports for developing countries will have adverse affect. These seven sectors include electronics and electrical goods, fish and fish products, footwear, leather goods, motor vehicle parts, and components, stones, gems and precious metals and textile and clothing. In all such items duties will be eliminated in a phased manner. Worst affected will be the textile sector under this proposal, which contributes about 30 per cent of total exports, 15 % of industrial output with employment to 65 million people. Although the gems and jewelry in the industrial sector being very important foreign exchange earner will get greater access in the international market in collaborations with foreign traders. So far as leather industry is concerned, it is loosing competitive strength in international market mainly due to poor infrastructure unfavourable and rigid labour laws and high rate of interest etc. but marine products of our country will get export jump and it has bright prospect.

In global game of trade negotiations, India will have to take advantage by being flexible in her approach, while mobilizing the developing countries will provide a better beginning counter in the global forum, the bilateral regional trade arguments with the neighbouring countries like China, Myanmar, Thailand, Indonesia and others will also be very crucial and instrumental for her development with advantageous position. Foreign investment has to be allowed in export oriented developing areas and the social and service sectors have to be strictly regulated. Development today is no longer a function of domestic resources and national policies alone rather it is inevitably linked to international economic environment and policies in order to face the on slaught of WTO. We need to find innovative sources of financing and access to technologies that are necessary to assist those who are on margins of globalisation. Economic prosperity cannot be sustained or protected by being walled in just as the curse of poverty cannot be banished to some invisible periphery. Therefore, it is warranted to evolve, equitable and rule based regimes to manage global trade, investment flows and movement of services. No doubt globalisation has posed new challenges for us but at the same time it has given us opportunities and new technologies to go ahead.

REFERENCES

Bhalla, G.S. and Gurmail Singh (1996), "Impact of GATT on Punjab Agriculture", Ajanta Book International, New Delhi.

Bhattacharya, B. (2000), "Food Security in India in the Context of Agreement on Agriculture", paper presented at the seminar on Consultation on Agreement on Agriculture, Ahmedabad, 31st January.

Bihar Economic Journal (2003), Conference Volume.

Brown, M.B. (1993), Unfair Trade, Zed Book, London.

Chadha, G.K. (2001), "India and WTO: Some Suggestions for Internal Corrections and External Initiatives" in G.K.Chadha (ed.) WTO and the Indian Economy, Deep & Deep Publication, New Delhi.

FAO Report (1999), The State of Food Insecurity in the World.

Government of India (2003), Economic Survey.

Gulati, Ashok and Anil Sharma (1994), "Agriculture Under GATT: What holds for India", Economic and Political Weekly, Vol. 29, No. 29.

Gulati, A. and Narayan, S. (1999), "Indian Agriculture in the Global Economy: What Should India Negotiate in Seatle and Why?", Focus WTO, Indian Institute of Foreign Trade, New Delhi, September.

Gulati, Ashok and Sharma, Anil (1997), Subsidies and Investment in Indian Agriculture, Rajiv Gandhi Institute for Contemporary Studies, Project No. 21.

Gulati, Ashok, Rajesh Mehta and Sudha Narayan (1999), From Marrakesh to Seattle, "Indian Agriculture in a Globalizing World." Economic and Political Weekly: Vol. 34, No. 41.

Panchamukhi, V.R. (2000), "World Trade Organisation and India-Challenges and Perspectives," Indian Economic Journal, Conference Volume.

Parikh, Kirti S. (1998), " Food Security: Individual and National", in Isher Judge Ahluwalia and I.M.D. Little (Eds.), India's Economic Reforms and Development: Essays for Manmohan Singh.

NEW GLOBAL SCENARIO AND INDIAN AGRICULTURE

Anjali Prasad

The post independence period have witnessed a veritable transformation in Indian agriculture what is most noticeable is the increase in agricultural production particularly the nearly four-fold rice in the production of food grain, which saved the country from one of the gravest crisis it, faced after independence. Expansion of irrigation, speed of new technology and additions of rural infrastructure like irrigation works, roads, market yards and warehouses made the increase in production possible. These changes in the physical feature of agriculture needed changes in the institutional structure. The cumulative effect of these changes has been reflected in the farmers, perceptions, attitudes and behaviour and in the changing features of the rural communities, such as stratification diversification, commercialization and exposure to outside influences.

Neo-classical economists are champions of the free trade/ lassaize faire policy who developed various economic models and provided policy prescriptions during 1700-1930 but at the time of world wide economic depression, all the prescriptions of classical were proved frivolous. This is how Keynes postulations were invoked. Subsequently, interventionist polices came into existence. Again in the name of macro economic stabilization structural adjustment programs the World Bank economists have recently switched back to the neo-liberal philosophy of free market economy and free trade, calling for a change in the policies, which has led to withdrawal of support to agriculture.

The New Economic Policy of 1991 initiated with the objective of LPG of the economy and later on in 1994, GATT accord was signed by 125 countries including India. This accord aims at substantial progressive reduction in support and protection so as to prevent restrictions and distortions in the world market. It includes establishment of WTO. The establishment of World Trade Organization (WTO) is an important landmark in the history of international trade. Installed as comprehensive dispute settlement machinery with a wider ambit covering international trade in both goods and services. It contains the single most important set of governing rules. The WTO formally came into being on January 1, 1995 and the implementation of the Uruguay Rounds resulted from the same date. The WTO is embodied with five essential functions:

(1) Administering and implementing multilateral trade agreements and legal instruments negotiated in connection with the Uruguay Round.
(2) To provide a form for multilateral trade negotiation.
(3) Administering the understanding on rules and procedures governing the settlement of disputes.
(4) Reviewing national trade policy mechanism.
(5) Co- operating with other international institutions like IMF and IBRD that are involved in global economic policy making.

WTO reiterates the objectives of GATT and improves the general discipline to clarify the provisions with greater precisions and to prescribe the procedures for their implementation. The "Marrakesh" Declaration affirmed that the results of the Uruguay Round would strengthen the world economy and lead to more trade investment, employments and income growth throughout the world. The WTO is the culmination of Uruguay Round result and successor to GATT.

Indian agriculture has come a long way since the inception of planning in 1951. All along there was obsessive concern of development policy with the attainment of self-sufficiency in food. This is perfectly understandable because we have lived with the nightmare of absolute shortage of food grains supply in the 1960. Although the Indian economy has achieved certain landmark developments during the post independence day its development processes so for seem to have deviated from the established pattered followed in the past by the developed countries of today.

The transformation of Indian agriculture from a chronically shortage sector to the so- called "Surplus" sector, would have made a fascinating story, if only the problems facing Indian agriculture had evaporated, as it were along with the food grains deficit. Alas, this is not so. Indian agriculture in the new millennium faces a far more complex set of problems though they are of a different genre. For instance, Indian remains the abode of the largest number of underfed and undernourished population in the world. Now the issue in how beneficial is the stepping in of the new-liberalists into aspects related to the agricultural sector? Why are international institutions eating this sector? It is to protect this primary sector if so why do we need to have free trade policy which has hailed earlier in 1930's. In fact, in India with the support of the government several agro support programs have been the polices have helped in implementing and successfully achieving the targets during 1950- 1990 As a result the present Indian agriculture accounts for 1/4th of the GDP and source of livelihood for more than 2/3rd of the population. Food production has also increased by more than the increase in the population leading to food security. Under these circumstances, what is the need to deviate form the protectionist policies? Does WTO agreement really offers a helping hand to farming community consisting of 91 per cent small farmers and 8 per cent of medium farmers or does it protect the interest of only one per large farmers in India?

Agricultural Growth

Our strategy for future agricultural growth should be anchored in broader vision. The twin objectives of accelerating agricultural growth and ensuring food security for all at the household level warrant a new paradigm of development, which is a new pro-poor and pro-environment in term of sustainability of growth. This strategy should ensure that higher growth is accompanied by a narrowing down of disparities in regional growth and of productivity differentials among different farm size groups.

Agricultural productions have two components – food grains and non-food grains. The former contributes approximately 2/3rd of the total agricultural production. Analysis of the growth represents the fact that there has been a decline in average annual growth rate during the pre- reform & post reform period i.e. from 3.9 per cent per annum to 3.6 per cent. Growth rate in food grains during 1980 -1990 was 2.9 per cent and it has declined to 2.0 percent during 1992-2000. Similarly, there was a decline in the growth rate of non-food grain from 4.3 per cent to 2.4 per cent during the same period as is shown in Table-1.

Table 1
Pre & Post Globalization Growth in Agriculture Sector
(Average Growth Rate)

	Crop	*1980 - 91*	*1991- 00*
1.	Agriculture and allied activities		
	(a) Agriculture	3.6	3.9
	(b) Forestry	4.2	3.7
	(c) Fishing	-0.1	0.8
2.	Crops		
	(a) Food Grains	2.9	2.0
	(b) Cereals	3.1	2.1
	(c) Rice	3.7	2.2
	(d) Wheat	3.6	3.6
	(e) Coarse Cereals	0.0	-1.6
	(f) Pulses	1.4	0.8
	(g) Non-food grains	4.3	2.4

Source: Economic Survey, 2000-01, Govt. of India, p.152.

There is inadequate investment in infrastructure and technology to boost quality agro processing and remunerative marketing at home and broadly lack of adequate diversification of agriculture and even more serious neglect of allied activities as sources of gainful income and employment opportunities within a generally neglected agriculture.

The country has conducted several revolutions, green, blue, white and so an and so forth, but none of these has been taken to their logical ends that is applying them to the length and breath of the country. As a result, there is a large disparity in average yield rates across the country, as can be seen from inside gaps in yield rates of most agricultural crops in Table 2.

Table 2
Comparative Perspective on Crop Yield Rates within India and vis-à-vis the World

	Crop		*India*		*World*	
1.	*Cereals*	*Average yield (kg/ha)*	*Maximum as % of average*	*Minimum as % of average*	*Average as% of India*	*Maximum as % of India*
	1.1. Rice	1990	163.14	56.68	112.97	257.10
	1.2. Wheat	2775	170.45	45.95	95.25	275.97
2.	Coarse Cereals	1034	253.70	48.45		
	2.1. Jowar	852	141.31	36.62		
	2.2. Bajra	639	210.49	51.64		
	2.3. Maize	1785	178.26	58.38	246.22	522.24
3.	Pulses	630	153.17	56.83		
	3.1. Gram	806	137.84	62.03		
	3.2. Tur	797	189.21	45.17		
	3.3. Lentil	732	207.10	70.90		
4.	Food grains	1697	237.42	54.74		
5.	Oilseeds	856	165.54	51.52		
	5.1. Groundnut	774	214.34	50.78	168.00	385.79
	5.2. Rapeseed & Mustard	982	134.83	46.03		
	5.3. Soyabean	1135	122.34	78.50		
	5.4. Sunflower	601	249.58	69.72		
6.	Cotton	226	180.53	65.49		
7.	Jute & Mesta	1830	121.20	49.78		
8.	Sugrancane	70825	149.32	56.02	90.96	156.44
9.	Potato	18643	127.41	48.94		
10.	Onion	9932	228.03	47.63		
11.	Tobacco	1419	458.07	44.05	110.43	195.28
12.	Coconut (no.of.nuts/ha)		6922	234.04	58.75	

Source: Agricultural Statistics at a Glance, Ministry of Agriculture, Government of India, 2001.

Apart from this, the country has been able to sustain continuous technological innovations to bring the country's yield closer to the highest in the world (Table -2) the widening gap between the overall rabi yield rate and kharif yield rate in Indian agriculture is the pointer to the failures of our agricultural technology, research and extension.

Plan Allocations

Plan outlays on agriculture and allied activities have been gradually declining during the plan period from 14.9 percent in the first plan to 5.2 percent in the tenth plan. This clearly shows governments withdrawals from the agriculture sector development (Table -3).

Table 3
Plan Outlay in Agriculture and Allied Sectors
(Rs in Crores)

	Plan	*Total Outlay*	*Agriculture & Allied Sectors*	*Percentage of Agriculture & Allied Sectors*
I.	Plan	2378	354	14.9
II.	Plan	4500	501	11.3
III.	Plan	8577	1089	12.7
IV.	Plan	15779	2320	14.7
V.	Plan	39426	4865	12.3
VI.	Plan	97500	5695	5.8
VII.	Plan	180000	10525	5.9
VIII.	Plan	434100	22467	5.2
IX.	Plan	859200	42462	4.9
X.	Plan	398890	20668	5.2

Source: Tenth Five-Year Plan, 2002-2007

Capital Formation

Despite the secular decline in the construction to national income, the centrality of agricultural growth to Indian economic development cannot be de-emphasized. In the Indian economy, the importance of agriculture transcends its primary function of more crop production. Agriculture continues to hold the key to higher GDP growth, employment expansion, reduction in poverty and equitable distribution of income. The larger than sectoral role of Indian agriculture stems from the basic fact that a large proportion of the population, about 60 percent continued to depend on agriculture for its livelihood. That is despite the sustained growth of GDP of some 6 percent in recent years. The non-agricultural sector has not been able to siphon off surplus labour from the agriculture sector. This is in sharp contrast to the empirical experience of developed countries. In India, specific confugation of circumstance which places agricultural or rural development in general in a per-eminent position in the development agenda.

Gross domestic formation in agriculture has undergone a secular decline due to steady erosion in the shade of public investment. More and more investment must be fueled into farm sector in the field of research, extension, infrastructure development, marketing, etc. to attain higher production and productivity. It will raise the income position of rural population.

Table 4
Gross Capital Formation in Agricultural Sector,
(At 1993-94 prices)

	Gross Capital Formation			*Investment in Agriculture*
Year	*Public Sector*	*Private Sector*	*Total*	*as % of GDP*
1993-94	4467 (33.0)	9056 (67.0)	13523 (33.0)	1.6
1994-95	4947 (33.0)	10022 (67.0)	14969 (33.0)	1.6
1995-96	4849 (28.9)	10841 (69.1)	15690 (28.9)	1.6
1996-97	4668 (28.9)	11508 (71.1)	16176 (28.9)	1.5
1997-98	3979 (25.0)	11963 (75.0)	15942 (25.0)	1.4
1998-99	3869 (26.0)	11026 (74.0)	14895 (26.0)	1.3
1999-00	4112 (24.8)	12470 (75.2)	16582 (24.8)	1.3
2000-01	4007 (24.2)	12470 (75.8)	16545 (24.2)	1.3

*Quick Estimate: Figures in brackets are percentages
Source: Central Statistical Organization, New Delhi.

Public investment in agriculture was at higher levels in the initial years but it has been declining particularly after 1980's. Investment in agriculture as percentage of GDP has remained at 1.6 percent during 1993-1996 after that it declined to 1.3 percent by 1999 and remained the same till 2001. This fall was due to decline in public investment. Since private investment to be compensating for decline in public investment in agriculture, it is being voiced that there is no need to expand public investment in agriculture. But these cannot be considered to be mutual substitutes in view of their current composition. In the name of macro economy, many enclosures have been introduced, though these liberalization measures would do nothing to raise the level of investment. The present rate of capital formation is far below the rate that is required to transform India's low-level agricultural economy into high-level agricultural economy instead to raise the investment in agriculture sector; government is withdrawing from the sector.

Rural Employment

All developed countries of the world have not only performed the necessary homework but also done everything possible during WTO negotiations to protect their domestic employment. India on the other hand, seems to be talking a different language in spite of an alarming unemployment situation at home. The following trends in rural employment have been observed with the implication of WTO agreements for Indian agriculture:

- The level of underemployment in rural areas shows a tendency of increasing in recent times.
- The extent of self-employment in rural India is showing a tendency to fall at the expense of increasing casualisation.
- Open rural unemployment is showing a tendency to increase.
- Inter industry share in rural employment is increasing in favour of the primary sector.
- In recent time, there has been steady decline in employment opportunities per unit in the agro-industries in general and more so in the agro food segment. This decline is quite sharp per unit of capital investment, though lesser as compared to similar trend in non-agro industries as a whole.

Table 5
Rural Employment Growth

(per cent)

Employment	*1987- 88 to 1993-94*	*1993-94 to 1999- 00*
Total Employment (PS + SS)	2.14	0.66
Agriculture Employment (PS + SS)	2.17	0.18
Non-Agricultural Employment (PS + SS)	2.02	2.34

Source: Human Development South Asia, 2002

According to the NSS current daily status, rural unemployment rate for male worker was 4.58 percent in 1987-

88. Since then unemployment among rural male workers has been 7.2 percent in 1999-2000 against 5.64 percent in 1993-94. Table 5 depicts that agricultural employment has declined between 1987-94 and 1994-2000 and total employment also has shown declining trend during the same period. Thus, it can be concluded that the globalization has failed even in improving employment position in agricultural sector.

Agricultural Exports and Imports

Since economic liberalization in 1991, countries followed up joining the WTO as one of its founding members, they turned toward exports and imports as a priority sector for growth.

Table 6
Percentage Change in Main Agriculture Export & Import Trade Indices

Indices	*Periods*					
	1961-67	*1968-73*	*1974-79*	*1980-85*	*1986-91*	*1992-97*
Agriculture Products						
Exports value	0.25	11.66	5.98	-3.08	5.34	16.04
Exports quantity	0.89	8.71	5.52	-3.76	12.89	10.37
Exports unit value	-0.63	2.71	0.44	0.71	-6.69	5.15
Import value	12.81	-5.37	-3.54	4.53	-13.91	25.76
Import quantity	18.09	-15.86	-27.9	10.8	-19.77	20.51
Import unit value	-4.47	12.47	33.79	-5.66	-7.31	4.39
Food excluding fish						
Exports value	0.79	14.37	0.51	-3.41	2.67	20.54
Exports quantity	-1.01	9.08	7.19	-4.02	7.98	24.58
Exports unit value	1.82	4.84	-6.23	0.63	-4.87	-3.10
Import value	17.07	-7.82	-4.8	4.61	-17.28	31.75
Import quantity	18.95	-17-05	-28.77	11.65	-20.31	21.61
Import unit value	-1.58	11.13	33.65	-6.3	3.79	8.56

Source: Yojna, Government of India, January 2002.

As Table 6 suggest in spite of high expectations of growth in India's agriculture, growth in India' agricultural exports, the evidence so far is very modest, if not altogether disappointing.

Table 7
Percentage Change in US $ Value of Major Agriculture Exports

	Items	*1995-96*	*1996-97*	*1997-98*
1.	Agriculture & allied	44.7	12.0	-6.6
	1a. Tea	12.7	-16.6	38.6
	1b. Coffee	34.0	-10.6	8.6
	1c. Cereals	264.3	-25.4	-19.9
	1d. Oil meals	22.6	40.2	-7.0
	1d. Marine products	-10.3	11.7	2.8
2.	Manufactured goods	16.5	2.7	4.7
	2a. Leather	8.1	-8.0	-11.6
	2b. Leather footwear	6.2	-42.2	-19.6
	2c. Cotton yarn, fabrics etc.	15.4	21.2	4.2
	2d. Readymade garments	12.0	2.1	0.6
3.	Grand total	20.7	5.3	1.5

Source: Yojna, Government of India, January 2002.

Table 7 also shows a declining growth rate in major agribusiness export from India. The share of agricultural exports in total export was 44.2 per cent in 1960-61, which was declined to 19.4 percent in 1990-91 and further to 13.5 percent in 2000-01 as it is evident from Table 8.

Table 8
Agricultural Exports ($ Million)

Year	*Agricultural Exports*	*Total Exports*	*% of Agricultural Exports to Total Exports*
1960-61	596	1346	44.2
1970-71	644	2031	31.7
1980-81	2601	8486	30.6
1990-91	3521	18143	19.4
1995-96	6320	31797	19.8
1997-98	6840	35006	18.5
1998-99	6205	33218	18.2
1999-00	5773	36822	15.2
2000-01	6246	44560	13.5
2002-03	6734	52719	12.8
2003-04	7533	63843	11.8

Source: Economic Survey, Government of India, Various Issues.

Though agriculture provides almost 25 percent of India's GDP, agricultural exports are insignificant. Lack of awareness, appropriate farmer organizations, technology, R & D and infrastructure, all these add to the worries of Indian agribusiness exporters. Thus; the external or trade sector, instead of providing a strong source of demand for a Indian agriculture, seem to have pose further challenges to its existence and growth.

India had expected that with the dismantling of domestic support in developed countries and widespread reduction in export subsidies by the countries market access for Indian agricultural product in developed countries would expand. The developed countries have played their cards very cleverly and have taken effective steps to block agricultural exports from developing countries including India behind various loopholes in AoA and other agreements.

Implications

The Agreement on Agriculture (AoA), which forms a part of final act of Uruguay Round of Multilateral Negotiations (1986-93), was signed by member countries including India in April 1994 in Marrakesh in Morocco. The AoA contains provisions in areas regarding clarification domestic support and export subsidies.

The two major factors are responsible for the present downfall of India's agriculture. First; in its eagerness to reduce fiscal deficit, the government has substantially reduced the development expenditure in agricultural sector. Secondly, import liberalization has contributed in a big way to reduction in prices of agricultural products. Having failed in getting remunerative price of their products, many farmers have curtailed either their products or farm operations, which in turn has increased unemployment among the agricultural workers. These import liberalization is a major cause of existing plight of the peasantry.

Indian farmers are worried, as they do not know about the WTO, GATT, Dunkel and Genetically Modified Crop. They are trying to understand what it means to live under the WTO regime. They have not yet achieved clarity on future trends in Indian and international agriculture and who exactly will help them in reaching the international standard of quality and costs. These related questions trouble them.

The overall impact of economic reform and WTO on agriculture is positive as well as negative. Positive impacts are seen in areas like floriculture, horticulture, dairy, etc. due to opening up of the agricultural trade. But the reform measures have not yielded the desired results in agricultural exports and improving the production and productively. Further, the WTO regime brought new problems like insecurity in food and seeds, loss of bio-diversity, ecological imbalance and bio-piracy. Due to globalization international trade has proved to be beneficial to the developed economies, rather than developing economies like India.

The developed countries have played their card very cleverly and have taken effective steps to block agricultural imports from developing countries including India behind various loophole in AoA and allied agreement. Therefore, to protect the Indian agriculture and Indian farmers from evils of globalization, the Indian agricultural policy needs to be built up with adequate "safety nets".

REFERENCES

Kapila, Uma (2002), Indian Economy Since Independence.

Datta, S. K. (2002), "Indian Agriculture: Retrospect", Yojana, January.

Yadav, S.S. (2001), "WTO and Its Impact on Indian Agriculture", Yojana, December.

Rao, C.H. Hanumantha (2005), "Crisis in Indian Agriculture", Mainstream, August.

Phougat, Sunil (2006), "Economic Reforms and WTO Implication for Farmer", Kurukshetra, March.

Vasudevacharya, A.K. (2006), Indian Agriculture in New Global Sacarid, Southern Economist, January.

Bhattacharya, B. (2002), "Global Competitiveness of Indian Agriculture "Yojana, January.

GOI, Economic Survey, Economic Division, New Delhi (Various Issues).

GOI (2002-07), Tenth Five-Year Plan.

GOI (2001), Agriculture Statistics at a Glance.

SECTION - III

WTO AND INDIAN ECONOMY

SOME ASPECTS OF PRODUCT PATENT REGIME IN INDIAN PHARMACEUTICAL INDUSTRY

Kuldip Kaur and Kushwinder Kaur

Over the last three decades, the pharmaceuticals industry in India has been a glowing example of success. It has shown tremendous progress in terms of infrastructure development, technology base and a wide range of production. Even while undergoing restructuring, it has established its presence and determination to flourish in the changing environment. India has emerged as one of the largest producers of the therapeutics in the world, accounting in volume nearly 12 per cent of the world drug requirements. The Indian pharmaceutical sector has achieved global recognition as a low cost producer of bulk chemicals and formulation products, with a significant international marketing presence in nearly 60 countries in Asia, the Middle East, Africa and South America; exports to the US and Europe are continually on the rise. The Indian pharmaceutical industry today manufactures practically the entire range of therapeutic groups, is nearly self-sufficient in raw materials and operates on a par with international standards in production, technology and quality. India now produces 80 per cent of the bulk drugs and nearly 100 per cent of the formulations available worldwide. India is a country with very low prices of high quality medicines. The quality of the products is reflected in the fact that India has the highest number of manufacturing plants approved by the US Federal Drug Authority (60 plants), which is next to that in the USA.

The secret of this success is the Indian Patent Law of 1970, that exempted 'food or medicine or drug' from product patenting. Since then India has done without product patents for pharmaceuticals, with the exemption of production processes that could be patented for seven years. In addition, the law allowed for compulsory licenses granted by the state in case a patent holder did not grant voluntary licenses on fair conditions. India thus profited from a large section of well-qualified experts who made good use of the new opportunities. More units larger in size and capacity set up in the 1970's and 1980's started producing drugs, which were primarily imported till then. Share of multinationals in domestic markets for pharmaceuticals declined considerably i.e. from 85 per cent in 1970 to 40 per cent in 1999.

Table 1 shows the percentage increase in market shares of top ten firms from 1998-99 to 2003-04. Thus, the market shares of the top ten firms except Novartis and Glaxo Smithkline (where marginal decrease in market share can be noticed) increased over the period. Furthermore, due to price controls imposed by the government and stiff competition among the big pharmaceutical firms, there has been a declining trend in their profitability.

Table 1
Year-wise Market Shares of Top 10 Pharmaceutical Firms In India

Sr. No.	*Name of the Firm*	*Market Share (Per cent)*							
		1996-97	*1997-98*	*1998-99*	*1999-00*	*2000-01*	*2001-02*	*2002-03*	*2003-04*
1.	Ranbaxy	4.74	5.77	5.58	5.87	5.88	5.97	8.59	10.23
2.	Dr. Reddy's Labs	1.04	1.35	1.49	1.64	3.04	4.83	4.60	4.89
3.	Glaxo Smithkline	2.96	3.18	3.12	3.26	2.92	3.08	3.11	2.48
4.	Aurobindo Pharma	-	-	1.90	2.38	3.01	2.94	3.17	3.57
5.	Alembic Chemicals	1.19	1.30	1.34	1.33	1.48	1.46	1.53	1.62
6.	IPCA	1.06	1.15	1.19	1.22	1.19	1.29	1.36	1.71
7.	Orchid	0.81	1.01	1.20	1.22	1.15	1.23	1.45	1.72
8.	Novartis	1.01	1.13	1.11	1.09	1.14	1.14	1.16	0.96
9.	Abbot India	0.93	0.96	0.90	0.92	0.96	0.96	0.95	0.98
10.	Pfizer	0.96	0.76	0.72	0.80	0.87	0.91	1.32	1.14

Source: Industry: Market Size & Shares, CMIE, February 2005.

Table 2
Introduction of New Drugs and Relative Prices of Patentable Drugs in India

Brand & Dosage (pack)	*Year*				*Times Costlier*		
	World Intro-duction	*Indian Market-ing Approval*	*Intro-duction Lag*	*Euro-pean Patent Expiry*	*Pakis-tan*	*USA*	*UK*
Antibiotic/ Antibacterial							
Ofloxacin 200 mg (4 tab)		1990		2001	1.3	4.4	2.4
Ciprofloxacin 500 (4 tab)	1985	1989	4	2001	8.3	15.4	10.3
Norfloxacin 400 mg (10tab)	1984	1988	4	1998	3.2	23.2	6.5
Pefloxacin 400 mg (4 tab)		1991		1998	3.8		
Anti-ulcer							
Rantidine 300 mg (10 tab)	1981	1985	4	1997	14.1	56.7	26.1
Famotidine 40 mg (10 tab)	1984	1989	5	1999	14	54	27.1
Omeprazole 20 mg (10 tab)		1991		1999		43.8	23.1
Cardiac care							
Lisinopril 5mg (10 tab)				1999		7.6	5.2
Enalapril Maleate 5mg (10 tab)	1984	1989	5	1999	2.3	19.9	9.4
Ketoconazole 200mg (10 tab)	1981	1988	7	1997	3.8	18.7	4.8
Anti-histamine							
Astemizole 10mg (10 tab)	1986	1988	2	1999	10.1	54	11.9
Others							
Ondansetron HCl 4mg (6 tab)				2005		56.8	32.6

Source: Economic and Political Weekly, January18, 2003, pp. 209.

As it can be seen from Table 2 that Indian enterprises have been able to introduce newer medicines within a short time lag i.e. most of the drugs could be introduced within 4-5 years of their introduction in the world market. The table also shows that the prices of these drugs in India have been much lower as compared to rest of the world. For instance, Ranitidine, Famotidime, Astemizole and Ondansetron are being sold in the US at prices as much as 50 times more than Indian prices. Due to their low prices, the Indian drugs have been affordable to the poor masses and thus, have served an important social cause of providing access of modern medicine to poorer people.

However, despite the good performance of the Indian pharmaceutical sector in the absence of product patents, India, like many other developing countries, has been forced to shift from process to a product patent regime that must provide for product patents of twenty years duration.

The new patent laws have come into force from January 1, 2005 as part of the Trade Related Intellectual Property Rights (TRIPS) agreement, negotiated under the WTO regime. TRIPS prescribe worldwide minimal standards for patent protection. No country adopting a market economy and keen to be integrated in the World economy can do without WTO membership and has to swallow the TRIPS pill as well. Now when TRIPS agreement has come into effect in India, major changes are being expected in the pharmaceuticals industry in coming time period. Evidences suggested that a country's level of IPRs influences a variety of social and economic factors, which range from common people's access to medicine to the functioning of the domestic industry, investment in R&D, technology, etc. In the absence of health cover for the majority of the population, prices of the drugs in the WTO regime in India is an issue of concern. In this paper, an attempt has been made to present the possible impact of product patent regime on prices of medicines; to study the relationship between product patents and R&D activity in the light of some studies and to suggest some measures so as to reduce the intensity of the adverse effects of product patent regime on the Indian pharmaceutical industry and the masses at large.

PRODUCT PATENT REGIME AND PRICES OF MEDICINES

Much of the debate on the impact of product patents on the pharmaceutical industry in India has centered on the issues of prices of the patented products and their accessibility. While it is a matter of fact that a positive association is observed between stronger patent protection and prices of drugs, it is also true that prices decline with the expiry of the patents. In US, Frank and Salkever (1995) report of rapid reduction in the prices of drugs after the expiration of the patent. Though more competition among generic drugs producers results in substantial price reductions for those drugs, yet increased competition from generics does not result in aggressive response in price behaviour by established brand name products. Danson and Chao (2000) on the other hand, opine that generic competition has a significant negative effect on prices of the branded products in the US and other countries with relatively free pricing like in UK, Germany and Canada, whereas for the countries with strict price regulation like France, Italy and Japan the number of generic competitors has either no effect or a positive effect on prices of branded products. In India when amoxycilin was first introduced by a multinational, the price of the drug was very high. However, when the local manufacturers entered to produce indigenous version, the prices of the same declined sharply. Hence, the severe competition resulted in relatively lower prices of medicines in India.

Julio Nogues (1990) argued that unlike other industrial countries, Japan and Italy in 1975, had not provided patent protection for pharmaceuticals and still showed quite a high price of pharmaceuticals. This observation lends support to the assertion that pharmaceutical companies charge what the market will bear. However, based on India's own experience and on a selective comparison of prices (given in Table 2) of some drugs in countries where product patent is in force, intellectuals forewarn that the stronger protection would result in increase in the prices of drugs and thus medicines will be inaccessible to common people. This fear of high prices and probable exploitation by the multinationals in India grew high when the vested multinationals tried to prevail on the South African Government to stop the passing of the bill to permit parallel import of the HIV-AIDS drugs which would ensure the availability of those drugs at lower rates.

According to the TRIPs agreement, drugs that were already available in India by 2005, will not get retrospective patent protection. Thus, initially the TRIPs agreement will only affect a small proportion of drugs available in India. However, the impact will gradually increase over time as virtually all new drugs entering the market in future would be patent protected and many old drugs will become ineffective over time as the disease causing bacteria or viruses develop resistance to them, thereby forcing people to switch to the new, more expensive drugs.

It is further suggested by various examples that patented drug prices have little to do with the cost of production or even invention. This is evident from the fact that the new combination drug therapy for AIDS patient being marketed in western countries at about $10,000 to $15,000 per patient per year was recently offered by the Indian company CIPLA, for $300 per patient per year. This is because the patented pharmaceuticals are essentially priced at monopolistic profit maximizing levels, taking into account the paying capacity of the consumers.

Further, it will also be very difficult for the multinational pharmaceutical firms to offer lower prices for essential drugs in developing countries based on their purchasing power. Because such disparities in price would be easily revealing the extent of profits involved and may lead to pressure to reduce prices in developed countries as well, especially for life saving and mass consumption drugs.

As per the pharmaceutical policy 2001, the Maximum Allowable Post-Manufacturing Expense (MAPE) would be 100 per cent for indigenously manufactured drugs. For imported formulation the selling price can be upto 150 per cent of the landed costs. The provision as per the Third Schedule of the Drug Price Control Order 1995, of limiting the profitability of drug companies has been done away with. There are some exemptions, even for the limited number of 37 bulk drugs to be under price control. Thus overall, the drug companies have been given a free hand to jack-up prices.

It is certain that through introduction of TRIPs, the prices of drugs will increase in long term. A number of studies have examined the effect of prices on medicines after introduction of product patents and have simulated welfare losses for consumers in developing countries. Watal (1999) computed that static price impacts of patent coverage in India could raise average patented drug prices by at least 26 per cent from 1994 base. Similarly, Lanjouw (1997) suggested that prices could increase in the range of 9 to 76 per cent. Lalitha (2002) argued that adherence to quality standards can increase cost by Rs. 30 lacs to Rs. one crore for small-scale units.

PRODUCT PATENT REGIME AND R&D ACTIVITY

The main argument in favour of stronger IPR regime is based on the premise that it will lead to increase in R&D expenditure, which is very low in India as compared to the developed countries like the USA and UK. But it may be argued that a legal protection as provided by the patent system for a rather longer term of 20 years is likely to erode the threat of potential competition and hence, the need for continuous improvement (Kumar and Siddharthan, 1997).

A number of studies have empirically demonstrated the ability of rather weaker IPRs in stimulating domestic innovative activity in developing countries. Kumar and Saqib (1996) found Indian chemicals industry enterprises to be among the more innovative ones in the Indian industry. They attributed this to weak patent laws. Haksar (1995) in his study argued that the larger return to R&D in Indian pharmaceutical industry was due to the highly successful adaptive R&D effort of Indian firms directed at development of alternative processes of known drugs made possible by the absence of patents on pharmaceutical products. Scherer and Weisburst (1995) examined the impact of strengthening of pharmaceutical patent protection in Italy since 1978. They concluded that the regime change had little or no impact on the trend of inflation adjusted R&D expenditures or on the introduction of new chemical entities. Moreover the research priorities of MNEs are determined by the purchasing power and very little R&D has been done on tropical diseases (World Bank, 2002).

Despite knowing the fact that strict IPRs protection will adversely affect the Indian pharmaceutical industry, leading to the closure of small scale and some medium scale, generic firms, also does not guarantee of increased FDI inflows and access to R&D investment in tropical diseases, India was not left with any option but to bring in legislation to recognize product patents. Now when IPR regime has become a permanent feature of India, it is imperative to find ways and means for providing medicines at affordable prices to the Indian populace on one hand and also leveraging the Indian intellectual prowess on the other, through which India could create its own intellectual property.

For this, some concrete steps have to be taken. These can be discussed as under:

1. The government should take concrete steps to improve the primary healthcare infrastructure in the country. Stress should be laid on higher investments in the health sector, well-directed policy initiatives to improve the quality and safety standards and fiscal incentives to carry out R&D on tropical diseases.
2. The pharmaceutical giants should be persuaded to invest more on R&D for drugs for diseases like Malaria, T.B., AIDS, etc., either by moral suasion or by sharing costs by the government. They can also be provided with desirable rewards to encourage them to carry out more R&D. These rewards can be in the form of (i) tax incentives for undertaking research and development of new drugs and (ii) reimbursement of research cost for specific discoveries, for the firms that are willing to undertake their research efforts. These measures may provide long term benefits without imposing severe price increase for medicines.
3. In India, 60-80 per cent of patients seek remedies from traditional medical practitioners or alternative medicines, so there is substantial potential for India to be competitive in this sector. The traditional medicine (Ayurvedic, Siddha and Unani) is the field wide open for Indian pharma sector, for R&D activity. Although the Indian government has launched a programme with objectives to promote and protect its traditional medicines sector, big Indian pharma entities should also come up in this field.
4. The Indian laws should support the development of clinical trial services, which it, until recently, has not encouraged. As compared to western countries, India has an abundance of people, who have never been treated for their ailments, along with abundance of physicians, investigators and support staff to conduct trials and also cost of conducting

clinical trials is much lower than US or Europe. So, India can become a generator of new intellectual property and more business may move to India, especially in pre-clinical and clinical area.

5. The combination of a lower cost base as well as the availability of skilled and knowledgeable manpower should make India an attractive destination for contract manufacturing. If successfully undertaken, it would provide a steady income stream for Indian companies. Moreover, as such arrangements are typically long-term and of strategic importance, the Indian firms would also stand to gain from the know-how inputs of the foreign partner.
6. To increase the efficiency of research in India, interaction of research laboratories with the pharmaceutical industry should be improved.
7. Collaboration between pharmaceutical firms and universities should be encouraged to inculcate research attitude and efficiency in the young researchers.
8. Post-2005 requires that Indian companies have to get their act together as regards R&D.
9. India pharmaceutical sector should embrace the role of IPRs in kick starting innovation by developing and strengthening the base of scientists through training them in world-class drug discovery skills.
10. The private sector should come up with models that can render an acceptable level of quality and wholesome healthcare to the masses at affordable prices.
11. The application of new age technologies like high throughput screening, genomics, combinational chemistry and bioinformatics are capable of increasing R&D productivity which will further reduce prices.
12. More attention should be paid to biotechnology, new drug discovery, novel drug delivery systems and chemical research.
13. The Indian pharmaceutical firms should move beyond the product production model and share in the significant financial benefits stemming from co-development and ownership of new patented products.

14. The Indian Government needs to ensure that India will be a place safe for FDI and for the development of the drug discovery process (i.e. new drugs, R&D and clinical trials, etc.).
15. There is need to pay more attention to quality and leverage the global recognition we have earned for our IT (Information Technology) skills.
16. The marketing and distribution infrastructure developed and refined over coming time period will lead as a key to success.
17. Over the next few years, drugs worth close to $40 billion would be off patents in the US. This provides a big opportunity for generic manufacturers to target the US market with their offerings at lower costs. This would also translate an opportunity to bulk drug manufacturers in India to supply inputs to other formulation companies abroad eyeing the US generics market (Balakrishnan, 2003).
18. Size is the most important factor to overcome the barriers imposed by high R&D costs and also benefit from economies of scale that apparently exist in R&D process, so the norms for acquisitions and mergers should be simplified.
19. Domestic drug price controls can be used to apply 'Tiered' or 'Differential' pricing of drugs through selective application of controls and provision for normal profits in the cost-plus formulae used to set price ceiling.

Indian pharmaceutical companies will inevitably be affected by turbulent conditions now confronting the global industry. In such an increasingly competitive and rapidly changing environment companies need a strategic approach that enables them to respond to current challenges as well as future uncertainties. The pharmaceutical companies may identify "core" strategies, which are expected to be critical for success under any future scenario. Keeping in view the future scenario, there is need on the part of the Indian Government and the Indian pharmaceutical companies to recognize a broader range of fundamental uncertainties that can exert a major impact on the pharmaceutical industry over the longer term. Examples of these critical uncertainties include, among other things, India's infrastructure development (be it power, export zones or education), stance towards international investment and trade, sustenance of reform agenda over a 20-year timeframe and proper interpretation of exemptions and exceptions provided in various articles of the TRIPS agreement in accordance with domestic conditions.

REFERENCES

Aggarwal, Pradeep and P. Saibaba (2001), TRIPS and India's Pharmaceutical Industry," *Economic and Political Weekly*, September 29-October 5, pp. 3787.

Balakrishnan, Nath (2003), "Pharmaceutical: A Growth Prescription", *Business Line, June.*

CII (2000), '*Report on the Pharmaceutical Sector in India*, Presented to International Trade Centre, Geneva.

Deloitte Research (2002), *Collaborative Knowledge Network: Accelerating Pharmaceutical R&D in the New Millennium* (New York: Deloitte Consulting and Deloitte and Touche LLP, 2002.) September 29-October 5, pp. 3787.

Frank, Richard and Salkever David (1992), 'Pricing, Patent Laws and the Market for Pharmaceuticals,' *Southern Economic Journal*, Volume 50, No. 2.

Govindraj, Ramesh and Gnanaraj Chelaraj (2002), '*The Indian Pharmaceutical Sector: Issues and Options for Health Sector Reform*,' World Bank Discussion Paper No. 437, September, The World Bank, Washington, D.C.

Haksar, Vikram (1995), 'Externalities, Growth and Technology Transfer: Application to the Indian Manufacturing Sector, 1970-90', Washington, DC: *International Monetary Fund (mimeo).*

Kumar, Nagesh (2003), "Intellectual Property Rights, Technology and Economic Development", *Economic and Political Weekly*, January 18, pp. 209.

Kumar, Nagesh and Mohammed Saqib (1996), 'Firm Size, Opportunities for Adaptation and In-House R&D Activity in Developing Countries: The Case of Indian Manufacturing', *Research Policy*, 25 (5): 712-22.

Kumar Nagesh and N.S. Sidharthan (1997), '*Technology, Market Structure and Internationalisation: Issues and Policies for Developing Countries*, UNU/INTECH, Routeledge: New York, USA.

Lanjouw, Jean (1998), *The Introduction of Pharmaceutical Product Patent in India: Heartless Exploitation of the Poor and Suffering*', NBER, Working Paper No. 6366.

Lalitha, N. (2002), 'Indian Pharmaceutical Industry in WTO Regime: A Swot Analysis', *Economic and Political Weekly*, August 24, pp. 3542, 3555.

Nogues, Jolio (1990), *"Patients and Pharmaceutical Drugs: Understanding the Pressures on Developing Countries"*, International Economics Department, The World Bank, WPS 502, September.

Phadke, Anant (2002), "Pharmaceutical Policy, 2001: Industry Wish List," *Economic and Political Weekly*, February 9-15, pp. 528.

Scherer, F.M and S. Weisburst (1995), 'Economic Effects of Strengthening Pharmaceutical Patent Protection in Italy,' *International Review of Industrial Property and Copyright Law*, 26 (6): 1020-4.

Watal, Jayshree (1997), 'Introducing Product Patents in Indian Pharmaceuticals Sector: Implication to Price and Welfare', *World Competition*, 20, pp. 5-21.

World Bank (2002), *Global Economic Prospects and Developing Countries 2002*, Washington D.C.

Online References

www.blonnet.com

www.deloitte.com

www.chemicals.nic.in

www.pharmabiz.com

www.epharmaceuticalnews.com

www.piribo.com

www.bbriefings.com

www.intracen.org

www.pubs.acs.org

WTO: SOME TASKS AND CHALLENGES

Mahesh Chandra Prasad

INTRODUCTION

The World Trade Organisation (WTO) oversees a multilateral system that deals with the rules of trade between nations on a global level. The working of the WTO is largely based on the Uruguay Round of negotiations that took place from 1986 to 1994. The WTO, which came into effect on January 1, 1995, has its origins in the General Agreement on Tariffs and Trade (GATT) of 1947, and subsequent round of negotiations. The GATT had mainly dealt with trade in goods, whereas the WTO agreements cover trade in services and in intellectual property besides dispute settlement procedures.

An important task facing the WTO is that of making the new multilateral trading system truly global in scope and application. While the present membership accounts for more than 90 per cent of world trade, a number of nations are still outside. Many of them have requested accession to the WTO. Twenty-eight governments ranging from China, the Russian Federation, Ukraine and Vietnam to the Baltic States, Bulgaria, Mongolia, Panama, and Vanuatu are set various stages of a process that has become more involved because of the WTO increased coverage relative to the GATT. With many of the candidates currently undergoing a process of transition from centrally planned to market economies accession to the WTO offers, these countries in addition to the usual trade benefits, a way of underpinning their domestic reform processes. Hence, the so-called "new agenda" containing issues which, may be regarded as likely subjects for the WTO work programme of the future.

WTO AND INDIA

Globalisation brings in a change in the competitive setting of a country. As any change in the competitive setting requires a change in the business strategy, it requires knowledgeable individuals to work out the changes required and to frame a strategy to make the necessary shifts so that, the firm's competitive advantage is maintained or ideal situations improved. Specifically this means that the macro-economic changes that are the results of the globalization process must be converted to industry–level implications and then to firm-level implications. A suitable strategy must be developed in order to keep the firm competitive. This requires the entire firm to use the existing knowledge or to generate new knowledge that could be useful in the development of such a strategy.

This is a matter of fact that with India's signing of GATT and becoming a founder member of WTO, globalisation of agricultural production will experience global competition and global market forces will play a leading role in determination of investment level, cropping pattern, prices, quality and level of international trade. The provisions and agreements made under GATT and WTO will speed up the process of globalisation and allow free play of market forces and the global trading and agro-based companies in India.

Therefore, WTO provides for an opportunity to introspect which is quite essential for a country like ours to take stock of our efforts to come into our own–to know where we have flourished and where we floundered.

That the country has made admirable strides in various sectors during globalization is obvious for anybody to see, but then, it is also equally true that the development has not been as evenly spread as the founding fathers of planned development had visualised. This is at the root of the general perception that there is a need to look a fresh at the development process, at its approach and refix priorities if necessary so that the benefits of development reach the desired sections of the people and the parts of the country which it is said to have by passed. Additional efforts to restructure a number of sectors of the economy so as to enable them to interact through a process of liberalization and become competitive are underway. The critics, often suspicious of the new deal economy pursued by the national and state governments, complain for having yielded to the design of the IMF, the World Bank and multi-national corporate sector in squeezing the socialistic objective out for an alternative in laissez-faire. In its defence, the policy makers point to a unique balance being maintained to ensure both growth and equity especially by being careful in maintaining a low tempo of reforms on the one hand and trying to increase the social sector spending on the other.

WTO's TRIPS AND INDIA

Knowledge has become a direct competitive advantage for companies selling ideas and relationships (professional services, software and technology driven companies) and an indirect competitive advantage for all companies attempting to differentiate themselves by how they serve their customers. Economists have examined physical and human capital as key resources for the firm that facilitates productive and economic activity. However, economists have also recognized knowledge as a valuable resource. Marshall, for example, suggests, "Capital consists in a great part of knowledge and organisation.... Knowledge is our most powerful engine of production." He further goes on to note, "Organisation aids knowledge." More recently, Quinn has expressed a similar view suggesting that, with rare exceptions, the economic and producing power of the firm lies more in its intellectual and service capabilities than its hard assets – land, plant and equipment virtually all public and private enterprises including most successful corporations –are becoming dominantly the repositories and co-coordinators for intellect.

Intellectual capital refers to the knowledge and knowing capability of a social collectivity, such as an organisation, intellectual community or professional practice.

BASIC OF TRIPS

The agreement on Trade Related Aspects of Intellectual Property Rights (TRIPS Agreement) establishes minimum standards of protection for a wide variety of intellectual property. Intellectual property rights can be defined as the rights given to people over the creation of their minds. They provide the creator an exclusive right over the use of his/her creation for a specified period of time. Intellectual property rights are traditionally divided into two main categories:

(a) Copyrights and rights related to copyright: i.e., rights granted to authors of literary and artistic works and the rights of performers, producers of phonograms and broadcasting organisations. The main purpose of protection of copyright and related rights is to encourage and reward creative work.

(b) Industrial property which includes trademarks, geographical indications, patents, industrial designs and trade secrets. Industrial property is protected primarily to stimulate innovation, design and creation of technology.

For the purpose of the TRIPS agreement, "intellectual property" refers to all categories of intellectual property that are the subject of section 1 through 7 of part II of the agreement (Article 1:2). This includes copyright and related rights, trademarks, geographical indications, industrial designs, patents, integrated circuit layout-designs and protection of undisclosed information. The TRIPS Agreement is applicable to all WTO members as it is a part of the total package of WTO agreements. However, different members have been allowed different time spans for applying its provisions keeping in view their economic circumstances. The main periods of transitions from existing provisions to TRIPS allowed under the agreement are as follows.

(a) Developed countries were granted a transition period of one year following the entry into force of the WTO Agreement, i.e. until 1 January, 1996.

(b) Developing countries were allowed a further period of four years (i.e. to January 2000) to apply the provisions of the agreement other than Articles 3, 4 and 5 which dealt with general principles such as non discrimination.

(c) Transition economies, i.e. members in the process of transformation from centrally-planned into market economies, could also benefit from the same delay (also until 1 January 2006), with the possibility of an extension. For pharmaceutical patents, this has been extended to 1 January 2016, under a decision taken by ministers at the Fourth Ministerial Conference in November 2001.

Basically, Intellectual Property Rights (IPRs) was formed to serve the following two purposes:

1. To control the growth of international trade in "counterfeit" goods. Such trade is supposed to be facilitated by widely varying national laws and standards for protection and enforcement of IPR and absence of any multilateral framework of principles, rules and disciplines to deal with this problem.
2. To reduce tariff and non-tariff barriers to cross border trade obliging every nation to accord most favoured nation treatment to all trading partners and reducing discrimination between domestic and foreign enterprises.

These two factors constitute the entire objective of the TRIPs Agreement as stated in Article 7 of the agreement entitled "objectives" which states: "The protection and enforcement of intellectual property rights should contribute to the promotion of technological innovation and to the transfer and dissemination of technology and to the mutual advantage of producers and uses the technological knowledge and in a manner conducive to social and economic welfare and to a balance of rights and obligations."

IMPACT OF WTO AND TRIPS

The General Council decision of August 30, 2003 under Para 6 of the Doha Ministerial Declaration on TRIPS and Public Health enables manufacture and export of pharmaceutical products under compulsory license to countries with limited or no manufacturing capacity in pharmaceutical sector by granting suitable waivers from various articles under this mechanism. Currently, discussions are going on in the TRIPs Council on the method of incorporation of the Decision in the TRIPS Agreement, i.e. whether this may be effected by inserting a footnote to Article 31 or by creating an Article 31bia, or by adding an annexure or by incorporating the full text of the relevant provisions of the Decision in the text of the TRIPS Agreement. The target for completing the process was set up for the end of March 2005.

In 1995, India agreed to adopt the "Product Patents Regime" by 2005 as a part of its WTO commitments. This encouraged our pharmaceutical companies to adopt a strategy of R&D based innovative growth. This can transform the Indian Chemical and Pharmaceutical Industry particularly, the biotech sector in which it has good prospects. The Government of India has already issued the patent (Amendments) Ordinance, 2004 on December 26, 2004 to further amend the Patent Act, 1970. The Ordinance amends the Indian Patents Act, 1970 for the third time (i.e. the earlier two amendments were enacted in 1999 and 2002) to introduce product patents for drugs, food and chemicals. With this, Government. of India has already adhered to the January 1, 2005 deadline for implementation of the Product Patent Regime, in conformity with the Trade-Related Intellectual Rights (TRIPS) Agreement of the World Trade Organisation.

The salient features of the third amendment to the Patent Law are as under:

(a) Extension of product patent protection to all fields of technology, by extending it to drugs, food and chemicals;

(b) Deletion of the provisions relating to Exclusive Marketing Rights (EMRs) which would now become redundant and introduction of a transitional provision for safeguarding EMRs already granted;

(c) Introduction of a provision for enabling grant of compulsory licence for export to medicines to countries which have insufficient or no manufacturing capacity to meet emergent public health situations (i.e. in accordance with the Doha Declaration on TRIPS and Public Health);

(d) Modification in the provisions relating to opposition procedures with a view to streamlining the system by having both pre-grant and post-grant opposition in the Patent Office;

(e) Addition of a new proviso to circumscribe rights in respect of mailbox applications so that patent rights in respect of the mailbox shall be available only from the date of grant of patent and not retrospectively from the date of publication;

(f) Strengthening the provisions relating to national security and to guard against patenting abroad or dual use technologies;

(g) Clarification of the provisions relating to patenting of software related inventions when they have technical application to industry or are in combination with hardware;

(h) Rationalisation of provisions relating to time-lines with a view to introducing flexibility and reducing the processing time for patent applications, and simplifying and rationalising procedures.

Some of the exporters/importers are having the apprehensions that the Patent Amendment will drive up drug prices by ruling out access and availability of medicines at low cost. However, such apprehensions are unfounded. In the first place, the fact remains that 97 per cent of all drugs manufactured in India are off-patents and so will remain unaffected. These cover most of the life saving drugs as well as medicines of common ailments. In patented drugs also, in most of the cases, there are always alternatives available. Further, the country has 13 Sections under Chapter XVI pertaining to Compulsory Licensing in place and the Act has strong provisions under Chapter XVII for outright acquisition of patents to meet national requirements. Besides, there is also the Drug Price Control Order administered by the National Pharmaceuticals Price Authority. With such a framework in place, the concerns and fears relating to rise in drug prices are misplaced. Besides, there are adequate safeguards to protect the interests domestic and the common man from any increase in the prices of drugs.

WTO's TRIMS AND INDIA

The Agreement on Trade-Related Investment Measures (TRIMS) under the WTO regime is another sensitive areas in the context of the Indian economy. The very purpose of TRIMS is to monitor investment measures which may have the effect of restricting and distorting trade. It aims at making it free and easy for investment to move across international frontiers. While doing so, it takes note of the development and financial needs of developing countries. The Article relating to the Agreement on TRIMs mandates national treatment to international investments on trade in goods.

TRIMS restrict the power of the Government to regulate and control foreign investment. Foreign investors have been given advantageous position vis-à-vis our domestic investors. Foreign investors enjoy full freedom to operate with the backing of their Government.

In the period of liberalization, the performance of the industrial sector has been better in comparison to agriculture sector but still it is far below the desired level. The overall index has increased by 176.4 points in 2003-04 by taking 1993-94 as base year, but the growth is still single digit and lot of efforts is required to achieve double-digit growth.

One of the key arguments made by advocates of stronger global IPRs is that such a system, as embodies in the TRIPs agreement, would increase FDI in and associated technology transfer to developing countries. But earlier studies undertaken had not shown any increase in flows in countries where IPRs laws and regulations were updated. Besides, India and the EU are already in formal WTO consultations in trade disputes on an Indian order on the import or raw hides and skins, which trade is of vital interest to India as a foreign exchange earner. It is also in consultation on the Indian requirement of foreign exchange neutrality from automakers and India's schedule of import restrictions imposed on grounds of health, environment and security, etc.

New trade talks will begin. No country including India, can afford not to participate. The MFN status and non-discrimination, the fundamentals of the Uruguay Round and WTO will be lost, if one were to stay away. There is, however, no unity in approach among the developing countries towards the new Round. Many amongst the developing countries find it more convenient to be pragmatic in their decision making. They prefer to keep their options open and then go along with the country or countries that can offer them more.

Given the emerging situation in Geneva, the biggest challenge for India is how to push forward its agenda on services in the Doha round of trade negotiations. The chances of using the G-20 alliance to further its interest took remote as India is facing opposition from Brazil, the leader of the G-20 alliance. Other members are also not very keen to go along with India on this issue.

CONCLUSION

India's biggest interest in new round of talks in liberalization in the services sector, something even most developing countries are not in favour of India, had come up with a plurilateral approach which basically fast-tracked the commitments that various countries would given on opening up their markets. This is something India soft-pedalled on at Hong Kong to maintain the unity of developing countries. So, the way ahead would depend purely on the negotiations India is able to have from now on.

No doubt, despite various criticisms, these proposals and agreements have been signed world over. Hence we cannot leave it. The only effort, which is sincerely needed at this juncture, is to find out a way that could minimize the damages and maximize the benefits. This needs sincere and continuous efforts towards the improvement and upgrading of technology applicable to agriculture and rural development.

The WTO has a leading role to play in the interconnected world. There is a clear and indivisible relationship between the dynamics of technological progress in our time and the dynamics of liberalization in the world economy–the WTO's future agenda is key to keeping this trend on track. There is also a clear link between deeper economic and technological integration and the global rules need to manage our interdependence–rules which only the multilateral trading system can provide. Thus, WTO provides opportunities to all and challenges to many.

REFERENCES

Gill, S.S. and Brar; J.S. (1996), Global Markets and Competitiveness of Indian Agriculture, E.P.W.

Indian Express–Various Issues.

Nayar, D.R. (2001), Globalization and Nationalism, Sage Publication, New Delhi.

Panchamukhi, V.R. (1996), World Trading System: Challenges for Rural India, Pigmy Economic Review.

Quereshi, Asif N. (1996), World Trade Organization.

Rao, M.B. (2002), WTO & International Trade, Vikas Publishing House Pvt. Ltd.

The Economic Times–Various Issues.

Todaro, Michael P. (1997): Economic Development in the Third World, Longman, London.

WTO (2004), Annual Report.

Yojana–Various Issues.

IMPACT OF WTO ON INDIAN ECONOMY

Md. Murshid Alam and Kumkum Jha

INTRODUCTION

The World Trade Organisation (WTO) has made useful contributions in shaping the world trade order based on its philosophy of market access. The World Trade Organisation (WTO) provides a firm institutional basis for the application and enforcement of multilaterally agreed trade rules on goods and services and on the protection of intellectual property rights. Over the past 57 years ever since the creation of the General Agreement on Tariffs and Trade (GATT) in 1947, trade has been a powerful engine for growth. After the eight rounds of trade negotiations and with GATT Agreement 1994, the WTO was established on January 1, 1995. At present, 148 countries are the members of WTO and about 40 more countries are in the line for becoming the members and about 95 per cent of the global trade is governed by the rules and regulations of the WTO. The scope and coverage of WTO is much wider than the GATT. The former was a multilateral treaty meant for fostering trade liberalisation among the member nations and it dealt only with trade in goods, the latter on the other hand, covers trade in agriculture, trade related investment measures (TRIMs), trade related intellectual property right (TRIPS), trade in service and host of other things which were earlier the subject matters of the respective nation states. WTO contains various trade procedures acceptable to developed and developing countries. In the globalised context, WTO also takes note of matters incidental and ancillary to trade and investment such as, employment standards, reduction of tariff rates, investment protection, trade and investment, and trade and employment. In order to see that these provisions are effectively implemented, WTO has provisions for sanctions in case of default by member countries. The purpose and objective of the WTO was to create a fair and equitable rule based multilateral trade system, which world ensure greater trade flows for all its participating members thereby ensuring fair distribution of the fruits of global economic development.

HISTORICAL PERSPECTIVE

The WTO came into existence in 1995 but its history goes back to the World War-II. The world trade experienced massive disruptions during the Great Depression of the late twenties and the early thirties when economic nationalism reigned supreme. In these years, the governments of many nations indulged in competitive devaluations of their currencies, raised their import duties to abnormal height and imposed various types of trade restrictions to balance their payments, undermining the world trading system. During the World War-II, it was feared that the depressed economic conditions of the 1930s may return after the cession of War as nations, like in the past, would attempt to return to balance budget. This would create problems for international trade. Therefore, plans for reform in the international trading system began to take shape during the war. As the war ended, the allied powers met in Bretton Woods, New Hampshire in 1944 to set some guidelines for the operation of the world economy in the post war years. The International Monetary Fund (IMF) to promote international monetary cooperation and trade and the International Bank for Reconstruction and Development (World Bank) to finance economic reconstruction and development were conceived at this conference. This conference also generated plans for the establishment of an International Trade Organisation (ITO) to frame rules eliminate restrictions and settle disputes relating to international trade. But the ITO fails to take shape due to the non-approval of its charter by the US Congress. Instead the US and some other countries agreed to adopt as treaty obligations a set of rules for conducting international trade among them. This treaty was called the

General Agreement on Tariffs and Trade (GATT). The GATT was signed in 1947 at Geneva by 23 countries including India and became effective from January 1, 1948.

The GATT framed rules of conduct of international trade among member nations and provided forum for multilateral negotiations on issues relating to it. Its members agreed to abide by the principle of non-discrimination embodied in the most-favoured-nation (MFN) clause and national treatment. They committed to protect their domestic industry by tariffs only and bind the tariff levels negotiated among them. The GATT also established a framework for settlement of trade disputes. Over the years, the GATT pursued trade liberalization by sponsoring a series of negotiations or rounds and achieved remarkable success in reducing tariffs all around the globe especially in the developed countries. Continued reduction in tariffs helped spur an unprecedented expansion in world trade surpassing the rate of growth of world output. But despite these achievements, grievances against the working of the GATT appeared in the early 1980s. Its credibility and effectiveness began to be questioned on grounds of its limited success in eliminating non-tariff barriers (NTBs) to international trade and ignoring trade in agricultural goods, textiles and clothing and services. Its weak institutional structure and defective dispute settlement system were considered responsible for impeding further progress in trade liberalization. Its members wanted it to be improved and absorb the complexities of world trade, encompass additional areas of trade and address increasingly the concerns of developing countries. The developing countries, called GATT as the "rich men club."

These realizations led to a fresh round of trade negotiations —the eighth in the series under the aegis of GATT at Punta del Este, Uruguay in September 1986 with the principal objective "to halt and reverse protectionism, and to reverse distortions in trade." This round of trade negotiations popularly known as the Uruguay Round (UR) concluded in 1994 and "was unique in several respects. It covers many new areas such as agriculture, textiles, technology, intellectual property rights (IPRs), trade-related investment, services, etc. It included in its scope of liberalization, non-tariff barriers (NTBs), along with tariffs and conceived many new norms and disciplines such as sanitary and phyto-sanitary measures, anti-dumping measures, dispute settlement procedures, safeguard measures, etc. with a view to ensuring liberalised effective market access and rule-based trade". The conclusion of the Uruguay Round saw the transformation of the GATT into a more formal organisation called the WTO in 1995.

GATT & WTO

The WTO is not a simple extension of GATT. It is a legal and institutional foundation of multilateral trading system. It provides the principal contractual obligations determining how governments frame and implement domestic trade legislation and regulations. It is the platform on which trade relations among countries evolve through collective debate, negotiation and adjudication. In many ways, the WTO is different from the GATT. For instance, unlike the GATT, the WTO commitments are full and permanent. In additions to goods, the WTO covers trade in services and TRIP's. The WTO dispute settlement system is faster, more automatic, and thus less susceptible to blockages. The implementation of WTO dispute findings will also be more easily assured. The GATT lives on as "GATT 1994", amended and up dated version of GATT 1947, which is an integral part of the WTO agreement and which continue to provide the key disciplines affecting international trade in goods.

IMPACT OF WTO ON INDIAN ECONOMY

India's signing of GATT agreement in 1994 and joining of WTO as a founder member in 1995, raised a number of issues relating to its impact on our nation's interest. There are major four provisions of the GATT accord relating to agriculture and other sectors as under: (i) Reduction in domestic support; (ii) Market access; (iii) TRIPS; and (iv) Sanitary and phyto-sanitary provisions.

The agreement on agriculture provides a first and welcome step in reducing the protectionist production and dumping practices particularly those of the EU and USA. A potentially negative consequence of the proposals is that developing countries like India will be more constrained in setting up supportive measures for their agricultural production. The government of India has taken several steps to implement policy commitments made under some of the agreements, particularly under the Agreement on Tariffs and Quantitative Restructions, Agreement on Agriculture (AoA), Trade Related Intellectual Property Rights (TRIPS), Trade Related Investment Measures (TRIMs), General Agreement on Trade in Services (GATS), apart from others. However, a strategy for tariff negotiations is required. Further, the additional 'non-trade' issues relating to transparency in government procurement practices, trade and competition policy, trade and environment, and trade and labour standards proposed in the Singapore and the Geneva Ministerial need to be addressed for negotiations.

Further, the commitments regarding the technical barriers to trade, social agenda covering labour standards and environmental and phyto-sanitary issues also require establishment of certain national standards and technical regulations in a standardized and transparent system. There are some of the issues on which India has already expressed certain reservations to the WTO. Some of them are as under:

1. During the process of implementation of WTO agreements in the last ten years, India has experienced certain imbalances and inequities in the WTO agreements. It has been observed that some of the developed countries have not fulfilled their obligations in letter and spirit of the WTO agreements and many of the special and Differential Treatment clauses in favour of developing countries, added in various WTO agreements have remained inoperational.
2. Taking advantage of the exception clauses provided in the WTO, most of the industrialised countries are still enforcing various regulations on foreign produces and suppliers.
3. It has been observed that extending the scope of the investment regime in WTO beyond Trade Related Investment Measures and General Agreement on Trade in Services is not appropriate for the developing countries like India.
4. India has also experienced and observed that a multilateral framework cannot guarantee an increase in FDI inflows, although, it threatens to adversely affect the quality of the inflows.

5. Further, it has observed that the WTO does not address the responsibilities of corporations, which often impose trade restrictive clauses on their subsidiaries.
6. WTO has not been able to ensure abolition of non-trade barriers being imposed on labour and environmental considerations, including the linkage in certain Generalised System of Preferences (GSP) schemes of these issues.

(A) WTO and Agricultural Trade

Indian share in total world trade is about 0.8 per cent out of which agricultural export accounts 11.8 per cent of total merchandise of export in 2003-04, of which the export of food grain (rice and wheat) have acquired considerably significant place in recent years accounting 12 and 6.9 per cent of total agricultural export respectively. Volume of export of agriculture has increased significantly during last one decade. It was about US $ 6828 million in 1996-97 and in the year 2003-04, it has reached to US $ 7533 million. But share of agricultural export has declined significantly from about 20 per cent to 11.8 per cent. Estimates for the year 2004-05 (April–September) indicates further decline to 9.7 per cent whereas during April-September 2003-04, it was 11.2 per cent. The share of export of rice has declined significantly from 18.1 to 12 per cent and that of wheat has increased marginally from 5.4 to 6.9 per cent. If we add up the two components of major food grains, total export has declined from 23.5 per cent in 2002-03 to 18.9 per cent is 2003-04. Thus, despite increase in volume of export, relative position of agricultural export has declined because of expansion of other sectors of the economy.

Volume of agriculture import has also increased considerably from US $1428 to 3282.3 million. However, the share of agricultural import in total merchandised of import has increased from 3.7 to 4.6 per cent, of which import of cereals have nominal share of 0.5 per cent. World trade in rice is less than 5.0 per cent of total production, yet it is one of the most important agricultural commodities in the world trade, which is dominated by Thailand, United States, Pakistan, China and Australia. Despite the fact that India has the largest area under the rice production and is the second largest producer of rice, share of rice export in total agricultural export is only 12 per cent. This is due to inter-alia limited and unsteady surplus-caused partly by low productivity, poor quality, price policy and internal restrictions like ceiling on stock and Essential Commodities Act, etc. In case of wheat, India contributed about 8 per cent of total world production. India has the fourth largest area under wheat production and is the second largest wheat producer of the world. Table 1 reveals that export of agricultural commodities has increased. However, Coffee, tea and mate, tobacco, cashew kernels, spices, raw cotton have shown their decline. Table 2 also confirms this finding.

Table 1
Commodities Indian Exports of Agricultural

(in US Million $)

Sl. No.	Item	1980-81	1990-91	1999-2000	2002-03
1.	Agriculture	2601	3521	5773	6962
1.1	Coffee	271	141	331	205
1.2	Tea and Mate	538	596	412	341
1.3	Oil Cakes	158	339	378	382
1.4	Tobacco	178	147	233	211
1.5	Cashew Kernels	177	249	568	424
1.6	Spices	14	133	408	342
1.7	Sugar and Molasses	50	21	9	375
1.8	Raw Cotton	209	471	18	10
1.9	Rice	283	257	721	1205
1.10	Fish and Fish preparation	274	535	1183	1432
1.11	Meat and Meat preparations	70	78	189	284
1.12	Fruits, Vegetables and pulses (Excl. cashew Karnels Processed fruit and juice	101	120	288	350
1.13	Miscellaneous processed (Incl. Processed fruits and juices)	45	119	154	307

Source: Government of India, Economic Survey (various issues).

Indian agricultural trade has been facing serious challenges under the globalisation. Though Indian agriculture contributes one-fourth in country's GDP, and source of livelihood of more than two third of the population but its share in global agro trade has been diminished to about 9 per cent only over the period of time. Agricultural trade was an exception to liberalization before the WTO agreement. It was the highly protected sector in the developed countries. Remunerative prices, subsidies, quantitative restrictions were the order of the day. As a result, the agricultural exports of the developing countries like India suffered a lot.

Table 2
Percentage of India's Agriculture and Allied Commodities in World Exports and Imports

Sl. No.	*Item*	*1980-81*	*1990-91*	*2000-01*	*2002-03*	*2003-04**
A.	**Export**					
1.	Rice	3.7	6.4	9.3	18.4	12.3
	Vegetable and Fruits	1.1	0.8	1.3	4.5	5.9
	Coffee and Coffee Substitutes	2.1	1.7	2.2	5.1	4.9
	Coffee, Tea, Coca, Spices	4.0	4.0	3.4	3.1	3.1
	Tea and mate	27.7	22.1	14.3	5.1	3.2
	Sugar, Sugar Preparations and Honey	0.3	0.1	0.0	5.6	4.0
	Meat and Meat preparations	0.4	0.2	0.7	4.2	4.8
	Feeding Stuff for animals	1.6	2.2	2.3	3.2	4.0
2.	Fish crustaceans and Molluscs and preparations	2.0	1.6	2.8	–	–
3.	Cereal and Cereal Preparation	0.5	0.6	1.4	–	–
10.	Spices	14.5	7.7	9.7	–	–
12	Tobacco and Refuse	4.4	2.1	2.3	–	–
13.	Oilseeds and oleaginous fruit	03	0.8	1.3	–	–
14.	Leather	10.0	4.8	2.5	–	–
15.	Woven Cotton Fabrics	5.3	3.7	5.0	–	–
B	**Import**					
1.	Cereals	–	–	1.0	0.9	0.5
2.	Pulses	–	–	5.9	20.2	12.7
3.	Milk and Cream	–	–	0.1	0.1	0.6
4.	Cashew Nuts	–	–	11.3	9.1	8.9
5.	Fruits and Nuts (Excl. cashew Nuts)	–	–	9.4	4.7	4.6
6.	Sugar	–	–	0.4	0.2	0.3
7.	Oil Seeds	–	–	0.1	0.1	0.1
8.	Vegetabie Oils Fixed (edible)	–	–	71.8	64.7	71.4

Source: Government of India, Economic Survey (various issues).
*Data relate to 2003–04 (April–February)

(B) WTO and TRIPS

The General Council decision of August 30, 2003 under Para 6 of the Doha Ministerial Declaration on trade related intellectual property right (TRIPS) and Public Health enables manufacture and export of pharmaceutical products under compulsory license to countries with limited or no manufacturing capacity in pharmaceutical sector by granting suitable waivers from various articles under this mechanism. Currently, discussions are going on in the TRIPS Council on the method of incorporation of the Discussion in the TRIPS Agreement, i.e. whether this may be effected by inserting a footnote to Article 31 or by creating an Article 31 bia, or by adding an annexure or by incorporating full text of the relevant provisions of the decision in the text of the TRIPS Agreement. The target for completing the process was set up for the end of March 2005. In 1995, India agreed to adopt the "Product Patents Regime" by 2005 as a part of its WTO commitments. This encourages our pharmaceutical companies to adopt a strategy of R & D based innovative growth. This can transform the Indian chemical and pharmaceutical Industry particularly, the biotech sector in which it has good prospects. The Government of India has already issued the Patent (Amendments) Ordinance, 2004 on December 26, 2004 to further amend the Patent Act, 1970. The Ordinance amends the Indian Patent Act, 1970 for the third time (i.e. the earlier two amendments were enacted in 1999 and 2002) to introduce product patents for drugs, food and chemicals. With this, Government of India has already adhered to the January 1, 2005 deadline for implementation of the Product Patent Regime in conformity with the Trade-Related Intellectual Rights (TRIPS) Agreement of the World Trade Organisation.

The salient features of the third amendment to the Patent Law are as under:

(a) Extension of product patent protection to all fields and technology by extending it to drugs, food and chemicals;

(b) Deletion of the provisions relating to Exclusive Marketing Rights (EMRs) which would now become redundant and introduction of a transitional provision for safeguarding EMRs already granted;

(c) Introduction of a provision for enabling grant of compulsory license for export to medicines to countries, which have insufficient, or no manufacturing capacity to meet emergent public health situations (i.e. in accordance with the Doha Declaration on TRIPS and Public Health);

(d) Modification in the provisions relating to opposition procedures with a view to streamlining the system by having both pre-grant and post-grant opposition in the patent office;

(e) Addition of a new provision to circumscribe rights in respect of mailbox shall be available only from the date of grant of patent and not retrospectively from the date of publication;

(f) Strengthening the provisions relating to national security and to guard patenting abroad or dual use technologies;

(g) Classification of the provisions relating to patenting of software related inventions when they have technical application to industry or are in combination with hardware;

(h) Rationalisation of provisions relating to time-lines with a view to introducing flexibility and reducing the processing time for patent applications and simplifying and rationalizing procedures.

Some of the exporters/importers are having the apprehensions that the Patent Amendment will drive up drug prices by ruling out access and availability of medicines at low cost. However, such apprehensions are unfounded. In the first place, the fact remains that 97 per cent of all drugs manufactured in India are off-patents and so will remain unaffected. These cover most of the life saving drugs as well as medicines of common ailments. In patented drug also and in most of the cases, there are always alternatives available. Further, the country has 13 sections under Chapter XVI pertaining to compulsory Licensing in place and the Act has strong provisions under Chapter XVII for outright acquisition of patents to meet rational requirements. Besides, there is also the Drug Price Control Order administered by the National Pharmaceutical Price Authority. With such a framework in place, the concerns and fears relating to rise in drug prices are misplaced. Besides, there are adequate safeguards to protect the interests domestic and the common man from any increase in the prices of drugs.

In India just after independence, there was no pharma industry. During 1950's and 60's pharma section development started but it was not able to meet the domestic demands. There were two ways to improve the pharma sector either by importing medicines or by providing incentives to domestic industry. Indian government opted to provide incentives to domestic industry. The Indian Patent Law of 1970 recognised only process patent instead of product patent.

The global genetic market is projected to grow from present \$36 billion to \$ 50–55 billion by 2008 and India will be in a favourable position being one of the most cost effective producers of genetic drugs. With their cost effective process innovations, Indian companies have emerged as competitive suppliers in the world of a large number of genetic drugs that are now outside the patent protection. Pharmaceutical exports from India have grown at a significant rate since the seventies as shown in Table 3. As a result, their share in India's exports has increased from 0.55 per cent in 1970-71 to over 5 per cent in 2002-03. India's share in world pharmaceuticals exports has also risen steadily but even today, it is only around one per cent (Table 4).

During 1994-95 and 1999-2000 taken together, price index of drugs and medicines increased by 78.1 per cent as against overall increase in price index by 29.4 per cent. However, the fear that drug prices will rise due to the introduction of product patent regime appears overstated since almost 97 per cent of the medicine including certain life saving drugs is off patent.

(C) WTO and Indian Textiles and Clothing

Another significant development in the world trade is the expiry of Agreement on Textiles and Clothing (ATC) at the end of 2004, ending a historic anomaly in the world trading system by putting textiles and clothing on the same footing as other industries under the WTO. Now, Indian textiles industry is at the cross roads with the phasing out of quota regime on January 1, 2005 and the full integration of the textiles sector in the WTO. We know that on January 1, 1995, the WTO Agreement on Textiles and Clothing (ATC) replaced MFA with a commitment to a 10 years transitional process for the ultimate removal of these quotas and fully integrating the sector into WTO rules by January 1, 2005. The main implication of this for the Indian

Table 3
India's Trade in Pharmaceutical Products
1970–71 to 2002–03 (current prices)

(In Rs. Crores)

Year	*Trade in Medicinal and Pharmaceutical Products*			*Pharmaceutical Exports as a per cent of India's Total Exports*
	Exports	*Imports*	*Trade Balance*	
1970-71	8.5	24.3	–15.8	0.55
1975-76	22.2	36.3	–14.1	0.55
1980-81	67.4	84.6	–17.2	1.00
1985-86	157.9	177.2	–19.3	1.45
1990-91	1014.1	468.4	545.7	3.11
1995-96	3408.7	1358	2050.7	3.21
1996-97	4341.8	1089.2	3252.6	3.65
1997-98	5419.3	1447.1	3972.2	4.17
1998-99	6256.07	1615.2	4640.87	4.48
1999-2000	7230.16	1616.22	5613.82	4.07
2000-01	8757.47	1711.81	7045.66	4.30
2001-02	9834.68	2026.58	7808.10	4.70
2002-03	12826.10	2865.20	9960.9	5.00

Source: RBI (2003-04), Handbook of Statistics on Indian Economy, Reserve Bank of India, Bombay.

Table 4
India's Pharmaceutical Exports in World Trade
1970-2001 (current prices)

(in US $million)

Year	*Share of India in World Exports*	
	All Merchandise	*Pharmaceuticals*
1970	0.6	0.4
1975	0.5	0.4
1980	0.4	0.8
1985	0.5	0.8
1990	0.5	1.2
1995	0.6	1.0
1998	0.6	1.0
2000	0.7	1.2
2001	0.7	0.9

Source: Government of India, Economic Survey, 2003-04 and UN International Trade Statistics Year Book.

Textile Industry is the threat from the China, which is poised to grab the lion's share of global trade in clothing. China has a cap of 7-8 per cent annual increase in exports of clothing to the US and EU until January 2008 by value of their being late signatory to the WTO. India needs to concentrate on this window of opportunity from January 1, 2005 till December, 2007 to gain serious market share, while China's exports of clothing is still restricted. Further, it has been observed that most of the studies conducted to estimate the impact of ATC expiry on textile trade, share the finding that some of the Asian countries are most likely to benefit from the dismantling of the quotas. They predict a substantial increase in market shares for China. According to a recent study conducted by CRISIL the Indian textile and apparel industry can achieve a potential size of US $85 billion by 2010 with a domestic market size of US $45 billion and nearly 60 per cent of exports comprising of garments. Moreover, the potential translates to creation of 12 million job opportunities, 5 million in the textile industry and 7 million in allied sectors. Further, India has a natural competitive advantage in terms of a strong and large multi-fibre base, abundant cheap skilled labour and presence across the entire value chain of the industry ranging from spinning, weaving and made ups to manufacturers of garments. But, with prices expected to fall in the post quota regime with increased international trade and competition, such as advantage may not be enough. Enhanced efficiency and productivity is a must to meet this emerging challenge of global competition.

(D) WTO and Trade in Financial services

The WTO negotiations on financial services, which extended beyond the Uruguay Round through repeated rounds of discussions and concluded as late as December 1997 with the signing of the Financial Services Agreement, clearly reflect the competing considerations and concerns associated with liberalization of the financial services sector. The WTO commitments in financial services reflect the various kinds of market access and national treatment barriers that effect trade and investment in financial services. The GATS negotiations on financial services were fraught with difficulties. While the developed countries sought access to important emerging markets in Latin America and Asia for their banking, insurance, brokerage, and other financial services firms the developing countries, although eager to strengthen and modernize their financial systems and cognizant of the associated benefits, were wary of making liberal binding commitments to guarantee such market access in their financial sectors. As a result, commitments were often limited in scope. India was one of the developing countries, which offered only limited liberalization in this sector under the GATS. This is a sector where India has limited export prospects and where the focus of the negotiations is on India's offers, especially on commercial presence. India is under a lot of pressure from various developed countries to open up its financial services sector to foreign investment. However, India has not been prepared to bind in its existing policies in this sector under the GATTS, although unilaterally it has undertaken considerable liberalization in recent years in banking, insurance and non-banking financial activities. To some extent, this negotiating stance reflects prudential and macroeconomic concerns about liberalizing financial services and the possibility of rolling back such liberalization if circumstances so required. These concerns largely stem from recognized structural and regulatory deficiencies in India's financial system and the general perception that these deficiencies need to be addressed and the financial system strengthened before binding multilateral commitments can be made under the GATTS.

(E) WTO and Human Resource Development

WTO introduced a detailed programmed for free and fair trade both in goods and services. It created international competitiveness in world economies. Those countries adjusting their resources and upgrading their technology could be able to survive in the highly competitive world market. Out of total trade, services began occupying larger and increasing share both in developed and less developed countries. The main channel of WTO for bringing out competition in services is the General Agreement on Trade in Services (GATS), which made Most Favoured Nations (MFN) and National Treatment (NT) obligatory to all the member countries. MFN (Article II, Sub-section 1 of GATS) requires non-discriminatory practices with regard to the supply of products from one country to another. Impact of WTO on HRD in India is to be analysed in terms of educational attainments, health profile and poverty reduction. India has made substantial progress providing education to its people at defficient levels. The adult literacy rate increased from 34 per cent in 1970 to 50 per cent in 1992. During reform period and the post WTO period there is only marginal improvement that is 52 per cent rise in 1995 and 58 per cent rise in 2001. It is appreciating that literacy rate in India is highest in SAARC countries except Sri Lanka and Maldives. India's educational success in even more interesting in the case of female adult literacy rate, which doubled during 1970 and 1995 and rose to 68 per cent up to 2001. India has not made much progress in the educational attainment during post WTO era both in absolute form as well as at the regional level. Moreover, the quality of education continues to be low as compared to the international standards. India's educational success may be understood from Table 5.

Table 5
Selected Indicators of Human Resource Development in India

Indicator / Year	*1992*	*1995*	*2001*
Life expectancy at birth (years)	60	62	63.3
Adult literacy rate (% age 15 yrs. & above)	50	52	58
Infant mortality rate (per 1000 live births)	89	73[1]	67
Population with access to safe water (%)			
Rural	61[2]		79[5]
Urban	88[2]		95[5]
Gross enrolment ratio primary level (%)	85	89	96
Gross enrolment ratio for all levels (%)	50[2]	56	56
Population below poverty line (%)	51.34[3]	35	26.15
GDP per capital (PPP$)	1150	1422	2840
Children reaching grade 5(%)		62	68[4]
MDI Value	0.382	0.451	0.59
Public expenditure on education as % of GDP	3.9[2]		4.1[6]
Public expenditure on health as % of GDP	1.3[2]		0.9[6]

1. Figure relates to 1996. 2. Figure relates to 1990. 3. Figure relates to 1977-78. 4. Figure relates to 1998-99. 5. Figure relates to 2000. 6. Figure relates to 1998-2000.

Source: UNDP, Human Development Report (various issues).

In the case of health profile also, there are both progress and deprivations in India after WTO. The life expectancy, which increased to 62 years upto 1995, shows marginal rise 63.3 years in 2001. The gap between crude birth rate and crude death rate still continues to be quite large reflecting non-adoption of family welfare programmes. In the year 2002, birth rate stood 25 while death rate was 8.1 both per 1000 population. The fertility rate declined from 6.0 in 1960 to 3.2 in 1995 but in 2001 it remained 3.1, which is much higher causing high rate of population growth in India. Similarly, maternal mortality rate per 1,00,000 live birth shows little decrease from 437 in 1992-93 to 407 in 1998. Infant mortality rate per 1000 live births declined from 80 in 1991 to 63 in 2002. The health profile of India may be studied from Table 6.

Table 6
Selected Health Indicators in India (Person years)

Indicator / year	*1951*	*1981*	*1991*	*Current level*
Crude Birth Rate (Per 1000 population)	40.8	33.9	29.5	25.0 (2002)
Crude Death Rate (per 1000 population)	25.1	12.5	9.8	8.1 (2002)
Total Fertility Rate (Per woman)	6.0	4.5	3.6	3.1 (2001)
Maternal Mortality Rate Per 1,00,000 live births)	N.A.	N.A. (1992-93)	437	407 (1998
Infant Mortality Rate Per 1000 live births	146	110 (1951-61)	80	63 (2002)
Child (0-4 years) Mortality Rate (Per 1000 live births)	57.3 (1972)	41.2	26.5	19.3 (2001)
Couple Protection Rate (%)	10.4 (1971)	22.8	44.1	48.2 (1998-99)
Life Expectancy at birth				
Male	37.2	54.1	59.7	63.9 (2001-06)
Female	36.2	54.7	60.9	66.9 (2001-06)

Source: Economic Survey, 2004-05, Table 10.9.

In spite of the enough progress made by India in the health sector, it is still much behind of the industrial and world level.

There is impressive decline in the overall poverty in the country due to the numerous poverty alleviation measures and strategies undertaken. According to Planning Commission quinquennial Sample Survey on Household Consumer Expenditure conducted by National Sample Survey Organisation (NSSO), the poverty ratio in India was 26.1 per cent in 1999-00 showing significant decline from 36.0 per cent in 1993-94 and particularly from 51.3 per cent in 1977-78. The Tenth Plan target is to reduce poverty ratio by five percentage points to 19.3 per cent upto 2007 and by 15 percentage point upto 2012. Even the absolute number of poor people on a nutritional norm of per capita daily intake of 2400 calories in urban areas and 2100 in rural areas decreased from 328.9 million in 1977-78 to 320.3 million in 1993-94 and to 260.3 million in 1999-00.

Albeit, there is poverty decline in the country yet; disparities are large at the rural-urban and regional/states level. India's global position in terms of human and gender development indices is unsatisfactory as it is fourth largest economy of the world.

CONCLUSION

From the above analysis, we find that WTO put its impact on Indian economy. India is failure in new system in absence for preplanning in negotiations. Preparation for negotiation requires three basic things:

(i) Clarity in our perceptions regarding our goals and development strategies.

(ii) Clarity in regard to the mapping of the strategic options available with us and the identification of bargaining points and negotiation strategies.

(iii) Effective co-ordination with like-minded countries and negotiations both in the developing and the developed world.

It may be unfair if we pronounce that India has been failing on all three fronts in the various stages of negotiations in the past. It was assumed that becoming a member of WTO, India's market share in world export will improve from 0.5% to 1% and its share in export market will range from 3.5 to 7 billions US dollars per year. The WTO agreement is an emergence of world parliament and imposes international trade laws on the member countries and takes away the matters that were under national jurisdiction so far. But unfortunately the WTO trespasses the sovereignty of nations. It is necessary to face the challenges of developed countries, the first and the foremost thing that India should do is to strengthen the process of preparedness for various issues of negotiations that continue to come forward in the WTO for a instrument of coercion and exploitation. Non-trade items cannot and should not be brought into the WTO jurisdiction to give a longer rope to the US and other developed countries to encircle the developing third world countries to squeeze their economies in the name of environment, labour standards and exploitation.

If India is to take advantage of the opportunities of the WTO system and achieve the target of increasing the relative share in World exports to 1.5 per cent by the year 2009 as set forth in the Foreign Trade Policy of India 2004-09, India should strengthen the infrastructure facilities of the economy in a big way and improve the efficiency and competitiveness of the industrial sector by removing complex domestic and state interventions. In respect of agricultural exports, continuing efforts have to be made to persuade and pressurize the developed countries to bring down the heavy subsidies given in various forms to their agriculture sector.

REFERENCES

Srinivasan T.N. (1999), "WTO and the Developing Countries" Journal of Social and Economic Development, Vol. II, No. 1.

Economic and Political Weekly, March 25, 2003.

WTO, Trade Policy Review—India, 1988.

WTO Report, "Global Trade: WTO's Assessment of Recent Trends", WTO Report, International Trade, 1995.

Panchamukhi, V.R. (2001), "World Trade Orgnisation and India, Challenges and Perspectives", in Chadha, G.K. (ed.), Deep and Deep Publications Pvt. Ltd., New Delhi.

Wardha, H. (2002), "WTO and Third World Challenges", Commonwealth Publishers, New Delhi.

Government of India (2002), Economic Survey, 2001-02, New Delhi, Ministry of Finance.

Government of India (1995), Economic Survey 1994-95, New Delhi, Ministry of Finance.

Claessens, S. and Jansen M. (eds.) (2000), Internationalization of Financial Services, World Bank and WTO, Klumer Academic Press, Washington, D.C.

Mehta, M.M. (1976), Human Resource Development Planning, Macmillan, Delhi.

UNDP, Human Development Report (various issues).

Ahluwalia, Montek S. (1996), "New Economic Policy and Agriculture: Some Reflections", Indian Journal of Agricultural Economics, Vol. 51, No. 3, July-September.

Gulati, Ashok and Sharma, Anil (1994), "Agriculture under GATT; What It Holds for India", Economic and Political Weekly, Vol. XXIX, No. 29, July 16.

WTO: World Trade Reports for the years 2003, 2004 and Prospects for 2005.

Hoda, A. (1987), Developing Countries in the International Trading System, Allied Publications, New Delhi.

WTO AND ITS IMPACT ON INDIAN ECONOMY

Krishna Kant Jha & Usha Jha

INTRODUCTION

The World Trade Organization (WTO) is the only global international organization dealing with the rules of trade between nations. At its heart are the WTO agreements, negotiated and signed by the bulk of the world's trading nations and ratified in their parliaments. The goal is to help producers of goods and services, exporters, and importers conduct their business.

A policy agenda for the Indian economy should be determined by looking at the existing strengths and weaknesses and building on the strength while correcting the weakness. However, the corrective measures we have taken up hitherto are related to growth leaving the development aspects.

Growth does matter but it is means not end. End is development and development is about people rather than economic statistics. The process of development is, therefore, focus on human welfare and well being rather than capital output ratio of its derivatives. Any move towards eradication of poverty should now be a process of development involving reorientation of the entire economic, social and political system towards improving the quality of life of each individual of the entire society resulting welfare of mankind. So a break through in Indian economy is required.

OBJECTIVES OF THE PAPER

The following are the main objectives of the paper:

- To examine the role of WTO in development process
- To clarify some misconception about W.T.O.
- To give a new concept of development
- To examine the development of Indian economy
- To suggest a development model for Indian economy
- To draw conclusion regarding impact of W.T.O on Indian economy

METHODOLOGY

The paper has been written on the basis of some primary data collected using observation method. Secondary data has also been collected to supplement the work. Some laboratory type tests, unique in social science, have also been conducted before writing this paper.

ROLE OF WTO IN DEVELOPMENT PROCESS

The following are some important functioning, which helps the development of world economy:

The basic principles make the system economically more efficient and they cut costs

Many of the benefits of the trading system are more difficult to summarize in numbers, but they are still important. They are the result of essential principles at the heart of the system, and they make life simpler for the enterprises directly involved in trade and for the producers of goods and services.

Trade allows a division of labour between countries. It allows resources to be used more appropriately and effectively for production. But the WTO's trading system offers more than that. It helps to increase efficiency and to cut costs even more because of important principles enshrined in the system.

The system shields governments from narrow interests

The GATT-WTO system, which evolved in the second half of the 20th Century, helps governments take a more balanced view of trade policy. Governments are better placed to defend themselves against lobbying from narrow interest groups by focusing on trade-offs that are made in the interests of everyone in the economy.

One of the lessons of the protectionism that dominated the early decades of the 20th Century was the damage that can be caused if narrow sectoral interests gain an unbalanced share of political influence. The result was increasingly restrictive policy, which turned into a trade war that no one won and everyone lost.

The system encourages good government

The rules include commitments not to backslide into unwise policies. Protectionism in general is unwise because of the damage it causes domestically and internationally, as we have already seen. Particular types of trade barriers cause additional damage because they provide opportunities for corruption and other forms of bad government.

The system helps to keep the peace

Peace is partly an outcome of two of the most fundamental principles of the trading system: helping trade to flow smoothly, and providing countries with a constructive and fair outlet for dealing with disputes over trade issues. It is also an outcome of the international confidence and cooperation that the system creates and reinforces.

The system allows disputes to be handled constructively

There could be a down side to trade liberalization and expansion. More trade means more possibilities for disputes to arise. Left to them, those disputes could lead to serious conflict. But in reality, a lot of international trade tension is reduced because countries can turn to organizations, in particular the WTO, to settle their trade disputes.

The system based on rules makes life easier for all

The WTO cannot claim to make all countries equal. But it does reduce some inequalities, giving smaller countries more voice and at the same time freeing the major powers from the complexity of having to negotiate trade agreements with each of their numerous trading partners.

Decisions in the WTO are made by consensus. The WTO agreements were negotiated by all members, were approved by consensus and were ratified in all members' parliaments. The agreements apply to everyone. Rich and poor countries alike have an equal right to challenge each other in the WTO's dispute settlement procedures.

This makes life easier for all, in several different ways. Smaller countries can enjoy some increased bargaining power. Without a multilateral regime such as the WTO's system, the more powerful countries would be freer to impose their will unilaterally on their smaller trading partners. Smaller countries would have to deal with each of the major economic powers individually, and would be much less able to resist unwanted pressure.

Freer trade cuts the cost of living

We are all consumers. The prices we pay for our food and clothing, our necessities and luxuries, and everything else in between, are affected by trade policies. Protectionism is expensive: it raises prices. The WTO's global system lowers trade barriers through negotiation and applies the principle of non-discrimination. The result is reduced costs of production (because imports used in production are cheaper) and reduced prices of finished goods and services, and ultimately a lower cost of living.

It gives consumers more choice and a broader range of qualities to choose

Let us think of the things people in other countries can have because they buy exports from elsewhere and us. Look around and consider all the things that would disappear if all our imports were taken away from us. Imports allow us more choice –both more goods and services to choose from, and a wider range of qualities. Even the quality of locally produced goods can improve because of the competition from imports

Trade raises incomes

Economists estimate that cutting trade barriers in agriculture, manufacturing and services by one third would boost the world economy by $613 billion—equivalent to adding an economy the size of Canada to the world economy. In Europe, the EU Commission calculates that over 1989–93 EU incomes increased by 1.1–1.5% more than they would have done without the Single

Market. So, trade clearly boosts income. Trade also poses challenges as domestic producers face competition from imports. But the fact that there is additional income means that resources are available for governments to redistribute the benefits from those who gain the most–for example to help companies and workers adapt

Trade stimulates economic growth and that can be good news for employment

Trade clearly has the potential to create jobs. In practice there is often factual evidence that lower trade barriers have been good for employment. There is strong evidence that trade boosts economic growth, and that economic growth means more jobs.

BLAMES AGAINST WTO–NOT TRUE

We have the following answers against some blame against the WTO:

The WTO does not tell governments what to do

The WTO does not tell governments how to conduct their trade policies. Rather, it's a "member-driven" organization. That means:

- the rules of the WTO system are agreements resulting from negotiations among member governments,
- the rules are ratified by members' parliaments, and
- decisions taken in the WTO are virtually all made by consensus among all members.

In other words, decisions taken in the WTO are negotiated, accountable and democratic.

The WTO is not for free trade at any cost

It's really a question of what countries are willing to bargain with each other, of give and take, request and offer. Yes, one of the principles of the WTO system is for countries to lower their trade barriers and to allow trade to flow more freely. After all, countries benefit from the increased trade that results from lower trade barriers.

But just how low those barriers should go is something member countries bargain with each other. Their negotiating positions depend on how ready they feel they are to lower the barriers, and on what they want to obtain from other members in return. One country's commitments become another country's rights, and vice versa.

The WTO is not only concerned about commercial interests

The answer to this blame is that the WTO agreements are full of provisions taking the interests of development into account. Underlying the WTO's trading system is the fact that freer trade boosts economic growth and supports development. In that sense, commerce and development are good for each other.

At the same time, whether or not developing countries gain enough from the system is a subject of continuing debate in the WTO. But that does not mean to say that the system offers nothing for these countries. Far from it, the agreements include many important provisions that specifically take developing countries' interests into account.

The WTO does not destroy jobs or widen the gap between rich and poor

The accusation is inaccurate and simplistic. Trade can be a powerful force for creating jobs and reducing poverty. Often it does just that. Sometimes adjustments are necessary to deal with job losses, and here the picture is complicated. In any case, the alternative of protectionism is not the solution.

Small countries are not powerless in the WTO

Small countries would be weaker without the WTO. The WTO increases their bargaining power. In recent years, developing countries have become considerably more active in WTO negotiations, submitting an unprecedented number of proposals in the agriculture talks, and working actively on the ministerial declarations and decisions issued in Doha, Qatar, in November 2001. They expressed satisfaction with the process leading to the Doha declarations. All of this bears testimony to their confidence in the system.

At the same time, the present rules are the result of multilateral negotiations (i.e. negotiations involving all members of GATT, the WTO's predecessor). The most recent completed negotiation, the Uruguay Round (1986–94) was only possible because developed countries agreed to reform trade in textiles and agriculture–both issues were important for developing countries.

Weaker countries do have a choice; they are not forced to join the WTO

Most countries do feel that it's better to be in the WTO system than to be outside it. That's why the list of countries negotiating membership includes both large and small trading nations. China, for example has laboured hard to join WTO.

The WTO is not undemocratic

Decisions in the WTO are generally by consensus. In principle, that's even more democratic than majority rule because no decision is taken until everyone agrees.

The above description suggests that before we blame WTO, we should accept a new concept of development.

NEW CONCEPT OF ECONOMIC DEVELOPMENT

The Nobel Laureate, Amartya Sen (1986) rightly suggests that traditional development economics has been useful in analyzing factors in economic growth but has been less successful in characterizing economic development. The process of economic development according to him is best seen as the process of expanding the capabilities of people. According to him, process of economic development has to be concerned with what people can do and what cannot do.

Thus, Sen's way of development refers to a process of expansion of capability. Capability has a functional relationship with entitlement. The individual himself produces entitlement. So, one is capable of living better life by earning entitlement. In the mean time, these well being of people should not depend on chance or circumstance. Circumstance should not dominate the individuals but they should dominate the circumstances.

The above mentioned view of Sen regarding individual's dominance of circumstances matches with the individuality concept of R.M. Maciver (1962) He points out that when the possessor of individuality does as other do, at least in matters he deems important, he does it not simply because others do it, but because his own self approves that particular behaviour.

He has some independence of judgment, some initiative, some discrimination, as we often say some strength of characters. Thus individuality is individual's ability to exercise freedom of choice. He also observed that we find less individuality in less developed and primitive societies with their relatively rigid customs than in more organized ones

Sen, therefore, rightly remarks that the traditional development economics has been failing on account of its concentration on supply of goods rather than on ownership of entitlement. Sen himself has given example of 1974 famine of Bangladesh when large number of people died of hunger when food availability was at peak between 1971-75 in the country, They died because their services were not required for planting and transplanting of paddy. The poor workers lost entitlement firstly not getting an opportunity to selling their labour power and secondly losing purchasing power due to price hike of food grains. Similarly growth of total income or redistribution of income can provide inadequate basis for analyzing person's entitlement. For example, a person having very high earning of income lives in a village where there is no school or hospital and there is a custom that female member cannot go outside the village for study and treatment this curtailment of entitlement limits the development of the villagers.

There is, therefore, nothing wrong to accept Sen's explanation that a person in real sense, cannot be affluent and developed unless she is capable to earn entitlement but if we drop further explanation at this point, we fail to understand that who is and what is responsible for non-capability of a person. We can find solution to this problem after a close examination of rationality of behaviour on the part of the members of different groups of a society.

Rationality of Human Behaviour: A Pre-Condition for Development

If we examine the aforesaid example of Bangladesh minutely we find that the irrationality of behaviour on the part of different groups of persons was responsible for the tragedy. Thè labours lost capability by depending on paddy farming only. This decision was irrational act on their part. On the other hand the State did not behave rationally by not offering proper opportunities for them to work somewhere else. It was also irrational behaviour on the part of food grain dealers to increase the prices.

Now the question arises why people in the society behave irrationally? The reason is obvious. Our society is divided into weaker and stronger groups. Women for example belong to weaker group. A majority of ignorant and poor persons belong to weaker group whereas a powerful minority group is stronger one. This creates a situation where one person or a group of persons consider genuine right to exploit others. They feel there is no power where power is equal, the weaker section or a weaker person suffer voluntarily and gladly.

According to Richard Grabowski and Michael P. Shields (1996), an individual may actually calculate the pleasures and pains derived from alternative courses of action and chooses to act in a way that maximizes net pleasure such behaviour is an example of strong rationality. They further observe that within the concept of rationality it is not difficult to think of examples of individual behaviour that is irrational. We behave irrationally out of angers, habits, ignorance, laziness, fear or lust.

The weaker sections of our society generally behave irrationally out of ignorance, habit, laziness and fear whereas stronger group does so for lust of power and self-interest. For example, woman is habituated to suffer due to ignorance and fear of men who are stronger than the women. Men on the other hand feel powerful and superior to women by curtailing entitlement of women.

Joyce Jacobsen (1994) observes the following symptoms of irrationality of behaviour:

1. An irrational behaviour has no pattern and is apparently completely random in nature or responds erratically to outside influences.
2. It is responsive to the desire of others, behaviour that does not lead to maximizing one's self interest, but that may result of self-respect on the part of others.
3. It was one's own past behaviour and social custom as a guide to current behaviour regardless of changing circumstances.

When we keep these symptoms of irrationality of behaviour in mind we find, in less developed countries like India, that people in all walks of life behave irrationally engulfing themselves and the society into poverty.

State and its Behaviour

Now, the question arises that all the states behave rationally to eradicate poverty of their citizens? The function of state depends on the particular conditions of individual state. Unfortunately, many states mainly act as an exploitative power in the interest of dominant class controlling the rest of the population. It may on the other hand be a positive agency of the social welfare.

But it is recognized that the reforms that the state takes up often does not act with social welfare in mind. We can see states as obstacles, either passive or active to economic development. The first view argues that the policy made by the state is determined by the interplay competition and struggle between interest groups within the society.

It is not out of place to mention Olson's theory of group behaviour (1971). He argues that smaller groups remain more organized than the larger groups. Hence, the smaller groups are likely to have greater influence over policy making. As a result, state policies are likely to be disastrous for long-term economic development.

Robert H. Bates and Rogerson (1980) have argued that a more active view of state should be taken. The state should be taken as group as a coalition of groups with its own interests that may be separate from the interests of the most of the society The state seeks to pursue these interests, chief of which is to maintain itself in power. For example in Indian state instead of beginning development work adopts divide and rule policy. In principle it claims to be secular but calls influential Muslims minority group on the basis of religion and exploit their religious weaknesses. Cast politics spoils Indians. Political parties in lust of power try to appease them on religion and caste ground instead of making them development oriented. Similarly in Pakistan state appease people on Kashmir and anti-India issues instead of taking up development work. These are irrational behaviour on the part of state.

In this way, development of any economy cannot be seen in terms of gross national products only; rather it is about the people. It provides people better quality of life. We must adopt some principles as a framework for development process. Rationality of behaviour on part of each citizen and that on state is a pre condition for this. For that we will have to believe that human being is end not means. It is human being who utilizes other means. Principle of providing opportunity for empowerment to all should be the essence of the theory of development. Without having an opportunity for empowerment to earn entitlement for expansion of capability, better life is impossible. In Indian case providing opportunity for empowerment to all is a social problem. It requires cultural education to change attitude of people. Access to equal opportunity for all should be based on the principle of equity. Security of job and meaningful education should be fundamental right of each citizen of a country.

DEVELOPMENT OF INDIAN ECONOMY AT PRESENT

An American author made the following remark on development of Indian economy-"If it were possible to transplant overnight all the factories of Michigan, Ohio and Pennsylvania to India without changing of attitude of the people, two decades later the country would be as poor as it is now." This is not a casual statement rather it may be treated as a hypothesis to be tested. Let us examine India's present position regarding its growth and development.

Growth of Indian Economy

So far as economic growth in terms of GDP is concerned, our position is not so bad which is clear from the Table-1. The table shows the growth of 11 nations in terms of GDP during a period of twenty years at the close of 20th century.

The above table has been extracted from the data of PWT, which is an ambitious attempt, by researchers in the United States of America to arrive at micro economic agencies for long time series, which are comparable across countries. The PWT estimates are better at showing difference in purchasing power between countries.

Table 1
GDP of Top 11 Nations of the World

Rank	*Rank*	*Countries*	*Million$*	*Million$*	*Growth. Average*	*Growth Average*
1970	*1990*		*1970*	*1990*	*1970-80*	*1980-90*
1	1	USA	1008650	5392210	10.29	8.24
3	2	China	256950	3060944	14.22	13.19
2	3	Japan	308339	2197970	11.86	10.32
4	4	USSR	255151	1740161	13.25	10.08
5	5	Germany	225318	1125231	10.08	8.37
9	6	India	146778	1062592	10.85	10.41
6	7	France	190496	941475	10.13	9.32
7	8	U.K.	163168	882390	10.67	8.81
8	9	Italy	160228	868520	11.07	8.82
10	10	Brazil	88370	689888	16.47	10.82
11	11	Canada	80881	549846	12.44	10.05

Source: CMIE Report, Mumbai, 1994

In the table, USSR occupying 4th position stands dissolved now, hence not in picture. So India shifts from 6th to 5th position and Canada from 11th to 10th. . These are 10 largest countries of the world in respect of their DGP.

When we compare the rank, these countries possessed during 1990, with that of 1970 we see USA and Germany are maintaining status quo. China has slightly improved from 3 to 2. Japan has also shifted back from 2 to 3. France, U.K,. Italy, Brazil and Canada are not only behind India but also they are losing their rank occupied earlier. India, on the other hand has shifted on its rank from 9 to 6. We are occupying number one position in rank shifting process. When we throw light on the average rate of growth India is almost maintaining its trend from 10.85% to 10.45% whereas USA has fallen from 10.29 % to 8.24%, Canada from 12.44% to 10.5%, U.K. from 10.67% to 8.81%. Thus taking improvement in rank and improvement in rate of change together India is occupying number one position in respect of growth of GDP in the year 1990.

Now, let us see India's position in terms GDP in 2003.

Table 2
GDP of India and High Ranking Countries in terms of HDI Rank, 2003

		GDP (PPP US$ billions)	
HDI Rank	*GDP Rank*	*Country*	
1		Norway	171.9
2		Iceland	9.0
3		Australia	589.1
4		Luxembourg	27.9
5		Canada	970.3
6		Sweden	239.6
7		Switzerland	224.6
8		Ireland	150.7
9		Belgium	294.0
10	1	United States	10,923.4
11	3	Japan	3,567.8
12		Netherlands	476.5
13		Finland	144.0
14		Denmark	169.5
15		United Kingdom	1,610.6
16		France	1,654.0
17		Austria	243.5
18		Italy	1,563.3
19		New Zealand	90.5
20		Germany	2,291.0
21		Spain	920.3
22		Hong Kong, China (SAR)	185.3
23		Israel	134.0
24		Greece	220.2
25		Singapore	104.0
127	4	India	3,078.2
85	2	China	6,445.9 5

Source: Human Development Report, 2003

The table shown above makes it clear that India today occupy fourth position in terms of GDP leaving behind 23 top HDI ranking countries where as its own HDI rank is 127th.

DEVELOPMENT OF INDIAN ECONOMY

Our performance from this angle is dismal. India though at the top in terms of GDP production lies at the bottom in respect of per capita income (172nd). This is due to population explosion, unemployment, lack of proper education, economic dependence etc. Most of our citizen lose entitlement and lead a miserable life due to irrational behaviour on their part. Majority of our citizens voluntarily or compulsorily lead very poor quality of life.

Women are the most sufferers. They acquire 'ardhangani' status after marriage. Their livelihood earning limbs are socially handicapped, on the other hand their reproduction organs are made so strong that they can downpour causing flood of children.

The State is involved in electoral politics. Leaders keep eyes on vote bank only to continue in power. For that they divide the society in different. They divide people in religious groups and castes. Instead of taking up core issues of development they take up schemes to appease a particular group in which they are interested. For example recently our government announced the subsidy to all applicants of Haz pilgrimage knowing that Muslim votes remain almost undivided.

DEVELOPMENT MODEL SUGGESTED FOR INDIAN ECONOMY

It is clear from the perusal of above mentioned facts that our economy has grown but development of our people is yet a great challenge. For that we must train up our coming generation. Let us limit our population according to resources available with us. Give every one equal opportunity for earning entitlement. Give employment to every man and woman according to capacity. We require the following actions in this direction-

Ascertainment of Standard of Development Oriented Persons and State

On the basis of a laboratory type test and other observation the standard of development oriented woman, man and state has been fixed which as follows:

(i) Woman

A development-oriented woman must not be orthodox and blind follower of old practices. She views old and new with wisdom. Concept for womanhood for her is home, marriage and reproduction but also various other important activities of life. She is able to face critical problems both personal and global. She remains serious about education and career to avoid dependence and contribute in prosperity of herself and of her nation and of the world at large.

(ii) Man

A development-oriented man appreciates women of above said character. Instead of being involved in exploitation of woman or a weaker person for his personal gain, helps them for a better quality of life. He remains serious towards his own education and earning entitlement for a better quality of life. He must be broad minded and generous towards others.

(iii) State

It is up to those who guide the destinies of nation to create conditions which will enable all people to lead successful and happy lives. So a state must ensure education and training of its each citizen to make them development oriented persons as mentioned above.

In order to achieve persons of above mentioned standard the state is responsible for setting the following targets in the three different areas, namely-Women, Population and Education.

Targets for Women Empowerment

- Produce only development oriented women
- Avoid the situation where anti-development oriented girls are brought up.
- Remove liability status of women.
- Do not glorify marital status of women and make them financially independent.
- Give them full opportunity to compete with men in earning entitlement for capability.
- Marriage be linked with job not with dowry.
- Amend the institution of marriage where a superior girl may marry an inferior boy to bring him to her house and vice versa.

The above mentioned policy if fulfilled will also be a bid to promote population control besides other measures for the purpose.

Population Policy

- India, in long run, has to bring down its population to 50 crore

- Adopt one child policy.
- In the first phase a couple having only one child (male or female) be given free education and job guarantee.
- Young couple promising to ever remain childless must be given job guarantee.
- No woman be left for household work only
- Agriculture be made to avail business status and less than 10% working force be absorbed in it.
- Population in long run be brought to match the need of working force.
- All children must get cultural education for attitudinal change and vocational education for getting job
- Equal opportunity first, be given to all without any bias and then job be offered according to qualification.
- No relief be granted to any one on the basis of caste, religion etc.

Education Policy

Without having a sound education policy both women and population policy will fail. So there is a great need to streamline the education system in the following way:

- Education must be compulsory for all
- To maintain uniformity education must be centrally controlled.
- School education must be free and compulsory.
- One and similar arrangement of education should be made for all.
- For that all the school of the nation should fall under one organization.
- Education should be so designed to change the present social order.
- It should produce only development oriented people
- Cost of schooling must be borne by the state
- University students must be forced to adopt earning and learning process.

- Educational institution should attract the most talented personnel.
- Educational institution must be entrusted with the task of job recruitment.
- Such institution should also work as information centre for other wings.

Thus, education wing of the development model is the most important for providing equal opportunity to all for earning capability in the interest of true social justice.

Development Commission

As the political leaders running the government, directly cannot adopt the aforesaid development policies, not affording to lose vote bank, the task should be entrusted with a strong autonomous body 'Development Commission' to be created for the purpose. This commission should be made even stronger than Election Commission. An honest non-political person should head the Development Commission. The main functions of the commission will be to coordinate the three development wings, to formulate policies, to implement the policies and to keep control on the performance. The present Planning Commission should be dissolved or merged with the Development Commission.

CONCLUSION

Thus, we see that the WTO has a great role to play in the development of world economy. Though some powerful nations dominate the organization to some extent but it cannot affect Indian economy adversely. Now economic development of any nation is not only about the growth of productions but also about the people and their quality of life. India has already acquired fourth position in terms of growth yet it is an underdeveloped country in terms of development. We should, therefore, adopt the development model suggested in this paper instead of blaming the WTO for a sustainable development of Indian economy.

REFERENCES

Bates, Robert (1980), Government and Agriculture Market in Africa, Harvard University Publishers, Massachusetts, USA

Grabowski and Shields (1996), Development Economics, Blackwell Publishers. Massachusetts, USA.

Jacobsen, Joyce (1994), Economics of Gender, Blackwell Publishers Massachusetts, USA.

Human Development Report, 2003.

Maciver, R.M. and Page Charles, H. (1962), Society, McMillan and Co., London.

Mill, J.S. (1863), Utilitarianism, http//www utilitarianism.com

Mill, J S. (1869), Subjugation of Women, http//www.la.utexas

Olson (1971), The Logic of Collection Action-People and Theory of Groups.

Sen, Amartya (1986), Resources Value and Development, Oxford Blackwell Basil.

WTO Reports: http//= www.wto.int.org

IMPACT OF WTO ON RURAL DEVELOPMENT

Mridula Kumari

INTRODUCTION

65 per cent of India's labour force engaged in farming and allied activities make it chiefly an agrarian society. As per 2001 census, 72 per cent of its total population resides in around 5.67 lakh villages which are more or less categorized with high levels of illiteracy, ignorance, low level of quality of life and so on. Therefore, it is essential to concentrate more on rural development.

Rural development helps to utilise the energies of the rural masses to improve their capacity by realising their full potential. It inspires them to be committed to the development and attainment of a higher quality of life for the individual and for the entire community. The need for rural development has been emphasised by our policy makers ever since the advent of planning process in the country. Accelerated economic growth with equitable distribution of its gains were the ultimate objective of the rural development.

It this era of globalisation, rural sector has an important role to play but it has been left behind. Indian rural sector has the potential to provide the base for the planners and policy makers on which they can stand and bargain a better deal with international players.

This paper proposes to understand the pace and pattern of rural development since the beginning of present day globalisation of world economics. The study is organised into four sections. The second section evaluates major programmes of rural development since Seventh Five Year Plan. Issues of WTO related to rural development has been evaluated in the third section. Fourth section suggests measures to enhance and empower rural sector so that it can play its due role in the growth process and provide an environment of justice and equity with improved standard of living.

RURAL DEVELOPMENT PROGRAMME: A REVIEW

Though, several approaches like top-bottom planning, planning from below, micro level planning, resource based planning and multilevel planning have been formulated to attain faster rural development, it was only from Sixth Plan onwards that more and more emphasis was laid in building rural India as real India.

Budgetary outlay on rural development has increased substantially during last one and a half decade. It is indicative of Government's serious concern and effort towards empowering rural sector.

Central Government expenditure on rural development has increased manifold from 1995 to 2006-07 as indicated in Table 1 below:

Table 1
Central Governments Expenditure on Rural Development

Year	*1995-96*	*2000-01*	*2001-02*	*2002-03*	*2003-04*	*2004-05*	*2005-06*	*2005-06*	*2006-07*
Expenditure in Rs. Cr.	6609	4449	6241	10991	11537 (R.E.)	17001*	24480 (B.E.)	27490 (R.E.)	31444 (B.E.)

Source: Economic Survey, 2004-05, Budget 2006-07.

* Including allocations meant for certain rural development programme in the lump sum provision of Rs. 10000/- cr. provided to the Ministry of Planning.

Seventh Plan witnessed the introduction of two programmes aimed at providing employment opportunities in the rural sector. These were NREP and RLEGP. Later on these programmes were merged to form Jawahar Rozgar Yojana. Various other schemes have been implemented and are still going on such as Indira Awas Yojana, Million wells scheme, Employment. Assurance Schemes. These are aimed at building infrastructure and providing employment to persons below poverty line in rural areas.

Eighth Plan was more focused on building up of rural infrastructure and people's participation in rural development programmes. During this plan; all weather rural roads, minor irrigation works, social forestry, water harvesting and soil conservation schemes were the priority areas.

Increase in agricultural and rural sector income was thought an essential pre condition for rural development during Ninth Five Year Plan. A serious attempt was made in this regard. Agricultural and rural development with a view to generating adequate productive employment and eradication of poverty was given top most priority. Other priorities included ensuring food and nutritional security for all, environmental sustainability of the development process, empowerment of women and socially disadvantaged groups as agents of socio-economic change and development. Promotion and Development of people's participatory institution like Panchayats, co-operatives and self-help groups were too on rural development agenda during Ninth Plan.

Many more programmes were launched and implemented recently aiming to strengthen rural sector such as Swarn Jayanti Gram Swarojgar Yoyana (SGSY) and the National Food for Work Programme (NFWP) as wage employment. Accelerated Rural Water Supply Programme and the Swajaldhara for providing safe drinking water and the Total Sanitation Campaign (TSC). All these schemes are meant for over all development and upliftment of rural poor.

The National Rural Employment Guarantee Scheme provides an indispensable lifeline to the millions of poor in rural areas. The Government, through this act, aims at removing poverty in the rural areas and thus improve infrastructure.

It is remarkable to note that most of these target based developmental programmes performed poorly to achieve desired results. Agricultural employment which was 2.57 per cent during 1987-94 declined to 0.02 per cent during 1994-00 period. It is the period which saw the birth of WTO. These developmental programmes failed to eradicate poverty as even today one third of our rural population is reeling under conditions of abject poverty. Our rural sector is still struggling with illiteracy, low socio economic growth and inequality of income and employment opportunities. Between 1993-94 to 2004 unemployment rate for males in rural areas increased from 5.6 per cent to 9.0 per cent and for females it increased from 5.6 per cent to 9.3 per cent during same period.

WTO: ISSUES AND IMPACT ON RURAL DEVELOPMENT

Agriculture is the major component of rural sector. All roads to rural development pass through agricultural development in India. Agricultural still contribute around 20 per cent of the national income and provides employment to almost 2/3rd of the labour force in rural India. Rural development and reduction in rural poverty is the direct outcome of increase in agricultural growth rate.

Some of the issues of WTO may be mentioned here which directly or indirectly influence free and fair trade in agriculture and subsequently income and employment in rural sector. These are:

(i) Market Access

(ii) Reduction in Export Subsidies

(iii) Reduction in Domestic Support

(iv) Agreement on Sanitary and Phytosanitary Measures (SPS)

(v) Agreement on Technical Barrier to Trade (TBT)

(vi) Trade Related Intellectual Property Rights (TRIPS)

Market access requires that any restrictions on agricultural trade should be in the form of tariffs. Non tariff barriers were to be replaced by tariffs on imports and then were to be followed by progressive reduction of tariff levels.

Developing countries are required to reduce the subsidy on exports by 14 per cent in volume terms and 24 per cent in budgetary expenditure over a period of 10 yrs.

Domestic support measures are taken to fix some acceptable measures of support to farmers. These support may be categorised under.

(a) Green box and blue box measure. These have non distorting effects on agricultural trade.

(b) Amber box measures having trade distorting effects. Assistance given through environmental assistance programme services like research, training and extension marketing, information and certain types of rural infrastructure etc. are included in green box measures. These assistances are exempted from any reduction commitment. Support under blue box is also exempted from any reduction commitment, but it has an upper limit.

The domestic support under Amber box measures are measured in terms of total aggregate measurement of support (Total AMS) and includes both product specific and non-product specific support. Domestic support given to the agricultural sector upto 10 per cent of the total value of agricultural produce in developing countries is allowed. Hence, India's farm sector is not under any effect on cut in subsidies. Non-product specific support such as subsidies on power, irrigation, fertilizers, etc. is well below permissible level of 10 per cent of the value of agricultural output.

Sanitary and phytosanitary measures allows countries to fix higher standards than international standards if there is a scientific justification or as a consequence of consistent risk decisions based on an appropriate risk assessment. Developed nations are using these measures to block the exports of agricultural and agro processed commodities from developing countries.

Under TRIPS agreement, seven types of intellectual properties are covered for protection. These are patents, copyrights, trademarks, industrial designs, geographical indications, design layout of integrated circuit. As far as agriculture is concerned, the agreement requires members to provide for protection of plant varieties either by patents or by an effective sui-generic system or by any combination thereof. IPR regime may affect the interests of the poor farmers through increase in seed price. Cheap import substitutes for small scale rural industrial products and processed foods are hampering the rural sector in part of the north-east and southern India.

The market access for Indian agricultural products in developing nations did not expand as was expected. Share of agriculture in total exports is declining continuously and now forms a very insignificant proportion of the total exports. In 1995-96, agriculture contributed 19.8 per cent of total exports of India, which declined to 9.7 per cent during 2004-05 (April-September).

SUGGESTION

Globalization and trade liberalisation has multi dimensional impact. But it is true that WTO has no visible agenda for the resourceless, illiterate, poor farming families in rural sector. Developing countries like India have not been able to derive much benefit from a free trade regime. In fact trade liberalization without increased investment in agricultural and rural development will not help us strengthen our bargaining power at WTO forum and get an enhanced share in world trade. What is needed is major investment in the following areas:

1. Rural infrastructure, especially rural connectivity and irrigation.
2. Development of post-harvest technology and value addition
3. Scientific storage capacity in rural areas and establishment and development of markets.
4. Soil conservation and water harvesting.
5. Development of eco-friendly technologies of cultivation and production.
6. Development of agro-industries
7. SPS measures
8. Research and development
9. Education and health.

Investing in rural infrastructure including the development of rural roads that connect areas of production to markets and connecting rural India through the emerging information and communication technologies are essential for reaching out to the rural population. Information and communication technologies should be used to sensitise panchayats and rural families on the implication of the protection of plan varieties and Farmer's Rights Act (2001) and the Biodiversity Act (2002), since they contain provisions for recognising and rewarding the contributions of the primary conservers of biodiversity and holders of traditional knowledge. The innovations, traditional knowledge in this sector and biodiversity should be documented and patented to contribute to the rural development.

Utmost care on quality control in our agricultural production must be taken to improve our capacity in areas of sanitary and phytosanitary measure. India has to play an active role in the process of determination of SPS standards at international level to stop the use of these measures as trade barriers against exports.

Increasing agricultural productivity is fundamental for rural economic growth and requires development of new and improved technologies through higher investment in agricultural research and development.

Along with such investment, emphasis should be made to develop and promote institutions that would ensure transparency and accountability of effectively using such rural investments in order to benefit the most needed group of the population.

Devolution of power to the grassroots institutions such as panchayats are in the right direction. They should be provided more power in the use of resources according to local needs.

Another area which has the high income and growth potential is crop diversification. Farmers should be encouraged to go for crop diversification. Their income can increase by growing high value fruit and vegetable crops, livestock and dairy products, going for epiculture, sericulture, wormiculture and horticulture along with agriculture. Cultivation of medicinal and aromatic plants is suggested as a viable solution to stabilise and increase agricultural income, increase employment opportunities and enhance the natural resources at micro level where as at macro level it is sure to lead for rural prosperity manifested in declining poverty level. Agricultural diversification in this field (MAP cultivation) along with high returns and employment generation also provides ample scope to earn foreign exchange. Mentha cultivation in India alone constitute 70-80 per cent of global menthol mint oil production. It may substantially increase the income of the farmers and reduce the level of poverty in the rural areas as well as all these activities are labour intensive. However, step towards crops diversification needs to be made smooth by removing the hurdles like inadequate storage facilities, lack of credit facilities for agro-processing, poor connectivity of farmers to the markets etc.

Health and education are the two major challenges remain to be addressed. Multiple of programmes are there but what is needed is their reorientation to provide social security to the poor people in rural India. Children should be encouraged to join and attend schools. Mid-day meal schemes in schools and employment guarantee schemes may go a long way in providing social security and creating physical infrastructure effectively.

High economic growth rate is a pre-requisite for poverty alleviation and rural development. But high economic growth rate itself depends upon high growth rate in agriculture. Hence the major challenge is to make Indian agriculture globally competitive and thus, using it as a tool for rural development, poverty reduction and providing our expanding economy a solid base.

REFERENCES

P. Jagadish Gandhi (ed.) (2003), Globalised Indian Economy: Contemporary Issues and Perspectives, Deep & Deep Publications (P) Ltd., New Delhi.

A.K. Vasudevachary, Indian Agriculture in the New Global Scenario, Southern Economist, January 1, 2006.

G.K. Chadha (ed.) (2001), WTO and the Indian Economy, Deep & Deep Publications Pvt. Ltd., New Delhi.

B. Mishra, G.C. Kar, S.N. Mishra (eds.), Agro Industries and Economic Development, (2002).

GOI, Kurukshetra, Ministry of Rural Development, New Delhi. (Various Issues).

GOI, Survey of Indian Agriculture, 2004-2005.

GOI, Economic Survey, Ministry of Finance, New Delhi, 2004-2005.

INDIAN STANDARD SETTING INSTITUTIONS AND TECHNICAL BARRIERS TO TRADE

Md. Imteyaz Hassan

INTRODUCTION

The world has witnessed a significant reduction in import tariffs during the rounds of multilateral trade negotiations promoted by the General Agreement on Tariffs and Trade (GATT), especially since the Kennedy Round in the 1960s. Lately, there has also been a reduction in the unilateral application of quotas and other forms of non-tariff barriers (NTBs). A considerable number of NTBs still exist in the shape of technical regulations and standards. Though technical regulations and standards (including sanitary and phytosanitary controls) are not in trade barriers, but their use or adoption may create new obstacles to trade and provide protection to domestic products.

The Agreement on Technical Barriers to Trade (TBT) and the Agreement on Sanitary and Phytosanitary Measures (SPS) agreements define the international rights and obligations of member countries with respect to the development or application of standards related measures that affect trade. They are based on the principle that countries have a right to adopt and apply such measures as long as they do not restrict international trade more than is necessary or unavoidable. Although these agreements have established certain standards for their application, disagreements among countries about these measures often involve complex issues not specifically addressed by the text of the agreements.

The perceptions and the institutional capacities of developing countries are significantly different from those of industrial countries in implementation of the TBT and SPS agreements under the World Trade Organization (WTO). Developing countries fear that technical barriers may become increasingly important in the future and thereby become significant barriers to trade. Among the difficulties in the technical aspects of trade identified by the developing countries are the high cost of adaptation, irrelevance of foreign standards to local conditions, lack of timely and adequate information and consequent transaction costs, difficulties in understanding the requirements and in testing for and monitoring them, perceived lack of scientific data for specific threshold or limiting values and the uncertainty that arises from rapidly changing requirements in overseas market.

The major issue facing developing countries is implementation, which leads to the question of domestic capacity building. This paper reviews the existing institutional or infrastructure framework created to comply with the TBT/SPS Agreements and the approach for addressing NTB measures. It also highlights the areas in which India should seek international technical and financial assistance to implement fully the TBT/SPS Agreements.

SPS AGREEMENT

The SPS Agreement establishes international rules on how to apply sanitary and phytosanitary measures. It acknowledges a country's right to protect itself from risks to human, animal and plant life and health and it confirms the need to constrain countries from using such measures as excuses to create unnecessary barriers to trade. In short, the purpose of the agreement is to enable the legitimate protection of life and health while not giving rise to illegitimate protectionism. Protectionism in this regard is defined as trade barriers beyond what is required to meet a country's desired protection levels. The approach taken to address these two issues simultaneously is to require SPS measures based on sound science. In this way; only measures truly aimed at protecting life and health are allowed, and measures that are either not related to life and health issues at all or excessively strict are ruled out.

The two basic principles of the agreement are non-discrimination and scientific justification. The principle of non-discrimination is described in Article 2.3 of the agreement. It states that a measure shall not discriminate against or between trading partners more than necessary to reach the goal of sanitary and phytosanitary protection. This principle is equivalent to the GATT basic principle of most-favored-nation privileges. The principle of scientific justification of SPS measures is spelled out in Article 2.2. Any SPS measure must be backed by scientific justification.

The special concerns of developing countries are addressed explicitly in the agreement in several regards. The general functioning of the agreement is the same for industrial and developing countries. The differences occur mainly in the implementation of the agreement and in the obligations to provide technical assistance to other members.

The regulation of SPS agreement can be divided into four cases:

1. In areas where international standards already exist, the agreement encourages international harmonization based on international standards. It must be clear that this does not necessarily imply identical worldwide standards but rather standards that have some basic relationship to the same reference points.
2. In areas where no international standards exist, measures for individual member countries are permitted if they are based on a risk assessment and are non-discriminatory.
3. If a country does not find that the protection level provided by an international standard is high enough, it may implement stricter measures. Again, this right is conditional on a formal risk assessment and the obligation that measures are to be non-discriminatory.
4. Finally, when not enough scientific evidence enables a proper risk assessment, temporary measures are allowed. This right is also conditional. Temporary measures must be reviewed after a certain time and the implementing country must seek additional evidence.

NON-TARIFF BARRIERS

The SPS and TBT Agreements were added to the WTO so that at whatever levels are deemed appropriate, no country would be prevented from taking measures necessary to ensure the quality of its imports; human, animal and plant life and the health of the environment would be protected; and deceptive practices would be prevented. But these agreements are subject to the requirements that measures are not applied in a manner that constitutes arbitrary or unjustifiable discrimination between countries where the same conditions prevail or a disguised restriction on international trade and that measures are otherwise in accordance with the provisions of the agreements. Experience, however, has been contrary to the requirements. Barriers in the name of technical regulations exist along the boundaries of trading nations.

SPS and TBT technical specification have been a major source of NTBs and are likely to continue to be so in the future. This fact is not difficult to infer because the SPS Agreement specifies that a country may introduce or maintain a higher level of SPS protection that has been achieved by an international standard if there is scientific justification or when the country determines that a higher level of protection would be appropriate. In fact, the latter is often chosen to explain many stringent SPS measures in the EU and the United States.

PRODUCT-RELATED NON-TARIFF BARRIERS: PEANUT EXPORTS

Peanut exporters believe that foreign governments put NTBs on their imports of agricultural products in order to sustain their domestic agriculture. Exporters also may have to make distress sales when buyers refuse shipments based on domestic import standards. Indian exporters therefore may have to depend on the domestic market or the South Asian Association for Regional Cooperation for business sustenance. Their foreign customers have informed them that new and stricter regulations have become applicable after December 31, 2000.

Some of the problems faced by exporters appear to be genuine. For example, they find that different testing procedures and conformity assessment standards are required in different markets. Each test costs Rs. 6,000. Nobody has told them of the justification for most of the tests. In fact, the EC tests exports from the Arab Republic of Egypt and India but not from Argentina and the United States. Exporters also face problems regarding genetically modified peanuts. Although some years ago one foreign government encouraged the use of genetically modified organisms (GMOs), another now has asked for an assurance that the peanuts supplied do not contain GMOs.

The European Snack Association's Nut Working Group has already expressed concern about the testing program and analytical methodologies through the European Food and Beverage Association. The American Peanut Council has submitted documents showing significant increase in costs and rejections arising from the use of a multisampling system. In the United Kingdom, where approximately 25 per cent of the peanuts imported into Europe are consumed, the Ministry of Agriculture has stated that the proposals were more stringent than were required by current UK regulations and could result to unacceptable costs to both industry and enforcement without any prospect of improved consumer safety. Despite these protests, the revised draft of the sampling plan still recommends a multiple sampling system. It is evident that such a change will have very serious implications for the peanut industry. It is also important to note that the EU proposal may contravene the GATT/WTO agreement by erecting artificial barriers and seriously discriminating against a number of producing countries, particularly developing country such as India.

BARRIERS RELATED TO PRODUCTION AND PROCESS METHODS

Mango Pulp

Many codes of regulation as well as European SPS measures link the quality of a product with its production processes. In India, where most primary production takes place in unorganized, small-scale units, such primary level quality assurance is difficult to attain. Thus, the EU demand that each mango farmer keep records of the use of its mangoes in processing mango pulp is cumbersome. The EU justification for this measure is that the farmer whose mangoes were had can be traced in case a consignment of mango pulp is found to be harmful. However, as long as a pulp processor observes strict quality checks at the point where mango pulps from various orchards enter the processing unit, records of farmers may not be necessary. In such a situation, a pulp processor and exporter can ensure strict compliance with quality norms at the factory's entry point.

Milk Products

The EU standard for milk and milk products requires checks originated from the level of primary production, and it lays down the conditions of maintaining animals, types of feed to be given, and the monitoring of these regulations. Under Indian conditions, a dairy farm may have just one or two draught animals and milk from a number or such holdings is commonly pooled before it is processed. It is impossible to monitor every animal. Therefore, the quality is determined at the processing unit's entry point and the milk is appropriately treated to ensure the destruction of any pathogens. The final product is thereby safe. It is necessary to stress the quality of the final product, which may be attained through a flexible system approach. It is neither feasible nor desirable to standardize a specific systems approach.

Likewise, the EU has directed that raw milk mostly originate from cows or buffalos, which in the case of cows yields at least 2 litres of milk a day. In the Indian situation this is simply impractical. Similarly, the animal health requirements stipulated by the EU are far in excess of the requirements of the International Animal Health Code of the International Office of Epizootics (IOE). The International Animal Health Code does not include any conditions specifically related to milk and milk products for diseases like rinderpest, pestedes petits ruminants, bluetongue, sheep pox and goat pox. But EU animal-health-attestation conditions specify that the animals must belong to holdings that were not under restrictions due to food-and-mouth disease (FMD). Therefore, whereas IOE requirements for FMD are specific in nature, the EU directives are general and have included the conditions for livestock diseases like rinderpest.

In 1997, the EU circulated a directive stating that when dry milk was exported, the package should clearly mention that buffalo milk was used and that, ideally, there should be an illustration of a buffalo on the package. This is likely to create a psychological barrier in the mind of a consumer who is used to drinking cow's milk, although in terms of health both cow and buffalo milk are perfect substitute for making milk powder. On opposition from countries like India, the EU directive was withdrawn.

BARRIERS RELATING TO TESTING PROCEDURES: EGG PRODUCTS

The acceptance of a sanitary standard is based on the acceptance of certain test results. Some test results, however, can be disputed. For example in 1997, Company O, a Bangalore-based egg products-exporting company, sent egg powder to Japan. Japan reported BHC (beta isomer) levels in the Indian product far in excess of permitted levels of 0.01 parts per million (ppm). To investigate this report, composite samples were analyzed in laboratories in Bangalore and Belgium. Both analyses reported that the BHC level was below the detectable limit of 0.01 ppm. The inference to be drawn from this case is that if laboratory results can vary, then products that have been tested as fit for export in Indian laboratories, can be declared unfit for acceptance at international borders. When both parties stick to their test results, how can credibility be brought about in laboratory tests?

BARRIERS RELATED TO CERTIFICATIONS: TIRES

Brazil requires that tires being exported to Brazil have "En-Metro" (EM) marking on them. EM is the national standard for tires in Brazil, rather like the "Agmark" for foods in India. For the Indian tire exporter, however, obtaining EM certification is expensive. To receive the EM certificate, an Indian exporter must defray the lodging and miscellaneous expenses of a Brazilian team of experts who travel to India and visit the prospective exporters tire plant. The Automotive and Tyre Manufacturers Association of India quotes the sum total of these expenses at an average of US $ 20,000 ($ 1,100 of which is the direct cost for the certificate). Certification lasts only one year, so the exporter must invite and pay for the Brazilian team of experts every 12 months. Except for a few major Indian tire manufacturers (e.g. Apollo, JK and Modi Rubber), many smaller potential the exporters from India cannot export tires to Brazil because certification is prohibitively expensive. Assuming that Brazilian tire manufacturers also must be certified, it is apparent that the cost they would incur would total little more than the $1,100 for the certificate itself. It is interesting to note that although the EM team has been traveling from Brazil to do inspections in India every year, formal EM certificates have not been issued at all for the last two years, and exports of Indian tires to Brazil have continued.

Mexico offers another example of a certification barrier; Imported tires must carry "Norm" certification, which is awarded to each tire imported rather than to the tire company. To get this certificate, $40,000 -$50,000 has to be paid to different certifying agencies of Mexico.

ENVIRONMENTAL BARRIERS: STEEL

Australia and New Zealand have imposed extremely stringent environmental laws and raised objections to the usage of wooden dunnage by an Indian steel company. As a consequence the company has used treated wood and wood substitutes, which are more expensive and in short supply. Furthermore, fumigation of containers is required and the cost for that is $400 per container.

PACKAGING, MARKING AND LANGUAGE BARRIERS

Barriers related to packaging, marking and language include printing of minimum import prices in countries like Brazil and Syria, and the requirement that texturized yarn be supplied in equal-length packages in some European markets. It has also been reported that Germany poses significant problems for Indian exporters of engineering products because German technical regulations are rarely made available in English. Indian exporters employ translators at their own expense, but the Germans argue that the translations do not accurately present the German specifications. Indian exporters, therefore, are always apprehensive of falling short of German norms. This apprehension obviously damages export potential.

DOMESTIC INSTITUTIONAL FRAMEWORK

The domestic institutional framework is the most important aspect of implementing the SPS and TBT Agreements. A week institutional framework adds to the woes of exporters who are already facing NTBs from other countries. In India, trade is regulated by a plethora of policy announcements and multiple regulatory authorities. This section of the paper, which describes the significant domestic policies and institutions, is based on interviews and government reports.

EXPORT/IMPORT POLICY OF INDIA

The Export and Import Policy (EXIM Policy) of India is drawn up for a period of five years, with some changes being effected in an annual review in April and other changes taking place when necessary. The current EXIM Policy is applicable for the years 2002-2007. There is a negative list for exports and for imports comprising prohibited, restricted (licensed) and canalized items. India's domestic environmental concerns (related to health and conservation) and multilaterally agreed environmental measures (e.g. CITES and Montreal Protocol) are implemented through these lists. There are many export-promotion measures built into the EXIM Policy including the grant of special import licenses for firms having ISO certification.

Export promotion councils and certain (commodity) boards and (export development) authorities are given special status in the EXIM Policy. They grant membership to exporters so that some exporters become eligible to receive certain licenses and benefits such as duty-free advance licenses for inputs for export production. Other relevant incentives include duty concession on import of capital goods used for export production, duty-free imports for 100 per cent export-oriented units and units in export-processing zones, some fast track mechanisms for import clearances, and additional benefits for export and trading houses showing export performance beyond a certain threshold.

RULES AND REGULATIONS ON PRODUCT STANDARDS

The Ministry of Food and Consumer Affairs is the main government agency dealing with product standards, although each ministry or department also has its own system of framing and publishing product standards. State governments also have systems for adopting standards, notably in the area of weights and measures. For the products under consideration in this paper, the main rules and regulations are contained in the Prevention of Food Adulteration Act, the Export Inspection and Quality Control Act, and regulations for spice quality. A notable point in product standardization in India is that, although the enforcement agencies have means of enforcing these rules in domestic units, there is little possibility of enforcing them on imported goods. One reason for this could be that the Indian consumer market was comparatively closed until recently and few imported goods entered. With the passage of time, it would be advisable for the concerned agencies to devise systems to enforce the rules on imported goods. Today the producers of imported goods seem to receive even better than national treatment because they are seldom subjected to the same enforcement procedures, as are the domestic producers of similar goods. A review of the packaging rules has been initiated by the Ministry of Food and Consumer Affairs in 1999 order to apply the same rules to imported goods as are applied to domestic goods.

EXPORT PROMOTION INSTITUTIONS

The Indian Government has been emphasizing export promotion since the late 1960s. One of the results of this emphasis has been the proliferation of export promotion councils and authorities. These agencies have been playing a dual role for product promotion – first, as nodal agencies for disbursement of export subsidies (a function that has declined considerably since liberalization and the removal of subsidies like the cash compensatory scheme) and second, as the nodal points for interaction between the industry and the government. Some of these agencies, notably, the Marine Product Export Development Authority and Agriculture Produce Export Development Authority have been actively involved in Implementing policies related to product standards.

STANDARD-SETTING BODIES

Indian goods have repeatedly faced restrictions on entry into foreign countries because of alleged non-compliance with certain standards, norms, or regulations established by the importing countries. Apparently products made under Indian standards were not fit to be accepted abroad, so either Indian standards and hence, the products made under them were not good enough or the Indian standards were reasonable but the product was being harassed at international borders on the pretext of unduly stringent foreign standards.

There are approximately 24 standard-setting bodies (SSBs) and a host of regulating agencies at the central government level as well as at state levels. Some of the most important domestic standard-setting and implementation authorities are the Bureau of Indian Standards (BIS); the Food and Agriculture Department (FAD); the National Accreditation Board for Testing and Calibration Laboratories (NABL); the Central Committee for Food Standards (CCFS); the Ministry of Food Processing Industry; the Standardization, Testing and Quality Certificate (STQC) and the National Quality Council (NQC).

In the following discussion, an attempt has been made to identify the procedures of standard setting, their implementation and problems that occur with them. It will also access the coordination among various standard-setting bodies and how well equipped these organizations are to meet the challenges posed by the WTO.

BUREAU OF INDIAN STANDARDS

Among 24 standard-setting bodies in India, the Bureau of Indian Standards (BIS) is the premier organization. It sets voluntary standards, which may be made mandatory by government action. The procedure for setting up a standard in the BIS is the same as anywhere in the world. The request for a standard comes from a consumer or organization. A divisional council of the BIS considers the request. The BIS then puts together a committee with a convener and members from interested groups and that committee drafts a standard. When approved, the standard is circulated for comments before its adoption. All BIS standards are voluntary unless they are adopted by the central government and made mandatory by the concerned ministry.

The BIS has been identified as the "enquiry point" for all TBT-related issues under Article 10.1 of the TBT Agreement, which states:

> "Each member shall ensure that an enquiry point exists which is able to answer all reasonable enquiries from other members and interested parties in other member countries as well as to provide the relevant documents".

In the simplest terms, notification means that whenever an Indian SSB sets a technical regulation that differs from the existing international regulation on the same item, the rest of the world must be informed about it. This is helpful for any country wishing to export that item to India. Such notification informs the exporting country of the minimum technical requirements that it must meet specifically for the Indian market. Notification can be made to the WTO via the BIS or through the Ministry of Commerce and it must be made in a format prescribed by the WTO and readily available from BIS or the WTO. According to Article 10.6 of the TBT Agreement:

> "The WTO Secretariat will, when it receives notifications in accordance with provisions of this Agreement, circulate copies of the notifications to all members and interested International standardizing and conformity assessment bodies".

Suggested alterations (deletions or additions) to the draft reach the concerned foreign member by the same route back. This is a tedious process so the BIS is trying to expedite the mechanism by enabling downloading of notifications directly from the Internet. Only technical regulations (TRs) that are at slight or major variance with the prevalent international norm need to be notified.

Some basic infrastructure is needed for an organization entrusted with the responsible status of an inquiry point. Essentially, an inquiry must be able to answer all questions regarding standards set within the country's national boundary. To the extent possible, SSBs should have a well-integrated information system to minimize the duplication of standards. Such a system also would prompt more harmonization of standards along the lines of international standards.

To this point, however, nothing much has been done about creating such an integrated process. The stark absence of a national notification system in India is noteworthy. The BIS reported an effort that it was making in conjunction with the Ministry of Commerce to create an awareness program for evolving a national notification system but the response of other SSBs has been lukewarm.

NATIONAL ACCREDITATION BOARD FOR TESTING

NABL is India's premier laboratory accreditation center. It performs testing and calibration of laboratories. The testing is repetitive in nature, i.e., the tests may be done again either under a surveillance program or otherwise. NABL exists under and is funded by the Ministry of Science and Technology. Following a period of five years, however, NABL is supposed to begin garnering its own resources, chiefly through revenues generated in the form of charges from laboratories seeking accreditation. An accreditation certificate expires after three years.

NABL accredits laboratories, not products. It does not certify research and development laboratories because tests in those facilities are not repeatable (Standards for products are certified by the BIS). Experts are either on the permanent payroll of NABL or are hired for their consultancy to provide accreditation. The TBT and SPS Agreements encourage use of international standards where such standards exist instead of reliance on national standards that are specific to only one market. Customers increasingly are fusing international standards when specifying technical requirements.

The International Laboratory Accreditation Cooperation (ILAC), which is an informal international forum of laboratory accrediting bodies, has played a major role in establishing international standards for laboratory testing. In 1993 the ISO/IEC published ISO/IEC Guide 5B, developed by ILAC, as the standard system for the accreditation of testing, calibration, and measurement laboratories. To avoid expensive and unnecessary retesting of goods, ILAC promotes the concept of bilateral and multilateral recognition arrangements among laboratory accreditation bodies in various countries. Multilateral agreements are based on international peer evaluation by an international assessment team of accreditation experts in quality assurance and different technical fields.

Thus, NABL's current role in facilitating international trade is rather non-functional. What good is lab accreditation if all goods have to be tested at both places-at port of exist and at port of entry? NABL must get its accreditation system recognized by more countries so that Indian goods carrying test reports issued by NABL accredited labs are accepted readily without additional tests in foreign countries. Such recognition would greatly reduce the interim time between shipping and final consumption of Indian goods, thereby reducing the chances of decay and increasing the credibility of the Indian goods.

CENTRAL COMMITTEE FOR FOOD STANDARDS

The CCFS set up at the federal level, has nine sub-committees dealing with different subjects such as cereals, oils and fats, milk and milk products and so forth. The sub-committees first generate data to support a new proposal or a revision to existing standards in cooperation with laboratories, industry and consumers. Then the proposal is sent to the CCFS, which is chaired by the director general of health services and comprises five consumer members, two government experts, three representatives from industry, and representatives from all states, the BIS and related ministries. If the new or revised standard is agreed on at the CCFS level, a notice period of 60-90 days is open for public reaction before the standard is notified. Standards generated by this committee are mandatory unlike those of the BIS.

NATIONAL QUALITY COUNCIL

A national scheme for the formation of national quality councils was prepared in 1992 to serve the following chief purposes:

- To mobilize resources to ensure that goods and services are designed to match consumer needs, expectations and desires in terms of their specifications, delivery and competitive price, and that goods and services produced consistently conform to standards and are produced at the optimum cost at which the consumer will buy.
- To raise quality consciousness in the country, both in industry (manufacturing and service) and among consumers, by launching a nationwide quality campaign and establishing a national standards information inquiry service.

- To encourage third-party certification of goods, services and quality-management systems (ISO 9000 standards or equivalent) at the enterprise level with a view to minimizing the need for multiple assessments by the consumers.
- To facilitate the upgrading of testing and calibration laboratories and encourage the development of a unified national laboratory accreditation system to ensure that the test reports becomes acceptable in the world market.
- To raise the level of training for personnel engaged in quality control activities including assessors and trainers and to encourage their third-party certification.
- To obtain mutual recognition with similar national schemes of India's major trading partners.
- To meet effectively the challenge of new and demanding European accreditation standards and legislation. Its most advantageous aspect would be the fact that all efforts would be made to bring about maximum possible national and international recognition of the scheme. This would greatly help in increasing the acceptance of Indian goods abroad.

The structure of the NQC has been established but its effects have not yet started to percolate at levels where it is required. At this time, it is non- operational.

INTERNATIONAL INSTITUTIONAL FRAMEWORK

(A) World Trade Organization

The General Agreement on Tariffs and Trade has been the beacon of the multilateral trading system since 1948. As a result of the Uruguay Round of multilateral trade negotiations, the World Trade Organization came into being on January 1, 1995 subsuming GATT under it. Article XX of the GATT allows member countries to deviate from their obligations under the agreement in the case of three types. A trade measures, animal or plant life or health; ones relating to the conservation of exhaustible natural resources if such measures are made effective in conjunction with restrictions on domestic production or consumption and ones necessary to secure compliance with laws or regulations not otherwise inconsistent with GATT rules. Such unilateral measures, however, have to pass a composite trade test. The trade test has three components; no arbitrary discriminative, no unjustifiable discrimination and no disguised trade protection. It is also called the least-trade-restrictiveness test. Jurisprudence has shown that the second type of trade measure has become the most potent tool for making GATT-compliant unilateral trade measures pursuant to environmental objectives.

(B) International Organization for Standardization

The ISO is the most important of the international standard-setting organizations. It is a world federation of 123 national standards bodies, an international non-government organization with a majority of its members coming from the public sector. Its core business is the development, approval and promulgation of consensus-based international standards. Unlike the WTO, however, majority voting is practiced in this organization.

The ISO develops standards through 200 technical committees split into about 650 sub-committees and 2,000 working groups. It also develops guides for standard setting. In preparing these guides, the ISO works with specific users of standards including those in the private sector. All of its standards and guides are voluntary in nature but given the organization's international credibility and wide acceptance, its standards have considerable trade effects. Those who can afford it apply for ISO certification. The certification is a costly process by Indian standards. It may take Rs.100,000–Rs.500,000 to get certified, apart from the cost of maintaining the certificate. The ISO 9000 series is the general quality certification standard but there also is an environmental management standard–the ISO 14000 series. India has about 5,000 ISO 9000 companies, some 10 companies have received ISO 14000 certification.

CODEX ALIMENTARIUS COMMISSION

The Codex Alimentarius Commission, a UN body, compiles agreed standards, guidelines and other recommendations into the Codex Alimentarius, the Codex Food Code (CFC). The CFC tries to create harmonized standards. Prior to the SPS Agreement, the CFC could be adopted, applied or ignored at the discretion of a government. Within the agreement, however, CFC has been adopted as the benchmark. Therefore, countries that do not impose standards higher than those of the CFC have the right to seek these standards for their imports. The Codex Alimentarius has incorporated Hazard Analysis Critical Control Point (HACCP) plans and principles as an integral part of the CFC. Volume V of the Food Code sets standards for a number of specific fish and fish products. The EU banned marine export in 1997 and HAACP was adopted officially as the standard by government agencies for the first time in the marine sector.

HAZARD ANALYSIS CRITICAL CONTROL POINT SYSTEM

The Hazard Analysis Critical Control Point System is being used increasingly as a food safety system all over the industrial world. When properly applied, it is a set of preliminary steps and principles that yields a systematic method for identifying significant hazards and properly applying preventive measures so that food-borne hazards are prevented, eliminated, or reduced to an acceptable level. With emerging international and national agreement on HACCP principles, their application would create a commonality of understanding of the development, implementation, and maintenance of a food safety system. Having these commonly understood principles, many food processors require their suppliers to have an HACCP system for producing the ingredients that they supply. Application of the system offers widely understood principles for identifying significant risks and means of controlling them. Being able to identify the most likely sources of food-borne hazards by implementing effective, documented systems will enable the industry to focus more attention on those sources.

CONCLUSIONS AND RECOMMENDATIONS

The study on which this paper is based, indicates that Indian exports face a number of NTBs in the forms of very high standards, testing procedures, environmental considerations, packaging requirements and so on. It is also evident from the survey that these prohibitive standards lack sufficient scientific proof of a protective effect on the health and environment of the importing country. For the impact of these barriers on the value of trade for a broad range of Indian exportable commodities is potentially extensive, results to a variety of trade effects and creates additional costs for Indian industry and government. Therefore, India is increasingly concerned that certain technical and sanitary/phytosanitary measures may be inconsistent with WTO provisions and may unfairly impede the flow of trade.

It is evident from the study that the Indian Government is not well positioned to address these issues. Trade associations and key government officials have identified these barriers as an increasingly important issue in trade but they have difficulty in defining the nature and scope of the problem, partly because of the complex nature of the issue itself and partly for other reasons. For example, they lack complete information on the number of measures that affect India's exports, they are unsure how many measures that have been identified may be inconsistent with WTO provisions and they do not have reliable estimates of the effects such measures have had on exports.

Many governments, trade, regulatory and research entitles have some responsibility for addressing such measures, but there is no single entity directing and coordinating overall government efforts. Roles and responsibilities of some entities regarding these measures are not clearly defined and these entities have had difficulty coordinating their activities. Government entities lack comprehensive data on which to address these measures and they do not know what progress has been made to address them.

One important recommendation for all of the standard-setting and implementation bodies is to create an exclusive set-up for documenting data on WTO compliance activities. These organizations have to be made aware of their responsibilities in the WTO and they must learn how they can play a more active part in setting standards at the international level.

The Bureau of Indian Standards as a nodal agency for standards coordination and notification for the WTO is well aware of its obligations under the TBT and SPS Agreement. But the BIS, structured today with multiple responsibilities and lacking authority and coordination with other SSBs, may find it difficult in cope with increasing demands of the WTO. Therefore, a separate body–something like a national quality council in collaboration with the BIS–should be established so that there is a body fully committed to standard-related matters in the WTO.

To upgrade quality in India, expertise is needed from countries that have tested quality measures on their farms but inviting such expertise is a costly preposition. Therefore, WTO/FAO should promote and perhaps sponsor experts to assist developing countries improve their quality. India has resented in international standard-setting meetings. Repeatedly, it has been reported that most of the Codex standards are set even when there is very little participation by developing nations including India. The Codex committees are dominated by members from industrial countries so the standards set by them, are most often not viable for the developing countries. Standards set by Codex are made with the food and agricultural practices of the industrial economies in mind but these practices are vastly different from the practices prevalent in developing economies. India must be better represented in standard-setting procedures.

As far as testing facilities are concerned, India's existing laboratories are poorly equipped with machines and skilled manpower and that has led to the poor reputation of test results in international markets. Exporters therefore resort to multinational testing facilities, which are more expensive. Laboratory accreditation is voluntary and carries no accountability, so the number of inappropriately equipped and staffed laboratories has mushroomed and many of the laboratories resort to issuing fake certificates. India, therefore, should invoke technical and financial assistance provisions in the WTO agreements to upgrade its testing facilities.

Apart from these, India must set her house in order as far as WTO commitments are concerned. Various government and semi-government authorities responsible for implementing these commitments do still not recognize the seriousness of the WTO commitments. The lack of coordination, communication and interaction among government agencies is leading to delays and duplication of efforts and that leads to suffering of business unable to exploit the benefits of globalization.

REFERENCES

Bhagwati, Jagdish, (1997), "The Demands to Reduce Domestic Diversity Among Trading Nations". In Jagdish Bhagwati and Robert E. Hudec, (eds.) Trade and Harmonization; Prerequisites for Free Trade, Vol. 2, Cambridge, Mass: MIT Press.

Bhattacharya, B. (1999), Non-Tariff Measures on India's Exports; An Assessment Occasional Paper 16, New Delhi, Indian Institute of Foreign Trade.

Federation of Indian Chambers of Commerce and Industry (2000), "Study on Comparative Trade Policy Analysis to Assess Barriers to Trade", New Delhi Processed.

Government of India, Ministry of Commerce (1999), "Non-Tariff Barriers (NTBs) Faced by India; Preliminary Report", Economic Division, New Delhi, Processed.

Gupta, Deepak (1999), "Codex Alimentarius Commission and SPS Agreement", Delhi; Ministry of Health Unpublished paper.

Mehra, Rajesh, and S.K. Mohanty (1999), WTO and Industrial Tariffs: An Empirical Analysis for India, New Delhi, Research and Information System for the Non-Aligned and Other Developing Countries.

APPENDIX

A GLOSSARY OF WTO AND RELATED TERMS

The Basics

The World Trade Organisation (WTO) deals with the rules of trade between nations at a global level but there is more to it than that. It is an organization for liberalizing trade. It is a forum for governments to negotiate trade agreements. It is a place for them to settle trade disputes. It operates a system of trade rules. Above all, it is a negotiating forum. Essentially, the WTO is a place where member governments go to try to sort out the trade problems they face with each other. The WTO was born out of negotiations and everything the WTO does is the result of negotiations. The bulk of the WTO's current work comes from 1986-94 negotiations called the Uruguay Round of multilateral trade negotiations and earlier negotiations under the General Agreement on Tariffs and Trade (GATT). The WTO is currently the host to new negotiations under the "Doha Development Agenda", launched at the Ministerial Conference of the WTO at Doha (Qatar) in 2001.

Accounting Rate: In telecoms, the charge made by one country's telephone network operator for calls originating in another country.

ACP: African, Caribbean and Pacific countries, Group of countries with preferential trading relations with the EU (European Union) under the former Lome Treaty now called the Cotonou Agreement.

Ad Valorem Tariff: A tariff rate charged as percentage of the price of value of an imported product. See "specific tariff".

Agricultural Product: Defined for the coverage of the WTO's Agriculture Agreement by the agreement's Annex 1. This excludes, for example, fish and forestry products. It also includes various degrees of processing for different commodities.

Agreement on Agriculture (AoA): One of the agreements of the Uruguay Round of negotiations that led to the establishment of the World Trade Organisation (WTO) in 1995. The AoA became operational with the establishment of the WTO from 1st January 1995. It brought agriculture under the purview of substantive multilateral trade rules for the first time. Developed and developing countries got six and nine years respectively for the implementation of commitments under the AoA. The AoA comprises three pillars namely, domestic support, market access and export competition. The AoA also contains provisions for reviewing the agreement. Presently, the AoA is being renegotiated on the terms agreed by the WTO member countries at the Fourth Ministerial meeting at Doha in 2001 and the July 2004 Framework decision adopted by WTO's General Council on 1 August 2004.

Aggregate Measure of Support (AMS): An index that measures the monetary value of the extent of government support to a sector. The AMS, as defined in the Agreement on Agriculture, includes both budgetary outlays as well as revenue transfers from consumers to producers as a result of polices that distort market prices. It consists of two parts product specific and non-product specific. If AMS is positive, agriculture is subsidized. If the AMS is negative, agriculture has negative subsidy.

Andean Community: Bolivia, Colombia, Ecuador, Peru and Venezuela.

Anti-Dumping Duties: GATT's Article 6 allows anti-dumping duties to be imposed on goods that are deemed to be dumped and causing injury to producers of competing products in the importing country. These duties are equal to the difference between the goods' export price and their normal value, if dumping causes injury.

APEC: The Asia Pacific Economic Cooperation forum (APEC) region was founded in 1989 as a regional institution arrangement among member countries linked by Pacific Ocean trade. Member countries include Australia, Brunei, Canada, Chile, China, Hong Kong, Indonesia, Japan, Malaysia, Mexico, New Zealand, Papua New Guinea, Philippines, Singapore, South Korea, Taiwan, Thailand and the United States.

Applied Tariff: Tariff that is actually levied on an imported product.

Appellate Body: An independent seven-member body that consider appeals in WTO disputes. When one or more parties to the dispute appeals, the Appellate Body reviews the findings in panel reports.

Article XX (i.e.20): A GATT article listing allowed "exceptions" to the trade rules.

ASEAN: Association of South East Asian Nations. Seven ASEAN members are members of the WTO–Brunei, Indonesia, Malaysia, Myanmar, the Philippines, Singapore and Thailand. The other ASEAN members Cambodia, Laos and Vietnam are negotiating WTO membership.

ATC: The WTO Agreement on Textiles and Clothing, which integrates trade in this sector back to GATT rules. The Agreement on

Textiles and Clothing replaced Multi-Fibre Arrangement (MFA) and integrated trade in this sector back to GATT rules within a ten-year period i.e., by the year 2005. It prohibits imposition of quota restrictions and discrimination on imports by textiles and clothing importing countries.

Automaticity: In disputes, the "automatic" chronological progression for settling trade disputes in regard to panel establishment, terms of reference, composition and adoption procedures.

Average Tariff: The simple average of all applied ad valorem tariffs (tariffs based on the value of the import) applicable to the bilateral imports of countries. This rate is calculated by adding up all the tariff rates and dividing by the number of import categories.

Basel Convention: A multilateral environmental agreement dealing with hazardous waste.

Berne Convention: A treaty administered by WIPO for the protection of the rights of authors in their literary and artistic works.

Bindings: (see also bound rate) When a country commits not to raise the tariff on an item above a specified level, the level is called a "binding". The levels at which Member bind their tariffs is agreed to through negotiations in the WTO. Thus a binding (also called a concession) is a legal obligation not to raise tariffs on particular products above the specified rate agreed to in negotiations. This rate is incorporated into a country's schedule of concessions. WTO Members can break a commitment (i.e. raise a tariff above the bound tariff), but only through negotiations with the countries affected by this measure, which may require payment of compensation for trading partners' loss of trade.

Bound Tariff: Refers to the tariff or maximum tariff that can be levied on a particular imported product. For instance, if an imported product has a bound tariff rate of 100 per cent-it means that the maximum tariff that can be levied on this particular product is 100 per cent. Countries can levy tariff rates less than or equal to 100 per cent but not more than 100 per cent on this particular product. Binding or binding commitment is a commitment by WTO members for not raising tariffs above a certain level.

BIT: Bilateral Investment Treaties.

Border Protection: Any measure, which acts to restrain imports at point of entry.

Box: In agriculture, a category of domestic support. Green Box: Supports considered not to distort trade and, therefore, permitted with no limits. Blue Box: Permitted supports linked to production but subject to production limits and therefore, minimally trade-distorting. Amber

Box: Support considered to distort trade and therefore subject to reduction commitments, i.e., prohibited.

BTA: Border Tax Adjustment.

Cairns Group: Group of agricultural exporting nations lobbying for agricultural trade liberalization. It was formed in 1986 in Cairns, Australia just before the beginning of the Uruguay Round. Current membership: Argentina, Australia, Bolivia, Brazil, Canada, Chile, Colombia, Costa Rica, Guatemala, Indonesia, Malaysia, New Zealand, Paraguay, Philippines, South Africa, Thailand and Uruguay.

CAP: Common Agricultural Policy The EU's comprehensive system of production targets and marketing mechanisms designed to manage agricultural trade within the EU and with the rest of the world.

Caricom: The Caribbean Community and Common Market comprising 15 countries.

CBD: Convention on Biological Diversity.

Circumvention: Getting around commitments in the WTO such as commitments to limit agricultural export subsidies. Includes: avoiding quotas and other restrictions by altering the country of origin of a product; measures taken by exporters to evade anti-dumping or countervailing duties.

CITES: Convention on International Trade in Endangered Species. A multilateral environmental agreement.

Codex Alimentarius: FAO/WHO commission that deals with international standards on food safety.

Commercial Presence: Having an office, branch or subsidiary in a foreign country. In services, "mode 3" (see "modes of delivery").

Compulsory Licensing: For patents: when the authorities license companies or individuals other than the patent owner to use the rights of the patent to make, use, sell or import a product under patent (i.e., a patented product or a product made by a patented process) without the permission of the patent owner. Allowed under the WTO's TRIPS (intellectual property) Agreement provided certain procedures and conditions are fulfilled. (See also government use)

Contractual Services Suppliers (CSS): Refers to those who provide services on a contractual basis. One of India's main demands is for inclusion of this category in the liberalization offers in Services from its trading partners.

Counterfeit: Unauthorised representation of a registered trademark carried on goods identical or similar to goods for which the trademark is registered, with a view to deceiving the purchaser into believing that he/she is buying the original goods.

Countervailing Measures: Action taken by the importing country, usually in the form of increased duties to offset subsidies given to producers or exporters in the exporting country. (See subsidies and countervailing measures agreement).

CTD: The WTO Committee on Trade and Development.

CTE: The WTO Committee on Trade and Environment.

CTG: Council for Trade in Goods oversees WTO agreements on goods, including the ATC.

Customs Union: Members apply a common external tariff (e.g., the European Union).

De Minimis: Refers to the de minimis provisions of the WTO Agreement on Agriculture, under which there is no requirement to reduce trade-distorting domestic support in any year in which the aggregate value of the product specific support does not exceed 5 per cent of the total value of production of the agricultural product in question. In addition, non-product specific support, which is less than 5 per cent of the value of total agricultural production, is also exempt from reduction. The 5 per cent threshold applies to developed countries whereas in the case of developing countries the de minimis ceiling is 10 per cent.

Deficiency Payment: A type of agricultural domestic support paid by governments to producers of certain commodities and based on the difference between a target price and the domestic market price or loan rate, whichever is the less.

Distortion: When prices and production are higher or lower than levels that would usually exist in a competitive market.

Doha Ministerial Conference: The Fourth WTO Ministerial Conference at Doha in 2001 adopted the text of the Ministerial Declaration, a decision on Implementation Related Issues and Concerns and the Declaration on the TRIPS Agreement and Public Health.

Doha Development Agenda (DDA): This is the name given by the WTO Secretariat to the trade negotiations that WTO Members agreed to embark on when they met in Doha for the WTO's Fourth Ministerial Conference in November 2001. It used the term "development agenda" as opposed to "round" to make the negotiation seem less threatening to those (particularly developing countries) who had opposed the launch of a new round of trade talks. However, the term "Doha Development Agenda" is not defined or even mentioned in the text of the Doha Declaration. Many members prefer the use of the term "Doha Work Programme", which is technically correct.

Doha Declaration: The Declaration in the form of a Work Programme, laid down the fundamental elements of a new round of multilateral trade negotiations, which aimed at concluding the negotiations not later than 1 January 2005. The new round is often called as a Development Round in view of the special emphasis it places on issues related to economic development in both the preamble and the operative parts of the Declaration. These elements include the recognition of the role of international trade in the promotion of economic development and the alleviation of poverty; special and differential treatment enhanced market access, balanced rules and sustainably financed technical assistance and capacity building programmes. The particular vulnerability of the Least Developed Countries was also recognized and the Declaration included the commitments of WTO members to address the marginalization of LDCs in international trade and improve their effective participation in the multilateral trading system.

Domestic Support: (Sometimes "internal support".) In agriculture, any domestic subsidy or other measure, which acts to maintain producer prices at levels above those prevailing in international trade; direct payments to producers, including deficiency payments and input and marketing cost reduction measures available only for agricultural production.

DSB: Dispute Settlement Body when the WTO General Council meets to settle trade disputes.

DSU: Dispute Settlement Understanding, the WTO agreement that covers dispute settlement in full, the Understanding on Rules and Procedures Governing the Settlement of Disputes.

Dumping: Occurs when goods are exported at a price less than normal value, generally meaning they are exported for less than they are sold in the domestic market or third-country markets, or at less than production cost.

EC: European Communities (official name of the European Union in the WTO).

EEP: Export Enhancement Programme of US export subsidies given generally to compete with subsidized agricultural exports from the EU on certain export markets.

EFTA: European Free Trade Association.

Electronic Commerce: The production, advertising, sale and distribution of products via telecommunications networks.

Enabling Clause: The WTO Framework permits the developed countries to give more favourable treatment to the developing countries, notwithstanding most-favoured nation provisions. (see also Special & Differential Treatment, MFN Treatment).

EST: Environmentally-Sound Technology.

EST & P: Environmentally-Sound Technology and Products.

EU: European Union, in the WTO officially called the European Communities.

Ex ante, Ex post: Before and after a measure is applied.

Exhaustion: In intellectual property protection, the principal that once a product has been sold on a market, the intellectual property owner no longer has any rights over it. (A debate among WTO member governments is whether this applies to products put on the market under compulsory licenses.) Countries' laws vary as to whether the right continues to be exhausted if the product is imported from one market into another, which affects the owner's rights over trade in the protected product. (See also parallel imports).

Export-Performance Measure: Requirement that a certain quantity of production must be exported.

Export Subsidies: The issue of export subsidies is part of the export competition pillar of the WTO agriculture negotiations. Export subsidies refer to special monetary incentives, such as cash payments, extended by governments to encourage increased sales abroad, often used when a country's domestic price for a good is higher than the world market prices.

FDI: Foreign Direct Investment.

FIPS: Five Interested Parties—a group consisting of Australia, Brazil, The European Commission (EC), India and the US.

Food Security: Concept, which discourages opening the domestic market to foreign agricultural products on the principle that a country must be as self-sufficient as possible for its basic dietary needs.

Free Trade Area: Trade within the group is duty free but members set their own tariffs on imports from non-members (e.g., NAFTA).

Free-Rider: A casual term used to infer that a country which does not make any trade concessions, profits, nonetheless, from tariff cuts and concessions made by other countries in negotiations under the most-favoured-nation principle.

G-4: Refers to a group consisting of Brazil, EC, India and the US.

G-7: Group of seven leading Industrial countries: Canada, France, Germany, Italy, Japan, United Kingdom, and United States.

G-8: G-7 plus Russia.

G-10: A group of mostly developed countries that have defensive interest in agriculture includes Iceland, Israel, Japan, Korea, Liechtenstein, Mauritius, Norway, Switzerland, Chinese Taipei.

G-15: Group of 15 developing countries acting as the main political organ for the Non-Aligned Movement.

G-20: A group of agricultural exporting countries, which came together during the 5th Ministerial Conference of the WTO, held in Cancun (Mexico) in 2003. The G-20 is led by Brazil, China, India and South Africa, and other members include Argentina, Bolivia, Chile, Costa Rica, Cuba, Ecuador, Egypt, Guatemala, Indonesia, Mexico, Pakistan, Philippines and Thailand. Together, these countries make up over half the world's population and two thirds of its framers.

G-33: A group of 42 developing countries which calls for safeguarding their food and livelihood security and rural development needs through designation of an appropriate number of Special Products (SPs) (which will attract more flexible treatment than the sensitive products) and protection against import surges or depressed prices through the Special Safeguard Mechanism (SSM).

G-77: Group of developing countries set up in 1964 at the end of the first UNCTAD (originally 77, but now more than 130 countries.)

GATS: The WTO's General Agreement on Trade in Services. It is the first multilateral agreement to provide legally enforceable rights to trade in all services. Covers about 12 service sectors and 155 sub-sectors. This is an open-ended agreement requiring members to make sectoral liberalization commitment before enforcement of its provisions. Members choose services and limit the degree to which they provide market access and national treatment commitments.

GATT: General Agreement on Tariffs and Trade, which has been superseded as an international organization by the WTO. An updated General Agreement is now the WTO agreement governing trade in goods. GATT 1947: The official legal term for the old (pre-1994) version of the GATT. GATT 1994: The official legal term for new version of the General Agreement, incorporated into the WTO, and including GATT 1947.

General Obligations: Obligations, which should be applied to all service sectors at the entry into force of the GATS agreement.

Geographical Indications: Place names (or words associated with a place) used to identify products (for example, "Champagne", "Tequila" or "Roquefort"), which have a particular quality, reputation or other characteristic because they come from that place.

Government Use: For patents: when the government itself uses or authorizes other persons to use the rights over a patented product or process for government purposes without the permission of the patent owner. (See also compulsory licensing.)

Green Room Meeting: A concept used commonly for initiating informal meetings within the WTO. Important breakthroughs are rarely made at Ministerial Meetings but Green Room meetings play a vital role in bringing vastly diverse membership around to an agreement. These meetings involve like-minded negotiating groups to bring a general consensus among participating members via informal discussions on a trade issue. Usually, 6-12 member countries discuss the issue in the Green Room Meetings and evolve a reasonable negotiating agenda and proposal. Once the consensus is reached, the group invites other members to discuss the issue informally. Once the proposal receives a larger group's approval, the proposal is tabled before the General Council for inclusion in the Ministerial Meeting. For example, market access negotiations during the Uruguay Round were first initiated at the Green Room Meetings.

GSP: Generalised System of Preferences programmes by developed countries granting preferential tariffs to imports from developing countries.

Harmonised System: An international nomenclature developed by the World Customs Organisation, which is arranged in six-digit codes allowing all participating countries to classify traded goods on a common basis. Beyond the six-digit level, countries are free to introduce national distinctions for tariffs and many other purposes.

Harmonising Formula: Used in tariff negotiations for much steeper reductions in higher tariffs than in lower tariffs, the final rates being "harmonized" i.e. closer together.

Horizontal Commitment: Commitment that applies to multiple services. An example is the obligation to provide most favoured nation treatment in the GATS. Regardless of whether a country has agreed to subject a service sector to GATS disciplines, it is bound to MFN treatment for all services sectors. Thus, by merit or being a WTO member, a country is required that if it privatizes a service or has private services, it must give companies or investors from all WTO member nations the same rights and privileges it gives a company or investor from any foreign country.

Initial Commitments: Trade liberalizing commitments in services which members are prepared to make early on.

Initial Negotiating Rights (INRs): It is a right held by a WTO member country to seek compensation for an impairment of a given bound tariff rate by another WTO member country. INRs stem from past negotiating concessions and allow the INR holder to seek compensation for an impairment of tariff concessions regardless of its status as a supplier of the product in question.

Integration Programme: In textiles and clothing, the phasing out of Multifibre Arrangement restrictions in four stages starting on 1 January 1995 and ending on 1 January 2005.

Intellectual Property Rights: Ownership of ideas, including literary and artistic works (protected by copyright), inventions (protected by patents), signs for distinguishing goods of an enterprise (protected by trademarks) and other elements of industrial property.

Internal Support: See "domestic support" (Agriculture).

International Office of Epizootics: Deals with international standards concerning animal health.

IPRs: Intellectual Property Rights.

ITA II: Negotiations aimed at expanding ITA's product coverage.

ITA: Information Technology Agreement or formally the Ministerial-Declaration on Trade in Information Technology Products under which participants will remove tariffs on IT products by the year 2000.

ITC: The International Trade Centre, originally established by the old GATT and is now operated jointly by the WTO and the UN, the latter acting through the UN Conference on Trade and Development (UNCTAD). Focal point for technical cooperation on trade promotion of developing countries.

ITCB: International Textiles and Clothing Bureau Geneva-based group of some 20 developing country exporters of textiles and clothing.

July Framework: Refers to the 1st August 2004 Decision of the WTO General Council Adopting the Framework Agreement, which marked the recommencing of negotiations after the stalemate of Cancun. Commonly known as the "July Framework" (signed a little after midnight of July 31, 2004), it provides a road map for the WTO negotiations up to the Sixth Ministerial Conference of the WTO in Hong Kong, China scheduled to be held from 13-18 December 2005.

LCA: Life Cycle Analysis (a method of assessing whether a good or service is environmentally friendly).

LDCs: Least-Developed Countries.

Lesser Duty Rule: A concept, which promotes moderate penalty in terms of additional duties for protecting domestic industry under the Anti-dumping Agreement. The respective provisions attempts to impose additional duties to the extent of dumping margin or to the margin of injury. The rule encourages levying lesser anti-dumping duty if it is adequate to remove the injury to the domestic industry. But the ultimate prerogative between the two options lies with the importing government.

Less than full reciprocity: Refers to the flexibilities for developing countries such as offering less than the formula reduction. This is an element of the special & differential treatment for developing countries.

Lisbon Agreement: Treaty, administered by the World Intellectual Property Organisation (WIPO) for the protection of geographical indications and their international registration.

Local-Content Measure: Requirement that the investor purchase a certain amount of local materials for incorporation in the investor's product.

Madrid Agreement: Treaty, administered by the World Intellectual Property Organisation (WIPO) for the repression of false or deceptive indications of source on goods.

Mailbox: In intellectual property, refers to the requirement of the TRIPS Agreement Applying to WTO members, which do not yet provide product patent protection for pharmaceuticals and for agricultural chemicals. Since 1 January 1995, when the WTO agreements entered into force, these countries have to establish a means by which applications of patents for these products can be filed. (An additional requirement says they must also put in place a system for granting "exclusive marketing rights" for the products whose patent applications have been filed.)

Market Access: This refers to the extent to which a good or a service can compete with locally produced products or services in another market. Market access is expressed in WTO terms as border measures, i.e., tariff and non-tariff measures in the cross border supply of goods and regulations inside the market in the case of services and intellectual property rights.

MEA: Multilateral Environmental Agreement.

Members: WTO governments (first letter capitalized, in official WTO style).

MERCOSUR: Argentina, Brazil, Paraguay and Uruguay.

MFA: Multi Fibre Arrangement (1974-94) under which countries whose markets were disrupted by increased imports of textiles and clothing from another country were able to negotiate quota restrictions. The Agreement on Textiles and Clothing (ATC) replaced the MFA, laying down rules for phase-out of MFA quota restrictions within a 10-year period by the year 2005. The ATC/MFA ceased to exist on 1st January 2005 with complete integration of textiles and clothing in the multilateral trading system.

MFN: Most-favoured-nation treatment (GATT Article I, GATS Article II and TRIPS Article 4), the principle of not discriminating between one's trading partners.

Ministerial Conference: It is the highest decision making body at the WTO, which meets once in every two years. This body can take decisions on all matters related trade. It is empowered to waive an obligation imposed on a particular member under any multilateral agreement. Usually, trade and commerce ministers of members represent the Ministerial Conference. Till date, five WTO Ministerial Conference have been held Singapore (1996), Geneva (1998), Seattle (1999), Doha (2001) and Cancun (2003) while the Sixth Ministerial Conference in Hong Kong has been held in December 2005.

Modality: A way to proceed. In WTO negotiations, modalities set broad outlines such as formulas or approaches for tariff reductions for final commitments.

Modes of Delivery: How international trade in services is supplied and consumed. In other words, ways in which a service can be rendered. They may include sales through establishment, cross-border sales and the movement of persons involved in the provision of services. The General Agreement on Services (GATS) identifies the supply of services under Mode 1: cross border supply (provision of the service from the territory of a member to the territory of another member); Mode 2: consumption abroad (movement of the consumer from his country of origin to the country of supply of such services as tourism, hotel services, etc.; Mode 3: commercial presence (right of establishment i.e., through foreign direct investment); and Mode 4: movement of natural persons. (See for more in Article 1 of GATS Agreement).

Montreal Protocol: A multilateral environmental agreement dealing with the depletion of the earth's ozone layer.

Movement of Natural Persons: It is an Annex to the GATS Agreement specifying that natural persons who are themselves service providers or employed by the service providers are allowed to supply service abroad in accordance with the specific commitments made in the National Schedule relating to the entry and stay.

Multilateral Trade Negotiations: A term describing the multilateral rounds of negotiations held under the auspices of GATT and WTO since 1947. Each Round represented a lengthy series of interacting and bargaining sessions among the participating Contracting Parties in search of mutually beneficial agreements. Under the GATT regime, eight multilateral trade negotiations took place between 1947 and 1994. The first trade negotiations between 23 members took place under GATT in Havana in 1947, followed by subsequent negotiations at Annecy (1949), Torquay (1951), Geneva (1956), Dillon Round (1960-61), Kennedy Round (1964-67), Tokyo Round (1973-79) and Uruguay Round (1986-93). Under WTO, the Doha Round was launched in 2001. Over the period of time, multilateral negotiations saw rising number of membership. Besides, under the aegis of WTO sectoral negotiations under GATS were carried forward and successfully concluded Agreement on Basic Telecommunication Services, Agreement on Financial Services, etc.

Multilateral Trading System: This system came into force with effect from 1st January 1995 with the establishment of the WTO. The multilateral trading system provides legally enforceable rules of international trading for members. This system covers rules of trade for goods and services including protection of intellectual property rights. Besides, it has a unique feature of time-bound trade related dispute resolution system.

Multi Functionality: Idea that agriculture has many functions in addition to producing food and fibre, e.g., environmental protection, landscape preservation, rural employment food security, etc. (See non-trade concerns.)

Multi-Modal: Transportation using more than one mode. In the GATS negotiations, essentially door-to-door services that include international shipping.

NAFTA: North American Free Trade Agreement, comprising Canada, Mexico and the US.

NAMA: Non-Agricultural Market Access. Refers to negotiations in the WTO that relate mainly to industrial tariffs.

National Schedules: In services, the equivalent of tariff schedules in GATT, laying down the commitments accepted voluntarily or through negotiation by WTO members.

National Treatment: The principle of giving others the same treatment as one's own nationals. GATT Article 3 requires that imports be treated no less favourably than the same or similar domestically-produced goods once they have passed customs. GATS Article 17 and TRIPS Article 3 also deal with national treatment for services and intellectual property protection.

Natural Persons: People, as distinct from juridical persons such as companies and organizations.

Newly Industrialised Countries (NICs): Relatively advanced developing countries whose industrial production and exports have grown rapidly in recent years. Examples include Brazil, Hong Kong, Korea, Mexico, Singapore and Taiwan. The term was originated by the Organisation for Economic Cooperation and Development (OECD).

NG: Refers to negotiating group in the WTO e.g., NGBT (Negotiating Group on Basic Telecommunications).

Non-Agricultural Product: In the non-agricultural market access negotiations, products not covered by Annex 1 of the Agriculture Agreement. Fish and forestry products are, therefore, non-agricultural along with industrial products in general.

Non-Trade Concerns: Similar to multi-functionality. The preamble of the Agriculture Agreement specifies food security and environmental protection as examples. Also cited by members are rural development and employment and poverty alleviation.

NTBs: Non-tariff barriers, such as quotas, import licensing systems, sanitary regulations, prohibitions, etc. (Same as "non-tariff barriers").

Nuisance Tariff: Tariff so low that it costs the government more to collect it than the revenue it generates. Sometimes, a tariff that does not have any protective effect, some countries defend this as necessary in order to raise revenues.

Nullification and Impairment: Damage to a country's benefits and expectations from its WTO membership through another country's change in its trade regime or failure to carry out its WTO obligations.

OECD: Organisation for Economic Cooperation and Development, based in Paris, is a forum for governments of the industrialized countries for the discussion of common economic and social issues confronting the US, Canada, Western Europe, Japan, Australia and New Zealand.

Offer: In a negotiation, a country's proposal for its own further liberalization usually an offer to improve access to its markets.

Outsourcing: Procurement of sourcing of raw material, component parts and finished goods from outside a business organization. It is the opposite of in sourcing.

Over-quota Tariff Rate: The rate of customs duty to be applied to quantities in excess of the quantity specified under a tariff rate quota.

Panel: In the WTO dispute settlement procedure, an independent body is established by the Dispute Settlement Body, consisting of three experts to examine and issue recommendations on a particular dispute in the light of WTO provisions.

Parallelism: Parallelism is a commonly used term in NTB negotiations under NAMA. It means that NTBs should be addressed in parallel to reduction in tariffs, as NTBs in many occasions have nullified existing market opportunities.

Parallel Imports: When a product made legally (i.e., not pirated) abroad is imported without the permission of the intellectual property right-holder (e.g., the trademark or patent owner). Some countries allow this, other do not.

Paris Convention: Treaty, administered by the World Intellectual Property Organization (WIPO) for the protection of industrial intellectual property, i.e., patents, utility models, industrial designs, etc.

Peace Clause: Provision in Article 13 of the Agriculture Agreement saying agricultural subsidies committed under the agreement cannot be challenged under other WTO agreements, in particular the Subsidies Agreement and GATT. It expired at the end of 2003.

Piracy: Unauthorized copying of materials protected by intellectual property rights (such as copyright, trademarks, patents, geographical indications, etc) for commercial purposes and unauthorized commercial dealing in copied materials.

PPM: Process and Production Method.

Preferential Agreement/Preferences: Economic integration in which access to a larger market generally in a more developed country is offered without demands for reciprocity.

Price Undertaking: Undertaking by an exporter to raise the export price of the product to avoid the possibility of an anti-dumping duty.

Product-Mandating: Requirement that the investor export to certain countries or region.

Protocols: Additional agreements attached to the GATS. The Second Protocol deals with the 1995 commitments on financial services. The Third Protocol deals with movement of natural persons.

Protectionism: The deliberate use of encouragement to restrictions on imports to enable relatively inefficient domestic producers to compete successfully with foreign producers.

Prudence, Prudential: In financial services, terms used to describe an objective of market regulation by authorities to protect investors and depositors to avoid instability or crises.

PSI: Pre-Shipment Inspection. The practice of employing specialized private companies to check shipment details of goods ordered overseas i.e., price, quantity, quality, etc.

QRs: Quantitative Restrictions specific limits on the quantity or value of goods that can be imported (or exported) during a specific time period.

Quad: Canada, EU, Japan and the United States.

Reform Process/Programme: The Uruguay Round Agriculture Agreement starts a reform process. It sets out a first step in the process i.e., a programme for reducing subsidies and protection and other reforms. Current negotiations launched under Article 20 are for continuing the reform process.

Rome Convention: Treaty, administered by the World Intellectual Property Organisation (WIPO), United Nations

Educational Scientific and Cultural Organisation (UNESCO) and International Labour Organization (ILO) for the protection of the works of performers, broadcasting organizations and producers of phonograms.

Rounds (of Trade Negotiations): Cycles of multilateral trade negotiations under the GATT and its successor WTO, culminating in simultaneous agreements among participating countries to reduce tariff and non-tariff barriers. Uruguay Round was the 8th Round (1986-93), which was the last round to be held under the aegis of GATT. The current Round is the 9th Round, which was launched under the WTO at the Ministerial Conference at Doha (Qatar) in 2001.

Rules: The negotiations in the Rules area are aimed at clarifying and improving disciplines under the Agreement on the Implementation of Article VI of GATT 1994 (Anti-Dumping Agreement) and Subsidies and Countervailing Measures Agreement.

Rules of Origin: Laws, regulations and administrative procedures, which determine a product's country of origin. A decision by a customs authority on origin can determine whether a shipment falls within a quota limitation, qualifies for a tariff preference or is affected by an anti-dumping duty. These rules can vary from country to country.

RTAs: Regional Trade Agreements.

S & D: (Sometimes "SDT") "Special and Differential Treatment" provisions for developing countries. (Contained in several WTO agreements).

SACU: Southern African Customs Union comprising Botswana, Lesotho, Namibia, South Africa and Swaziland.

Safeguard Measures: Action taken to protect a specific industry from an unexpected build up of imports generally governed by Article 19 of GATT. The Agriculture Agreement and Textiles and Clothing Agreement have different specific types of safeguards: "special safeguards" in agriculture and "transitional safeguards" in textiles and clothing.

Schedule: In general, a WTO member's list of commitments on market access (bound tariff rates, access to services markets). Goods schedules can include commitments on agricultural subsidies and domestic support. Services commitments include bindings on national treatment. (Also: "schedule of concessions", "schedule of specific commitments.")

Schedule of Concessions: List of bound tariff rates.

Sectoral Approach: Cutting or eliminating tariffs on certain sectors independent of the tariff cutting formula that is followed for other sectors.

Services: The WTO defines the term "services" as a wide range of non-tangible economic activities covering major sectors, services like business services including professional and computer services, communication services, construction and engineering services, distribution services, educational services, environmental services, financial (banking and insurance) services, health services, tourism and travel services, recreational, cultural and sporting services and transport services.

Singapore Issues: Four issues introduced to the WTO agenda at the December 1996 Ministerial Conference in Singapore: trade and investment, trade and competition policy, transparency in government procurement and trade facilitation.

Special Commitments: See "Schedule".

Special Products or SPs: These refer to agricultural products on which there will be either nil or marginal tariff reduction.

Specific Tariff or Specific Rate of Duty: A tariff rate charged as fixed amount per quantity such as $ 100 per ton. (See "ad valorem tariff".)

SPS: Sanitary and Phytosanitary measures or regulations implemented by governments to protect human, animal and plant life and health, and to help ensure that food is safe for consumption.

Special Safeguard Mechanism (SSM): Refers to a mechanism to safeguard agriculture against import surges and price fall. During the on-going negotiations, some developing countries, including India, have sought a special safeguard mechanism to be used by developing countries for addressing situations of import surges or swings in international prices of agricultural products.

Standstill: It is also known as 'non-backsliding clause'. It refers to a commitment of the GATT contracting parties not to impose new trade restrictive measures during the Uruguay Round negotiations. For instance, in the TRIPS agreement member countries are required to not to take any measure that will result in a lower level of protection to IPRs than that already existing in their territories during the transition period.

Subsidy: There are two general types of subsidies: export and domestic. An export subsidy is a benefit conferred on a firm by that government that is contingent on exports. A domestic subsidy is a benefit not directly linked to exports.

Sunset Clause: It is specifically directed at keeping a constant review of restrictive measures such as anti-dumping and countervailing measures. Under the sunset clause, such measures automatically expire after five year from the date of imposition, unless the review determines that in the absence of such measures domestic industry is threatened by injury.

Sustainable Development: It is the Bruntland Commission's recommendations seeking to meet the needs and aspirations of the present without compromising the ability to meet those of the future. Sustainable development is included in the preamble of the WTO. In other words, recognizing the problems of poverty and underdevelopment along with need for economic growth and economic development but without compromising the ecological balance as adopted by the Rio Summit in 1992.

Swing: In textiles and clothing, when an exporting country transfers part of a quota from one product to another restrained product.

Swiss Formula: A tariff reduction formula that requires that WTO Member narrow the gap between high and low tariff (known as "harmonizing the tariffs."). Discussions in NAMA on the tariff reduction formula have focused mainly on two variations of the Swiss formula, namely the simple Swiss formula with one or two coefficients (as proposed by the US, EC and some other developed countries) and a tariff average based Swiss formula (as put forward by Argentina, Brazil and India). Under a simple Swiss formula, the higher the tariff, the greater the cut. Developing countries are generally opposed to the simple Swiss formula, as they tend to have higher tariffs on industrial goods than developed countries. The Swiss formula is T1=(B*T0)/(B+T0) where T1 is the new tariff rate, T0 is the initial tariff rate and B is the reduction coefficient.

Tariff: A tax or levy imposed at the (national) border on imported products. Tariffs can be imposed in two ways. First is the ad valorem tariff, where the tariff rate is based on the value of the import i.e., it is based on the price of the imported product. Second is the specific tariff rate, where tariff rates are imposed on the basis of weight/volume or number of items of the imported product irrespective of the price of the product.

Tariff Binding: Commitment not to increase a rate of duty beyond an agreed level. Once a rate of duty is bound, it may not be raised without compensating the affected parties.

Tariff Escalation: Higher import duties on semi-processed products than on raw materials, and higher still on finished products. This practice protects domestic processing industries and discourages the development of processing activity in the countries where raw materials originate.

Tariff Peaks: Relatively high tariffs, usually on "sensitive" products, amidst generally low tariff levels. For industrialized countries, tariffs of 15 per cent and above are generally recognized as "tariff peaks".

Tariffication: Procedures relating to the agricultural market-access provision in which all non-tariff measures are converted into tariffs.

Tariffs: Customs duties on merchandise imports. Levied either on an ad valorem basis (percentage of value) or on a specific basis (e.g., $ 7 per 100 kgs.). Tariffs give price advantage to similar locally produced goods and raise revenues for the government.

Tariff Reduction Formula: This refers to different approaches or methodologies for cutting or reducing tariff rates on different agricultural products or tariff lines.

- **Uruguay Round Formula:** This formula or approach to cut tariff rates was adopted during the Uruguay Round of negotiations. This is a linear reduction formula, requiring an average total reduction of 36 per cent (24 per cent for developing countries) and a minimum of 15 per cent (10 per cent for developing countries) in each tariff line. This formula does not lead to steep reduction in the tariff rates.
- **Swiss Formula:** This formula aims at harmonization of tariffs (bringing all tariffs at the same level) between member countries of the WTO. It cuts higher tariffs more steeply than the lower tariffs. It does not support the cause of developing countries and LDCs as most of these countries have high tariff rates.
- **Banded Formula:** According to this formula, all tariff lines are to be divided into different bands or categories and then each band or category is to be subjected to tariff reduction by applying the Uruguay Round Formula.
- **Blended Formula:** This formula mixes the Uruguay Round Formula and the Swiss Formula.
- **Tiered Formula:** The WTO General Council adopted this approach on 1 August 2004, as a part of the framework for establishing modalities for future negotiations. According to this, the tariff lines are to be divided into different bands or categories. Bands or categories comprising of higher tariff rates would be subjected to steeper reductions. However, the number of bands, thresholds for each band and the extent of tariff cut in a particular band are yet to be decided.

TBT: The WTO Agreement on Technical Barriers to Trade.

TMB: The Textiles Monitoring Body, consisting of a chairman plus 10 members acting in a personal capacity, oversees the implementation of commitments under the Agreement on Textiles and Clothing.

TPRB, TPRM: The Trade Policy Review Body is General Council operating under special procedures for meetings to review trade policies and practices of individual WTO members under the Trade Policy Review Mechanism.

Trade Facilitation: Removing obstacles to the movement of goods across borders (e.g. simplification of customs procedures). It is one of the Singapore issues that was included as part of 'New Issues' for multilateral negotiations under Singapore Declaration. As a result of the July Framework of 2004, all the Singapore Issues barring Trade Facilitation were dropped from the agenda of WTO negotiations.

Trade-Balancing Measure: Requirement that the investor use earnings from exports to pay for imports.

Traditional Knowledge: It is the centuries old knowledge of indigenous or local communities like parts of plants (root, bark, leaves, flowers and fruits) have been used in developing countries to relieve pain and treat infections and other complaints. They have also been used as insecticides and pesticides. Local knowledge of these varied uses is not recorded but it is a part of communal heritage and usually known as traditional knowledge. The TRIPs agreement is silent on this issue and developing countries are grouping to extend the IPR protection regime to traditional knowledge.

Transitional Safeguard Mechanism: In textiles and clothing, it allows members to impose restrictions against individual exporting countries if the importing country can show that both overall imports of a product and imports from the individual countries are entering the country in such increased quantities as to cause or threaten serious damage to the relevant domestic industry.

Transparency: Degree to which trade policies and practices and the process by which they are established, are open and predictable.

Triggers: The criteria involving either a rapid surge in import volume of agricultural goods (volume trigger) or a fall of the import price below a specified reference price of agricultural goods on a shipment-by-shipment basis (price trigger).

TRIMs: Trade-Related Investment Measures (note small "s").

TRIPS: Trade-Related Aspects of Intellectual Property Rights (note capital "S").

TRQs: Trading mechanism that provides for the application of a custom duty at a certain rate to import of a particular good up to a specified quantity (in quota quantity) and at a different rate to import of that good that exceed that quantity.

Unbound: Unbound tariff means tariffs, which are not subject to binding commitments or limits.

UNCITRAL: United Nations Centre for International Trade Law, drafts model laws such as the one on government procurement.

UNCTAD: The UN Conference on Trade and Development.

UPOV: International Union for the Protection of New Varieties of Plants.

Uruguay Round: Multilateral trade negotiations launched at Punta del Este, Uruguay in September 1986 and concluded in Geneva in December 1993. Signed by Ministers in Marrakesh, Morocco in April 1994.

Variable Levy: Customs duty rate, which varies in response to domestic price criterion.

VRA, VER, OMA: Voluntary restraint arrangement, voluntary export restraint, orderly marketing arrangement. Bilateral arrangements whereby an exporting country (government or industry) agrees to reduce or restrict exports without the importing country having to make use of quotas, tariffs or other import controls.

Waiver: Permission granted by WTO members allowing a WTO member not to comply with normal commitments. Waivers have time limits and extensions have to be justified.

Washington Treaty: Treaty for the protection of intellectual property in respect of layout designs of integrated circuits.

Water in Tariff: The difference between bound tariff rate and the applied tariff rate is called water in the tariff.

WCO: World Customs Organisation, a multilateral body located in Brussels through which participating countries seeks to simplify and rationalize customs procedures.

WIPO: World Intellectual Property Organisation.

WTO: Refers to World Trade Organisation, which in brief is the only international organization dealing with the global rules of trade between nations. Its main function is to ensure that trade flows as smoothly, predictably and freely as possible.

Location: Geneva, Switzerland.

Established: 1 January 1995.

Created By: Uruguay Round Negotiations (1986-93 signed at Marrakesh in 1994).

Membership: 149 countries (with the accession of Saudi Arabia in 2005).

Budget: 169 million Swiss Francs for 2005.

Secretariat Staff: 630

Head: Pascal Lamy (Director-General)

Functions:

- Administering WTO trade agreements
- Forum for trade negotiations.
- Handling trade disputes
- Monitoring national trade policies
- Technical assistance and training for developing countries
- Cooperation with other international organizations.

Zero-for-Zero Approach: Tariff reduction approach, which implies that in identified sectors all countries should bring down their tariff rates to zero. For instance, in the fish and fish products category, India and Pakistan have 87 per cent and 90 per cent of tariff lines unbound. When such a high proportion of tariff lines is unbound in a sensitive sector it would not be prudent for these countries to support the zero-or-zero approach.

Source: (i) WTO/UNCTAD

(ii) Government of India (2005): India & The WTO, A Monthly Newsletter, Ministry of Commerce and Industry, New Delhi, Vol. 7, No. 12, December.